SOVIET
POLITICS
IN THE
BREZHNEV
ERA

SOVIET POLITICS IN THE BREZHNEV ERA

edited by
Donald R. Kelley

PRAEGER SPECIAL STUDIES • PRAEGER SCIENTIFIC

Library of Congress Cataloging in Publication Data

Main entry under title:

Soviet politics in the Brezhnev era.

   Includes bibliographical references and index.
   1. Russia--Politics and government--1953-
2. Brezhnev, Leonid Il'ich, 1906-   I. Kelley,
Donald R., 1943-
DK274.S651957 1980   320.9'47'085   79-24741
ISBN 0-03-046626-1

ISBN 0-03-046621-0 pbk.

Published in 1980 by Praeger Publishers
CBS Educational and Professional Publishing
A Division of CBS, Inc.
521 Fifth Avenue, New York, New York 10017 U.S.A.

© 1980 by Praeger Publishers

0123456789 038 98765432

Printed in the United States of America

CONTENTS

LIST OF TABLES

SOVIET POLITICS IN THE BREZHNEV ERA

1

SOVIET POLITICS IN THE BREZHNEV ERA: "PLURALISM" OR "CORPORATISM?"

Valerie Bunce
John M. Echols III

The study of Soviet politics is first and foremost a study of eras, periods associated with specific leaders doing specific things. As William Welsh has observed, "The process of political change in the Soviet Union is characterized in terms of moving from the era of one leader to another."[1] Indeed, Alfred Meyer has suggested that the Soviet system in fact has been "a succession of political systems, differing from each other in purpose, structure and functioning."[2] If this is so—and most scholars agree with the notion of eras—then how might we characterize the Brezhnev years? How does it differ from the Lenin, Stalin, and Khrushchev eras?

It is precisely this issue, the nature of Soviet politics under Brezhnev, that we will address in this chapter. While we will agree with the dominant position in the field—that Brezhnev has put a definite stamp on his administration—we wish to diverge somewhat from common scholarly views about the content and effect of that imprint.[3] Specifically, we will argue that politics under Brezhnev can be characterized best not as "petrification" or "pluralism," to use two well-known descriptions,[4] but rather as a variant on a type of politics common in many advanced industrial societies. The Brezhnev era, we will contend, can be understood best in terms of *corporatist politics.* Thus, in this paper, we will describe both the concept "corporatism" and recent trends in Soviet politics and attempt to demonstrate how well this concept summarizes those trends.

THE NAME GAME

If our purpose, then, is to justify a new label for the current Soviet system and, in elaborating that label, provide a better description of that system than previous attempts have offered, it might be reasonable to ask, why not simply do the latter and skip the label? One reason is that there is a tradition in the study of Soviet politics of devising some word or phrase to describe "the system." Even Brezhnev has attached a name to the current era: "developed socialism."[5] As long as scholars and leaders continue to depict the Soviet Union in a word or phrase, it obviously would be best to use the most appropriate characterization available. More generally, however, labels like "pluralism," "totalitarianism," and "corporatism" can be both very convenient shorthand devices and good starting points for breaking the system down into its essential elements. Moreover, labels facilitate comparisons across different political-economic systems, thereby allowing us to bring Soviet studies into the comparative politics fold, as well as highlighting key characteristics of the Soviet system.

The question then becomes *which* model best captures the central components of current Soviet politics? To date, we have witnessed several attempts to model the Soviet system. These models reflect seemingly divergent trends under Brezhnev. On the one hand, some scholars see conservative trends—continued suppression of dissent, an expanded role for the Communist Party (and, concurrently, no withering away of the "state"), and the development of routinized, indeed, "hide-bound" decision processes. Thus, the system has been termed, for example, "petrified" and even still "totalitarian."[6] In contrast to these notions, other scholars have observed distinctly liberalizing trends since 1964. Whether they refer to it as "groupism," "pluralism," or "welfare state authoritarianism," they argue that under Brezhnev the welfare state has grown and that the decision-making arena has expanded. For example, they have pointed to increasing opportunities for mass participation at the local level, the growing representation of workers and experts in the party, the increasing inclusion of expert advice in decision making in the upper reaches of the party and state, and, finally, the rapid expansion of social welfare benefits to include previously ignored groups in society, particularly those in rural areas.[7]

It would seem that scholars emphasizing liberalizing trends have had the upper hand in recent years. Certainly the most prominent yet controversial attempt to incorporate these liberalizing tendencies in a coherent model has been Jerry Hough's description of politics under Brezhnev as "institutional pluralism."[8] This term refers to the emergence of the party and the top leadership as political brokers reconciling major institutional interests within the system. This is a pluralist system, in Hough's view, because the party is no longer (and perhaps never was) a dictatorship. Elites have limited power and limited consensus about policy priorities, groups must compete for influence, and no one group or elite coalition can dominate the policy-making process. Rather, elites are held in check by their conflicts with each other, by the diversity of their institutional interests and competencies, and, finally, by the dispersion of power among them and among major interest groups in the system. Under conditions of institutional pluralism, then, the power of the party and the first secretary in particular, like the power of the U.S. president, is in large part the power to listen, resolve, and persuade.

While Hough's evidence for institutional pluralism is tempting, it leaves one with some uncertainties about the true nature of the Soviet system and qualms about employing the term "institutional pluralism" to describe recent trends. Specifically, we would argue that, while Hough's model is a most welcome corrective, there is evidence as well for some of the conservative trends noted above. These must be taken into account, and the term "corporatism," as we hope to demonstrate, can encompass these seemingly divergent trends. In our view, then, "corporatism" will provide us with a more accurate and more complete description of the politics of the Brezhnev era.

"CORPORATISM" AS AN ALTERNATIVE TO "PLURALISM"

The task before us, then, is to set out the concept of corporatism and illustrate its utility in describing the Soviet system, especially as it has developed in the Brezhnev era. Though the major use of corporatism has been to describe recent trends in major advanced industrial societies, such as Germany, Britain, Sweden, and France, corporatism also has been used to summarize politics in several authoritarian systems—for example, Brazil.[9] In fact, Philippe Schmitter has distinguished the two basic corporatist types: liberal or "societal" and authoritarian or "state" corporatism.[10] However, there is a core to the concept, and we shall argue that the Soviet Union fits this core as well as some elements peculiar to each of its subtypes.

Essentially, corporatism refers to a decision-making structure in which major functional interest groups are incorporated into the policy process by the state and its leaders. Phillippe Schmitter provides a more formal definition:

> Corporatism can be defined as a system of interest representation in which the constituent units are organized into a limited number of singular, compulsory, non-competitive, hierarchically ordered and

functionally differentiated categories recognized and licensed (if not created) by the state and granted a deliberate representational monopoly within their respective categories in exchange for observing certain controls on their selection of leaders and articulation of demands and supports.[11]

This model contrasts with a pluralist perspective on decision making, as Schmitter elaborates:

> Pluralism can be defined as a system of interest intermediation in which the constituent units are organized into an unspecified number of multiple, voluntary, competitive, nonhierarchically ordered, and self-determined (as to type or scope or interest) categories that are not specifically licensed, recognized, subsidized, created, or otherwise controlled in leadership selection or interest articulation by the state and that do not exercise a monopoly of representational activity within their respective categories.[12]

The contrast between these two models and the improvements the corporatist approach offers are summarized by Leo Panitch: "As a working model in political analysis, [corporatism] has manifest advantages over pluralist theory, unencumbered as it is by the latter's unwieldy assumptions of extensive group multiplicity, passive state behavior, and stability as a product of overlapping membership and the unseen hand of group competition."[13]

Working from these basic formulations and their elaboration by Schmitter, Panitch, and others, we can set out four important clusters of components that epitomize the corporatist polity: these involve, respectively, the role of the state and interest groups, planning and rationality, the mass publics, and goals in the system. Once these are delineated, we will briefly describe the development of a corporatist system.

The Role of the State and Interest Groups

A number of important elements of corporatism are subsumed by this issue of the role of the state and interest groups. First of all, the state takes an active role in the decision-making process. It works with groups to make public policy and does not, as in the pluralist model, simply act as a passive broker, mediating interests; interest groups are not the autonomous, independent actors they are in pluralism. Rather, they are linked integrally with the state for access and even survival through constant interaction in the policy process. In addition, there is an important distinction regarding the nature of the state-group and intergroup interaction. In pluralist models, the emphasis is on conflict; in corporatism, consensus and cooperation. Groups do not compete with one another through the state to obtain more for themselves. Instead, they are brought together by the state in active cooperation to achieve more for all; harmony is the watchword of a corporatist regime.

The notion of cooperation makes corporatism sound rather ideal; unfortunately, however, that conclusion is premature. For one thing, there are definite biases in a corporatist power structure. For the most part, only those groups deemed necessary to making the system work are included; thus, *functional* interest groups—most notably, business and labor—are the centerpiece of a corporatist system. Others, primarily attitudinal groups, are left out. Under classical pluralism, of course, no group is left out except of its own volition. Second, conflict is still present, but held in check by the state's promise that all will get something and few, if any, will lose. So corporatism is a system wherein conflict is reduced but not eliminated; group interests are channelled into the policy process.

The Role of Planning and Rationality

As to the role of planning and rationality, under corporatism, groups and the state coalesce to pursue what they see as more rational (that is, more informed and systematic) procedures for making major political and economic decisions. Specifically, they work together through the *planning* process. As Charles Lindblom and Aaron Wildavsky have pointed out, a successful pluralist system does not, indeed, cannot, plan.[14] A corporatist system will not accept an absence of planning; growth cannot be assured, the society, the polity, and the economy cannot be stabilized, and the power structure cannot be maintained without planning and other forms of systematic decision making.[15]

The Role of the Masses

The economic and political role of the masses in a pluralist system is rather limited; they are to provide for themselves economically and periodically make their political demands known by selecting leaders and agitating for their interests through various groups. By contrast, in a corporatist system (a "liberal" corporatist system, at least—this is perhaps where the two types of corporatism differ most significantly), the masses are protected by a welfare state in which a minimal standard of living is guaranteed by the government through income policies, transfers, and social services. In a sense, the masses are bought off (or more charitably, rewarded) in corporatist states by the social welfare state. The political role of the masses—again, in a "liberal" corporatist order—also diverges from that in pluralism. The public is expected not just to vote but also to participate as representatives of group interests in decision-making areas of particular competence and concern. Certain kinds of participation in local and administrative decision making by the mass publics, then, are often encouraged in liberal corporatism (primarily in Scandinavia).[16] In return for this participation and socioeconomic security the state receives political stability, economic and political compliance, and, as a result, continued economic growth and the maintenance of the prevailing distribution of political power. There is, therefore, a deal struck between elites and masses, a deal which meets many of their respective needs.

Finally, pluralist and corporatist orders can be contrasted with respect to their system's goals. A pluralist polity, of course, has no explicit goals. Instead, the presumption is that a pluralist *process* is the major concern; optimal public policy will necessarily follow. By contrast, a corporatist system does tend to feature explicit policy goals, and the system is designed to ensure the fulfillment of these ends. The goals are economic growth, political, economic and social stability, and the maintenance of the prevailing distribution of economic and political power (and, perhaps, of the particular incumbents).[17] So politics—that is, the activist state, the cooperation among groups, the planning and sharing of benefits such that no one loses (Pareto optimality)—is set up to *ensure* the fulfillment of these goals.

These, then, are the major aspects of corporatism and the ways in which that system contrasts with pluralism. But *how* and *why* does corporatism develop? For the first question we must return to Schmitter's differentiation of the two corporatist patterns, "societal" and "state." These differ fundamentally with respect to how corporatism is established. The key variable is the degree of voluntarism involved. Corporatism is either entered into voluntarily by the relevant groups or is imposed by the state; it is a product either of "reciprocal consensus on procedure and/or goals, or of an asymmetric imposition by the 'organized monopolists of legitimate violence.'"[18]

But why would a state wish to establish such a system, or, alternatively, why would certain groups want to enter into such an arrangement? Western literature on the subject suggests that there are several rather attractive features of corporatism. One common argument is that corporatism is the state's response to the deficiencies of pluralism, a way of forcing mechanical solidarity in a seemingly uncontrollable mass society.[19] Another contributing factor is thought to be the growing complexity of the decision process, the pressing need for expert information, and the increasing dominance of bureaucracies over legislatures in shaping public policy.[20] In this view, corporatism is a way of linking bureaucracies with their clienteles in order to rationalize the policy process and to give credence to an already developing symbiotic relationship. A third interpretation is that corporatism is a way of handling class conflict in industrial society by co-opting management and labor into a coalition with the government.[21] Fourth, it has been suggested that corporatism is a way of enhancing group input and, at the same time, forcing those groups' compliance with the resulting policy decisions. Here the argument is that co-optation is a mechanism for at least limited democracy and central control; co-opted groups both have more to say in decisions yet are pressured by their complicity to stand by most of the decisions that eventually result.[22] Thus, corporatism seems to be a force for both democracy and authoritarian control.

Finally, keeping all the above reasons in mind, we should return to the goals set out above for corporatism. This system is designed to provide something for everyone, especially for those crucial to the system's operation and most particularly for those at the top. It is a system for preservation and protection, *with* growth, through planning, co-optation, and the sharing of benefits. It is, *ideally*, a comfortable and convenient coalition of interests, achieving growth and influence without stress.

CORPORATISM AND THE BREZHNEV ERA

Scholars familiar with politics in the Brezhnev era already may have begun to recognize some aspects of this era in our elaboration of the corporatist model. Our task in the remainder of this paper is to make that connection explicit, to establish the Brezhnev regime as a good example of corporatist politics. To facilitate the presentation, we shall once again break the model down into its four main components. As above, we will begin with the central issue of the role of the state (in this case, the state and the party) and its relationship to other groups in the system.

The Role of the State and Other Actors in the System

To reiterate, this first cluster of traits in a corporatist system places a premium on cooperation among politically important groups and institutions, the incorporation of functional interest groups and specialists into the policy process, and, simultaneously, a dominant role for an activist state. Let us look at these three components in the Brezhnev era, beginning with the notion of cooperation.

Nikita Khrushchev was removed from office for a number of reasons, but surely none was more important than his handling of policy change. Khrushchev's approach was to attack the pillars of the Soviet state; neither individuals nor structures were sacred. Conflict and reorganization were the order of the day, at all levels of government. State and enterprise officials were watched ever more closely by new or expanded party and public bodies. It was not, to put it simply, a regime based on trust.[23]

The contrast with the Brezhnev era on these issues is quite explicit. The post-Khrushchev leadership quickly rescinded or cut back several of those Khrushchev initiatives which had exacerbated intra-elite conflict and undermined elite job security—for instance, compulsory rotation (as introduced in the 1961 Party Platform) and the bifurcation of the party into agricultural and industrial sectors. In direct contrast to Khrushchev, then, the new regime instituted a policy of "trust in cadres."[24] Conflict among elites and between the party and other elements has been replaced to a significant extent by cooperation and a search for consensus. We can see evidence of this trend in the declining rate of personnel turnover in the Central Committee and the Politburo since 1964. For instance, in 1961, at the Twenty-Second Party Congress, some 70 percent of the members were reelected. At the Twenty-Fifth Congress in 1976, the comparable figure was over 90 percent.[25] Even party membership is far more secure than it has been in the past; in the very recent party purge only 2 percent of all members did not receive new cards.[26] Thus, while we would hardly suggest that political conflict is over in the Soviet Union or that tenure is guaranteed, we would simply stress that both removals and conflict are significantly *less* evident in Soviet political life today than they were under Khrushchev. Party and state life has become more pleasant and cooperative under Brezhnev's tutelage.

This contrast between the Khrushchev and Brezhnev eras is exemplified in a comparision of the two leaders' styles and personalities, the one combative and conflictual, the other consensual and conciliatory. This comparison can be illustrated nicely by examining, as Jerry Hough has done, the content of accolades addressed to the two leaders at the peak of their powers. In 1961, at the Twenty-Second Party Congress, "almost no one spoke of [Khrushchev] with real affection, and the words of praise stressed his 'tireless energy,' 'revolutionary fervor,' 'daring,' 'decisiveness,' 'principles' and 'demanding' nature, and so forth. The words 'smelyy' (bold) and 'smelost' (boldness) appeared with particular frequency."[27] In contrast, at the Twenty-Fifth Party Congress in 1976, the strongest emphasis in the effusive praise for Brezhnev, was placed upon such personal qualities as "deep humanity, considerateness, and attentiveness to people," as well as his modesty. In particular, it was often said that Brezhnev has "established comradeliness, trust, and a respectful relation to people in the party," has created "a good atmosphere for work," a "situation in which people can breathe easily, work well, and live peacefully"; "has an ability to establish an atmosphere of trust, respect, and dedication to the standards among people" and "to coordinate (nalazhivat) strong and friendly common work by a large number of people"; under his leadership, "the Central Committee consistently raises the role of the local party organs, widely consults with them, alternatively examines initiatives and proposals from the localities."[28]

These comments not only illustrate the cooperative spirit of the Brezhnev era, they also point to a second component of a corporatist order: the inclusion of major interests in the policy process. Numerous elements in the system seem to have achieved a degree of influence or at least some of the prerequisites (or indicators) of influence that they did not hold before. In particular, scholars have emphasized the growing role—though they debate the extent of influence—of interest groups, or at least of *functional* area specialists in the system. This has been demonstrated (with some qualifications) in the cases of environmental, educational, and criminal justice policy.[29] This trend toward group participation reflects concern among the leadership with obtaining more and better information and extracting compliance.[30] It has expressed itself in two ways: as a process whereby experts are regularly consulted in the making of policy and as a more subtle procedure whereby party members take group interests into account by virtue of their being group representatives themselves ("virtual representation").[31] Thus, groups can be seen as being part, though clearly not the center, of much policy making in the Soviet Union.

Cooperation, consensus, stability, and inclusion of nongovernment elements in the policy-making process—the outlines of a corporatist order are beginning to take shape. We can see these aspects summarized well in Donald R. Kelley's explication of the present era and its Soviet label, "developed socialism":

> As a conservative, or perhaps more generously, as a cautious projection of a slowly evolving institutional order, developed social-ism offers a stable institutional and political milieu within which limited and careful modernization may be safely attempted; in effect, it is a tacit promise that the rules of political battle and the institu-tional setting within which it occurs are unlikely to be capriciously altered. . . . In this vein developed socialism as a theoretical frame-work is in reality a mechanism to contain and manage certain kinds of conflict while simultaneously providing a greater space for limited reform.[32]

What Kelley is suggesting is that consensus is greater and conflict, while still part of Soviet high politics, is now contained to a greater extent than it was in the past. While under Khrushchev conflict was rampant and involved disagreements over means *and* ends, under Brezhnev disagreements are moderated. In the present era, value questions—such as those dealing with the future of Soviet society and the ideal mode of intra-elite and regime-society relations—are generally settled. The future (and the present) is devel-oped socialism, and trust, cooperation, and conciliation are to char-acterize interpersonal and intra-elite relations. What is left and what fuels most disagreements now are issues having to do with bureau-cratic politics—defending one's turf and tinkering with current priorities—and those concerned with the optimal means by which mutually agreed upon goals can be achieved.[33] However, even these sources of friction do not ignite elite politics in the way they did in the Khrushchev era due to certain moderating influences: the reliance on experts to handle many technical policies and technical issues; the belief in cautious, consensual decision making; and broad consensus over policy priorities, with incremental shifts the dominant pattern.[34] Conflict, then, focuses primarily on pragmatic concerns and is there-fore more often easily mediated.

Gail Lapidus also has examined many of these trends, and in them she sees what she considers to be the major theme of the Brezhnev era as the system's "depoliticization."[35] This term summarizes much of the spirit of the Brezhnev era, given the emphasis on consensus and stability as opposed to conflict and instability. Depoliticization, how-ever, does not encompass one very important aspect of the system: the role of the party. Many scholars who saw "a change to change" in the Soviet system in the 1960s argued that the party might lag behind the pluralization brought on by modernization. The party, it was claimed, might not be able to keep up, and this inability would change the system. Contrary to these expectations, however, society diversified, as did the party, and, as a consequence, it does not seem likely to wither away in the near future. In fact, as the party has expanded in size, its infiltration of society has increased. In addition, the ability of party members to handle the growing complexity of decision making has risen, thanks to a sharp rise, faster even than that of the general population, in their levels of education and in the range of their technical and administrative training.[36]

The party, seeking a microcosm of the best and brightest, is viewed as more necessary than ever for rational decision making. As Brezhnev put it at the Twenty-Fifth Party Congress, the party must combine party spirit (*partiinost*) with competence, to be red and expert.[37] The general point is that there is *no* evidence that the Brezhnev regime envisions any significant reduction in party influence in Soviet policymaking. On the contrary, it has been argued explicitly that "now, more than ever, the responsibility of the party for all aspects of the economy, state affairs and social life has grown."[38]

Thus, the activist "state" (in this case, the Communist Party)—a central tenet in the corporatist model—is very much present in the Soviet Union. The party's role is not to dominate wholly, but to be the activist, the catalyst, in leading and coordinating the various sectors of the Soviet system. There is no doubt that the party is primary. The power of appointment (*nomenklatura*) over other units—a facet of some other corporatist polities as well[39]—is sufficient to ensure the party's standing. That power, though, is now used, even more than before, to bring other elements together in a cooperative effort to determine and implement public policy.

Though what we are describing is characteristic primarily of the Brezhnev era, we should stress, of course, that what we are describing has important roots in previous regimes. In essence, all Brezhnev has done is implement the notion that Lenin stressed upon the establishment of the Bolshevik administration, that under socialism, antagonism among groups is ended. In its place arises a common purpose, the transition to communism. It was this rationale that originally "permitted" the emasculation of all independent entities in the system, from trade unions to agrarian associations. These organizations were restructured into subordinate bodies, subservient to and infiltrated by the Communist Party.[40] They remain subordinate and infiltrated, and antagonisms still are presumed not to exist. What Brezhnev has done is to encourage and even regularize some influence on policy by representatives of nonparty bodies and to stress more genuine as opposed to forced cooperation. The Brezhnev era, then, has witnessed a trend toward a relationship of equals, though still far from equality. The party remains the leading partner.

The Power of Planning and Rationality

The original Leninist corporatist arrangement—massive state and party intervention in major sectors of the society and economy—was designed most immediately for the purpose of control in a time of civil war. More generally, however, its purpose was to take hold of those sectors to facilitate the planning and the controlled development of Soviet society. Of course, this concern was manifest to an extreme under Stalin, to the point where control was in fact hard to find in the drive to transform the system. Greater policy stability began to return to the Soviet scene under Khrushchev, yet "hurrah planning" and "hare-brained schemes" were as characteristic of that regime as were signs of more measured and cautious policymaking. Brezhnev has been the one to restore control, in the sense of stability and informed decision making, to the policy process. As he has repeated time and again, "We must put an end to subjectivism"[41] and "guard against extremes, proceeding in a rational economic manner, taking all aspects and implications of each measure into account."[42] It is the present leadership, therefore, that has instituted the Stalinist dictum that socialism is not created by "explosions." Rather, it is created by careful, informed decision making. This approach is reflected, first, in a greater emphasis on knowledge and scientific analysis in policymaking; second, a greater use of specialists and experts in the policy process; third, more realistic policymaking; and, fourth, greater stability and evenness in policy outputs.

The first two trends are subsumed under what has been termed the "scientific-technical revolution" in the Soviet Union. It was Khrushchev who began the process of trying to make Soviet decision making more systematic, but it has taken Brezhnev to make this a full-fledged movement. It is difficult to assess to what extent modern decision-making techniques, such as systems theory, have actually been introduced in the Soviet Union, but they are certainly being discussed, and calls for their use are numerous.[43] As for the general role of expertise, there is clear evidence simply in the tremendous growth noted above in education, technical training, and experience among party and government officials. Beyond that, we have, again, the several studies documenting, within certain limits, the significant role of nonparty and nongovernment specialists in many areas of policymaking.

The greater realism in policymaking in the Brezhnev era is reflected in such trends as the smaller gaps in the current period between goals in the economic plan and the plan's actual fulfillment. Under Khrushchev, the plan was used as a spur to productivity; it was often unrealistic and unfulfilled. Given its inflated expectations, it became less of an economic aid than a hindrance and a source of great resentment among party and state officials. With Brezhnev, however, the plan has become a better guide to action and a more realistic set of inputs and targets. While both consumer goods and agriculture have lagged behind planned investment, in general plan fulfillment is much more pronounced now than under Khrushchev.[44] Thus, the plan is one more indication of Brezhnev's pragmatism and his concern for rationalizing the policy process, setting realistic goals, promoting consensus, and keeping morale high.

A similar conclusion could be drawn from analyses of other policy areas as well—for example, dissent, relaxation of foreign tensions, Comecon relations, the formation of agricultural-industrial complexes, land reclamation, pension reform, reduction of socio-economic gaps between the city and the countryside, and the like. Khrushchev oversold and underfinanced his innovations, often quickly abandoning them to move on to new projects. By contrast, Brezhnev has made longer term and more realistic commitments and has been more successful in terms of fulfillment. Thus, both regimes have been innovative, but in different ways; many of Khrushchev's ideas foundered, only to be picked up and implemented more effectively by Brezhnev—for example, détente, the concept of the all-people's state, and many agricultural innovations.[45]

Closely related to this emphasis on more realism in policymaking is evidence of greater stability and evenhandedness in policy outputs. The conflict embedded in the zero-sum game of resource allocation—characteristic of the Khrushchev years—has been reduced, replaced by a generally positive-sum game in which all, or at least most, can win. The scientific-technical revolution is designed to maintain a steady if not spectacular economic growth rate, and that growth is to be distributed in roughly constant patterns across the various sectors of the society and economy; few are asked to sacrifice unnecessarily. In the vast majority of cases, incremental adjustments are the most that will occur.

This stability of politics and policy under Brezhnev is evident in a number of areas, most prominently in the relative lack of administrative reorganizations since 1964. It also can be illustrated in a comparison of the magnitude of shifts in priorities under Khrushchev and under Brezhnev. In Table 1.1 we present the average annual changes in shares of all capital investment for the major sectors of the

TABLE 1.1

Average Annual Changes in Shares of Total Capital Investment, Khrushchev and Brezhnev Eras (Percentage)

Investment Sector	Khrushchev Era 1956-64	Brezhnev Era 1965-75
Total industry	1.40	0.30
Heavy industry	1.47	0.40
Light industry	0.35	0.09
Agriculture	1.00	0.50

Sources: *Sovet Ekonomicheskoi Vzaimopomoshchi statisticheskii ezhegodnik stran-chlenov ekonomicheskoi vzaimopomoshchi* (SEV) (Moscow: Statistika, 1976), pp. 130-59; *Narodnoe khozyaistvo SSSR za 60 let: yubileinyi statisticheskii ezhegodnik* (Moscow: Statistika, 1977), pp. 272-73, 653-56.

economy. As is readily apparent, priority shifts have been significantly less year-to-year under Brezhnev.[46]

We should note, however, that the Brezhnev years have not been characterized only by marginal adjustments. There have been some dramatic policy changes as well, although most of these were designed to create a more stable, corporatist system. Many occurred very early on and involved retractions of Khrushchev's policies: the 1962 bifurcation of the party into agricultural and industrial sectors was rescinded, as were the regional economic councils (*sovnarkhozy*); the 1958 education reforms were dealt a final blow; and Lysenko was dethroned. Policies such as these gave the new administration an image simply of being opposed to Khrushchev's innovations. Yet these changes, in addition to more positive moves (for example, substantial increases in the amounts paid by the state for agricultural deliveries), involved extending an olive branch to many important and discontented elements of society that had been alienated by Khrushchev: the party, industrial managers, the government bureaucracy, scientists, and the agricultural sector. Placated, these elements became the base upon which the new coalition strategy of cooperation, harmony, and corporatism developed.[47] These innovations mended the fences Khrushchev had broken, and the measured and positive-sum policy change that ensued has cemented this strategy.

Of course, there have been times when the consensus has broken down, when the conflicts among groups has resurfaced. This has occurred, for example, in agricultural policy—over the nature and size

of state investment in agriculture and that sector's optimal organization.[48] Similarly, the failure of the 1965 economic reform indicated
that not all policies since 1965 have been a source of consensus,
either in terms of how they were formed or how they were implemented.[49] Corporatist politics do not preclude conflict. They merely
provide the psychological and institutional milieu for encouraging,
even forcing greater consensus.

The Role of the Masses and the Welfare State

The fence mending and appeasement described above have not
been restricted to the more narrow, identifiable and/or organized
sectors of society. The general public has been brought in as well,
their lot considerably improved by a vast expansion of consumer
goods and services for all and redistributive wage and subsidy
policies for those on the bottom of Soviet society.

The Soviet Union has always projected an image of a welfare
state, but this was not at all deserved until very recently. Stalin's
beneficence, such as it was, ignored a number of policy areas, such
as wages and housing, and many sectors of the population, especially
those unable to work. Khrushchev began the long process of remedy-
ing this situation. Brezhnev continued and expanded it, engaging in a
war on poverty that made Lyndon Johnson's effort look more like a
skirmish. Indeed, Peter Wiles has claimed, "I doubt if any country
can show a more rapid and sweeping progress towards equality."[50] As
a result, Wiles further concludes, income inequalities across the
various strata of Soviet society have finally been brought to levels
significantly below what we find in the West. The Soviet Union is still
far from an egalitarian society, but it is much closer than it once
was.[51]

The redistributive thrust of recent Soviet incomes policy differs
significantly from corporatist practices in the West. There the workers
have been rewarded only in an absolute and not a relative sense;
income inequalities have not been reduced since World War II.
Instead, the average citizen, at least in the *liberal* corporatist society,
is provided with the newest products of the consumer society and
with a lengthening list of guaranteed, universalized benefits in education, health care, housing, and income security.[52] The Soviet Union is
currently engaged in a campaign to expand these benefits as well for
its citizens. The last two decades have witnessed a tremendous
housing boom, an effort to implement universal secondary education
(evidenced in a sharp increase in educational levels), attempts to

improve general medical care and expand basic care to rural areas (a more intractable problem than the others), and programs to provide minimum income levels for all citizens.[53] For the most part, these programs simply have continued priorities set under Khrushchev. The Brezhnev innovation in this area (besides the redistributive incomes policy) has been in consumer goods, where a veritable revolution has taken place. Television sets, refrigerators, washing machines, all rare commodities only 15 years ago, are now flooding the Soviet Union.[54] Perhaps the epitome of the concessions to Soviet consumerism has been the decision to expand greatly the production of private cars. Khrushchev had attempted to hold the line on that issue, but the new regime has given in.

What we are describing is part of an effort to extend to the masses what the party, government, enterprise officials, and other higher-level bodies have received, that is, a more comfortable and secure position in the social, economic, and political order. The efforts in the consumer sector—"goulash communism," as some have termed it—are to combine with the continued easing of political pressures on all who do not overtly criticize the regime to promote a more satisfied, quiescent public. Again, as Brezhnev himself has stressed, his regime is creating an atmosphere where those who do not dissent can "breathe freely, work well, and live quietly."[55]

This effort to tie the masses into the system with positive benefits has its political aspects as well. Most notably, Brezhnev has further expanded the Khrushchev policies of increasing the size of the party, debate in the mass media about public policies, and popular involvement in local bodies. Much of the activity of these participants is symbolic and orchestrated from the top, yet a good deal of this participation may be meaningful. At the least, such activity is heavily encouraged and brings more and more people formally into the system.[56]

Thus, with the expansion of the welfare state, the consumer society, and opportunities for political involvement, the Brezhnev regime has made a substantial effort to tie the masses into the system, to make them more comfortable, and, it is hoped, more productive. The masses, like the other elements in society, are seen as vital to the system, worthy of trust and greater responsibility (to a point), and to be rewarded and encouraged accordingly. Stalin once argued that "the people do not want to fight for socialism; you must make them fight for socialism." The Brezhnev regime has decided that a little more trust, and a lot more benefits, will make the people, not fight perhaps, but at least work harder.

The Goals of the System

What does "working for socialism" mean in the Brezhnev era? What are the goals of this regime? Ultimately, of course, the expressed goal is a communist society, with all that entails. In the meantime, however, certain ends and means are stressed over others, and the Brezhnev administration has set some clear priorities.

When we discussed corporatism in the West, we stressed that that system's central goals are economic growth, political and social stability, and maintenance of the prevailing distribution of power. It is not unreasonable to suggest that these are the ends of the Soviet corporatist system as well. The first goal, of course, is not new; economic growth has been at the center of Soviet policy making since the end of War Communism, when the regime committed itself to "Soviet power plus electrification." The debate has been over means. Both Stalin and Khrushchev had their methods, and now Brezhnev is offering his—the approach we have been setting out in this paper: greater satisfaction of wants, more systematic and informed decision making, political and social stability, maintenance of the existing order, and greater participation. These are all important components of that approach as well as ends in themselves. If one can maintain stability in the system *and* achieve reasonable growth, then all the better. In fact, the argument is more forceful than that. Growth, according to contemporary Soviet thinking, is *aided* by stability and participation.[57] Stability and participation breed trust and cooperation, which, combined with the scientific-technical revolution, promote growth—not spectacular growth, but steady advances of 3–5 percent per year. This rate is sufficient to generate continuous, albeit incremental increases for all sectors, which further ensure stability and the existing order; thus the circle is complete. This indeed is the promise of a corporatist arrangement, and it is the essence of the Brezhnev era.

Summary

In the early 1960s, it seemed as if the Soviet Union were on the verge of a major transformation. Growth rates were declining, several major structural reforms were attempted, and economic reforms, often of a distinctly revisionist nature, were proposed and discussed. Many Western scholars saw these developments as the necessary result of pressures for change within the system. The Soviet Union, it was felt, could not survive without major modifications.

It has survived, of course, and in part because of modifications
that were made by the leadership to help ensure that survival. Those
changes, however, were not the stuff Western predictions were made
of. Instead, they have paralleled changes many non-Communist systems have made, albeit from a different direction and with some
different emphases, in order that *they* might survive and even flourish.
We have subsumed these changes under the label employed for the
Western systems—"corporatism"—a system of participation and cooperation among major elements in the policy, society, and economy,
enforced and coordinated by the state (or the party) and designed to
ensure continuous economic growth, political and social stability,
and the preservation of the existing order with at best incremental
adjustments.

Thus, the conflict and restructuring characteristic of the Khrushchev era and proposals for substantial reform of the economy in more
market-oriented directions were rejected. Adopted instead is what on
the surface may seem to be "muddling through" but in fact reflects a
somewhat more fundamental, systematic, and successful reorientation of the system. All this is not to argue that the Soviet Union has
become a well-oiled machine of shared interests, meshing smoothly
and moving toward continued further development. There is still, of
course, a good deal of conflict; in the system, inefficiencies, significant limits on participation by outside elements, a low standard of
living—even poverty—for many still exist. The Soviet Union is not
ideal; far from it. It is not even an ideal "corporatist" polity. However,
that word best describes the major characteristics of the present
order, and, given the "name game" in Soviet scholarship discussed
earlier and the utility of the label for many Western systems, it is a
useful characterization.

CORPORATISM: EAST AND WEST

Although we are employing the same concept to describe different systems, it must be stressed that this is not at all meant to imply
that corporatist practices in the West are *identical* with those in the
Soviet Union under Brezhnev. There are certainly important differences between corporatist politics in advanced capitalist societies
and the Soviet Union. Most notably, of course, we can point again to
Schmitter's distinction between "societal" and "state" subtypes. The
latter is meant to apply to "anti-liberal, delayed capitalist, authoritarian, neomercantilist" states, but it seems applicable to the Soviet case
as well:

The distinguishing structural and behavioral differences between the two are seen to depend on whether the nature of the constituent units, in terms of their limited numbers, singularity, compulsory character, and monopolistic representation of functional groups is a product more of general socioeconomic developments and voluntarist arrangements than of state imposition, and whether the state's controls on their leadership selection and interest articulation is a product of "reciprocal consensus on procedure and/or goals, or of an asymmetric imposition by the 'organized monopolists of legitimate violence.'"[58]

Corporatism in liberal Western politics is a *voluntary* arrangement, one which unions in particular can and indeed have broken in some cases. There is no question in the Soviet Union of the trade union federation or any other major association breaking off from the system. This is important particularly since it is often the independent, active, even violent interest group challenging the system that has been a major force for change in democratic polities.[59] The general point, then, is that liberal corporatist systems permit a far wider range of civil liberties and political rights than does the Soviet Union.

However, the Soviet Union does not fully fit the *state* corporatist model either. In particular, there is the development of a welfare state—with its guarantees of jobs, minimum incomes, and certain services—and the egalitarian revolution (at least with respect to income distribution by class). These differentiate the Soviet Union from the nonliberal (and, to some extent, even the liberal) corporatist orders.

Thus, the Soviet Union is a mixture of corporatist types, and it is in this mixture that we make sense of the seemingly contradictory trends, such as policy stability *and* an expanding welfare state, that scholars have been unable to reconcile in "liberal" or "conservative" models. "Corporatism" fits these trends much better, particularly the core characteristics of that model.

CONCLUSION: AFTER BREZHNEV

How permanent is this trend, and what will happen after Brezhnev? As always, predictions of this type are difficult to make. Certainly the impact of a new leader could be substantial, and past experience would lead us to predict such an impact.[60] We opened this chapter with a discussion of eras associated with first secretaries, and what reason have we to expect the next to be different?

Ironically, we have several reasons to expect the next era to be different, in the sense that it may very well *continue* the corporatist trend. First, corporatism has been successful, especially in terms of economic growth. What's more, it is plausible to suggest that the current growth rates of 3–5 percent per year can be maintained in the foreseeable future; even agriculture, despite popular notions, is hardly in dire straits.[61] In addition, this economic growth can be bought under corporatism at little or no cost to any major sector. On the contrary, the new order has been a boon to many groups, not just the economic managers and the party but also agricultural workers and the masses, who have gained a great deal under Brezhnev's tutelage.

Second, there is the importance of precedent. Almost one-fourth of Soviet history has taken place under Brezhnev; this is a lot to retract, especially when one remembers (and Soviet elites do remember) all the problems associated with trying to cancel the legacy of Stalin. More importantly, there would seem to be few reasons to believe that the Soviet leaders would *want* to erase the Brezhnev years. Given the accolades he received at the Twenty-Fifth Congress and the fact that he has been allowed to christen a new era— "developed socialism"—and a new constitution, it is very likely that Brezhnev will leave office a hero rather than a nonperson. (Lenin, of course, was the last person so honored.) Moreover, it would seem that the known alternatives would be worse. Life under Khrushchev was not as comfortable, either at the top or at the bottom.

Third, corporatism, under the label "developed socialism," would appear to be an acceptable system with which to head into the future. Few are hurt, many are helped, progress is being made, and a new stage is evolving. Communism, meanwhile, is put off for the indefinite future. The transition to communism is on track but not compelled to meet any pressing timetable.

Thus, corporatism would seem to be here to stay. It may undergo some strains, and conflict may surface, as has happened periodically since 1964; however, such a cycle is *common* in most corporatist states as group access is repeatedly readjusted to changing conditions.[62] It is also possible that in the Soviet Union fundamental conflicts over priorities or even the future of the system may split the leadership into irreconcilable camps, major economic dislocations may in fact occur, and certain unincorporated groups may become strong enough to demand inclusion in the policy process. Any of these developments could undermine corporatist arrangements. However, the logic of corporatism and its benefits to elites, groups, and masses are not insignificant. Brezhnev, therefore, seems to have been much more of an innovator than many scholars have argued;

like his predecessors, he has ushered in a new system. But, unlike his predecessors, this system may even outlive its founder.

NOTES

1. William A. Welsh, "Introduction: The Comparative Study of Political Leadership in Communist Systems," in *Comparative Communist Political Leadership*, ed. Carl Beck et al. (New York: David McKay, 1973), p. 1.

2. Alfred G. Meyer, "The Comparative Study of Communist Political Systems," in *Communist Studies and the Social Sciences*, ed. Frederic J. Fleron, Jr. (Chicago: Rand McNally, 1969), p. 193. Also see Jerry Hough, "The Brezhnev Era: The Man and the System," *Problems of Communism* 25 (1976): 14.

3. For a discussion of these issues and those immediately following concerning change in the Brezhnev era see, for example, Hough, "Brezhnev Era," pp. 1–17; Jerry Hough, "The Soviet System: Pluralism of Petrification," *Problems of Communism* 12 (1972): 25–45; George Breslauer, "Khrushchev Reconsidered," *Problems of Communism* 12 (1972): 25–45; George Breslauer, "Khrushchev Reconsidered," *Problems of Communism* 25 (1976): 18–33; George W. Breslauer, "On the Adaptability of Soviet Welfare State Authoritarianism," in *The Communist Party and Soviet Society*, ed. Karl Ryavec (Amherst; University of Massachusetts Press, 1978), pp. 3–25; Archie Brown, "Political Developments: Some Conclusions and an Interpretation," in *The Soviet Union Since the Fall of Khrushchev*, ed. Archie Brown and Michael Kaser (London: Macmillan, 1975), pp. 218–85; Zbigniew Brzezinski, "The Soviet System: Transformation or Degeneration," *Problems of Communism* 15 (1966): 3–9; Jerry Hough, *The Soviet Union and Social Science Theory*, (Cambridge; Harvard University Press, 1976), pp. 51–76.

4. See, in particular, Hough, "The Soviet System," and Brzezinski, "The Soviet System."

5. See Donald Kelley, "The Soviet Image of the Future," in *The Soviet Union: Problems and Prospects*, ed. Robert Wesson (Stanford: Hoover Institution Press, 1979); Alfred B. Evans Jr., "Developed Socialism in Soviet Ideology," *Soviet Studies* 29 (July 1977): 409–28; Paul Cocks, "Retooling the Directed Society; Administrative Modernization and Developed Socialism," in *Political Development in Eastern Europe*, ed. Jan Triska and Paul M. Cocks (New York: Praeger, 1977), pp. 53–92; B. N. Torpornin, "Gosudarstvo i demokratiya razvitogo sotsializma," in *Sotsializm i demokratiya*, ed. B. N. Torpornin (Moscow: Yuridicheskaya, 1976): 15–44; F. Burlatsky, "The Soviet Constitution on the Political System of Advanced Socialism," *Socialism: Theory and Practice* 2 (February 1978): 1924.

6. See Brzezinski, 'The Soviet System," William Odom, "A Dissenting View on the Group Approach to Soviet Politics," *World Politics* 28 (1976): 542–67.

7. For example, Hough, *The Soviet Union*; Breslauer, "On the Adaptability"; Chalmers Johnson, ed. *Change in Communist Systems*, (Stanford: Stanford University Press, 1970); H. Gordon Skilling and Franklyn Griffiths, eds., *Interest Groups in Soviet Politics*, (Princeton: Princeton University Press, 1971); Stephen White, "Communist Systems and the Iron Law of Pluralism," *British Journal of Political Science* 8 (1978): 101–18; William Taubman, "The Change to Change in Communist Systems: Modernization, Post-Modernization and Soviet Politics," in *Soviet Politics and Society in the 1970's*, ed. Henry Morton and Rudolf Tökes (New York: Macmillan, 1974), pp. 369–94; Peter Solomon, Jr., *Soviet Criminologists and Criminal Policy* (New York: Columbia

University Press, 1978); "The CPSU in Figures," *Soviet Law and Government* 3 (1976-77): 3-23; Robert Osborn, *Soviet Social Policies* (Homewood, Ill.: Dorsey Press, 1970); I. Matiukha, "The Rise in Living Standards of the Working People of the USSR," *Problems of Economics* 16 (1973): 60-71.

    8. Hough, *The Soviet Union*, esp. pp. 3-12, 23-24.

    9. For a discussion of corporatism, see Phillippe Schmitter, ed., *Corporatism and Policy-Making in Contemporary Western Europe, Comparative Political Studies* (Special Issue) 10 (1977); Phillippe Schmitter, "Still the Century of Corporatism" *Review of Politics* 36 (1974): 85-131; Robert Kvavik, "Interest Groups in a Cooptive Polity: The Case of Norway," in *Politics in Europe*, ed. Martin O. Heisler (New York: David McKay, 1974), pp. 93-116; Howard J. Wiarda, "Toward a Framework for the Study of Political Change in the Iberic-Latin Tradition: The Corporative Model" (Paper presented at the American Political Science Association Convention, Chicago, September 7-11, 1971); John T. S. Keeler, "Agricultural Corporatism in the Fifth Republic" (Paper presented at the American Political Science Association Convention, New York, August 31-September 3, 1978); James Wolfe, "Corporatism in German Political Life: Functional Representation in the GDR and Bavaria," in *Politics in Europe*, ed. Martin O. Heisler (New York: David McKay, 1974), pp. 323-40; Michael Brenner, "Interest Group Theory: Some Notes on British Practice," in *Politics in Western European Democracies*, eds., Gary Byrne and Kenneth Pederson (New York: Wiley, 1971), pp. 515-60; Francis Castles, "Policy Innovation and Institutional Stability in Sweden," *British Journal of Political Science* 6 (1976): 203-16.

    10. Schmitter, "Still the Century," pp. 103-05.

    11. Ibid., pp. 93-94.

    12. Ibid.

    13. Leo Panitch, "The Development of Corporatism in Liberal Democracies," *Comparative Political Studies* 10 (1977): 66.

    14. Charles Lindblom, *The Intelligence of Democracy* (New York: Free Press, 1965); Aaron Wildavsky, "The Political Economy of Efficiency: Cost Benefit Analysis, Systems Analysis, and Program Budgeting," *Public Administration Review* 26 (1966): 292-310.

    15. See, in particular, Leo Panitch, *Social Democracy and Industrial Militancy: The Labour Party, the Trade Unions and Incomes Policy, 1945-1974.* (London: Cambridge University Press, 1976); Brenner, "Interest Group Theory"; Keeler, "Agricultural Corporatism"; Rand Smith, "Institutionalization of Class Conflict? The State and Labor in Advanced Capitalism" (Paper presented at the American Political Science Association Convention, Washington, D.C., September 1-4, 1977).

    16. See Kvavik, "Interest Groups"; Norman Furniss and Timothy Tilton, *The Case For the Welfare State* (Bloomington: Indiana University Press, 1977), pp. 122-50.

    17. We should note that in recent years the goal of economic growth has become debatable in Sweden, as the issue of scarcity has arisen in that country. See Neil Elder, "The Swedish General Election of 1976," *Parliamentary Affairs* 30 (1977): 193-208. Also see, more generally, William Ophuls, *Ecology and the Politics of Scarcity* (San Francisco: W.H. Freeman, 1977.)

    18. Schmitter, "Still the Century," pp. 103-04, quoted in Panitch, "The Development of Corporatism, p. 65.

    19. Schmitter, "Still the Century."

    20. Jack L. Walker, "Knowledge into Power: A Theory of Agenda Setting" (Ann Arbor: Institute of Public Policy Studies, University of Michigan, 1973); Theodore Lowi, *The End of Liberalism* (New York: Norton, 1969).

    21. Panitch, *Social Democracy*; Smith, "Institutionalization."

    22. See Panitch. *Social Democracy*; "Political Change"; Wiarda, and some of the arguments made against workers councils as co-optive mechanisms; for instance,

Mauk Muldaur, "Power Equalization Through Participation?" *Administrative Science Quarterly* 16 (1971): 31–39.

23. Breslauer, "Khrushchev Reconsidered"; Merle Fainsod, "Khrushchevism," in *Marxism in the Modern World*, ed. Milorad Drakhovitch (Stanford: Hoover Institution Press, 1965), pp. 108–35; for typical Khrushchev statements on the need to challenge cadres, see N. S. Khrushchev. *Stroitelstvo kommunizma SSSR i razvitie selskogo khozyaistva*, vol. 1 (Moscow: Politizdat, 1962), pp. 390, 454–55.

24. Breslauer, "On the Adaptability."

25. Gail Lapidus, "The Brezhnev Regime and Directed Social Change; Depoliticization as a Strategy," in *The Twenty-Fifth Party Congress Assessment and Context*, ed. Alexander Dallin (Stanford: Hoover Institute Press, 1977), pp. 34–35.

26. Donald D. Barry and Carol Barner-Barry, *Contemporary Soviet Politics: An Introduction* (Englewood Cliffs, N.J.: Prentice-Hall, 1978 pp. 102, 104.

27. Hough, "Brezhnev Era," p. 5.

28. Ibid., pp. 5–6.

29. See Solomon, *Soviet Criminologists*; Skilling and Griffiths, *Interest Groups*; Philip D. Stewart, "Soviet Interest Groups and the Policy Process: The Repeal of Production Education," *World Politics* 22 (1969): 29–50; Donald R. Kelley, "Environmental Policymaking in the USSR: The Role of Industrial and Environmental Interest Groups," *Soviet Studies* 28 (1976): 570–89.

30. A. Gorskaya, "Leninskii stil i metody khozyaistvennogo rukovodstva," *Planovoe khozyaistvo* 11 (1975): 93–102.

31. It should be stressed that both these trends toward group influence did not begin with Brezhnev but with his predecessors. Brezhnev's contribution has been to expand and in a sense "regularize and institutionalize the process." (Solomon, *Soviet Criminologists*, p. 149). He wants both to expand input and to stabilize the decision-making process, as opposed to the Khrushchev strategy of expanding input as a way to shake up the system.

32. Kelley, "The Soviet Image of the Future."

33. For an attempt to categorize types of Soviet decisions and levels of elite conflict, see Donald R. Kelley, "Toward a Model of Soviet Decision-Making: A Research Note," *American Political Science Review* 68 (1974): 701–06.

34. Valerie Bunce and John M. Echols III, "Power and Policy in Communist Systems: The Problem of 'Incrementalism,'" *Journal of Politics* 41 (1978): 911–32.

35. Lapidus, "The Brezhnev Regime".

36. Hough, "Party Saturation," p. 126; Aryeh Unger, "Soviet Communist Party Membership Under Brezhnev," *Soviet Studies* 29 (1977): 306–16; Dale Chapman," A Note on the Ageing of the Politboro," *Soviet Studies* 29 (1977): 296–305; I. Kapitonov, "KPSS v politicheskoi sisteme razvitogo sotsialisticheskogo obshchestva," *Kommunist* 6 (1978): 29–43.

37. Leonid Brezhnev, "Otchet Tsentralnogo Komiteta KPSS i ocherednye zadachi partii v oblasti vnutrennei i vneshnei politiki," *Pravda*, February 25, 1976. Thus, Brezhnev's theory of correct leadership emphasizes objectivity, caution, and scientific sophistication, as well as party-spiritedness; also see N. Viklin and A. Davydov "Partiya i sovety," *Partinaya zhizn* 4 (1978): 26–33.

38. V. Stepanov, "Neuklannoe povyshenie rukovodyashchei i napravlyaiushchei roli KPSS," *Partinaya zhizn* 3 (1977): 15; G. Kh. Shakhnazarov, "O nekotorykh tendentsiyakh razvitiya politicheskoi sistemy sotsializma," *Sovotskoe gosudarstvo i pravo* 1 (1978): 4. The usual argument by the party is that the masses are still lagging and need to be prompted. See E.M. Kuznetsov, *Politicheskaya agitatsiya: Nauchnye osnovy praktiki* (Moscow: Mysl, 1974), pp. 280–81. Indeed, one could argue "objectively" that the role of the party should not be reduced if one notes Jerry Hough's argument for the

vital role the party plays in the system; see Hough, *The Soviet Prefects* (Cambridge; Harvard University Press, 1969).

39. See Schmitter, "Modes of Interest Mediation." This, of course, is far more common in the more authoritarian forms of corporatism, that is, the "state" form.

40. See, for example, Sheila Fitzpatrick, ed., *Cultural Revolution in Russia, 1928-1931* (Bloomington: Indiana University Press, 1977); Robert Vincent Daniels, *The Conscience of the Revolution* (Cambridge: Harvard University Press, 1960), pp. 108-18; Leonard Schapiro, *The Origin of the Communist Autocracy* (New York: Praeger, 1965), pp. 221-25.

41. Leonid Brezhnev, *Leninskim kursom*, vol. 1 (Moscow: Politizdat, 1972), p. 71.

42. Leonid Brezhnev, "Delo vsei partii, vsego naroda," *Pravda*, December 16, 1973.

43. See, for example, Robert Miller, "The Scientific-Technical Revolution and the Soviet Administrative Debate," in *Dynamics of Soviet Politics*, ed. Paul Cocks, et al (Cambridge: Harvard University Press, 1977): pp. 137-55; Donald R. Kelley, "American and Soviet Applications of Systems Theory," and Richard F. Vidmer and James C. Thompson, "Decision-Making in the Organizational Context: A Comparison of Soviet and American Perspectives," (Papers presented at the American Political Science Association Convention, New York, August 31-September 3, 1978).

44. Keith Bush, "Soviet Agriculture: Ten Years Under New Management," Radio Liberty Research Paper (Munich: Radio Liberty, August 21, 1974); also see Leonid Brezhnev, *Ob osnovnykh voprosakh ekonomicheskoi politiki KPSS na sovremennom etape*, vol. 2 (Moscow: Politizdat, 1975), pp. 5-20. In evaluations of Brezhnev's performance by the Soviets themselves, for example, much is made of Brezhnev's "realism," his "consistency" and his patience. See, for instance, A. Monov, "Agriculture During the Current Five Year Plan," *Problems of Economics* 15 (1972): 3-19.

45. In fact, the 1965 agricultural plenum is a very good example of the consensus and moderation of policymaking during the Brezhnev regime. See I. M. Volkov, "Novyi etap v razvitii selskogo khozyaistva SSSR," *Istoriya SSSR*, 22 (1975): 3-21. On the general point, see V. A. Golikov, ed., *Kursom Martovskogo plenuma* (Moscow: Politizdat, 1975).

46. Even areas in which innovation has been evident under Brezhnev illustrate the commitment to "measured policy change." A great deal of money has been poured into agriculture, with its share of total investment increasing substantially between 1965 and 1975. Yet except for 1965—the first year of the new regime and the year of a major plenum on the topic—the changes involved marginal upward adjustments. For a description of this strategy and how it compares with that of Khrushchev, see Leonid Brezhnev, *Voprosy agrarnoi politiki KPSS i osvoenie tselinikh zemel Kazakhstana* (Moscow: Politizdat, 1974) pp. 97-99; I.M. Volkov, "Nekotorye voprosy istorii selskogo khozyaistva i krestianstva v poslevoennye gody," *Istoriia SSSR* 20 (1973): 3-19; and Brezhnev, *Leninskim kursom*, pp. 68-70. In other words, policy change in this arena embodied Aaron Wildavsky's notion of "radical incrementalism"; small change over many years, resulting eventually in a radical readjustment of priorities. See his "Toward a Radical Incrementalism," in *Congress*, ed. Alfred de Grazia (Garden City, N.Y.: Doubleday, 1967), pp. 53-79.

47. This point is also made by Archie Brown in his "Political Developments."

48. Volkov, "Novyi etap"; "O dalneishem razvitii selskogo khozyaistva SSR: postanovlenie plenuma Ts.K. KPSS," *Kommunist* 10 (1978): 3-13; Bush, "Soviet Agriculture."

49. See Abraham Katz, *The Politics of Economic Reform in the Soviet Union* (New

York: Praeger, 1972); Gregory Grossman, "An Economy at Middle Age" *Problems of Communism* 25 (1976): 18-33.

50. Peter Wiles, *Distribution of Income East and West* (Amsterdam: North Holland, 1974), p. 25; cited in Hough, "Brezhnev Era," p. 12.

51. Wiles, *Distribution of Income*; however, the comparatively greater equality in the Soviet Union is limited largely to the area of income distribution by class. The status of women and minorities, for example, is no greater than in the West; see John M. Echols, "Does Communism Mean Greater Equality? A Comparison of East and West Along Several Major Dimensions" (Paper presented at the American Political Science Association Convention, Chicago, September 1-4, 1976).

52. For discussion of the welfare state, its performance and characteristics, see Furniss and Tilton, *Welfare State*.

53. For a discussion of the various social welfare reforms and their impact on various groups in Soviet society, see Hough, *The Soviet Union*; David Bronson and Constance Krueger, "The Revolution in Soviet Farm Household Income," in *The Soviet Rural Community*, ed. James Millar (Urbana: University of Illinois Press, 1971), pp. 214-58; A. Barkaiskas, "O prodelenii kulturno-bytovykh razlichii mezhdu gorodom i derevnei," *Kommunist* 8 (1973): 53-66; Osborn, *Soviet Social Policies*; Matiukha, "Living Standards", Hough, "The Brezhnev Era" op. cit.; V. Maier, "Rost narodnogo blagosostoyaniya v usloviyakh razvitogo sotsializma," *Kommunist* 9 (1974): 62-75; "Blagosostoyaniya naroda—glavnaya zadacha KPSS," *Pravda*, July 6, 1974. For a good summary, see George R. Feiwel, *The Soviet Quest for Economic Efficiency* (New York: Praeger, 1972), pp. 598-608.

54. Hough, "Brezhnev Era"; "The Party Leads the People to New Accomplishments," *Current Digest of the Soviet Press* 36, (January 15, 1975): 3.

55. Quoted in Breslauer, "On the Adaptability," p. 18. This theme also appears in Soviet discussions of the linkage between economic abundance, economic growth, and political satisfaction. See *Razvityi sotsializm: proizvodstvo materialnykh blag*, ed. M.S. Kukushkin (Leningrad: Lenizdat, 1975).

56. See Hough *The Soviet Union*, pp. 109-24; T.M. Rigby, "Hough on Political Participation in the Soviet Union," *Soviet Studies* 28 (1976): 257-61; Ivan Kapitonov, "Achievements and Problems of Democracy Under Developed Socialism," *World Marxist Review* 18 (1975): 46-51. James Oliver, "Citizen Demands and the Soviet Political System," in *Communist Systems in Comparative Perspective*, eds. Lenard Cohen and Jane Shapiro, (Garden City, N.Y.; Doubleday, 1974), pp. 379-99; D. Richard Little, "Mass Political Participation in the United States and the USSR," *Comparative Political Studies* 8 (1976); 437-60; P. Safarov, "Obshchestvennoe mnenie v usloviyakh razvitogo sotsializma" *Kommunist* 12 (1977): 29-40; Victor Turotsiev, *People's Control in Socialist Society* (Moscow: Progress, 1973), pp. 7-8; Ronald J. Hill, "Patterns of Deputy Selection to Local Soviets," *Slavic Review* 25 (1973): 196-212.

57. This is a major theme in tracts on developed socialism. See, for instance, P. Fedoseyev, "Developed Socialism: Theoretical Problems," *Social Sciences* 8 (1977): 8-23; Evans, "Developed Socialism"; also refer to Leonid Brezhnev, *Leninskim Kursom*, vol. 5 (Moscow: Politizdat, 1975), 527; *Leninskim Kursom*, vol. 2 (Moscow: Politizdat, 1972), p. 293.

58. Panitch, "The Development of Corporatism," p. 65.

59. See, for instance, William Gamson, *The Strategy of Social Protest* (Homewood, Ill.: Dorsey Press, 1975).

60. Valerie Bunce, "Elite Succession, Petrification and Policy Innovation in Communist Systems: An Empirical Assessment," *Comparative Political Studies* 9 (April 1976): 3-242.

61. James Millar, "The Prospects for Soviet Agriculture," *Problems of Communism* 26 (1977): 1–16. Since the 1950s, Soviet agricultural output has averaged an increase of 3.4 percent a year, a figure far above the 1.4 percent average growth in population and above U.S. growth for this period. Moreover, it is expected that a reasonable rate of interest (2-2.5 percent) can be maintained in the foreseeable future. It is true, however, that this growth is requiring an increasingly costly investment. This dilemma is also facing other sectors as well; see Grossman, "Economy."

62. See Olaf Ruin, "Participatory Democracy and Corporatism: The Case of Sweden," *Scandinavian Political Studies* 9 (1974): 171–88.

2

THE COMMUNIST PARTY

Donald R. Kelley

Western analysts of the Communist Party of the Soviet Union (CPSU) have long differed on the impact of Brezhnev's tutelage. While some have described his ascension to power as a conservative restoration and pointed to the growing immobilism of an aging "regime of clerks," others have stressed the cumulative impact of a decade-long upgrading of party cadres and noted the importance of interlocking reforms designed to rationalize and fine-tune the economy and state administration. Without question, substantial evidence can be mustered for either interpretation. But it would be simplistic to suggest that any single characterization of "conservative" or "reformist" would be adequate to describe the fifteen-year tenure of a general secretary who has headed the Politburo not only through a period of growing maturation for the society and economy but also through the gradual evolution of a style of leadership politics conducive to what Bunce and Echols have termed "corporatism." Rather, it is more appropriate to recognize that the many seeming contradictions of conservative and reformist tendencies are themselves the product of an attempt to deal simultaneously with three systemic dilemmas: (1) the need to maintain a reasonable level of stability within leadership circles while simultaneously upgrading the performance of party cadres; (2) the need to preserve the time-honored leading role of the party while modernizing both its role mission and self-image; and (3) the need to adjust membership policies to reflect the continued "proletarian" essence of the party while coping with the nation's changing social structure. In some areas, particularly those associated with high-level leadership politics, Brezhnev has moved with deliberate caution to preserve a stable working majority within the

Politburo, and although sometimes heated conflicts have occurred leading to the dismissal of dissident elements, the overall tone of Kremlin politics has been muted in comparison with Khrushchev's less-than-cautious forays against his opponents. Clearly both political realities and undoubtedly personal temperament have dictated a deliberate and cautious style easily interpreted by outside observers as innate conservatism, if not immobilism. Yet, in other areas, particularly those dealing with economic and administrative reforms and with the modernization of the party's leading role, the Brezhnev regime has shown a consistent reformist tendency, although opposition from varying sources has blunted the implementation of many reforms.

It is important to understand that the complex and often seemingly contradictory policies of the regime are best understood not as a manifestation of clearly dominant "reformist" or "conservative" trends or, for that matter, simply as the results of conflicting factional and institutional interests, although both obviously play some role. As Bunce and Echols argue in the previous chapter, the corporatist model presumes the existence of conscious, goal-directed political leadership; Brezhnev clearly has placed his own stamp on regime politics in terms of both his personal style of leadership and the overall orientation toward the system's modernization and rationalization. While the evolution of that style and orientation—and the nature of the resistance to them—will be discussed at length below, it is important to recognize at the outset that Soviet politics under Brezhnev is best understood in terms of the development of a complex *political formula* hammered out in the early post-Khrushchev era and adjusted only slightly over the years. As with any political formula, it combines elements of both hard-nosed elite politics—*kto kogo* in the traditional sense—and more diffuse, although no less political, struggles over social and economic priorities. And, as is commonplace with such formulas, the two dimensions overlap; one is never quite able with certainty to separate politics from purely programmatic concerns. Taken on the whole, however, the Brezhnev formula, if it may be termed that, has been essentially successful and forward looking. Relative peace has been maintained within top leadership circles, although some obviously politically motivated dismissals have occurred, and cautious reforms have been launched on a number of fronts. While the long-term success of many of these reforms is still an open question—in other words, whether the politics of elite stability and "respect for cadres" will prevail over the need to force reform measures on generally reluctant subordinate levels of the party apparatus and state bureaucracy—it remains clear that the top level of the regime has committed itself to recognizing the economic and social imperatives of a "developed socialist society."

LEADERSHIP POLITICS

While Brezhnev certainly does not possess the *élan vital* and ebullient style of his predecessor, he has established himself as *primus inter pares* within top leadership circles. Since 1973, he has always been listed out of alphabetical order at the head of the Politburo, and the treatment accorded his diplomatic and domestic pronouncements clearly suggests his preeminence in the hierarchy. Moreover, it is apparent that Brezhnev's relative power has grown since his original ascension to the post of first secretary in 1964; the seeming balance between Brezhnev as party chief and Kosygin as head of the state bureaucracy which characterized the first few years after Khrushchev's fall gradually gave way by the late 1960s to the cultivation of a restrained Brezhnev cult, and the general secretary's range of authority spread from limited party affairs to include foreign relations, the economy, agriculture, and virtually all other affairs of party and state.[1]

Brezhnev's emergence as the preeminent figure within the hierarchy must be read with some caution; while there is clear evidence that much of his ascent can be attributed to his skills at climbing the Soviet ladder of success—the ability to secure key appointments for his protégés, to identify with issues that draw support from diffuse elements, and to create the "mystification," as Marx would put it, of positive, forward-looking leadership while simultaneously projecting an image of stability—recognition must also be given to the fact that his long tenure in office has been enjoyed, at least in large measure, because of the tolerance and forbearance of his colleagues. His initial selection for the post of general secretary is best understood as the result of high-level deliberations among Khrushchev's opponents who chose him as the most generally acceptable candidate; there is little to indicate that he was himself the prime mover of the plot that ousted Khrushchev in 1964, nor did he incautiously overplay his hand to consolidate power in the immediate post-coup period. His growing preeminence in the late 1960s and his continued dominance of the Soviet scene, despite recurring illness in the last few years which seriously impairs his ability to deal with day-to-day affairs, are more a product of his cautious, partly conservative, partly reformist style and his ability to act as what Jerry Hough has termed a "broker" among competing factions and policy groups.[2]

This is hardly to say that Soviet politics since the fall of Khrushchev has been a seamless web of always congenial individuals and interests. Quite to the contrary, for while Brezhnev's personal style has muted conflicts among top-ranking Politburo figures—there have been few directly political dismissals not also tied to obvious failures of policy—in some ways the potential for conflict within the Politburo has been exacerbated by this body's gradual transition to a parallel cabinet within which a greater number of the important bureaucratic and regional interests are represented than ever before. In the hands of a skilled broker, and assuming a certain amount of mutual restraint on the part of the bureaucratic power centers and vested interests themselves, such a mechanism may well serve to channel and diminish conflict, in part by producing working compromises at the top level and in part by suppressing disruptive issues. But the potential for increasing conflict remains, especially when the "broker's" days are obviously numbered or the political formula defining the informal rules and limits of political battle is rejected.

The relative stability of top leadership circles has not obviated the regime's periodic need to impose its control forcefully in regional centers that have fallen victim to "localism" or simply have not met industrial or agricultural output goals. The most spectacular such incident was the extensive purge of the Georgian party apparatus in the early 1970s, an event triggered more by the recognition of widespread corruption and collusion among top Georgian party leaders than by any outstanding shortfall in production. Initial Georgian resistance was evidently vigorous, including, so the rumors that swept Moscow at the time said, threats of physical retaliation against central party officials and at least one bombing in the Soviet capital, and the Brezhnev regime was forced to conduct a protracted and frequently bitter cleansing process on top-level republic and lesser regional and local officials.

Far less spectacular but undoubtedly more common is the increasingly strong pressure being applied to regional and local officials to support the regime's efforts for economic reform and technological modernization. More often than not, regional party leaders have tacitly opposed such centralizing reforms and taken steps to block or weaken their implementation, in part certainly because they realize that the reforms are intended to diminish local party influence over crucial economic decisions within their regions and perhaps also out of a sense of innate conservatism that doubts the wisdom of extensive institutional reforms. Regardless of the motivation, the results—and the political implications for the center—are clear: political realities associated with the seemingly stable balance of institutional and personal forces within the Politburo and the need to preserve a high degree of stability among top-level party cadres have confronted the regime with the recurring dilemma of maintaining its "trust in cadres" while applying both economic and intra-party pressures to elicit support for the reforms. The record to date suggests that political considerations have dominated over the center's wish for reform, and while considerable rhetorical support for innovative measures is commonplace, the actual results are far less impressive. In most cases, attempts to alter or subvert the intent, if not the exact letter, of the reforms have been tolerated grudgingly by a central party leadership unwilling to apply the ultimate sanction of dismissal.

The evolution of the "trust in cadres" approach to intra-party stability itself requires further elaboration. While it was initiated shortly after the coup in 1964 essentially as reassurance to top and middle-level cadres that Khrushchev's capricious reorganizations of party and state bodies and frequent intervention into the affairs of local officials would be ended, it has persisted, with subtle shifts of emphasis, to this day. The need for such reassurance in the early days is evident. Khrushchev's bifurcation of the regional party apparatus, compulsory turnover of the personnel of elected party bodies at all levels, and efforts to force a redefinition of the party image along pragmatic managerial lines badly disrupted both the world view and personal security of many of the first secretary's previous supporters. It is understandable, then, that many of the new regime's first steps were directed toward reestablishing a sense of stability and purposiveness within party ranks. In organizational terms, the bifurcation was ended, with the former regional and local secretaries returning to unified command over their bailiwicks in most cases. At the Twenty-Third Party Congress the compulsory turnover on a portion of party committees was abolished, setting the stage for greater security of tenure on the part of middle-level party leaders. The Bureau of the RSFSR, a Khrushchev creation designed in part as a counterweight to the ·traditional apparatus and dominated by the first secretary's appointees, was also abolished. In similar fashion, the Party-State Control Committee, whose increasingly vigilant watchdog role had offended many within the party, was given more circumscribed tasks. Without doubt, at least the institutional vestiges of the Khrushchev era were quickly disassembled with little opposition from the state and party officials who had come to question their administrative wisdom and fear their political implications.

The style and tone of the early years of the Brezhnev regime came quickly to be expressed in the phrase "trust in cadres," which became the transparent code word for a policy which assured middle and lower-level party personnel that their views and prerogatives would be respected by the central leadership and that their careers would be reasonably secure. To be sure, party discipline and self-criticism remained important themes in the literature and at the Twenty-Third Party Congress in 1966, but the emphasis clearly fell on respectful attention to the needs and interests of the cadres. The first indications that excessive "trust in cadres" was resulting in a de facto blockage of economic reform measures came in the December 1969 plenum, when both party officials and state economic bureaucrats were criticized for the poor performance of the economy.[3] Such commentary intensified over the next several years, with the heaviest criticism falling on state officials who were unresponsive to reform proposals. Regional and local party bodies were far from immune, however, and the argument that the party itself was badly in need of an upgrading and modernization of its style of work was heard with increasing frequency.

The Twenty-Fourth Party Congress, held in 1971, at a time when the economic reforms of the mid-1960s clearly had failed and the 1973 reforms creating integrated industrial associations (obedinenie) were on the drawing board, gave clear evidence of the growing tension between the political wisdom of "trust in cadres" and its deleterious economic consequences. The decisions of the congress itself did little to resolve the dilemma; no significant changes were made in top-level personnel, and the high level of retention of regional and local party officials in the Central Committee suggested that extreme caution in such matters was still the rule of the day. Congress pronouncements on the themes of "trust" and "discipline," while stronger than those of the Twenty-Third Congress, still struck a balanced tone. In his opening remarks, Brezhnev spoke of the need for careful action "whereby trust in and respect for people is combined with principled exactingness toward them" to create a "businesslike, comradely atmosphere."[4] Several paragraphs later, he further underlined both the promise and the threat inherent in such "exactingness":

> Increasing the discipline and responsibility of cadres is one of our most important tasks. By this we have in mind discipline that is not built on fear or on methods of ruthless administrative fiat, which deprive people of confidence and initiative and engender overcautiousness and dishonesty. What is involved here is discipline that is founded on a high level of people's consciousness and responsibility. As regards officials who violate discipline, fail to draw conclusions from criticism and behave incorrectly, the necessary mea-

sures must be taken with respect to them. (Applause) In our country, executive posts are not reserved for anyone forever.[5]

Pressure for strengthened discipline of party and state cadres continued to grow after the Twenty-Fourth Congress. Within the party itself, the dual themes of "trust" and "exactingness" now received equal emphasis. New stress was placed on the heretofore slighted notions of criticism and self-criticism within party bodies, and in the mid-1970s the regime launched an extensive campaign against "subjectivism" (read: independence by regional and local cadres) and "a localist and departmental approach" in party and state activities.[6] Speaking to the Twenty-Fifth Party Congress, Brezhnev broadly sketched the process as one in which:

> all aspects of the activity of particular organizations and particular officials should receive an objective appraisal, that existing short-comings should be subjected to comprehensive analysis with the aim of eliminating them, and that a liberal attitude toward shortcomings and toward those responsible for them is impermissible. Trust and respect for people should be combined with high exactingness for the assigned task. This is the law of party work—indeed, not only of party work but of all our work. Of course, comrades, every instance of an improper response to criticism should bring a sharp and swift reaction from party agencies.[7]

Other speakers returned repeatedly to the same question, noting both that such criticism and self-criticism were meant to expose shortcomings within poorly functioning party bodies as well as on the part of recalcitrant state bureaucrats and that, while the situation had improved recently because of extensive pressures from top party leaders, many party committees still approached the tasks of criticism and self-criticism "formally [and] bureaucratically."[8]

Closely coupled with the new stress on "exactingness" was a subtle redefinition of the style of party leadership. While the larger questions of the party-society interface and party-state relations will be examined below, it must be noted now that great emphasis has been placed in recent years both on upgrading the leadership skills of party cadres through extensive reeducation programs and on the mastery of sophisticated managerial techniques borrowed almost wholly from the West. In pragmatic terms, "competetence" has become the watchword in the evaluation of party and state cadres. While other, more traditional aspects of leadership, such as a sense of *partiinost* ("partyness"), must also characterize the model executive,

Brezhnev made it clear in his comments to the Twenty-Fifth Congress that the themes of "thorough competence, discipline, and an initiative-taking, creative approach" to management were now clearly the operative standards.[9] While such calls for improved party work have been heard before, particular importance may be attached to recent efforts to upgrade cadre performance for both economic and political reasons. In economic terms, the call for improved performance is an inevitable result of the de facto ability of middle and lower-level party officials and state officials to blunt reform efforts; the flagging economy is blamed, at least in large measure, on the dilatory and inept performance of party and state operatives. In such a setting, the Brezhnev regime has strengthened its exhortations that the party must "constantly improve the forms and methods of its work" and foster the modernization of economic management within the state bureaucracy.[10] The "scientific approach to work [and] to the political leadership of society" easily translates in practical terms into the central leadership's attempts to compel both resistant party *apparatchiki* and state officials to accept new forms of industrial organization and a more rational perspective on long-range "scientific" planning.

In political terms, the increasingly strident tone of the regime's call for economic reform and a modernization of both the party and the state bureaucracy paradoxically has occurred simultaneously with the strengthening of Brezhnev's hand as the acknowledged leader of the Politburo. The political motivation of the modernization campaign is easily apparent: continued opposition by party and state officials coupled with the regime's unwillingness or inability to resort to forceful disciplinary measures and dismissals has meant that the only leverage left was an extensive campaign to sell the notion of modernization as the only appropriate response to the increasingly complex problems of a developed socialist society. As the scenario was planned, the party would put its own house in order and then rely upon its control and inspection capabilities to bring the larger and presumably even more reluctant state bureaucracy into line. The difficulty has been that the first step never has been fully taken; while there is credible support for the party's modernization efforts at the top level of the party hierarchy and among some state bureaucrats and planners, especially those in high-technology spheres, the resistance of others in both the party and state has proven highly effective. In response the tone of the exhortations for innovative leadership has grown even more extreme. In the almost plaintive words of the November 1978 Central Committee plenum:

What is needed . . . is persistence, selflessness and, if you like, courage. Here sometimes one has almost to learn things anew and to demand the same of others. He who is afraid of the new holds back development. It is from this position that one must proceed in evaluating cadres—both economic and party cadres.[11]

THE ROLE OF THE PARTY

No less important than leadership politics, at least in the longer perspective, is the issue of the CPSU's role within the system. As Brezhnev indicated at the Twenty-Fifth Congress, the party is expected to evolve with the further maturation of a developed socialist society:

Of course, there is nothing immutable about either the party itself or the nature of its activity. At every stage, the party's work is filled with new content. Therefore, it is natural that the new tasks the 25th Congress will pose will continue to require that the forms and methods of Party work be improved on a scientific basis.[12]

Considerable care must be exercised in understanding the limits placed upon the evolution of the party's role; the leading role of the party, as defined both by its traditional vanguard status and its dominance of the *nomenklatura*, remains the unquestioned lynchpin in the system. Indeed, party pronouncements since the Twenty-Third Congress have placed even greater stress on the party's increasing role in a developed socialist society, a development motivated as much by the desire to reassert party prerogatives with regard to state agencies and to use the party to foster modernization as by the concern with the ideologically defined role of a Leninist party in a "mature socialist society." The "new content" of which Brezhnev spoke is best understood as an attempt to redefine the tone and style of party operations within these traditionally defined guidelines.

At the base of the argument is the assertion that the further maturation of Soviet society places both greater and qualitatively different demands on the party in all phases of its activity. Expressing the tone typical in such pronouncements, a *Partiinaya zhizn (Party Life)* editorial in January 1978 spoke of a "deep transformation of the many aspects of practical activity of the party" and of the "massive scale" and "complexity" of the the changes to come.[13]

The increasing complexity of economic and social processes to which the party is summoned to respond is itself a product of an ongoing scientific and technological revolution. A recurring theme in party interpretations of contemporary Soviet society since the 1960s, the scientific and technological revolution refers in toto both to the further technological modernization of the economy similar to the "second industrial revolution" described by Western economists and to the more diffuse impact of such transformations on social structure and culture. In operative terms, it has been associated with an increasingly strident campaign for greater party activism, in part to overcome conservative resistance to such innovation and in part to provide the innovative and coordinating leadership necessary in an increasingly fractionalized setting, and with demands that the party master modern planning and administrative skills needed for a "mature level of scientific guidance by the CPSU of social and political processes" through "complex planning and technology"[14]

The party's growing role is also justified in terms of other changing aspects of the society, including (1) the increasing importance of the "subjective factor" in future growth, that is, the assumption that the conscious and purposive direction of economic and social change becomes more important in an era of developed socialism; (2) the increasing need for ideological guidance, although Soviet theorists leave no doubt that the mechanisms of state discipline and economic levers will remain of paramount importance; (3) the expanded role of public and mass organizations, in which the party is expected to play the leading role; and (4) the heightened consciousness and social involvement of the masses, which require a commensurate increase in political consciousness and activity among party cadres.[15]

While the traditional notion of the "guiding and directing" role of the party has remained a strong element in the recent literature, two other themes have emerged to characterize the party's efforts to redefine its role mission. The first is the party's role as the "initiator" of major reform efforts. To be sure, the party has always allocated to itself the function of determining general policy guidelines, a power which the new 1977 constitution reaffirms even more vigorously than have previous documents. The significant difference is, however, that the role of initiator has been closely tied to the attempts of top-level leaders to use the party as the cutting edge in the process of technological modernization and administrative reforms. As such, the shift to the "initiator" frame of reference, while subtle, nonetheless represents an important attempt—and one only marginally successful, if economic reforms are to be used as the key testing ground—to upgrade the activist and transformationist dimension of party activity.

The second major theme concerns the party's emerging role as a coordinator of an increasingly complex socioeconomic order. Again, the transformation is subtle but no less important than the return to the "activist" or "initiator" role. While the party has always placed emphasis on its penetration of all state and public organizations and its presumed ability to synthesize and articulate the general interest, the new emphasis on the party's coordinating role is closely tied both to the increasing complexity of the economy and society and to the proliferation—and undoubtedly the resistance—of the state bureaucracy. Recent attempts to place the party once again at the center of the planning and implementation process in the economy (the enhanced role of primary party organizations in ministries and other economic organizations will be discussed below) and to impose centralizing systems planning reforms within the party and state hierarchies testify to the increasing desire of top party leaders both to gain control of a fractious and commonly unwieldy bureaucracy and to improve the responsiveness of subordinate levels of both hierarchies to top-level command. Despite rhetorical support for the importance of local initiative and the promotion of local cadres, the principal thrust of recent reforms has been to centralize effective power at or nearer to the center and to provide, however incompletely, as in the case of the industrial associations, the opportunity for the coordination of widely scattered activities that all too frequently fall victim to the sins of "localism" or "departmentalism."

In such a setting, the party's experimentation with systems management reforms and its more recent interest in what Western analysts term matrix theory are best interpreted, as Paul Cocks has convincingly argued, as attempts to create a "mixed" organizational milieu in which the CPSU's political and leadership functions merge symbiotically with but are not wholly restricted by the routine administrative functions of the state bureaucracy.[16] In contrast to the strictly vertical organizational format of traditional bureaucracy, which stresses narrow rationality, incrementalism, and "departmentalism," a matrix format "entails a more untidy and fluid structure to secure cooperation and integration of effort in solving complex and critical problems. Designed as a 'web of relationships' rather than a pyramid of strict line and staff functions, this model allows for overlapping responsibilities and duplicated efforts."[17] The party's new-found stress on coordination casts it into the role of a "project expediter," combining both the functions of a "political *tolkach*" (expediter), whose mandate cuts across existing bureaucratic barriers, and of a comprehensive planner providing the coherent and integrative direction needed to compensate for the inherent conservatism of a deeply rooted and politically cautious bureaucracy. Thus, the intrusion of party officials into the affairs of their functional counterparts in the state bureaucracy is increasingly seen less as "petty tutelage," that is, unproductive interference, a transgression still condemned by party leaders, and more as a creative and compensatory endeavor made necessary in theoretical terms by the party's growing role as developed socialism matures and in practical terms by the need to overcome inertia and to provide an integrative mechanism tying together both programmatic leadership and administrative flexibility. In many ways this new role is far from inconsistent with the time-honored functions of high-level party officials in the past; both regional party secretaries and *apparatchiki* in the branch and functional departments of the Central Committee have operated de facto in just this manner, understanding well—for their careers frequently depended on it—how to manipulate the bureaucracy and how to exploit the informal organizational network to obtain the necessary flexibility. What is different is the degree to which such skills are now touted as necessary, laudable, and, indeed, key in providing the sort of creative leadership necessary in light of the scientific and technological revolution.

The reactivization of the party gradually evolved during the first few years of indecision of the Brezhnev regime. While Khrushchev's victory over his opponents in the state bureaucracy had set the tone for party dominance, despite the first secretary's limited reassertion of the latter's power shortly before his fall, the initial policy of the Brezhnev regime was to caution against excessive interference by party officials into the affairs of the state bureaucracy. Undoubtedly a product of the delicate political balance of the first few years, this policy quickly yielded to a reassertion of the party's "right of control" by the late 1960s and then to increasingly vigorous demands that it play an activist and transformationist role in the early 1970s. As T. H. Rigby has argued, more was at stake than the simple struggle of conflicting bureaucratic power centers; the assertion of greater party prerogatives was linked both to the consolidation of Brezhnev's power in relation to Kosygin and Podgornyi and, perhaps more importantly, to the growing perception within the party that reform efforts in the mid-1960s had fallen victim to institutional inertia.[18] At the organizational level, the primary response was to intensify the party's direct role in and responsibility for the implementation of reforms and the ultimate fulfillment of economic goals.

Although the increased responsibilities of and demands on party organizations emerged as a recurring theme in the literature in the late 1960s, it was not until the Twenty-Fourth Party Congress in 1971 that party organizations in ministries and departments were given a wide-ranging mandate to oversee the implementation of policy and to assert the "militancy and authority" of party cadres at that level.[19] While lower-level party bodies at the enterprise level and in other operational or production units were also instructed to play a more active role, the intent of the directive was unquestionable: party organizations in ministries and departments were to strike at the heart of the problem of bureaucratic inertia within the agencies, to "act as pacesetters in the introduction of scientific management methods and head up the struggle for the affirmation of a truly party style of work," and to provide a mechanism for party-led coordination of the sprawling bureaucracy.[20] This shift of emphasis to ministry-level party bodies paralleled the regime's new interest in further centralizing control and its growing disaffection with the modest impact of previous reforms targeted at lower-level operational units. Understandably, party leaders hoped that leverage applied at this critical juncture, especially when coupled with the subsequent formation of industrial associations and the emphasis on limited vertical integration, would result both in improved performance and, perhaps more importantly, in an enhancement of the party's ability to control the bureaucracy and to implement reforms.

While the level of party activism within ministries and other similar administrative bodies unquestionably has increased since the Twenty-Fourth Congress, recent party pronouncements strongly suggest that the results have fallen short of the regime's original hopes. Constrained once again by the political realities embodied in the "respect for cadres" approach, and increasingly mindful of the difficulties and complexities of effecting change within a firmly rooted bureaucratic milieu, Soviet leaders have complained repeatedly in recent years of the shortcomings and timidity of party bodies at the ministerial level and called in even more strident tones for an intensification of party control. Examples of "paper-shuffling and speechifying" instead of concrete leadership are frequently cited in the press, and some party bodies are sharply criticized for their "high-handed approach" and inability to engage in productive self-criticism in order to deal with their own inherent limitations.[21] Speaking at the Twenty-Fifth Party Congress in 1976, Brezhnev returned to the theme of party control over the ministries with particular force; condemning the "liberalism" which permits agencies nominally under party supervision to go their own way, necessitating resolution after resolution before policy is actually changed, he called again for intensified party control.[22] The November 1978 Central Committee plenum echoed the now familiar theme, this time with even further reaching implications:

> We must increase exactingness toward ministers and the executives of branches, especially those in which urgent tasks are still being accomplished at a slow pace. The Politburo deems it necessary . . . [to] intensify control over the fulfillment of adopted decisions and . . . [to] raise, promptly and in a pointed way, questions of the personal responsibility of those who fail to ensure their fulfillment.[23]

The creation of industrial associations combining several enterprises also provided an opportunity for the party to experiment with the organization and operation of factory-level party bodies. Since the separate primary party organizations in each of the elements of the association were themselves incapable of providing unified direction of party affairs or of obtaining the necessary overview of operations, special councils of party secretaries have been created at the association level, usually chaired by the party secretary of the most important enterprise. Overall direction is provided by the regional party bureau, especially when the enterprises are scattered throughout a territory. While the decisions of these councils are only advisory, they do provide an important element of coordination among the various units of the association and work in fairly close cooperation with the district or regional party bodies, whose authority is frequently invoked to strengthen the hand of the committee in relation to the state bureaucracy.[24]

The evident frustration of the Brezhnev regime in its efforts to foster reforms suggests a paradox which has been largely ignored by Western commentators. On the one hand, Brezhnev definitely has emerged as the leading figure in the Politburo. By all of the indicators traditionally closely watched by Kremlinologists seeking to understand the pecking order, more than any other figure, he enjoys wide-ranging powers in virtually all policy areas and is accorded a personal preeminence tempered only by the need to avoid the jarring freneticism of his predecessor or the sycophantism of an unrestrained cult of the personality. But he is clearly number one, and by all standards his powers seem to have increased from the mid-1970s onward, despite both his recurring illness and the questionable successes of his economic policies at home. For whatever reservations they may have in private—and there are no striking indications that internal disagreement is widespread, especially if the pulling and tugging of normal bureaucratic politics are allowed for—Brezhnev's colleagues on the Politburo have shown remarkable public unity, if not uniform enthusiasm, in pressing for the general secretary's priorities and pet projects in both foreign and domestic affairs. Moreover, the enactment of what was clearly intended as a "Brezhnev" constitution in 1977 and the articulation of developed socialism as a unique and inherently superior phase in the dialectical evolution of Soviet society characteristic of the Brezhnev years are both intended to impress the personal imprimatur of the general secretary on the decade and a half of his rule no less than his predecessor attempted to carve a discernible niche in history. Brezhnev's elevation to the presidency—itself a move considered and rejected for political reasons in earlier years and accomplished in 1977 only over some continuing opposition— must be read as the capstone of both his real and symbolic rise.

But the paradox remains. Despite this seldom-disputed preeminence of the general secretary, his reform efforts have more often than not floundered and fallen victim to quiet but unquestionably effective opposition emanating from within more conservative elements of the party itself—most notably the regional party secretaries, among whom turnover has been slight since the fall of Khrushchev, and who are least likely to favor Brezhnev's attempts to modernize the style of party work—and from the more conservative elements of the state bureaucracy. The tone of high-level party commentary in recent years suggests an increasing sense of frustration with continued opposition from these quarters, a frustration intensified by the inability to find effective and politically acceptable leverage against the resistance of subordinate units. Much of the problem undoubtedly is still linked to the "respect for cadres" approach; despite the ostensible strengthening of the general secretary's hand in most matters, he has been unable or perhaps merely unwilling to force extensive personnel changes in the middle to higher ranges of the party and state bureaucracies. Continued stability has remained the sine qua non of regime politics, and only marginal personnel shifts have occurred even in those areas in which attempted reforms or innovations have shown the least results. Even then, changes have occurred most frequently among the regime's acknowledged technocrats rather than hitting against high-level party generalists, the exceptions being the infrequent shake ups in regional or union republic party organs. To be sure, much of this stability in recent years may be attributed to some degree to a combination of Brezhnev's interest in preventing the emergence of any serious long-term heir-apparent (although the recent promotion of K. U. Chernenko to full membership in the Politburo raises many questions) and to the equally explicable resistance of his colleagues within the Politburo to accepting without opposition the elevation of one of their number to such status.

At a more fundamental level, however, much of regime's frustration may be the inherent product of the evolution of Soviet political institutions in recent years. Quite independently of the issue of Brezhnev's continued dominance or of the tacit arrangements for his succession, the evolution of the Politburo into a form of shadow cabinet within which all important bureaucratic power centers are represented and the development of "corporatist" politics may well have set the stage for a political stalemate in which no element is willing to risk the political costs of cutting through the deadlock. I have argued above that such "corporatism" may either facilitate the coordination of various interests and power centers and provide a mechanism for the effective exercise of purposive central leadership or, if the circumstances are right, merely provide an informal institutional mechanism for a de facto system of checks and balances, especially if the interests represented jealously guard their prerogatives and bailiwicks and the central leadership is constrained by political factors beyond its control. This situation, coupled with the inherent ability of any bureaucracy to resist change, is at the source of the paradoxical strengths and weaknesses of the current leadership. Bunce and Echols are quite correct that corporatism requires centralized, purposive leadership, and, as an analytic approach to Soviet politics, it is therefore a useful corrective to the almost laissez faire assumption that Kremlin politics has become merely the pulling and tugging of uncoordinated interest groups. But it also *restricts* certain kinds of leadership, especially to the extent that the fundamental interests, work styles, and self-images of important elements in the oligarchy are not amenable to "coordination." In such a setting, a de facto immobilism is the frequent result, an immobilism attributable not to the lack of imagination and stagnated minds of a "regime of clerks" but rather to the continued presence of unresolved political differences which go beyond the relatively simple issues of national priorities and reach deeply into the work styles, role missions, and fundamental self-perceptions of the elite.

The ability of any complex bureaucracy to resist change must also be considered as one of the important sources of the growing sense of frustration that has marked the Brezhnev regime in recent years. This resistance to charge is further complicated by the evident resistance not only within the state bureaucracy, which was to be the target for intensified and "scientized" party control, but also within the CPSU itself. As any student of complex organizations knows, problems of control, coordination, and effective leadership are endemic in such a setting virtually regardless of the nature of the larger political milieu; U.S. presidents have always had problems of commanding the respectful attention of what one commentator has termed the "permanent government," and Soviet party leaders have experienced similar difficulties. Subordinate units quickly come to articulate their own particular institutional goals, role perceptions, and self-images, which are usually only partially consonant with the mandates and perceptions of higher-level political authorities. As Western commentators on attempts to apply systems theory, program budgeting, and a host of other administrative panaceas to the seemingly uncoordinated and unresponsive bureaucratic maze of U.S. government now grudgingly admit, these once highly touted "fixes" have had little impact at all; the problems lay not so much with the intellectual frame of reference—although it did prove difficult to define what a "system" really was or to provide meaningful criteria for "optimum" decisions—but rather with the resistance of the subordinate units that were supposed to be controlled and converted to presidential direction. Simply put, systems reforms forgot the realities of bureaucratic politics and the complex interaction of bureaus and their constituencies, and it was this oversight that eventually did them in. Skilled bureaucratic entrepreneurs, while professing adherence to systems–inspired reforms and creating the appearance that they were being productively used, simply found ways of doing business as usual, in part because of their ability to cloak traditional behavior patterns in new systems terminology and in part because of their skill at exploiting traditional political allegiances to circumvent or at least blunt the drive for a higher level of centralized control. While the final verdict is not yet in, there is much in recent Soviet experience with such reforms to suggest that they will meet the same response when applied to the maze of Moscow bureaucracy.[25]

There is a second dimension to the organizational side of the problem, itself a part of the complex paradox of attempting to foster change within a highly bureaucratic setting: if the recent experience under Brezhnev's tutelage is any indication, it may well be easier to change the *goals* and *policies*, that is, the end results of party and state activity, than to change the deeply ingrained *procedures* and *work styles* of either bureaucracy. The reader has probably already noted another paradox about the Brezhnev regime, that the general secretary has had greater success in placing his stamp of personal leadership on the *content* of both domestic and foreign policies than on the *procedural questions* of party and state behavior at the planning and implementation stages. The growing frustration of recent years has not been directed so much at any opposition to the basic policy goals of the regime but rather at the dilatory performance of party and state bureaucrats, who ostensibly accept the general thrust of policy but are unwilling to alter their business-as-usual approach to daily affairs.

PARTY GROWTH

As a vanguard party cast in the Leninist mold, the CPSU has always viewed its social profile and admissions policies as important expressions of both its present level of sociopolitical maturity and its transformationist mission. During the Khrushchev era, the party grew rapidly, increasing by more than 70 percent from 1954 to 1964, with the largest growth noted among workers, minority nationalities, and technically trained people.[26] This rapid expansion, itself a product of the First Secretary's conscious efforts to alter the CPSU's social profile to reflect the heretofore paradoxical underrepresentation of the proletariat and certain nationalities, confronted the new Brezhnev regime with a party that was significantly different from that which existed at the time of Stalin's death and with clear and vexing dilemmas concerning the implications of future growth.

Before the dilemma of continued growth can be explored, however, it is wise to call the present profile of the CPSU into view. As of June 1, 1977, it numbered just over 16.2 million members, an increase of some 5 million since Khrushchev's fall in 1964.[27] While the implications of this growth will be considered below, it must be noted that these figures do represent a modest scaling down of the even more rapid expansion of party ranks during the Khrushchev era.[28]

In class terms, the 1977 figures show that 42 percent of party members are classified as workers (up slightly from 38.1 percent in 1967), 13.6 percent as collective farmers (down from 16 percent over the same period), and the remaining 44.4 percent as service and white collar personnel (also down from 45.9 percent in 1967). Within the latter category, the most rapid growth over the last decade occurred among engineering and technical personnel (38.1 percent to 44 percent), with lesser gains registered among workers in science, education, public health, literature, and art (23.6 to 24.2 percent). A decrease was noted among workers in trade and other public service posts, with their share of the total dropping from 5.5 percent to 4.3 percent.[29]

The educational level of the total party membership shows a marked improvement from 1967 to 1977. At the beginning of that decade, only 16.5 percent of the total membership possessed a completed higher education, a figure that was itself a slight drop from the previous decade, undoubtedly due to Khrushchev's attempts to stress worker and peasant recruitment. But by 1977, the figure for completed higher education had risen to 25.1 percent. A somewhat smaller increase was noted in terms of completed secondary education; in 1967, 31.5 percent of party members had such schooling, and the figure rose to 39.2 percent a decade later. Similar growth also occurred in the area of specialized secondary education—the Soviet equivalent of high-level vocational training—and although the data on that individual category are incomplete, the total of all party members in 1977 who possess either a completed higher education or a specialized secondary education was 49.5 percent, a sizable increase from the 36.8 percent registered only a decade earlier.[30]

Trends in the fields of study of party members are also an instructive lesson in adaptation to an increasingly mature economy. Among those individuals possessing a completed higher education, the most frequent field of study was engineering. In 1967, 37.8 percent of the group was trained initially as engineers (although, obviously, some of their number had gone on to administrative tasks as their careers developed), and that number rose to 43 percent in 1977. Only two other categories showed even modest increases: agronomists, veterinarians, and other agricultural specialists increased slightly from 7.7 to 7.8 percent, economists from 5.4 to 6.3 percent. Doctors and teachers—the only other fields specifically identified—experienced slight decreases, with the former falling from 6.9 to 5.3 percent and the latter from 25.5 to 22.6 percent.[31]

Among party members with specialized secondary educations, the most striking increase was noted among those identified simply as "technicians," a category best understood as covering both the Western sense of the term and also highly skilled blue-collar workers. Continuing their two-decade increase, they grew from 43.8 percent in 1967 to 56.1 percent in 1977, an expansion easily explained by the CPSU's interest in recruiting the best and brightest of the proletariat in compensation for its earlier attention to white-collar occupations.[32]

In terms of political "generations," that is, the date of recruitment into the party and hence the length of party service, the rank-and-file membership shows the clear impact of recent recruitment. As the 1977 figures demonstrate, more than one-third of the party members and then current candidates had been admitted to that status within the last ten years. Moreover, when the time frame is extended to two decades, that is, individuals recruited from 1957 onward and thus having no direct experience with the Stalin era, much less the purges of the 1930s and rapid industrialization, the formative political events for much of the present leadership, the figure increases to a remarkable 67.3 percent of total membership.[33] This is, however, a slight drop from the 68.5 percent which fell into the same category according to figures published in 1973, undoubtedly resulting from both the decrease in recruitment of new cadres and the passage of more senior members into the twenty-year-plus category.[34] But even this slight decrease does little to obviate the great generational differences separating the vast majority of younger party members from the relatively static and aging senior leadership.

The biological age of current party members also shows a similar "greening" process. While only 5.8 percent of current members are under 25—a situation explained by the fact that increasing numbers are joining in their late 20s or early 30s only after completing higher education and launching their careers and with considerable experience in the Komsomol—36.7 percent fall into the 26 to 40 age group. It must be noted, however, that when taken together the 26.4 percent in the 41 to 50 age group and the 18.1 percent in the 51 to 60 category still constitute the largest bloc of 44.5 percent, while those over 60 comprise some 13 percent of total membership.[35]

In terms of nationalities, the policies of the Brezhnev era have only moderately altered the trends established by Khrushchev. The decline in the overrepresentation of the Russians themselves has tapered off, undoubtedly in response to the regime's growing concern about their declining percentage of the national population. While the percentage of Russians in the party dropped from 62.4 percent in 1965 to 60.9 percent in 1973, the 1977 figures showed a much smaller reduction to 60.5 percent. Only modest increases have been noted among the other Slavic peoples, however, despite efforts to recruit more actively in these areas; from 1965 to 1973, the percentage of Ukrainians increased from 15.4 to 16 percent, but no new increment was reflected in the 1977 figures, which held constant at 16 percent. Among the Belorussians the increase from 1965 to 1973 was slight, 3.3 to 3.5 percent, and in 1977 they accounted for only 3.6 percent of total membership. The Georgians and Armenians, always overrepresented in terms of their numbers in the national population, remained at 1.7 and 1.5 percent respectively; this unquestionably represented a continuation in the decline of their overrepresentation because of overall population growth. Among the Central Asian peoples only modest increases were noted for the Uzbeks, from 2 percent in 1973 to 2.1 percent four years later, and the other nationalities remained static over the same period, despite rapid population growth in the region. No significant gains were registered for the Baltic peoples either, despite increased recruitment efforts.[36]

The underrepresentation of women within the CPSU has continued in the Brezhnev era, although their growth rate for the last decade has been the most rapid since the 1930s. In the ten years between 1957 and 1967, they increased from 19.7 to 20.9 percent of total membership, while from 1967 to 1977, they spurted ahead to 24.7 percent, obviously reflecting the regime's new interest in mobilizing support among women. Modest increases also have been noted in the number of women serving in lower and middle-level party executive posts. From 1971 to 1977 their representation as members or candidate members of *oblast, krai,* and union republic party committees increased modestly from 20.5 to 22.9 percent, while at the city and *raion* level their presence grew from 24.7 to 28.9 percent. Larger gains were recorded at lower levels of the party hierarchy, with female membership on party committees and bureaus of primary party organizations increasing from 21.4 to 25.2 percent in the same period and their standing as secretaries of primary party organizations growing from 27.6 to 31.9 percent. At the national level, however, women constitute only 3.3 percent of the Central Committee elected at the Twenty-Fifth Party Congress, and, of the 14 individuals involved, five are token workers with no real political role.[37]

The distribution of party members among the various sectors of the economy also provides an instructive view of the CPSU's profile. While 73.2 percent are involved in what Soviet figures label "material production," only 39 percent are listed as directly involved in industry and construction, a slight increase from the 1967 figure of 36.6 percent. Transportation and communication presently account for 8.3 percent (a drop from 9 percent a decade ago), and agriculture involves 20.4 percent (also a drop from 22.2 percent over the same period). The percentage of workers in trade, food processing, and various supply services accounts for another 4.4 percent (the same as ten years ago), with the remaining worker-party members scattered among other fields. In the "unproductive" sphere, that is, workers not directly involved with the production of material products or construction, 16.6 percent are in science, education, public health, and culture, a very slight increase from 16.5 percent in 1967. The percentage of workers in state and economic administration and in the *apparat* of party and public organizations has dropped slightly from 8.9 to 8.5 percent from 1967 to 1977, while the number of party members involved in domestic and communal activities has increased from 1.3 to 1.7 percent.[38]

THE DILEMMA OF PARTY GROWTH

With total party membership now approaching 10 percent of the adult population even according to official figures—and reaching even higher marks within the well-educated and urbanized strata, as Jerry Hough has noted in his comments on party "saturation"—the party is increasingly confronted with a dilemma. On the one hand, continued growth along several dimensions will be necessary not only to draw into the CPSU increasing numbers of well-qualified personnel and to maintain a high level of membership among social strata whom the regime does not wish to alienate but also to preserve an appropriate balance between the proletarian and white-collar elements. But, on the other hand, as Darrell Hammer has observed, the party remains conscious of its status as a "vanguard" reflective of but nonetheless distinctive from the mass of society; the preservation of the CPSU's elitist self-definition and sense of mission has long been dependent on the mystique of party membership, and current leaders have shown every intention of maintaining the facade of the party's special role even if they have hedged on hard decisions concerning the larger implications of the recruitment issue.[39]

The Brezhnev regime did attempt to cut back on the influx of new members in the mid-1960s, first beginning with widely publicized criticism of the Kharkov regional party organization for chasing after numbers and then reminding the local and regional party organizations, where effective leadership on the question had resided, that the "growth in numbers was not an end in itself."[40]

The Twenty-Third Party Congress, held in 1966, both reiterated the new tone of caution and provided easier mechanisms for expelling errant party members. Local and regional party bodies evidently responded at least in part to these new directives, for the annual rate of growth fell from a high of about 5 percent under the Khrushchev regime to around 3 percent from the 1966 to 1971 period, when it gradually began to creep upward once again.[41] Party leaders again returned to the question of growth at the Twenty-Fourth Party Congress in 1971, and although it was clear that the overall rate of increase had been slowed by the earlier decisions, they expressed continuing criticism of lower-level party officials who had not placed the "qualitative" expansion of the party, that is, emphasis on attracting both members of the technical intelligentsia and technically trained workers, above the desire for overall growth.[42]

The congress also ordered an exchange of party membership cards, itself the mechanism of previous purges of unqualified or inept cadres; it soon became clear, however, that no extensive cleansing of party ranks was intended. According to Brezhnev's report to the Twenty-Fifth Congress in 1976, 347,000 members were excluded in the course of the exchange, a number which must be further discounted by the normal attrition rate. Making such calculations, Rigby and Unger separately conclude that the exchange per se resulted in only a 1 to 1.5 percent reduction of the total membership, hardly a significant decrease in light of the party's rapid previous growth.[43]

A further perspective on the party's growth may be gained from the fact that, even with the decreased recruitment that resulted from the party's efforts since 1966, the rate of growth of party cadres in recent years is twice that of general population expansion. Even when the modestly increased attrition rates are taken into account—increases caused not only by tightened review standards but also by the increasing age of party cadres, among whom normal biological attrition is playing a more important role— the party will continue to expand to a point where the dilemma of continued growth will become an increasingly serious issue for party leaders. Either they will have to accept a serious alteration in the party's social profile as a consequence of limiting future growth—and this would entail choosing between its continued proletarian legitimacy or the co-optation of the society's functional elites—or they will have to live with the notion that the concept of a "vanguard" party has lost all practical meaning. A. L. Unger has summarized the dilemma best:

> As a ruling party, the CPSU must ensure a substantial representation among the educated technical and administrative strata that run Soviet society as they run modern societies everywhere; a ruling party which did not include those who rule would soon find itself "divorced from power". . . . Yet in order to substantiate its right to rule . . . the party also considers itself duty bound to manifest a proletarian social profile. Yet . . . these two aims—the representation of the party in the leading strata of society and the representation of workers in the party—can only be reconciled at the price of continuous expansion . . . and the consequent erosion of its vanguard status. For if party saturation levels of leading strata are to remain stable—and . . . they have remained remarkably stable in the period under review—then the growth of these strata in the population must necessarily entail a corresponding increase of party recruits from the ranks of the white collar intelligentisa, by occupation if not by origin.[44]

Unger calculates that, given the projected increase of persons with higher education, the party will have to recruit nearly a million new members each year (200,000 with higher education and over

750,000 manual workers), a rate far higher than at present. Barring a decision to expand recruitment to that level—a rate consistent with the influx of new members under Khrushchev but two to three times the new rate for the last decade—the party will have no choice but to accept an alteration in its social profile, undoubtedly to the benefit of the professional and technical strata and at the expense of the proletariat.[45]

In his comments on recruitment policy before the Twenty-Fifth Congress, Brezhnev rejected just such an acceleration of party growth:

> Over the past 30 years, the CPSU's size has almost tripled. It is perfectly obvious that the growth of its ranks will continue. This objective tendency stems from the entire course of social development under socialism and from the increase in the leadership role of the party and its prestige. However, the CPSU is not speeding up its numerical growth. It admits to its ranks only those who by their deeds have proved that they are entering the party, to use Lenin's words, not in order to obtain advantages of some sort but to do selfless work for the benefit of communism.[46]

Taking up the same issue shortly after the congress on the pages of *Kommunist*, the party's theoretical journal, I. V. Kapitonov noted that the party has no intention of "forcing its numerical growth" and cautioned local and regional party bodies against permitting their growth rates to exceed the national average for the party.[47] Party pronouncements since the congress have stressed repeatedly that candidates for membership are to be evaluated on an individual basis and that the qualitative upgrading of party cadres is of paramount importance.[48]

PARTY SATURATION

As Jerry Hough has noted, straightforward membership figures are, at first examination, quite misleading in terms of the party's representation among the better educated and more urbanized strata of the society. Speaking of the CPSU's "saturation" of these elements, he points out that of 35.5 percent of those individuals over 30 years old with a completed higher education are party members. Of those with an incomplete higher education slightly over 30 percent are members, and the figure for those with a completed secondary education drops only slightly to 23.6 percent. When the figures for men and women are disaggregated, the results appear even more significant. Among men over 30 with a completed higher education, between 50.3 to 54.5 percent, depending upon the assumptions used in the analysis, are members of the party; for those with incomplete higher schooling, the figure dips to somewhere between 41.7 to 45.1 percent, and for those with completed secondary training, the figures converge at 39.5 and 39.6 percent. Among women over 30 with completed higher schooling, between 17.8 and 13.6 percent are party members. Of those with incomplete higher educations, between 15.7 and 11.4 percent are members, and the figures for those with completed secondary schooling range between 10 and 9.9 percent.[49]

Setting aside the question of education and dealing solely with sex and age distribution, one still finds that party membership assumes widespread dimensions for some cohort groups. While among men between the ages of 18 and 25 party saturation amounts to only 3.5 to 4.1 percent, it increases sharply for older groups. Between 11.5 and 13 percent of men from 26 to 30 years old are members; the figures increase to 19.1 to 20.5 percent for the 31 to 40 group, 22.4 to 22.7 percent for the 41 to 50 group, and 22.9 to 24.8 for the 51 to 60 group. Factoring in the higher density of party members in urban areas, Hough concludes that somewhere in the vicinity of 25 percent of the men from 31 to 60 years of age living in urban areas are members of the CPSU. For women, on the other hand, party saturation figures are predictably far lower; only between 5.1 to 5.2 percent of women in the 31 to 60 age group hold party membership.[50]

These saturation figures suggest the severity of the growth and representation dilemma confronting the party over the next decade may be even more serious than originally thought. One need hardly agree with the figure of 1 million new recruits a year suggested by Unger to accept the basic premise of the argument that rapid growth would be needed to maintain proletarian legitimacy and also to sustain high levels of party saturation among urbanized, better educated males. A part of the solution undoubtedly lies in active recruitment of the best and brightest of the blue-collar working class itself, that is, highly skilled workers with vocational and technical training; in fact, emphasis has been placed in drawing greater numbers of such workers into the party, as previous figures have noted. However, the increasing representation of such elements does little to alleviate the basic problem that with rising educational levels for the population as a whole and increasing urbanization—to say nothing of

the professional upgrading of white-collar occupations themselves—
the pool of such individuals now accustomed to large-scale representation within the party will grow far more rapidly than the population on the whole. Any attempt to limit recruitment from this element
of the society would incur the serious political risk of alienating
important segments of the society, a risk which current leaders have
shown no willingness to take.

NOTES

1. Archie Brown, "Political Developments: Some Conclusions and an Interpretation," in *The Soviet Union since the Fall of Khrushchev*, ed. Archie Brown and Michael
Kaser (New York: Macmillian, 1975), pp. 240–42.
2. Jerry F. Hough and Merle Fainsod, *How the Soviet Union is Governed* (Cambridge: Harvard University Press, 1979), pp. 473–79.
3. T. H. Rigby, "The Soviet Government since Khrushchev," *Politics* 12 (May
1977): 14.
4. L. I. Brezhnev, comments to the Twenty-Fourth Party Congress, *Pravda*, March
31, 1971.
5. Ibid.
6. I. Kapitonov, "XXV sezd KPSS i aktualnye zadachi organizatsionno-partiinoi
raboty," *Kommunist*, no. 11 (July 1976): 35–36.
7. L. I. Brezhnev, comments to the Twenty-Fifth Party Congress, *Pravda*, February
25, 1976.
8. Kapitonov, "XXV sezd."
9. Brezhnev, Twenty-Fifth Congress.
10. Kapitonov, "XXV sezd." p. 32.
11. *Pravda*, November 28, 1978.
12. Brezhnev, Twenty-Fifth Congress.
13. "Deyatelnost KPSS i sovershenstvovanie politicheskoi sistemy SSSR," *Partiinaya zhizn* (January 1978): 11–18.
14. A. Egorov, "Kommunisticheskaya partiya v usloviyakh razvitogo sotsializma,"
Kommunist, no. 1 (October 1976): 56–57.
15. V. Sikorskii, *KPSS na etape razvitogo sotsializma* (Minsk: Belorussian State
University, 1975), pp. 39–47, 72–78, 118–19; G. E. Glezerman, ed., *Razvitoe sotsialis-
ticheskoe obshchestvo: sushchnost, kriterii zrelosti, kritika revizionistskikh kontseptsii*
(Moscow: Mysl, 1973), pp. 268–77; and V. S. Shevtsov, *KPSS i gosudarstvo v razvitom
sotsialisticheskom obshchestve* (Moscow: Politizdat, 1974), pp. 53–60.
16. Paul Cocks, "Administrative Rationality, Political Change, and the Role of the
Party," in *Soviet Society and the Communist Party*, ed. Karl Ryavec (Amherst: University
of Massachusetts Press, 1978), pp. 41–62.
17. Ibid.
18. Rigby, "Soviet Government."
19. Brezhnev, Twenty-Fourth Congress.
20. *Pravda*, February 11, 1974.

21. *Pravda Ukrainy*, January 11, 1976; *Pravda*, March 12, 1978; and A. P. Kirilenko, "Na glavnom napravlenie ekonomicheskogo stroitelstva," *Partiinaya zhizn*, no. 6 (March 1978): 8–21.

22. Brezhnev, Twenty-Fifth Congress.

23. *Pravda*, November 28, 1978.

24. *Pravda*, December 27, 1976; *Pravda*, August 26, 1976; and "Partiinaya rabota v usloviyakh proizvodstvennykh obedinenii v promyshlennosti," *Partiinaya zhizn*, no. 10 (May 1977): 22–37.

25. Donald V. Schwartz, "Recent Soviet Adaptations of Systems Theory to Administrative Theory," *Journal of Comparative Administration* 5 (1973): 233–64; Donald V. Schwartz, "Decisionmaking, Administrative Decentralization, and Feedback Mechanisms: Comparisons of Soviet and Western Models," *Studies in Comparative Communism* 7 (1974): 146–83; Paul Cocks, "The Policy Process and Bureaucratic Politics," in *The Dynamics of Soviet Politics*, eds. Paul Cocks, Robert V. Daniels, and Nancy Whittier Heer (Cambridge: Harvard University Press, 1976), pp. 156–78; and Donald R. Kelley, "Group and Specialist Influence in Soviet Politics: In Search of a Theory," in *Social Scientists and Policy Making in the USSR*, ed. Richard Remnek (New York: Praeger, 1977), pp. 108–37.

26. Darrell P. Hammer, "The Dilemma of Party Growth," *Problems of Communism* 20 (July-August 1971): 16–21.

27. "KPSS v tsifrakh," *Partiinaya zhizn*, no. 21 (November 1977): 21.

28. Hammer, "Party Growth," pp. 17–18.

29. "KPSS," p. 28.

30. Ibid., p. 29.

31. Ibid., p. 30.

32. Ibid.

33. Ibid., p. 32.

34. "KPSS v tsifrakh," *Partiinaya zhizn*, no. 14 (July 1973): 19.

35. "KPSS," 1977, p. 32.

36. T. H. Rigby, "Soviet Communist Party Membership under Brezhnev," *Soviet Studies* 28 (July, 1976): 325–27; and "KPSS," 1977, p. 31.

37. Gail Warshofsky Lapidus, *Women in Soviet Society: Equality, Development, and Social Change* (Berkeley: University of California Press, 1978), pp. 218–19; and "KPSS," 1977, pp. 32–33.

38. "KPSS," 1977, p. 34.

39. Hammer, "Party Growth," p. 19.

40. Ibid., p. 18.

41. Ibid., pp. 19–20.

42. Ibid., p. 20.

43. Aryeh L. Unger, "Soviet Communist Party Membership under Brezhnev: A Comment," *Soviet Studies* 29 (April 1977): 308; and Rigby, "Soviet Communist," pp. 322–23.

44. Unger, "Party Membership," pp. 314–15.

45. Ibid. For a conflicting interpretation that expansion will increase in the late 1970s and early 1980s and then taper off in response to population trends, see Rigby, "Soviet Communist," pp. 335–37.

46. Brezhnev, Twenty-Fifth Congress.

47. Kapitonov, "XXV sezd," p. 29.

48. I. Yunak, "Doverie i trebovatelnost v rabote s kadrami," *Partiinaya zhizn*, no. 21

(November 1977); 59-65; *Pravda*, April 1, 1977; and "Organizatsionno-partiinuyu rabotu—na uroven novykh trebovanii," *Partiinaya zhizn*, no. 24 (December 1977): 29-33. As Hough points out, some exceptions to this theme can be noted, as when the October 1976 issue of *Partiinaya zhizn* criticized the Kirghiz party organization for not admitting sufficient numbers of workers and peasants. However, the dominant tone of the discussion has continued to stress the qualitative dimensions of new recruitment rather than sheer numbers; see Jerry Hough, *The Soviet Union and Social Science Theory* (Cambridge: Harvard University Press, 1977), p. 137.

    49. Hough, *Soviet Union*, pp. 131-33.

    50. Ibid., pp. 128-29.

3

THE POLITICAL ECONOMY OF SOVIET AGRICULTURE UNDER BREZHNEV

Roy D. Laird

In our view, the single most distinguishing feature of Soviet agriculture is that it is the most politicized farming system in the world. Political considerations ultimately dominate decision making at all levels of Soviet rural affairs.

V. V. Matskevitch may well have been the most able of the long list of ministers of agriculture. Although this observer disagreed with many of the politically motivated policies he administered, nevertheless, when we had an opportunity to hear him speak in 1970, we were impressed. A brief postsession personal discussion with him further confirmed our view. Be this as it may, the need to find a scapegoat for bad policies, which really rested in Khrushchev's lap, resulted in his firing Matskevitch following the bad harvest of 1963. Brezhnev obviously knew better, recognizing Matskevitch's abilities. One of Brezhnev's first acts after succeeding Khrushchev in 1964 was to reappoint Matskevitch as the top agricultural official in the Soviet Union. Unfortunately, even Brezhnev has not been able (and probably has, not wanted) to remove politics from preeminance in Soviet agriculture. Thus, in spite of rather impressive advancements in output, when bad weather resulted in the 1972 crop failure, Matskevitch again became the goat and again was removed from office.

Soviet agriculture is bureaucratic politics with an underpinning of Marxist-Leninist ideology, guided by system goals set by the leadership in power. Moreover, as in politics everywhere, the bottom

The author wishes to thank the Hesston Foundation and the University of Kansas for assistance which helped make this study possible.

line is what policies and actions will keep the incumbent political leaders in office the longest period of time. A knowledge of this, plus a knowledge of the working of high state bureaucracies and an understanding of the peculiarities of bureaucracies in the Marxist-Leninist states is the essential base for an understanding of the political economy of agriculture under Brezhnev or any other politician who might succeed him.

SOME SOVIET AGRICULTURAL BASICS

Khrushchev effected significant changes from the Stalin era. As we shall record, Brezhnev has made important changes since the fall of Khrushchev. Nevertheless, there remain important givens that do not change:

Climate is a major negative factor in Soviet agriculture. The weather is less favorable for farming in the USSR than in Western Europe or the United States. The bulk of the sown area is subject to periodic drought. Unfavorable weather at the time of sowing and at the time of harvesting can be costly to yields. Having noted such natural limitations, however, one must add that Soviet farms consistently produce below their potential. Thus, Canada, with similar climate problems, continues to achieve twice the wheat yields of the USSR.

Soviet agriculture is above all else political. As Merle Fainsod noted before Brezhnev's leadership began, the early post-World War II history of Soviet agricultural policy was marked by a continued tightening of controls over the farms.[1] Brezhnev, however, was not satisfied with the Stalin-Khrushchev accomplishments, and the process has continued under his leadership.

Soviet agriculture has become fully enmeshed in the bureaucratic hierarchy. This task was completed in the 1950s, as a result of the Khrushchev changes, and to a man (with an occasional woman as *kolkhoz* chairman) the party-member chairmen have been fully disciplined to higher party control. *Kolkhoz* chairmen are on the *obkom* (oblast party committee) *nomenklatura* (appointments list). Thus, they remain in office at its pleasure.

By definition, Soviet farms are economic enterprises. After all, they are the source of most of the nation's food. However, the fundamental Marxist-Leninist doctrine is never completely obscured. He who controls the means of production controls all human activity. Thus, the state monopoly over virtually all economic resources is exploited continually to assure economic, political, and social control over the peasants and their product.

The kolkhozy and sovkhozy (state farms) are the answer to the ideological stricture that all Soviet citizens must enjoy the advantages of Marxist-Leninist socialism. They are "schools of communism in the countryside".

The farms dominate rural society. Not only are they the peasants' place of work, but they encompass their way of life as well. Village social affairs are nearly as important to the farm managers as are meeting the state-imposed production plans.

Soviet farms have been transformed into huge, impersonal rural factories. Table 3.1 represents some of the major changes that occurred from 1940 to 1976. For all practical purposes, the peasants who work in the fields and in the barns are hired hands. The com-

TABLE 3.1

Some Kolkhozy and Sovkhozy Averages

	1940	1960	1976
Kolkhozy			
Total number	235,500.0	44,900.0	27,300.0
Per farm			
Workers	110.0	445.0	542.0
Specialists	—	4.9	20.0
Sown area (hectares)	500.0	2,746.0	3,597.0
Head of livestock (cattle,			
hogs, sheep, and goats)	297.0	3,031.0	4,509.0
Tractors	4.4	14.4	39.0
Value of production			
(million/rubles/year)	0	0	1.7
Sovkhozy			
Total number	4,200.0	7,400.0	19,617.0
Per farm			
Workers	381.0	783.0	559.0
Specialists	—	22.0	33.6
Sown area	2,750.0	9,081.0	5,680.0
Head of livestock	3,033.0	10,279.0	6,171.0
Tractors	20.0	54.0	57.0
Value of production	0	1.6	2.0

Sources: Narodnoe khozyaistvo SSSR v 1961 (Moscow: Statistika, 1962); *Narodnoe khozyaistvo SSSR za 60 let* (Moscow: Statistika, 1977); and *Selskoe khozyaistvo,* (Moscow: Statistika, 1960 and 1971).

mands of their bosses are every bit as stringent as were the commands of the landlord's managers in the time of the tsars.

State purchase plans imposed from outside determine almost every major on-farm production decision. In effect, the purchase plans, which account for the bulk of a farm's output, are production plans. Moreover, even though the farms theoretically can dispose of above-plan production on their own decision, much of the above-plan output is also mandated by higher officials.

FROM KHRUSHCHEV TO BREZHNEV

Stalin's forced collectivization of agriculture provided the institutional form that satisfied ideological demands and paved the way for the maximization of political and economic controls. A most important consideration was that the resulting controls over agricultural output would allow a maximum extraction of rural capital (at a time when agriculture was the largest economic activity in the USSR) for the forced-draft construction of industry. Even though Khrushchev turned much of his attention to the serious problems of agriculture, urban industry continued to receive first priority under his rule.

In sum, the two most important elements of Khrushchev's agricultural policy were grandiose schemes to expand output (but at the lowest cost possible) and constant exhortation of the nation's farmers to produce more. Thus, he became enamored of the potential of corn as a solution to the shortage of livestock feed. At his urging, the feed grain was introduced over much of the countryside, including many areas lacking the moisture to allow it to mature.

The grandest of all his schemes was the plowing up of some 40 million hectares of grasslands in the "virgin lands" region of Kazakhstan and the neighboring RSFSR. As a result, the geographic center of Soviet grain growing has moved hundreds of kilometers eastward, from its former center in the Ukraine—long regarded as the breadbasket of the USSR—to in or near the arid steppes of Kazakhstan. The scheme, while quite successful in the early years, was grossly overdone. Needed moisture-replenishing fallow practices were not followed, and the extreme yield reversals in drought years, such as 1963, was a price to be paid.

After Khrushchev's ouster in 1964, one of the charges leveled against him was the practice of the "cult of the personality". He was guilty as charged as far as his agricultural performance was concerned. In spite of this, his exhortations, earthy remarks, and the sense of humor that often came forth in his constant barnstorming about the countryside had to be a welcome contrast to the Stalin style. Khrushchev visited scores (perhaps hundreds) of farms, while if Stalin ever visited the countryside it was only by way of retreating from the confines of the Kremlin. Nevertheless, Khrushchev could not restrain from poking his nose into local affairs, including giving orders to plant a particular crop or to adopt a different cultivation practice.

Perhaps documents buried in the Kremlin will surface some day to settle the argument over whether it was Khrushchev's defeat in his confrontation with Kennedy during the Cuban missile crisis or his failure to solve the food problem, that was most critical in the decision to oust him from power. However, at this juncture our view is that, coming as it did after the 1963 crop failure, his removal was, at the least, precipitated by the failure of his agricultural policies. Certainly, many of the first and more important changes made by the Brezhnev leadership were related to agriculture.

A NEW ERA IN SOVIET AGRICULTURE

Although the "agricultural basics" listed above have not changed, both the style and the substance of the Brezhnev rule over the countryside are as different from the Khrushchev way as Khrushchev's was from Stalin's.

Although Brezhnev occasionally has visited farms and rural provinces, he does not pose as the nation's leading agricultural specialist. Although his speeches often include concern for agricultural problems, and his policies have served further to tighten controls, he has not ventured to issue orders concerning when to plant and when to reap. Moreover, the Brezhnev leadership has exhibited a serious resolve to improve the people's diet.

The daily caloric intake of the Soviet citizenry is equal to that of U.S. citizens, some 3,200 per day. However, the demand for more livestock products has not been met. Currently the average per capita annual intake of meat is some 56 kilograms, while the Soviet medical academy has set a standard of 82 kilograms; in contrast, the U.S. average intake is over 100.[2]

Table 3.2 records the changed output of foodstuffs in the Soviet Union from 1955 (at the beginning of Khrushchev's tenure at the top), with 1965 (the first year after Brezhnev's takeover, but when his policies could not yet have had any important impact on production), and 1975 (after ten years of his leadership).

TABLE 3.2

Gross and Per Capita Changes in Food Production

	1955	1965	Percent over 1955	1975	Percent over 1965
Population (millions)	194.4	229.3	18	255.5	11
Meat (million tons)	6.4	9.7	52	14.3	47
per capita (kilograms)	33.0		27	56.0	33
Milk (million liters)	43.4	70.6	62	90.5	28
per capita (liters)	223.0	307.0	38	354.0	15
Eggs (millions)	18.4	29.1	58	56.1	93
per capita	94.0	127.0	35	220.0	73
Grain (million tons)*	105.0	148.0	41	187.0	26
per capital (kilograms)	540.0	645.0	19	732.0	13

*Three-year averages (e.g., 1955 is average for 1954, 1955, and 1956) to minimize year-to-year fluctuations in yields.

Sources: Narodnoe khozyaistvo SSSR (Moscow: Statistika, 1956 to 1975 volumes), Sel'skoe khozyaistvo SSSR (Moscow: Statistics, 1960 and 1971) and Narodnoe khozyaistvo SSSR za 60 let (Moscow: Statistika, 1977).

As shown, in the serious matter of meat availability, where Khrushchev's policies resulted in a 27 percent per capita increase in production, the Brezhnev leadership achieved a 33 percent increase based on a much more solid source of livestock feed. In spite of this achievement, our observations in Soviet stores in the fall of 1977 showed that meat supplies still are invariably short and with very little variety. Moreover, some of the state stores sometimes run out of meat altogether.

The most important of all the Brezhnev changes from the standpoint of production has been the increased priority given to agriculture. In the 1970s, instead of agriculture subsidizing the cities, the reverse has become true. According to N. T. Glushkov, the chairman of the USSR State Price Committee (thus the key person in charge of setting state prices for the whole of the Soviet Union), the annual subsidy to agriculture reached 22 billion rubles in 1978.[3]

Under Khrushchev, capital investment in agriculture during the 1961–65 plan period represented 19.6 percent of all investment in the Soviet economy. Under Brezhnev it increased to 23.5 percent for the 1966–70 period and 26.2 percent for the 1971–75 period. Moreover, during the current tenth five-year plan period (1976–80), investment in agriculture is slated to grow another 31 percent.[4]

The record of the early 1960s indicated that little by way of further output increases would be realized without a change in the Khrushchev policies. Certainly, there were no more new lands to be sown. Future advances had to come almost entirely from increased yields per hectare, which demanded the increase in investment in farming that has marked Brezhnev agricultural policies. *Intensifikatsiya*—more output per hectare—became the key slogan for agriculture.

The growth of major inputs mounted significantly and was responsible for the impressive output advances discussed earlier. In ruble terms, whereas during the 1961–65 plan period new investment in agriculture amounted to 48.2 billion rubles, during the 1966–70 period it increased to 81.5 billion and to 130.5 billion during the 1971–75 period.[5]

Unfortunately, in spite of the enormous increase in investment, the growth in grain output has lagged behind expectations. Grain, especially feed grain, is the primary key to the Soviet agricultural problem. Current levels of output remain far from the goal of 1,000 kilograms of grain per capita each year, which must be met if the dietary goal is to be reached. As shown in Table 3.2, the current achievement is only some 700 kilograms per capita. Grain occupies over half of the total sown area.

Moreover, while output grew by some 41 percent under Khrushchev, it grew by only some 26 percent during the first ten years of Brezhnev's leadership. Indeed, in a recent study made of the Soviet grain situation, we demonstrated that a point of diminishing returns in grain yields was reached in about 1968. Thus, while the yield growth from 1961–65 to 1966–70 (that is, the average yield per hectare for each of the five-year periods) was 34 percent, the growth from 1966–70 to 1971–75 was only 7 percent.[6] This signal that future yield growth probably will be less than what was once hoped for could not have been missed in Moscow and undoubtedly was a major factor behind the Brezhnev decision to make a long-term (five-year) import agreement with the United States as well as other important changes in crop policy, and in the treatment of the peasants' private subsidiary enterprise, which will be discussed later.

The downturn in yield advances also must have been a major factor influencing the decision to inaugurate a mammoth program to increase grain storage capacity in 1975. According to plans published at the time, grain storage capacity (largely for reserves in poor years) is slated to increase from an estimated 28 million to 40 million metric tons by 1980. As noted in the authoritative trade journal, *Milling and Baking News*, the costs involved are comparable to the Manhattan Project (which produced the first U.S. atomic bomb), and the scope rivals the construction of the pyramids in ancient Egypt.[7]

CROP AND LAND AMELIORATION POLICIES

With one major exception, the Brezhnev land-use policy has been markedly superior to the Khrushchev practices. As shown in Table 3.3, major shifts in sowings have been undertaken in the drive to produce more livestock feed. While the area sown to all grains has virtually stabilized, the area sown to the two major Soviet feedgrains, oats and barley, plus that sown for hay and other fodder crops has been increased by more than 20 million hectares, a 36.5 percent increase.

Considerable emphasis has been placed upon expanding the irrigated area and, especially, land amelioration projects to improve yields. The most costly—and sensible—of all such projects was the inauguration of the mammoth land amelioration program for the nonchernozem (non-black-earth) region of the Northwest. Yields in the region have remained far below those of neighboring Poland, where draining and liming of the land have long been practiced. These techniques now are being introduced into the nonchernozem

TABLE 3.3

Changes in Crop Policy: Sown Area
(millions of hectares)

Grain	1955	1965	Percent over 1955	1975	Percent over 1965
	185.9	209.1	12	217.7	4
All Grains	126.4	128.0	1	127.9	0
Wheat	60.5	50.4	-17	42.2	-16
Barley	9.3	18.3	97	30.9	69
Oats	14.8	6.6	-55	12.1	83
Fodder crops	35.7	55.2	54	66.3	20
Fallow	26.8	14.7	-45	11.7	-20

Sources: Narodnoe khozyaistvo SSSR (Moscow: Statistika, 1956 to 1975 volumes), *Selskoe khozyaistvo SSSR* (Moscow: Statistics, 1960 and 1971) and *Narodnoe khozyaistvo SSSR za 60 let* (Moscow: Statistika, 1977).

region. The bulk of the increased investment alloted to agriculture during the 1976–80 plan period is to go into this project. If the plans are fully implemented, by 1990 the Soviet Union should achieve the projected additional 20 million tons of grain from the area.[8]

Unfortunately, however, we agree with the geographer Paul Lydolph, who has analyzed the scheme extensively. Writing in 1976, he observed that what had been done up to that time left the impression that "as usual, deeds lag far behind plans."[9]

The serious 1972 shortfall in grain output not only precipitated the massive purchase of U.S. grain but also was followed by a return to sowing policies that had been most costly under Khrushchev. His new lands campaign had gone too far; the land was oversown, and the nation became dependent for too much of its food on land subject to frequent and devastating droughts. By 1964 Khrushchev had pushed the area sown to grain to a peak of 133.3 million hectares (see Table 3.4). Brezhnev listened to the soil scientists who warned against the droughts, and especially the depletion of the soils by the *sukhovy*, hot dry winds from the south which in the new lands area can devastate plowed land. As two leading Soviet authorities have recorded, "As much as 18 tons of soil an hour can blow away in the chestnut brown soil . . . and two tons of the saline chestnut brown soil areas of the region."[10] Thus, as another Soviet authority underscored, the overexpansion of the grain area in the 1960s brought about an "unjustifiable reduction" of the area left to fallow in the arid regions, which "did not produce a positive result."[11]

The sowing and fallow record reflects a recognition during the early Brezhnev years that until such major land amelioration projects as the nonchernozem scheme could be brought on stream the area sown to grains had to be held down, indeed reduced. The 1972 crop failure, however, resulted in throwing caution to the *sukhovy*. The area sown to grain was again expanded, and the area left to moisture-replenishing fallow was reduced. This return to an overreliance on marginal grain lands undoubtedly contributed to the magnitude of the serious yield reversals of 1975 and 1977.

KOLKHOZY AND SOVKHOZY

Although the pace has slowed, Brezhnev has continued the practice of enlarging the farms, reducing the number of *kolkhozy*, and transforming the weaker *kolkhozy* into *sovkhozy*. Although there were 36,300 *kolkhozy* in 1965, their number declined to only 27,300 by

TABLE 3.4

Area Sown, Sown to Grain, and Fallow
(millions of hectares)

Area	1950	1964	1967
Total sown	203.0	212.8	206.9
To grains	115.6	133.3	122.2
Fallow	32.0	6.3	17.7
% of sown area in fallow	15.7	3.0	8.6

Area	1968	1969	1970
Total sown	207.0	208.6	206.7
To grains	121.5	122.7	119.3
Fallow	18.2	16.9	18.4
% of sown area in fallow	8.8	8.1	8.9

Area	1971	1972	1973
Total sown	207.3	210.7	215.0
To grains	117.9	120.1	196.7
Fallow	18.8	16.2	13.5
% of sown area in fallow	9.1	7.8	6.3

Area	1974	1975	1976
Total sown	216.5	217.7	217.9
To grains	127.2	127.9	127.8
Fallow	12.7	11.2	11.7
% of sown area in fallow	5.9	5.1	5.3

Source: *Narodnoe khozyaistvo SSSR* (Moscow: Statistika, 1956 to 1975 volumes), *Sel'skoe khozyaistvo SSSR* (Moscow: Statistics, 1960 and 1971) and *Narodnoe khozyaistvo SSSR za 60 let* (Moscow: Statistika, 1977).

1975, while in the same time period the number of *sovkhozy* increased from 11,681 to 19,617.[12]

Important changes have included the institution of a guaranteed minimum wage for the *kolkhoz* peasants and increased incomes for all farm workers. (Prior to the institution of the guaranteed wage, made possible by a mandatory crop insurance scheme for all *kolkhozy*, a bad year could, and often did, mean that many farms paid no rubles to their worker members.) Nevertheless, the *kolkhoz* peasant still earns less than the *sovkhoz* workers, and both earn less than urban employees. Indeed, even if the 1976–80 plan for increased incomes is achieved, by 1980 the average *kolkhoz* worker will receive only 116 rubles per month from their work on the collective, while the urban worker's pay is projected to increase to 170 rubles per month.[13]

The average farm is now served by some five specialists with advanced training, for example, agronomists, zootechnicians, veterinarians, and mechanical engineers. The number of tractors has increased significantly, as has the availability of mineral fertilizer.

One of the most important of the early Brezhnev changes was the inauguration in 1965 of stable state purchase plans for the farms. The largest part of the farms output is destined, by plan, to be purchased by the state at set prices. Beyond the planned sales, additional amounts of produce are purchased by the state at premium prices. Prior to 1965, the farms were continually vexed by changes in the plan. Now the plans are set several years in advance, with the promise that they will not be changed until the end of the period. As a result there is less chaos in such matters as on-farm rationalization of sowings, crop rotations, and livestock herd expansion. This change, followed later by significant increases in prices paid to the farms (but not charged to the consumer), has meant that today most farms make a profit.

In spite of the above changes, the Brezhnev balance sheet does not point in the direction of more on-farm decision making. In fact, the balance rests on the side of increased external controls. For example, there has been an increase in the practice of outside authorities regarding the above-plan purchases as mandated. As Keith Bush has noted, such a practice leaves "little or no discretion to the farm management as to the output mix."[14]

From the standpoint of the peasant workers, the farm managers are enormously powerful individuals who order them what to do, and when and how they do it. From the managers' point of view, however, their own career depends upon fulfilling the overfulfilling state-imposed production plans, even though doing so often results in economic loss to the farm. This Soviet reality was made abundantly clear by the Soviet sociologist V. Perevedentsev in his accounting of an interview with the chief of economic planning for the Kuban, one of the best crop-growing regions in the Soviet Union:

> I asked why Kuban milk is unprofitable. Why not increase milk production in Estonia or Novosibirskiy Oblast, I asked, and allow Krasnodarskyi Kray (in the Kuban) the right to grow the most profitable crops?
>
> "No," I was told. "Economic indices, profitability, and law of cost don't mean anything here. There is not enough milk, it must be produced everywhere, in the largest amount possible, and at any price."[15]

Although the course is far from run, the call for specialization (e.g., creating huge livestock complexes on particular farms), more interfarm agrarian complexes (e.g., several farms producing feed for a specialized livestock farm) all work toward more outside controls. The agricultural daily, *Selskaya zhizn*, arguing that such change leads to greater rural industrialization, stated that such is the "main thrust in agricultural development today."[16]

PEASANT SUBSIDIARY ENTERPRISE

In the Soviet Union there must be well over 15 million private family plots, averaging somewhat less than one acre each. According to Karl-Eugen Wadekin, in the mid-1960s such activity engaged some 50 million people. The bulk of such entrepreneurs are rural residents, although Wadekin estimated that in 1964 some 13 percent of the nation's food was produced by "nonfarm workers and employees."[17] Most farm families also have a cow, a pig or two, and a poultry flock.

Stalin allowed the plots as a concession to the peasants at the time of forced collectivization. Although some Soviet commentators have implied that as a form of fresh air and recreational activity, some gardens may survive indefinitely, no one has dared openly challenge the oft-repeated observation that this survival of private enterprise as an important source of Soviet food is a serious anachronism. That they remain an important part of the economy is contrary to building socialism. At least in the past, the attitude has been, the sooner they disappear the better.

Khrushchev moved against the peasant subsidiary enterprise,

and local authorities were encouraged to reduce such activity. This included even building multistoried apartments in the villages, which did not allow adjacent buildings for private animals and nearby gardens for the tenants.

Until the October 1976 party plenum, Brezhnev remained relatively quiet on the matter. However, in his speech at that meeting, after a long listing of things needed to improve food output, he noted that at this time it would be "premature" to curtail such activity. He went further and stated that the private subsidiary food production should receive "more attention, more concern."[18]

As documented above, Brezhnev is bent upon improving the Soviet diet. Thus, his pro-private plot statement is not surprising in the face of Soviet reality. As of 1977 they produced 27 percent of all Soviet agricultural produce, 34 percent of all livestock products, nearly half the vegetables and potatoes. Moreover, in Belorussia in 1976 such activity accounted for some 40 percent of the farm workers' incomes.[19] Yet, even in 1978, articles appear in the Soviet press pointing to the shortage of simple hand tools, such as shovels, hoes, and rakes.[20]

The official party history admitted that collectivization had been a "revolution from above," that is, forced on the peasants below. Now, an announcement by the chief of legal administration of the USSR Ministry of Agriculture portends a new revolution from above, which the nation's peasants would fully welcome. He reported in the journal *Economics of Agriculture* that starting in 1978 the "appropriate ministries" have been instructed to develop and produce small garden machines for sale to the population.[21] Anyone who has used a Rototiller knows that such machines have revolutionized gardening in the West.

Private plots not only produce some one-third of the peasants' incomes; they are an important source of the urban population's food as well. Much of the produce from subsidiary farming is sold in urban *kolkhoz* markets. These are essentially free markets, and Wadekin estimated that in 1967 prices received for such food was some 50 percent higher than those asked in the state stores.[22]

Customers come to the peasant stalls for several reasons, not least of which is that the quality of the food is usually superior, and it is there that meat and vegetables can be found when the shelves in the state stores are empty. Another reason that people go to the markets is that there rural and urban relatives and friends meet. They are places for gossip and exchange of views on that great volume of events that never appear in the Soviet press. Indeed, in the leadership's never-satisfied attempt to control information, one can assume confidently that the uncontrolled information that circulates in the *kolkhoz* markets must be one of the major thorns in the leadership's side.

"INDUSTRIAL FUNDAMENTALISM"

We (and many other observers of the Soviet rural scene) have underscored for years that there were two major flaws in the Soviet system. One was that the lack of investment was most harmful to production, a matter which Brezhnev has moved massively to correct, even though more still needs to be done. The other flaw remains; agricultural success the world over depends upon the human ability to deal with living plants and animals, something that is not compatible with a system in which all work is done by people who are hired hands, lacking any personal investment in what they are doing.

As we have tried to point out at length elsewhere, much misunderstanding about agriculture, and the basis for a major flaw in the Soviet agricultural system, rests in what Professor T. W. Schultz described as a distorted faith in technological advance that is an "industrial fundamentalism."[23]

Lenin preached, and none of his successors have ever publicly doubted, that given a socialist base all agricultural problems could be solved by full industrialization of farming. Yet, as two leading students of U.S. agriculture, John M. Brewster and Gene Wunderlich, have emphasized, there has been no agricultural industrial revolution. "With minor exceptions of certain specialized poultry and livestock operations, a shift to machine farming leaves relatively undisturbed the sequential pattern of operations that have prevailed in farming since the domestication of plants and animals."[24] The essential role of the farmer as husbandman and not a machine operator remains. All of which, of course, is essential to understanding why, certainly at the expenditure of much more labor, the peasants coax relatively so much more out of their tiny private plots than they do out of the collective fields on which they have to labor.

Given the Leninist agricultural doctrine, one of the most extraordinary passages we have ever found in the Soviet press was a quotation of a remark by a collective farm chairman in the pages of *Literaturnaya gazeta*: "But how can one compare a mine or a factory to a collective farm? After all, the nature of production is entirely different."[25]

One wonders whether the local party bosses read the article and whether it cost the chairman his job.

NOTES

1. Merle Fainsod, *How Russia is Ruled* (Cambridge: Harvard University Press, 1953), p. 444.

2. N. Laguton, *Ekonomika selskogo khozyaistva*, no. 3 (March 1975): 97–104.

3. From an interview with Glushkov by David K. Willis, *The Christian Science Monitor*, June 21, 1978.

4. *Voprosy ekonomiki*, no. 7 (1976): 68.

5. *Narodnoe khozyaistvo SSSR za 60 let*, (Moscow: Statistika, 1977), p. 297.

6. Roy D. Laird and Betty A. Laird, "The Widening Grain Gap and Prospects for 1980 and 1990," in *The Future of Agriculture in the Soviet Union and Eastern Europe*, ed. Roy D. Laird et al. (Boulder, Colo.: Westview, 1977), pp. 27–47.

7. July 22, 1975.

8. Laird and Laird, "Grain Gap."

9. "The Agricultural Potential of the Nonchernozem Zone," in Laird et al., eds., *Future of Agriculture*, pp. 49–78.

10. G. P. Ozolin and M. I. Dolgilevich, *Vestnik selskokhyaistvennoy nauki*, no. 5 (May 1975): 123–31.

11. A. Novolotskii, *Ekonomika selskogo khozyaistva*, no. 3 (March 1975): 45–54.

12. *Narodnoe khozyaistvo SSSR za 60 let*, pp. 350, 369.

13. *Kommunist*, no. 16 (November 1976): 61–73. In 1974, the comparative average monthly pay in rubles was: *kolkhoz* farmers, 90.5; *sovkhoz* farmers, 124.7; and industrial workers, 155.0; G. Kostorand and V. Kracher, *Ekonomika sel'skogo khozyaistva*, no. 7 (July 1977): 86–90.

14. "Soviet Agriculture in the 1970s," Radio Liberty Research Paper, no. 42 (New York: Radio Liberty, 1971), p. 26.

15. *Nash sovremennik*, no. 1 (January 1974): 139–51.

16. April 5, 1974.

17. Karl-Eugen Wadekin, *The Private Sector in Soviet Agriculture* (Berkeley: University of California Press, 1973), p. 1.

18. *Pravda*, October 26, 1976.

19. A. M. Yemelyanov, "Means and Mechanism for Implementing the Party's Economic Strategy in Agriculture," *Vestnik Moskovskogo Universiteta*, no. 4 (July-August 1976): 3–16; and V. Tarasevich and V. Leshkevich, "Importance of Private Subsidiary Farming," *Ekonomika selskogo khozyaistva*, no. 2 (February 1978): 77–85. Much of the feed for the private animals does come from the collective fields.

20. *Pravda*, May 27, 1978.

21. A. A. Denisov, *Ekonomika selskogo khozyaistva*, no. 4 (April 1978): 123–26.

22. Ibid., p. 124.

23. Theodore W. Schultz, *Transforming Traditional Agriculture* (New Haven: Yale University Press, 1964), p. 113.

24. "Farm Size, Capital and Tenure Requirements," *Adjustments in Agriculture—A National Casebook*, ed. Charlton F. Christian (Ames; University of Iowa Press, 1961), p. 297.

25. K. Kozhevnikova, "But Why Did He Return," *Literaturnaya gazeta*, May 24, 1978.

4

ECONOMIC PERFORMANCE AND REFORMS IN THE SOVIET UNION

George R. Feiwel
with the assistance of
Ida Feiwel

GROWTH AND PERFORMANCE

Divergencies in quantitative dimensions among individual countries and in time notwithstanding, one of the key features of modern economic growth in industrialized capitalist countries is that high growth rates of per capita national product have been achieved primarily by qualitative improvements of factors; increases of labor and capital, as such, have played a relatively minor role. The high growth rate of productivity is essentially traceable to improved quality of resources, technical change, and evolving arrangements for diffusion and use of knowledge. Such a growth process is associated with capital accumulation, but the ratio of capital to output is compressed by capital-saving inventions, investment in human capital, and working arrangements conducive to a relative reduction of material and capital inputs. Thus, relatively high dynamic efficiency was partly instrumental in maintaining relatively modest shares of investment and relatively high shares of consumption in national product.[1] One of the striking contrasting features of the fairly impressive Soviet industrial growth is that it has been accomplished primarily by growing quantities of inputs with disappointing increases in productivity and efficiency.

Various criteria can be used for evaluating economic systems. From the vantage point of Soviet growth strategy, the growth rates of industrial output are the success criteria of economic performance. Whether measured by official or Western recalculations, until the

1960s the Soviet economy grew at fairly rapid rates. However, as illustrated in Tables 4.1, 4.2, and 4.3, a major secular deceleration in growth dynamics occurred over the last two decades. But this was not accompanied by a commensurate reduction in the growth of inputs.[2] Central planners were faced with the imperative of improving declining productivity and performance, especially in view of deteriorating factor endowments, proliferating priorities, and rising barriers obstructing the reallocation of resources to growth-forcing activities.

The cause of this phenomenon and the most effective cures—given the constraints on change—will continue to be a subject of dispute among economists and politicians. Probably the concentration on a single strategic determinant of growth and productivity is likely to be a misleading approach.[3] Indeed, growth and productivity are complex processes which have to be attacked on many fronts and with a multiplicity of instruments which, in a stochastic economy, tends to reduce the risks of misguided action.

Though space limitations prevent me from doing justice to the formidable questions of the potential sources of growth and productivity, I shall try to concentrate on some of the policy choices in the Soviet context. An appropriate revision of institutional arrangements for resource allocation is merely a necessary, but not sufficient, condition for major and sustained improvements. A radical and consistent revamping of the notorious static inefficiencies of the Soviet system will produce, with some time lag, more than transitional gains in growth rates. Yet it might not sufficiently foster dynamic efficiency. Half-measure reform cannot cope with instilling the system

TABLE 4.1

Growth Rates of National Income, Industrial Output, and Investment in the Soviet Union, 1951–75

Index	Average Annual Rates of Growth				
	1951–55	1956–60	1961–65	1966–70	1971–75
National income	11.3	9.2	6.5	7.8	5.7
Per capita national income	9.4	7.2	5.0	6.7	4.7
Industrial output	13.2	10.4	8.6	8.5	7.4
Per capita industrial output	11.3	8.5	7.0	7.4	6.4
Investment outlays	12.2	13.1	6.3	7.6	6.9
Ratio of 1:5	0.9	0.7	1.0	1.0	0.8
Ratio of 3:5	0.9	0.9	0.8	0.9	0.8

Source: Kraje RWPG 1977 (Warsaw: 1977), pp. 52–56, 61.

with a bold, innovative, and coherent approach to economic problems that would improve qualitative performance, uplift and diffuse
technology and managerial know-how, and stimulate creativity and
good workmanship.

The motivation and behavior of economic actors depends, among
other things, on the macroeconomic and institutional setting within
which they function. Rationality requires that dissonances among the
components of the economic process be removed by modifying the
discordant elements to satisfy the conditions of consistency and
efficiency. Given the political framework, the main villains here are
both the growth strategy and the system of functioning. Thus, it is my
main contention that the choice of an appropriate growth rate,
structure, techniques of production and distribution, and better
working arrangements together would produce results superior to
those that could be achieved by attacking the economic riddle on one
front only.

The centrally planned (socialist) economy provides an opportunity for resolving simultaneously the formidable problems of capital
accumulation, effective demand, income distribution, and working
arrangements. In principle, by setting an appropriate price-wage ratio
to achieve nearly full utilization of resources, the central planner
determines the partition of national income into accumulation and
consumption and solves the financing of accumulation. The central
planner tends to accelerate the tempo of economic growth by setting
as a target an immediate growth rate at the highest possible level. But
such a decision encounters a number of constraints: the consumers'
sensitivity to an adverse time distribution of consumption and various
technical and organizational barriers.

The traditional Soviet growth strategy featured stress on rapid
industrialization; priority of investment and other resources for heavy
industry and discriminatory allocation, with relative neglect of light
industry and agriculture; growth or investment faster than that of
national income (and, by that very fact, consumption); autarkic
tendencies; and the nationalization of industry and forced collectivization of agriculture. Progress was identified not only with maximization of the short-term growth rate of industrial output but also with
the rate of growth of key industries. Such growth strategy gave rise to
striking imbalances and incongruities in the growth process and
deleterious, ubiquitous disproportions between the development of
agriculture and that of industry; among branches of industry (broadly,
heavy versus light); between the sheer quantitative growth of output
and quality, production techniques, and costs; between investment in
new factories and the obsolescence of the underprivileged branches;

and between productive and unproductive activities, with the appalling neglect of the service sector. Consumption was considered largely a residue already at the planning stage and suffered further during implementation when it was treated as the shock absorber for planning blunders, unforeseen developments in unplannable activities, such as foreign trade and agriculture, and interim shifts in priorities.

Traditionally, investment was used as the principal growth propellent and accorded priority on all fronts. The institutionalized growth mania, permeating the whole system, compelled the economy to expand at a rate which heavily overtaxed its capacity; it was not counteracted by any endogenous mechanism to reduce the size and alter the composition of investment to the economy's actual possibilities. The most sensitive spot of the plan was the stupendous investment program. The taut investment plan induced unrealistic assumptions in other activities. As a result, bottlenecks emerged, promoted by forced and abrupt overexpansion of certain activities that were bound to prolong the gestation periods of investments and fruition of output, to raise the cost of an incremental unit of output, and to lower the investment-efficiency index. To sustain economic growth, with declining increases in productivity, a proportionately large share of national income had to be diverted to investment. If such policy were continued, it would entail encroachment on other uses of the national product, such as personal and collective consumption and military and administrative expenditures. Theoretically such a policy is conceivable, but it is not politically feasible within a more or less narrow range. The other alternatives (or combination thereof) available to the central planner were to take the necessary steps to increase productivity, to reconcile himself to a lower growth rate, or to secure external financing.

As the crash industrialization program unfolded, the maximization of output was the paramount task, with cost savings considered a subordinate constraint. The economy enjoyed relatively abundant natural and manpower resources which could be exploited freely. The advantages of backwardness enabled it to borrow technology extensively from the more developed countries. But this is a limited policy. Further extensive growth is circumscribed by scarcities of manpower and natural resources which become more acute with greater exploitation and the draining needs of the Council for Mutual Economic Assistance (CMEA) junior partners. The possibilities of borrowing new techniques diminish, and growing debt and service charges limit imports of new technology. With the growing complexity of the economy and planning, the central planner resorts indiscriminately to more capital-intensive techniques and encounters increasing, difficulties in substituting capital for labor. Working time is substantially reduced, and there is little opportunity for increasing the labor participation rate. Labor turnover increases, and workers become more demanding. Incentives are emphasized, but there is no sufficient quid pro quo in the form of consumer goods and services. The chronic weaknesses of agriculture plague the system intermittently. Thus, the irrational use of resources becomes responsible for the slowdown in the rate of growth, for mounting pressures and strains, and for recurring bottlenecks. As intensive forms of development become more imperative, it is increasingly evident that the dynamics of growth are limited not only by the size and structure of available resources, technological and organizational know-how, and decisions to allocate and reshuffle resources to priority areas, but also by virtual neglect and misguided economic calculation.

Some of the most flagrant inefficiencies of the Soviet system are: waste of capital frozen in protracted, ill-conceived, and dispersed construction projects; accumulation of idle equipment; underutilization of capacity; mismanagement of human resources; excessive labor turnover; and lack of stimuli for assimilating technical progress. Added to these are major fluctuations in output, poor quality and unsatisfactory composition of output, accumulation of huge stocks of unwanted consumer goods, dominance of seller over buyer, rationing, uncertainty of delivery, and a cumbersome supply system. To make matters worse, there is hoarding of materials by industrial producers (which slows down the turnover of working capital and decelerates production flow) and excessive factor and resource inputs in less productive employment. Finally, the system is overcentralized, rigid, and beset by inertia, lack of initiative, and bureaucratic proliferation. The planning system, with its choice coefficients, action parameters, and incentives, is a significant contributing factor to this state of affairs. It is a legacy of the period of extensive development and essentially has not evolved or been altered to meet the requirements imposed by intensive development with its stress on higher productivity, technical innovation, palpable incentives, and qualitative performance. Under the impact of an economy developing with increasing capital intensity, to maintain the same growth rates it is necessary to either increase the rate of investment; raise the efficiency of investment; and/or increase the weight of noninvestment factors of growth.

Although resulting from a combination of many factors, the slump of growth rates in the 1960s and 1970s (see Tables 4.1, 4.2, and 4.3) was severely aggravated and accelerated by anachronistic methods of planning and management. The burden of evidence indicates that these methods are incompatible with intensive development. Although deterioration of economic performance is the dominant factor determining the direction of policy changes (which may or may not entail system changes), it is not the only one. Pressures for economic reform also stem from noneconomic factors, such as the more articulate search for liberalization in all fields. Also, technological progress, economic performance, and the relatively high standard of living in the West are not without due influence. In addition, the infiltration of Western economic thought has been instrumental in reducing the dogmatic nature of Soviet economics. It would seem that the Western analysis of Soviet economic processes has not gone unnoticed. Generally, closer contact with the outside world and the variety of developments in economic reforms in other CMEA countries may also be partly credited for the new currents.

THE MAIN ECONOMIC PROBLEMS IN THE 1970s

The litany of complaints about inefficiency at the Twenty-Fifth Congress of the CPSU (1976) had the same ring as in the past, despite the reform that was being implemented since 1966. Of course, as illustrated in Table 4.2, the control figures of the 1971–75 five-year plan were badly underfulfilled. Brezhnev and Kosygin complained that one of the primary problems continued to be the wide construction front, the frittering away of investment funds on many projects, and delays in commissioning projects and bringing them to rated capacity. Problems continued to be solved by additional investments, labor, and other inputs. Introduction of technical progress was slow, and some R & D institutes were ineffective.[4] Construction was a serious bottleneck and responsible for underfulfillment of many plans.[5]

The construction plan is often drawn up with considerable shortages of resources. Hence these shortages pervade every construction site. When the dispersion of construction projects becomes intolerable, about 10 percent of the most crucial projects are selected for extra rapid completion with all needed resources diverted to them on a priority basis, while the completion of the remaining projects is postponed indefinitely. Such action effectively lengthens construction periods and disperses resources. Unfinished construction was 69 percent of total construction in 1965, 75 percent in 1975, and 80 percent in 1976.[6]

One of the most acute problems facing the Soviet economy is the

TABLE 4.2

Principal Aggregate Indexes of Plan and Performance, 1961-80

Indexes	1961-65 reported	1966-70 plan	1966-70 reported	1971-75 plan	1971-75 reported[a]	1976-80 plan
National income distributed	33	38-41	41	37-40	28	24-28
Gross industrial output	51	47-50	50	42-46	43	35-39
Producer goods	58	49-52	51	41-45	NA	38-42
Consumer goods	36	43-46	49	44-48	37	30-32
Gross agricultural output	12	25	21	20-22	13	14-17
Investment	45	47	42	36-40	42	24-26
Per capita real income	19	30[b]	33	30	24	20-22
Average wages	19	20[c]	26	20-22	20	16-18
Average earnings of collective farm members[d]	NA	NA	42	30-35	25	24-27
Retail goods turnover	34	43-48	48	40	36	27-29

[a] Preliminary results.
[b] Approximate.
[c] Minimum.
[d] From socialized sector only.

Sources: L. Brezhnev, Pravda, March 31, 1971; A Kosygin, Pravda, April 7, 1971; N. Lebedivsky, Planovoe khozyaistvo 3 (March 1971); 16; F. Kotov, Voprosy Ekonomiki 4 (April 1971); 33, 41; SSSR v novoy piatiletke (Moscow: 1966) pp. 126-34; Narkhoz 1967 (Moscow, 1967) p. 58; Narkhoz 1969 (Moscow: 1969) pp. 529, 539; Pravda, February 4, 1971, April 11, 1971; Pravda, December 14, 1975; Brezhnev, Pravda, February 24, 1967; Kosygin, Pravda, March 2, 1976.

declining efficiency of investment, as illustrated in Table 4.3 and frequently admitted by Soviet economists.[7] Probably among the outstanding causes for low investment efficiency are overexpansion of activity, slow gestation periods, underutilization of capacity, and construction of new plants rather than renovation of existing facilities. The gestation period of new facilities is inordinately slow because of the poor quality and technical level of equipment, unfinished construction and installation work, design errors, and shortages of materials, spare parts, and skilled labor.[8] Much attention is being accorded to the significantly higher and quicker returns on modernization, and in 1976–80 nearly two-thirds of investment outlays are supposed to be so channeled.[9] Yet many industries undertake little modernization, using only 10–12 percent of their investment funds for such purposes.[10] Labor shortages, especially in certain age groups, skills, and regions, are increasingly plaguing the Soviet economy. Whereas in the past increases in the Soviet labor force were derived primarily from agriculture and the increasing labor

TABLE 4.3

Recomputed Average Annual Growth Rates of GNP, by Sectors of Origin, End-Use, and Factor Productivity in the Soviet Union, 1951–75

Index	Average Annual Rates of Growth				
	1951–55	1956–60	1961–65	1966–70	1971–75
GNP by sectors of origin	5.8	5.8	4.9	5.3	3.7
Industry	10.3	8.9	6.6	6.2	5.9
Agriculture	4.1	4.1	2.4	4.2	-2.0
GNP by end use	6.0	5.8	5.0	5.5	3.8
Consumption	5.9	5.4	4.0	5.1	3.8
Fixed investment	12.2	10.3	7.1	6.3	5.4
Factor productivity in GNP	1.4	1.8	0.9	1.5	-0.2
Man-hours (labor)	4.6	5.1	3.4	3.4	1.8
Capital	-2.7	-3.6	-3.3	-1.9	-3.8
Land	1.9	4.4	4.4	5.8	2.9
Factor productivity in industrial products	3.6	3.2	0.6	1.3	1.5
Man hours (labor)	6.9	7.6	4.0	3.6	4.5
Capital	-0.6	-2.3	-3.8	-1.8	-2.4

Note: This is an essay by Greenslade in a Joint Economic Committee publication.
Source: Rush V. Greenslade, In Joint Economic Committee, U.S. Congress, *Soviet Economy in a New Perspective* (Washington, D.C.; 1976), pp. 272, 276, 279.

participation rate of women, more recently this increase has primarily come from population growth, which is on the wane because of the declining birthrate.[11] Labor shortages are intensified by inordinately high labor turnover, lack of mechanization (especially in auxiliary production), and mismanagement of labor resources.[12] Managers require labor reserves for: (1) meeting plan revisions upping targets during the year; (2) making up for workers seasonally withdrawn from production and assigned to help out on farms or construction sites; (3) coping with "storming" (short periods of frantic activity) mainly due to cyclical deliveries of inputs; (4) compensations for unreliable norms; (5) upgrading the classification of the enterprise which depends on the number of workers and on which, in turn, depend the salaries of managers; and (6) increasing the size of the wage fund to which the incentive funds are related.[13]

THE 1976–80 FIVE-YEAR PLAN

Do the slogan "the five-year plan of efficiency and quality" and the scaled-down growth rates in 1976–80 imply a rethinking of the growth strategy? I would be inclined to be rather pessimistic. Table 4.2 clearly indicates that the control figures are even lower than the reported growth indexes in the preceding quinquennium. Moreover, the consumption fund (27–29 percent) is to grow faster than the accumulation fund (17–23) percent.[14] But despite Brezhnev's assurances that the targets are less exacting in order to create better conditions for qualitative improvements, I believe that it is one of those sporadic periods of shift to a lower gear (like the famous New Course in the mid-1950s) and, rather, as Brezhnev admitted, a reflection of difficulties in the preceding years.[15] In his comments on the 1976–80 five-year plan, Brezhnev emphasized in particular: (1) faster growth of producer than of consumer goods, the responsibility of machine building in provisioning the economy with up-to-date equipment whose supply is to increase by 50 percent, and increasing the flexibility and amenability to technical progress; (2) elaboration of 10–15-year programs for leading industries taking into account progress in world technology; (3) rapid increase in productivity, cutting back drastically on manual labor and raising automation; (4) essential reorientation in the structure and technical level of the economy; and (5) improvements in quantity and quality of consumer goods.[16]

Whereas in 1971–75 labor productivity increased by 23 percent, in 1976–80 it is supposed to go up by 27 percent.[17] In 1971–75 labor productivity increased by 35 percent in industry, 22 percent in agriculture, 29 percent in construction, and 24 percent in the railroad industry. The corresponding figures planned for 1976–80 are 30–34 percent, 27–30 percent, and 18–20 percent.[18] But the results for the first two years of the 1976–80 five-year plan are not encouraging. Whereas the average annual target for increase of labor productivity in industry during the period is 8.8 percent, in 1976–77 it was only 7.5 percent. The respective figures for construction are 9.8 and 6.3 percent and for rail transport 5.6 and 1.7 percent.[19]

Overall, by 1978 the problems in fulfilling the 1976–80 five-year plan resembled those of the past. Among the most irksome are strained balances for raw materials caused primarily by delays in commissioning new facilities and continued waste of raw materials; continued scattering of resources in construction and waste of billions of rubles of uninstalled equipment; plaguing snags in transportation; and underfulfillment of plans for commissioning capacities to produce consumer goods, and underutilization of the potential for producing consumer goods at nearby enterprises.[20]

THE INITIAL REFORM

The transfer of enterprises to the reformed system began gradually with 43 enterprises on January 1, 1966, and a piecemeal shift continued thereafter which was to have been completed by the end of 1968. Yet even by mid-1971 some industrial enterprises remained unconverted, and the bulk of construction was not transferred until 1972. The delays were caused mainly by difficulties in transferring small-scale enterprises of below-average performance, the unwillingness to further dislocate an already taut construction program, and the hostility of the bureaucracy.

The converted enterprises received the following plan assignments from their ministries: volume of sales; key assortments in physical units, including production for export and output quality; the general wage fund; the size of profit and profitability (to capital); payments to and appropriations from the budget; centralized investment, singling out the amount of construction work, putting into operation centrally financed new capacities, assimilation of new types of products, introduction of new processes, and such technical progress that is of particular significance for the branch; and the central allocation of material and technical supply.

Profit was distributed by remitting the capital charge (about 6 percent), fixed rent payments, and interest on bank credits. The remaining profit was apportioned among the enterprises's decentralized funds: the material incentive fund (MIF), the welfare fund (WF), and the development fund (DF). Thereafter the balance was applied to paying off all sorts of loans and obligations. The difference between total profit and the above deductions was transferred to the budget as the "free" remainder of profit.

The MIF was supposed to stimulate the staff's material interest in raising efficiency. Its main source was the profit earned by the enterprise, determined on the basis of individual or group normatives, calculated on the basis of two indexes: growth of sales (or profit) planned for one year in comparison to the preceding year and the profitability planned for that particular year. The unused balance of the MIF could be carried over to the following year. The lack of an upper limit for MIF contributions was one of its positive facets.

Essentially the formation of the WF paralleled that of the MIF. But, whereas the MIF contained workers' premiums from the wage fund, the WF consisted entirely of profit, with the normatives set at about 2 percent of the wage fund.

The DF was formed for financing capital investment, for introducing new techniques, for mechanizing, automating, and modernizing equipment, for renovating fixed assets, and for improving organization. The DF consisted of part of depreciation earmarked for replacement of fixed assets, net revenue from the sale of fixed assets, and contributions from the enterprise's profits according to normatives related to the annual average value of fixed assets for each percent increase of sales (profit) and for each percent of profitability.

REORGANIZATION OF INDUSTRY

In the 1970s the focus shifted from reform of the functioning system to reorganization, which originally had begun as far back as the early 1960s with the emergence of the Lvov combines. For all intents and purposes, an attempt was made to concentrate and streamline the multilayered administrative system to reduce it to two, three, or four-tier administration of industry (disregarding the republican counterparts): ministry—industrial association—production association (or production-research association)—enterprise (with either the industrial association or the production association omitted in the three-tier system).[21]

Those enterprises and R & D units amalgamated into a production association lose their legal entity status, and the association operates according to the preexisting statute on state industrial enterprises, together with other prerogatives granted by the ministry. Since 1976 production-research associations were set up including both production and research units.[22] It seems that the aim of creating such associations was to rid large-scale production units of the responsibility of prototype production. Since the latter were so unwilling to undertake prototype construction because it interfered with the fulfillment of their overall plan assignments, this activity was shifted to units that would specialize in it and where its fulfillment could be more easily controlled.

The industrial association incorporates production and production-research associations, independent enterprises, combines, and R & D units. It functions on *khozraschet* (cost accounting) and is directly responsible to the ministry. The ministry is instructed to determine the location of associations, taking into account the necessary proximity to production.[23] In fact, however, as most were set up on the basis of preexisting chief administrations, which were located in Moscow within the precincts of the ministries, this is where they remained.

Some of the reasons that motivated Soviet planners to set up associations were:

In addition to other economies of scale, as a large unit the association is in a better position to make use of computer technology, and, above all, it is better suited to control from the center. The limited number of associations simplifies the information flow, thus permitting a smoother computerized central direction.

The association is presumably familiar with the conditions at each enterprise, so it can judge which indexes the enterprises are able to improve. The association can use individual settlement prices to allow for divergent quantity and quality of capital. It can provide its enterprises with an "equal start" by differentiating incentive normatives.

The incorporation of R & D institutes should draw a closer link between R & D and production. An institute within the association is much closer to production than it would be as a budgetary unit outside the production process.

The process of concentration is better served by the association than by a combination of several existing enterprises. Specialization can be developed easily under the tutelage of the association, which can compensate enterprises for temporary disadvantages, shift assets among enterprises, and ensure better coordination of production flows.

The association possesses an overview the enterprise lacks, yet it is not so far removed as the ministry and thus is able to make more

effective investment decisions, especially since it has a stake in
profitability.

The supply system could be streamlined. To ensure smoother production flows, the association would perform the supply functions
better than the traditional supply organs.

The association is better equipped to engage in domestic and foreign
market studies.

The association can employ skilled manpower more effectively and is
better equipped to retrain redundant workers.

The timetable for setting up associations has not been as swift as
anticipated. By 1978 their number had risen to 3,600, accounting for
43 percent of total industrial sales volume. The reorganization of
industry was expected to be completed by 1980.[24] Some of the
problems encountered were of a deliberate, bureaucratic, procrasti-
nating nature, but others had much to do with well-entrenched
relations, territorial scattering, subordination to different ministries,
and the like. Associations often decide on unimportant matters that
could be left up to the plants, whereas they refrain from such overall
questions as the study of demand for their plants' products, drafting
long-term technical development plans, and assigning clients to
producers. Moreover, bypassing of authority and duplication of
functions persist.[25] Reorganization on this pattern was much easier
for the more homogeneous production industries, such as gas, coal,
and petroleum, than for those producing a multiplicity of products.
The industrial associations strongly resemble the former chief administrations. They have the same staffs, the same work methods, and the
same loyalties.[26] The production associations consist of an amalga-
mation of enterprises that were previously under the same chief
administration, without much consideration to including enterprises
from other branches (more vertical concentration), thus hampering
specialization and concentration.[27]

INCENTIVES AND PERFORMANCE CRITERIA

In the 1970s there was a distinct return to prereform performance criteria. As the share of MIF premiums in wages grew, Soviet
planners realized that it would be mandatory to take into account in
planning the supply of consumer goods. By mid-1972 a new regulation on MIF formation was issued to ensure that premium payments be
included in the overall wage fund. The formation of the MIF was
related to the wage fund and labor productivity and adjusted if the

annual plan assignments were changed.[28] No matter how taut its plan, each enterprise was set a more or less equal incentive fund (calculated per worker) as an absolute sum for each year, to be paid out as long as the plan was fulfilled. When it was overfulfilled the funds were increased by means of fund-adjusting rather than fund-forming indexes which were related to planned profitability and sales and in time were joined by labor productivity, share of new or high-quality products, meeting deliveries, and so on.[29]

As in the past, whatever problem emerged at a given time, it was tackled by creating new premiums to counteract it, tending to a layering of premiums and affording management a wide range of choices for fulfilling specific premium-carrying assignments—if all could not be fulfilled—or even duplicating premiums for the same results. The special-purpose premiums still in existence include introduction of new equipment, production of export goods, collection of scrap metal, improvement of quality, and savings of materials.

The prerogatives granted the economic units since 1965 are being largely eroded. As the size of the DF grew, the decentralized investments began to compete for resources with the centralized investments. Starting in 1971 the volume of "decentralized" investments began to be planned by the ministry for its wards, and by 1973 the ministry imposed strict limits on decentralized investments. By 1977 the distinction between centralized and decentralized investments was abolished, and all investments are now planned by Gosplan for the ministries and by them for their subordinates, regardless of sources of financing.[30] Since decentralized investment funds are usually spent on renovation rather than new projects, central planners have effectively cut down on the desired renovation momentum.

In most enterprises the free remainder of profit is a disincentive.[31] The enterprise's time horizon is limited to one year at best. At the end of the year the enterprise's "free" remainder is confiscated by the budget, which also makes up deficits. At the start of the following year the enterprise's financial position does not depend on its previous performance. The free remainder confiscation nullifies the incentive effect of the capital charge. The former represents about 60 percent of the enterprise's total payments to the budget and the latter less than 30 percent. Economists increasingly are calling for a progressive profits tax which would then leave the rest of the profit at the enterprise's disposal to be accumulated over the years.[32]

The "equal start" also runs counter to the reform. In 1976 the minimum wage and that of "middle salary" categories were raised. The increase apparently had an excessive leveling and disincentive effect. However, the raises were often so conducted that premiums were cut to compensate for the raise.[33] As a rule, management receives premiums from the MIF that amount to about 20–30 percent of basic salaries, and production workers get 9–10 percent.[34]

Besides the changes introduced in the formation of the MIF, its formation and distribution have been shackled by additional conditions superimposed on one another in the course of time. The latest is the meeting of contractual deliveries. If at the beginning of a new quarter contractual obligations remain unfilled, the amount of nondelivered goods is subtracted from the planned volume of sales, and this now becomes the plan fulfillment report, reducing the share of incentive funds in profits. Moreover, this "penalty" is only a quantitative measure of nondelivery and in no way depicts the quality of output delivered.[35]

One of the reform criteria was the establishment of stable, long-term normatives for fund formation and profit taxes to enlarge the enterprise's time horizon.[36] Yet for more than a decade these were not introduced.[37] For many reasons stable normatives are at variance with a high pressure economy, mainly because under taut conditions central planners require great flexibility for ad hoc plan changes. Notwithstanding the scaled-down targets of 1976–80, the Soviet economy continues to show all the signs of a high pressure economy. So despite the pronouncements at the Twenty-Fifth Congress of the CPSU, there are still no stable normatives, and planning still starts from the notorious level achieved.[38]

Plan fulfillment as a performance criterion is famous for its many abuses, especially the incentive to obtain the lowest possible plan targets and the highest possible inputs. Profit shares remaining at the various production units are determined annually on the basis of bargaining and compromise among the various levels of the administrative hierarchy. Large investment continues to be financed by the budget, with little or no financial responsibility on the investor. Several factors militate against adoption of taut or even realistic plans at all levels of management: managers are deprived of premiums even if the plan is slightly underfulfilled; if the plan is overfulfilled, this will result automatically in even higher planned targets for the following year regardless of the enterprise capabilities; supply is erratic; reserves have to be kept for fulfilling plans raised during the year, for carrying out all sorts of counterplans and social measures, and for replacing personnel recruited for seasonal agricultural work; and extra funds have to be acquired for "socialist competition," shortages in working capital, and the like.[39]

According to Soviet experts, the sales volume performance criterion is not unlike gross value—the costlier the good the better. In addition it has given rise to problems of trying to collect payments so that "expediters" are sent to roam the country trying to collect payments owed their enterprises.[40] Although the total sales criterion is being shackled by additional product mix indexes, the enterprises often disregard the latter and concentrate on the former.[41] The sales value index is a potent obstacle to introduction of technical progress which often reduces current production growth rates and labor productivity and deteriorates a host of other related indexes.[42]

Performance criteria are frequently discussed in Soviet economic literature. Some economists advocate cost saving, but they admit that it is merely an additional and not a "synthetic" criterion.[43] Many economists suggest that gross value be replaced by value added. But although the methodological guidelines for drafting the 1976–80 plan of enterprises and associations recommended that "production efficiency" be measured in terms of value added, according to Professor Valovoi this index has not yet received its "civil rights," and these recommendations may remain "good intentions."[44] Although profit as the performance criterion is often criticized, the strongly profit-oriented school is not giving way. Self-financing as a means of solving some of the functioning mechanism's problems, ranging from technical progress to daily operations, is still strongly propounded by some economists.[45] Recently the influential mathematical school proponent, AcademicianlFedorenko, offered the following set of solutions to the Soviet quandry:

1. The plan should be balanced, but it should specify a set of final (specific purpose) targets, with deadlines for achieving them, and not intermediate products. For example, the volume of construction would not be considered a specific-purpose index; rather the achievement of rated equipment capacity or increase of output per planned volume of capital investments would be used.

2. Contrary to present-day financial five-year plan estimates, these plans should be firm and fully coordinated and integrated with the physical plans.

3. Stable five-year normatives (prices, payments to budget, interest rates) should be established for all economic units, guiding planning agencies in apportioning the production plans and the bank in distributing credits. All forms of gross output should be abandoned and replaced by a value-added criterion in determining labor productivity and computing the wage fund. In order to reinforce the influence of economic levers and incentives on production efficiency and achievement of end results, very large production associations on full *khozraschet* should be

working on the basis of stable and balanced plans, coordinated with stable normatives and long-term contracts, to do away with the practice of planning from the level achieved. The enterprises' inventives should be related to the degree of client satisfaction and net profits.

4. The wage fund should be related by stable normatives to value added so that there is a definite correlation between the growth of the wage fund and the growth of labor productivity. The managers should be allowed to funnel a larger share of the wage fund to progressive forms of pay (job-rate pay, pay for final results achieved by a brigade, and so on).[46]

At present an important experiment deals with the validity of value added vs. gross value. Since January 1, 1973, a group of machine-building enterprises has been experimenting with value added for measuring production volume and MIF formation. Gross value continues to be used for planning interbranch flows, setting working capital norms, and other tasks.[47] The value-added norm in the experiment is stable for five years and is usually computed by deducting from the wholesale price the "values" of materials, fuels, semifabricates, and depreciation and the average rate of profit for the entire product mix, since under the present price system "profitability levels are largely determined by factors unrelated to the efficiency of an enterprise's performance."[48] However, these norms are at an experimental stage and, as such, are usually overstated, thus allowing the managers considerable leeway in manipulating output. Managers of these enterprises seem more inclined to produce new goods, presumably because these are usually more labor-intensive and have more advantageous norms set for them.[49]

Experience thus far has indicated that value-added norms are more objective criteria for measuring output, especially at enterprises with a wide product mix, for enterprises then become more indifferent to the product mix they produce and there is less violation of the assortment plan. The use of this index also eliminates the incentive to produce the heaviest products and to use the most expensive material inputs.[50]

THE SUPPLY SYSTEM

In principle, the supply system is based on the customer's placing his order about one and one-half years before the goods are needed so that his detailed requirements can be incorporated in the producers' plans. It all seems quite simple on paper: what is produced is used. Yet many unneeded goods accumulate while many plants are obliged to interrupt operations for lack of materials. This seemingly foolproof system goes haywire simply because the detailed composition of plans changes. Plan changes are usually accompanied by allocation orders. But the issuing agency does not really worry about the availability of goods. The real shortages appear at the production level.

By 1978 Gosplan centrally allocated 2,000 product groups (including 1,300 types of equipment), and the State Committee for Material and Technical Supply 13,500 items. Allocation at the 42 ministries and departments comprised 25,000 product groups, which constituted about 7 percent of all centrally allocated goods.[51]

The reform relied on the establishment of long-term contracts between suppliers and users as a means of streamlining the supply system and reducing the centrally approved products lists. In the past decade the list of centrally distributed goods has grown, and there have been considerable difficulties in establishing and honoring long-term supply contracts.[52] It is expected, however, that most large-scale mass producers will be shifted to direct long-term contracts in 1976–80. But the transfer is being implemented slowly and half-heartedly. The supply agencies performing this transfer have no incentive. Nearly all these contracts limit themselves to deliveries only for the following year, and the customers have little to say about improvements in technology and quality of goods.[53]

The customer is entitled to levy fines on the delinquent supplier, but these often remain unexacted because they are inadequate and not proportionate to the loss suffered by the customer.[54] Arbitration agencies report that fines are being exacted in only one out of ten violations of contracts, mainly due to the customer's fear of retaliatory measures by the supplier.[55] The delinquent supplier is hardly affected by the fines levied, for they amount to no more than 1-1.5 percent of the enterprise's profits. Failure to make delivery costs the delinquent no more than 8 percent of the undelivered product.[56] As they presently stand, the fines neither penalize the offender nor compensate the victim sufficiently.[57]

PRICES AND TECHNICAL PROGRESS

The reform had to cope with blatantly outdated prices. Various proposals for price reform were advanced, ranging from the more orthodox average cost plus profit (related either to labor or capital) to the far-reaching mathematical school that would derive scarcity prices from an optimal plan. But Soviet planners were not prepared to stray far from the straight and narrow path of past experience. The new prices that went into effect on July 1, 1967, were based on 1965 or 1966 average costs and planned changes for 1968.[58] Yet at the very outset the prices were outdated. In the extractive industries (especially oil and gas) prices were based on the cost of enterprises working in relatively worse natural conditions. The enterprises working under better natural conditions had to pay a fixed (rent) payment set by the State Committee for Prices. In other branches the profit rates were to be determined as percentages of average branch stock of capital indispensable for operating under average conditions. The branch profit was established in relation to capital and the prices of individual goods in relation to costs, mainly for the sake of expediency.[59]

Since the 1967 price revision, several reductions in prices of machinery were made. Considerable and unintended divergencies in profitability have arisen in various production units and among different products. Due to worsening mining conditions, the coal industry is again unprofitable.[60]

A new approach to price setting, concentrating on improved quality and technical progress, was already evinced in the regulations issued by the State Committee for Prices in July 1969.[61] The regulations envisaged different methods for determining wholesale prices: products replacing (or interchangeable with) those previously produced, products similar to those previously produced but differing from them on a number of technical and economic parameters, and goods produced for the first time.

For replacement of interchangeable products, prices are determined on the basis of prices of existing goods, the relative advantages of the new product, and the expected economy-wide savings from its use. The savings are computed as the difference between the upper and lower limits of prices, taking into account the expenditures of putting the item into production.

For products similar to those previously produced but differing on a number of parameters, economic gain does not have to be established. It is sufficient to relate prices to the given group of products according to their "technical and economic indexes." The changes in expenditures on the production of a given item and its price in connection with the item's basic features (productivity, capacity, speed, and so on) are usually determined empirically.

For goods produced for the first time, prices are to be set on the basis of planned unit costs for the second year serial production plus the profitability normative set for the branch.

Once again the intractability of reforming prices by regulations has been demonstrated. These regulations were often disregarded, and prices continue to be set as before, that is, on the high costs of initial production plus a profit markup.[62] The price-setting organs encountered considerable difficulties in estimating the periods for the production of output, cost dynamics, and the degree of satisfaction of requirements.[63] The setting of graduated prices (with upper and lower limits) was difficult because of the intricate determination of the "beginning of obsolescence" and the intermediary stages for each specific article. There was a scantiness of data on future developments in given and related fields so that reliable forecasts could be made. Also, to set prices that discriminate for technical progress and quality requires reliable standards of modernity, which often are unavailable.[64]

A central problem seems to be determining technical parameters. The State Committee for Prices claims that the ministries together with the State Committee for Science and Technology and the State Committee for Standards, Measures, and Measuring Instruments are responsible for determining the entire complex of qualitative and other operational characteristics of various groups of products and should "reflect the optimal values of these parameters" in normative-technical documentation for a definite period. The State Committee aims at reflecting the "real national economic effect" of new products, thereby encouraging by means of higher prices the production of machines with improved operational characteristics.[65]

Still, according to the chairman of the State Committee for Prices, prices do not always stimulate production of sophisticated equipment and higher quality goods. At present the procedure followed for setting prices of new or updated products is as follows: In the case of goods that are technically superior or even equivalent to those previously produced but whose production entails savings of materials and fuels the profit remains the same as on the previously produced goods. If the goods qualify for the highest quality rating, an additional profit amounting to 50 percent of the savings on production costs is included in the price. This is also the case if the goods conform to the highest domestic or foreign technical standards. In cases where the cost savings are very substantial, the State Committee may grant the same wholesale prices as for the replaced product. Last, if the price for the new product is lower than that of the replaced one, Gosplan may allow the producing ministry to use the old price for planning production volume and labor productivity.[66]

Yet all this seems to be "music of the future." For example, the prices of rolling-mill equipment are based on the machinery's weight and take no account of productivity or end result savings.[67] Moreover, irrespective of price, the manufacturers of heavy machinery prefer to produce the heaviest products possible. The price markups for producing more efficient machines are received only if the weight index is met—and when it is not, not only the production workers but also management lose 40 percent of premiums.[68]

The experience of central planning so far has shown that centralized decision making is responsible for the following advantages and drawbacks to the introduction of technical progress:

By virtue of operating a command economy, planners should be able to order the implementation of technical progress at all levels. However, the average economic gain from introduced inventions has fallen by 60 percent in the last decade.[69]

A planned economy should operate with a wide time horizon, which would make it possible to take into account the directions of technical progress over a longer time interval. In practice, however, the extended time horizon often is obscured by current problems and by the short-run system of evaluating the performance of the entire hierarchy. A high pressure economy is incompatible with long-term planning.

State ownership provides a basis for disseminating technical information. Enterprises are obliged to transmit technical data to each other. But in practice there are significant barriers to spillover. The processes of acquiring superior know-how and making effective use of it are not equivalent. There are great problems of absorption. Rewards favor current plan execution. Also, the dissemination of either foreign or domestic technology is not only circumscribed by the unwillingness of managers to adapt it but also by the existing supply limitations and lack of flexibility and adaptation.

It is possible to plan and coordinate state development of science and technology. This is of essential significance from the standpoint of concentrating efforts on chosen activities. But, on the other hand, such concentration might be detrimental due to neglect of other subjects and a weakening of the spontaneity of innovation.

There is considerable stress on technical training and education, accompanied by continuous complaints that special training and education are not sufficiently rewarded in terms of salaries.

The plan, at least in theory, ensures realization of output. Although competition, which is essential to stimulate technical progress, has been largely eliminated and tremendous difficulties are encountered in reinstating some resemblance thereof, a positive role could be played by competition on the world market. But it is easier to sell to undemanding customers. The persistence of a buyer's market at home, and to a certain extent within CMEA, and the maintenance of rigid controls and lack of flexibility are largely responsible for the Soviet Union's inability to raise substantially its exports of manufactured goods to the West.

A good dose of conservatism is built into planning techniques since a large degree of uncertainty due to new technology and products creates difficulties for the central planners. One might also add that the perpetuation of established structure is an obstacle to introducing new technology. Experience has shown that in basic, centrally financed investments attempts were made to infuse technical progress. The constraining factors lay primarily in such areas as information, design, technological skills, and disposable resources. But there is also the danger of technocratic fascination with progress without sufficient consideration for real possibilities and needs. Relatively well-developed methods of investment efficiency calculation should permit, in principle, a rational choice of technology. However, in practice, these methods are not always satisfactorily implemented, particularly because the alternative variants are not elaborated.

One of the obstacles to technical progress implanted by the planning system involves the materials barrier. Because tremendous pressure is exerted for increased output at the early stages of production, the quality of raw materials and semifabricates is frequently sacrificed. This, in turn, hampers technical progress at the later stages of production and has widespread repercussions on economy-wide progress.

The dislocations and bottlenecks of production impose certain demands on R & D. Distribution of investment resources is partly determined by the need to overcome the existing limitations. In turn, the search for new solutions is influenced by the distribution of investment resources. Central planners place higher priority on concrete and immediate solutions to current bottlenecks. Such requirements subordinate R & D to the actual needs of production. Since the solutions to these assignments are urgent, not much attention is paid to their quality in comparison to world standards. R & D units require fairly stable operating conditions and a certain autonomy, even if the results do not remove current bottlenecks and do not find their way immediately into production. Conflicts often arise between management, oriented towards current production problem solving, and R & D executives, who interpret their mission with a longer time horizon.[70] Investments usually are not undertaken in response to new technology; quite the reverse, techniques are adapted to investments already decided upon. Frequently investments do not embody technology of the latest, or even recent, vintage. Changes in production techniques affect new investment with inordinate lags, and many investments merely copy outdated technology. Extraordinary difficulties are encountered in adapting even the imported, sophisticated, expensive, and presumably priority technology. Moreover, installed equipment is not updated, nor is there any preceptible spillover to other firms.[71]

In some cases small or even medium series production continues to dominate industry chiefly due to efforts to meet domestic requirements with domestic resources. On the one hand, this results in enormous diversity of production; on the other, it limits the size of production runs and effective specialization.

The problem of risk taking and aversion to risk associated with innovative activity is by no means confined to the Soviet Union. The solution is to provide palpable incentives not only to overcome the resistance to risk taking but to entice risk bearing. A primary function of planning is to reduce risk by reducing uncertainty in the future. But uncertainty is endemic to a high pressure economy. In such an economy the plan executant feels that "little change entails little risk." The prudent way is to perform the tasks that matter to one's superior and on which the largest rewards are based. At the present stage the Soviet system does not sufficiently reward those who bear risk, nor does it penalize those who avoid it. It is not quite clear exactly what it would take to elicit the desired response. In large organizations it is awkward to identify an individual's contributions. Premiums are often awarded for activities that would have been undertaken without them. Generally, it seems that to elicit the appropriate response the premium must be large. From the central planner's standpoint, this is objectionable not only on distributional grounds but also because it generates excessive purchasing power which has to be met with more and better consumer goods. In a nutshell, the essential shortcoming of all premium and incentive systems tried thus far is that they fall short of injecting a modicum of entrepreneurship without which incentives for technical progress cannot succeed.

The principal obstacles to technical progress erected at the enterprise level can be summarized as follows.

As we know, the enterprises are still driven to maximize gross output. This is one of the most potent obstacles to technical progress since the introduction of new products or new processes often involves a slowdown in output over the short run due to various ills that necessarily accompany such measures. Or the user of the new product might be penalized if its use reduces his gross output.[72] The calculation of the wage fund in relation to gross output also inhibits technical progress, which might require an enlarged R & D staff not otherwise available unless the enterprise increased its gross output. The relationship of the MIF, WF, and technical progress premiums to the wage fund also impedes technical progress. Enterprises might be reluctant to increase automation (especially in auxiliary production) since this would perforce reduce the number of workers and therefore the wage fund.

One of the tools useful in stimulating the introduction of new or substantially improved goods is an appropriate price system. When new goods are priced in relation to similar goods previously produced, the producer is discouraged from producing new goods since his profit on existing production is higher. As a rule, the financial indexes of the enterprise's performance deteriorate in the initial period of preparation and mastering of new products, and not only for the new products but for the entire activity of the enterprise.[73] Just as it is not profitable for producers to introduce new models, it is not convenient for the user to install new machinery, because in the initial period he encounters manifold problems of assimilation.

A special fund to cover the costs of mastering new technology compensates only a part of these costs; and it does not cover losses involved in reduced profits and reduced sales volume. The expenditures covered pertain primarily to the period prior to mass production and not the high costs of the first year or two of production.

A special premium fund for technical innovations has been in existence for several years, related to the wage fund. The plants with a larger work force tend to receive a higher premium which at any rate is relatively insignificant.[74] Moreover, at this juncture premiums for new technology are derived from increased profits and from funds which aim at defraying the additional costs of introducing new technology. The new technology assimilation fund formed at associations is now derived from profit, but it does not have the same incentive effect as premiums derived directly from profits realized on the new technology. In a number of branches specific technical progress premium funds are created. For example, in the electrical equipment industry about 40 percent of this fund consists of 50-60 percent of additional profits on new products; the remaining 60 percent of the fund depends on other criteria.[75]

Under conditions of an obligatory plan at all levels, central planners apply pressure for implementation of technical progress through technical coefficients, the technical progress plan, and the assortment plan. The pressure exerted by the plan could be very significant if the central planners control both autonomous sources of information for plan construction and means of ensuring plan execution (mainly effective instruments of quantitative and qualitative control). These conditions can be met fully only with reference to a relatively small number of high priority targets. In the majority of cases, planners must depend largely on information derived from the lower echelons, which may be subject to contamination and distortion. If, in practice, it is not easy to overcome the tendencies at the lower echelons to obtain easy plan directives, it is all the more difficult in connection with the technical progress plan. Therefore, there are greater dangers of misconceived targets in this area. The central directives may overlook possibilities of relatively insignificant modernization and improvements whose cumulative effect may be significant.

As a rule, the plan for technical progress is not integrated or coordinated with production and financial plans; the failure to fulfill the former does not preclude the enterprise from fulfilling the latter. Ironically, the failure to carry out the technical progress assignments usually helps the enterprise in carrying out its production and financial plans. This is mainly due to the year-by-year nature of short-term planning.

A key obstacle to the introduction of new production methods is the preeminence of the annual and even quarterly plans. Enterprise managers are simply apprehensive that any changes in production methods might mean a sacrifice of immediate benefits already planned for the given year. When planning output of newly built capacities, superiors usually allow for a progressive mastering of capacities. Such a period of adjustment is not taken into account when existing facilities are being modernized or are introducing new products. They are still expected to fulfill taut output plans.[76]

It was expected that industrial associations and production associations would have a better perspective for fostering technical progress and could be entrusted with greater investment decision making. However, these units are not overly interested in technological undertakings that would bear fruit in the distant future because, like enterprises, they have a short-run outlook due to the omnipotence of the short-term plan. In such a system any economic unit is reluctant to sacrifice a part of its resources for technical progress, fearing that the effects derived therefrom will be "confiscated" by the subsequent operative plans through an appropriate rise in assignments.

The spread of technical progress and efficiency clashes with the planner's manifest preference for centralized administration of the economy. A wide scope of decentralization is needed to make immediate decisions and to take action without delay, on the spot, unhampered by bureaucratic inflexibility. Even where greater scope for such action seems to be accorded in activities granted highest priority, the firm still does not operate in a vacuum; it depends on other links in the system, on even interenterprise flows, and on the quality of inputs. When innovative initiative is exhibited at the lower echelons, the centralized system may not provide the necessary means for realizing this initiative. If the enterprise does not dispose of some financial means, its innovative activity often requires a protracted process of requests and acceptance. It is only after such initiative has been included into the plan by the higher echelons that the possibilities of execution are open. The restrictions of the supply system make it extremely difficult for enterprises to modernize their equipment, improve production technology, introduce new products, or raise the quality of existing output. Moreover, although R & D organizations usually require relatively small quantities of materials and equipment, they have difficulty planning ahead of time.

Technical progress is severely handicapped by the protracted construction period. The investment cycle (from design to reaching planned capacity) usually lasts 8 to 12 years. In many cases the investment projects begin paying off only when they are already obsolete. With the scattering of construction projects, completion deadlines are delayed, although the machinery keeps coming in. Some of the equipment becomes not only obsolete but also inadequate for the project whose specifications might have changed during the course of construction.

Although some attempts have been to change the situation through reorganization, basically the R & D units have no stake in the results of their work. They do not bear responsibility if their projects fall short of expectations, nor are they recompensed if they meet or surpass expectations. The reform has not really touched on the operation of design organizations.

The reform blueprint was supposed to infuse qualitative improvement into enterprises. By increasing enterprises' interest in their profits, it was anticipated that they would become more sensitive to problems of cost reduction and increased sales. By limiting the number of directives, it was hoped the enterprises would be provided with greater possibilities for substituting factors of production, for adapting the structure of production flexibility to the structure of demand, and so forth. However, such actions were not stimulated, partly because the producer was not subject to the pressures of a buyer's market. It was still far easier to manipulate indexes so as to achieve one's ends than to revert to the arduous tasks of implementing modernization which, in the short run, still did not pay.

Even assuming that enterprises were vested with limited decentralized investment decisions, that they could obtain investment resources incorporating technology of latest vintage, and that the incentive problems were resolved, the system would still have to solve the intractable question of criteria for evaluating alternative projects. Given the obdurate problems of price and cost (including capital) coefficients, profitability can hardly be a guide for rational resource allocation. Without a concomitant and consistent reform of other system components, enlarged decentralization of investment is not always beneficial and is often the cause for a swing back to recentralization, as the experiences of many other CMEA countries show.

CONCLUDING REMARKS

It is hazardous to make comparisons, particularly when a host of various factors is at work. However, some striking similarities between the Soviet Union and Japan may be noted. Both succeeded in recording exceptionally high growth rates, both channeled a relatively high share of GNP to capital formation, and both gave priority to growth-promoting activities. But the differences were many. Japan energetically exploited the advantages of backwardness; its investments primarily embodied creatively adapted superior foreign technology. The Japanese exhibited a strong entrepreneurial spirit. Government policy and flexible working arrangements facilitated adjustment to change and a forceful penetration of foreign markets. The Japanese were phenomenally successful in extracting more marketable output from every unit of labor.and capital. The Soviet Union failed miserably in all these areas where the Japanese have been so successful. As we know, since the early 1960s the Soviet Union's growth momentum and rate of increase of productivity have flagged. Growth no longer can be propelled by relying on an increasing commitment of resources due to the relative exhaustion of resources and to the proliferation of competitive claims on them. More recently there have been disquieting signs about the continuation of Japan's success story. It appears that to some extent the remarkable Japanese and Soviet growth momentums were facilitated by "transitory" opportunities. In Japan the advantages of backwardness are receding, labor is becoming more demanding, and the need to improve housing and public services can no longer be postponed. Similarly, in the Soviet Union increasing attention has to be paid to the worker-consumer, limiting the share of GNP diverted to capital formation. However, aside from other possible improvements, the Soviet Union still has a vast source of potential growth in the better allocation of the investment fund, in an improvement of utilization of existing capacity, in borrowing and adapting foreign know-how, and in instilling the will to produce and the spirit of innovation—if only it could devise a means of doing so effectively.

Whatever the other differences, Japan's "growth miracle" was not burdened by the heavy Soviet military expenditures. The problem is not only one of sheer outlays but of the military's claim on the most advanced and qualitatively best resources. Thus, another source for improving the economy's performance is to cut military expenditures and to reallocate some of the superior material and human resources to civilian activities. Whatever their other differences, both the United States and the Soviet Union suffer from powerful lobbies that strongly oppose reduction of the military budget. Contrary to Japan, the Soviet Union has a vast but lopsided material base. But the growing needs for domestic and CMEA industrialization, more costly exploitation, and wasteful use of materials make future availabilities, especially of energy, a matter of critical importance. Here again the chronic weakness of Soviet agriculture is a major constraining factor. As a supplier of raw materials, the Soviet Union is being criticized for lagging in deliveries to its CMEA partners. Similarly, even at the cost of sophisticated foreign technology, the Soviet Union has had to cut back on the supply of raw materials to the West.

The Soviet planning system was designed to facilitate mobilization of resources and is ill-suited to the requisites of intensive growth. Mobilization and steering of resources into appropriate activities and the maintenance of production flows are signs of economic vitality; economic efficiency means employing resources to obtain as much output as possible by applying the best available techniques. The Soviet Union particularly needs to augment, spread, and utilize technical and organizational know-how and to reinforce incentives "in employing resources in a different way, in doing new things with them, irrespective of whether these resources increase or not."[77]

In part the economic reform movement owes its existence to the retardation of production growth rates and productivity in the 1960s. At first economists and later the leadership became increasingly aware that, with the growing complexity of the economy, proliferating priorities, the increasingly demanding consumer, shifts in factor endowment, and abated possibilities of extensive growth, the traditional ways of running the economy were becoming increasingly obsolete.

The economic reform blueprint referred to increased efficiency derived from economic reform as an additional source of economic growth or as a possible source for redressing some disproportions and increasing living standards. However, the essence of the inverse relationship between growth policy and reform, that is, that reform implementation requires an appropriate slack in the economy, was not really perceived. Reform will encounter intractable obstacles in an economy overheated by overcommitment of resources to investment.

Whatever their advantages in manipulating macroportions, the central planners are subjected to little immediate scrutiny, and the dangers of voluntarism are great. The system is rigid, lacks a microeconomic adaptive mechanism, and does not stimulate technical and organizational dynamism at the production level. Whereas the reform focuses on more effective input combinations, improved quality, and wider and better product mix, together with technical dynamism, a high pressure economy necessarily stresses quantity, is conducive to wasteful factor combinations, and insists on current production to the detriment of innovation. The insistence on high growth rates affects the ways of achieving such growth rates. Whereas the reform usually stresses economic calculation, the high pressure economy invalidates such calculation. The execution of an excessively taut plan involves supply shortages in one branch after another. Under such conditions economic calculation is forgone in favor of production at all costs, and central planners increasingly revert to central allocation of resources. Whereas the reform involves greater stress on material incentives to motivate the actors and, consequently, larger take-home pay, the high pressure economy encroaches on the volume, quality, and variety of consumer goods and services available on the market and so reduces the attractiveness of large pay.

The maximization of output pushes quality considerations aside. It is in the makeup of the directors of high pressure systems to overrate the favorable effects of growth and underrate the adverse effects of poor quality on the system's dynamic efficiency and welfare. This is partly due to their limited time horizon, for in politics immediate results count. The valuation scale affects the attitude toward the reform and the trade-off between gains in efficiency and deceleration in growth momentum. While central planners largely agree on the necessity to shift to intensive growth, they are unwilling to accommodate themselves to the accompanying costs in terms of a deterioration of extensive growth indexes. Whereas the reform ostensibly offers a set of stable norms to broaden the decision-making horizon of lower units, a taut plan contains the seeds of breakdowns and consequent shifts which undermine stability and reintroduce the short-term vantage point. While the reform features profit (or a variation thereof) as a key performance criterion, the high pressure economy, with its stress on quantity, increasingly reverts to forms of gross value of output as the most important criterion.

The reform tends to substitute profitability (achieved through increased output and/or reduced costs) for quantity of output as the enterprise's important performance criterion. But this is incompatible with physical planning which relies on material balance techniques in plan construction. It is not a matter of indifference whether increased profitability results from increased output or cost reduction and, in the latter case, whether the reduction is achieved in labor and/or material costs. All these enter into separate balances and are not interchangeable for this type of system. Whereas the reform gives greater leeway to horizontal relationships, an overheated economy requires increasing control over the lower units and consequently strengthens the vertical hierarchical apparatus. In the final analysis the system of functioning should be consistent and dovetailed with the development strategy. There is an obvious interaction between the plan's content and the modus operandi of the economy.

Theoretically the centrally planned economy provides opportunities for a wide gamut of arrangements for resource allocation. But in practice the choices are fairly circumscribed, and not only by political constraints. Broadly speaking there are at least three abstract possibilities of reforming the system: market socialism, indirect centralism, and modified centralism. In turn, each of these alternatives is open to a number of variations and different configurations. The present Soviet regime distrusts market socialism, which is largely incompatible with a dictatorial system. In the near future Soviet reforms are most likely to favor modified centralism coupled with a technocratic approach. Experience of their CMEA countries shows that as long as a high pressure economy is maintained, even if indirect centralism is adopted, it soon ends up as modified centralism at the implementation stage.[78]

The technocratic approach predominates in the structural, organizational, and functional reforms. The emphasis is on technology rather than people or overall system changes for dynamic efficiency. Yet the technological gap continues to be disappointingly large. As tentative and difficult to generalize as the results of such investigations are, detailed Western case studies conclude that while in certain activities Soviet technology is equal or even superior to that of the industrialized West, on the whole there was no discernible reduction in the technological gap between the Soviet Union and the West from the mid-1950s until the early 1970s.[79] Potentially, the greater the gap or "advantages of backwardness," the greater the opportunity for borrowing foreign technology. But central planners have also had to contend with the system-made obstacles to absorption, adaptation, diffusion, and effective utilization of expensive foreign technology. Moreover, they are reluctant to increase substantially the economy's "leading links" dependence on foreign sources of supply. After an initial spurt in the mid-1970s, imports of Western machinery have been on the wane. Moreover, imports on the scale thus far experienced appear to have made a fairly small contribution to boosting the growth rate of output and productivity.

In examining Soviet economic performance, the core of the issue is whether the results would have been better if the resources had been more efficiently used or whether the same results could have been achieved by tapping a smaller quantity of resources. In the latter case, the remainder could have been diverted to consumption, and it would not have been necessary to treat consumers as shock absorbers penalized for the shortcomings and failures in planning. The economy might have been able to approach an optimal rate of growth if it had not been overtaxed by excessive priority investments, a more proportionate and effective investment policy had been pursued, stimuli to generate innovation and to implement new techniques had been provided, efficiency and productivity had been induced, apathy had been overcome and incentives strengthened, and if some form of economic democracy or workers' participation had been introduced.

The costs of Soviet industrialization and economic system are not confined to obstacles to technical progress and organizational innovations at the micro level; they embrace the adverse effects on the quality of performance of the workers themselves. It is not at all improbable that the damage inflicted is much greater than is commonly perceived. Rapid industrialization has increased the working class tremendously, but it has not rid it of many sociological, psychological, and political characteristics of the peasantry. On the contrary, the nature of industrialization has not been conducive to uplifting the quality of life. The system has had indelible adverse repercussions on social consciousness, motivation, the attitude to work, and the attitude toward collective (state) property. It has encouraged mistrust of authorities and their promises, a lack of a sense of commitment or determination, general apathy and disillusionment, and indifference among the masses. It has also had a demoralizing effect by introducing or perpetuating the system of all sorts of economic crimes (bribes, petty theft, and large-scale larceny) and the complacency with which the population accepts them.

To repeat, the fundamental problem of the Soviet economy is not really one of quantity, but of quality. In only 60 years the Soviet Union has achieved a momentous transformation of the economy, military might, advances in technical progress in some priority areas, considerable improvement in health, education, and culture, reduction in working time, and a modest improvement in living conditions— however unevenly distributed they may be in favor of the ruling elite. This progress should be viewed in light of the initial low level in the Soviet Union and relatively greater economic upsurge in the West. The results probably would have been markedly better, with lower costs in terms of human and material resources, had an alternative growth strategy been adopted and had the system overcome its resistance to change and innovation. Part of the problem undoubtedly lies in the authoritarian, conservative, and ossified political system, the bureaucratization of life, and the stress on control rather than quality of performance. Probably the system's greatest failure was that it depressed the will to produce, to create, to "do a good day's work" for oneself and for society, and to create conditions for work to become a source of joy that would carry its own reward. To qualify as real reforms, changes must palpably improve daily living and working conditions, stimulate the willingness to produce and innovate at all levels, and profoundly affect the aspiration levels and structure of wants in all members of society.

NOTES

1. S. Kuznets, *Population, Capital, and Growth* (New York; 1973).

2. A. Bergson, *Productivity and the Social System of the USSR and the West* (Cambridge, Mass.; 1978); S. Gomulka, *European Economic Review* 10 (1977): 37–49; M. L. Weitzman, *American Economic Review* 4 (September 1970): 676–92.

3. R. M. Solow, *Review of Economics and Statistics* (August 1957): 312–20; D. W. Jorgenson and Z. Griliches, *Review of Economic Studies* (1967): 249–83; E. Denison, *Accounting for United States Economic Growth 1929-1969* (Washington, D.C.; 1974).

4. A. Kosygin, *Pravda*, March 2, 1976; L. Brezhnev, *Pravda*, February 24, 1976.

5. *Pravda*, June 13, 1976.

6. D. Valovoi, *Pravda*, November 11, 1977; B. Pokrovskii, *Pravda*, April 16, 1977; I. Dimitrieyev, *Pravda*, September 7, 1977.

7. L. I. Mokeeva, *Ekonomika i organizatsiya promyshlennogo proizvodstva* 4 (July–August 1978): 102; V. Mikhalev, *Pravda vostoka* 8 (August 1978): 110; Valovoi,

Pravda, November 11, 1977; V. K. Faltsman et al., *Izvestiya akademii nauk SSSR* 3 (May–June 1978): 44–54.

8. I. Pogosov, *Pravda*, July 29, 1977; E. Shklovskii and Ye. Saburov, *Materialno-tekhnicheskoe snabzhenie* (February 2, 1978): 48–53.

9. N. Budunova, *Pravda*, August 15, 1976.

10. A. A. Borovoi (Interview), *Ekonomicheskaya gazeta*, September 28, 1976; Ye. Ivanov and E. Eskina, *Ekonomicheskaya gazeta*, May 21, 1978; M. Berkovich, *Ekonomika i organizatsiya promyshlennogo proizvodstva* 2 (March–April 1978): 91–96.

11. L. Danilov, *Kommunist* 9 (June 1977): 39–50.

12. M. Ya. Sonin, *Ekonomika i organizatsiya promyshlennogo proizvodstva* 4 (July–August 1977): 3–12.

13. Ye. L. Manevich, *Ekonomika i organizatsiya promyshlennogo proizvodstva* 2 (March–April 1978): 75–87.

14. Kosygin, *Pravda*, March 2, 1976.

15. Brezhnev, *Pravda*, February 24, 1976.

16. Ibid.

17. Kosygin, *Pravda*, March 2, 1976.

18. *Pravda*, December 14, 1975.

19. A. V. Bachurin, *Voprosy ekonomiki* 8 (August 1978): 3–4.

20. L. Brezhnev, *Pravda*, November 28, 1978.

21. N. Drogichinskii, *Pravda*, February 7, 1976.

22. L. Pekarskii and N. Kolesnikova, *Kommunist vooruzhennykh sil* 16 August 1978): 36–37.

23. *Pravda*, April 3, 1973.

24. Pekarskii and Kolesnikova, pp. 35–36.

25. M. Kashirina, *Pravda*, June 11, 1977.

26. I. Ya. Kremenetskii (Interview), *Ekonomika i organizatsiya promyshlennogo proizvodstva* 2 (March–April, 1976): 154–156.

27. Yu. V. Subotskii, *Ekonomika i organizatsiya promyshlennogo proizvodstva* 4 (July–August 1975): 35–42.

28. *Ekonomicheskaya gazeta*, January 2, 1973.

29. P. C. Bunich, *Voprosy ekonomiki* 9 (September 1975): 67–85.

30. V. Ostapenko, *Planovoe khozyaistvo* 4 (April 1978): 124–25.

31. T. Zaleskis, *Voprosy ekonomiki* 1 (January 1977): 64–70.

32. Yu. Yarkin, *Kommunist* 4 (March 1977): 48–59.

33. Ye. G. Antosenkov et al., *Ekonomika i organizatsiya promyshlennogo proizvodstva* 3 (May–June 1976): 60–78.

34. Yu. Artemov, *Voprosy ekonomiki* 8 (August 1975): 38.

35. Ye. G. Liberman and V. P. Khaikin, *Ekonomika i organizatsiya promyshlennogo proizvodstva* 1 (January–February 1978): 30–40.

36. Yu. Artemov, *Pravda*, November 22, 1976.

37. A. V. Bachurin, *Ekonomicheskaya gazeta*, August 3, 1978.

38. Kosygin, *Pravda*, March 2, 1976; Brezhnev, *Pravda*, February 24, 1976, Valovoi, *Pravda*, November 11, 1977.

39. P. G. Bunich, *Voprosy ekonomiki* 9 (September 1975): 67–85.

40. Valovoi, *Pravda*, November 11, 1977.

41. N. Yegyazarov, *Pravda*, September 20, 1977.

42. Valovoi, *Pravda*, November 11, 1977.

43. V. Sobolev, *Pravda*, October 17, 1977; Yu. Yakovets, *Ekonomicheskaya gazeta*, February 9, 1977.

44. D. Valovoi, *Pravda*, August 17, 1976; A. Stepankov, *Pravda*, April 12, 1977.

45. A. M. Birman, *Ekonomika i, organizatsiya promyshlennogo proizvodstva* 1 (January-February 1978): 19-29; Mokeeva, pp. 97-108.

46. N. Fedorenko et al., *Pravda*, March 23, 1978.

47. P. G. Bunich, *Ekonomika i organizatsiya promyshlennogo proizvodstva* 5 (September-October 1976): 48-51.

48. G. Ya. Kiperman, *Ekonomika i organizatsiya promyshlennogo proizvodstva* 5 (September-October 1976): 51-63.

49. V. P. Ignatushkin and V. I. Parasochka, *Finansy SSSR* 4 (April 1978): 33-38.

50. Kiperman, K. P. Orinichev, *Ekonomika i organizatsiya promyshlennogo proizvodstva* 5 (September-October 1976): 67-70. N. Rogovskii and G. Ya. Kiperman, *Voprosy ekonomiki* 2 (February 1976). Gavrilov, *Voprosy ekonomiki* 3 (March 1976); N. Loiko, *Voprosy ekonomiki* 9 (September 1976).

51. *Planovoe khozyaistvo* 7 (July 1977): 117; M. Braginskii, *Materialno-tekhnicheskoe snabzhenie* 8 (August 1978): 31-32.

52. N. Sapozhnikov, *Pravda*, August 26, 1976.

53. B. Puginskii, *Pravda*, May 28, 1978.

54. V. Kamayev, *Ekonomicheskie nauki* 9 (September 1978): 54-55.

55. N. Sapozhnikov, *Pravda*, February 18, 1978.

56. N. Petrakov and V. Perlamutrov, *Pravda*, April 4, 1977.

57. Liberman and Khaikin, pp. 30-40.

58. V. Sitnin, *Ekonomicheskaya gazeta* 6 (1968).

59. A. Koshuta, *Ekonomicheskaya gazeta* 24 (1966): 16.

60. Yakovets, *Ekonomicheskaya gazeta*, February 9, 1977.

61. N. Orlov and I. Balabanov, *Ekonomicheskaya gazeta* 31 (1969).

62. V. Afanasyev, *Pravda*, May 18, 1971.

63. Yu. Borozdin, *Ekonomicheskaya gazeta* 26 (1970).

64. G. Triger, *Ekonomicheskaya gazeta* 36 (1970); A. Koshuta, *Ekonomicheskaya gazeta* 22 (1970).

65. A. Koshuta, *Izvestiya*, November 17, 1976.

66. N. Glushkov, *Sotsialisticheskaya industriya*, March 7, 1978.

67. V. Parfenov, *Pravda*, November 26, 1976.

68. Ibid.

69. Yarkin, pp. 48-59.

70. F. I. Mochalin, *Ekonomicheskaya gazeta* 18 (April 1977): 5-6.

71. E. Golland, *Ekonomika i organizatsiya promyshlennogo proizvodstva* 1 (January-February 1976): 75-87.

72. V. Smirnov, *Izvestiya*, April 29, 1970; *Kommunist* 5 (March 1976): 57-58.

73. G. A. Tsaritsina, *Finansy SSSR* 5 (May 1978): 25.

74. Ye. Sapiro, *Pravda*, June 22, 1978.

75. L. Shevchenko, *Planovoe khozyaistvo* 8 (August 1978): 104-07.

76. Yarkin.

77. J. A. Schumpeter, *The Theory of Economic Development* (Cambridge, Mass.: 1934), p. 68.

78. G. R. Feiwel, *Growth and Reforms in Centrally Planned Economies* (New York: 1977), pp. 237-40.

79. R. Aman et al., *The Technological Level of Soviet Industry* (New Haven; 1977); J. Berliner, *The Innovation Decision in Soviet Industry* (Cambridge; Mass.: 1976).

5

SOVIET CONSUMER POLICY IN THE 1970s: PLAN AND PERFORMANCE

Jane P. Shapiro

It turns out that documents show one thing, but reality another. . . . Why?

M. Lidina, in *Sovetskaya Torgovlya*, December 3, 1977

The past 15 years of the Brezhnev period have witnessed a continuing official effort to improve the standard of living for Soviet citizens, urban and rural dwellers alike. Attention and investment have been focused on expanded production and improved quality of consumer goods (including edibles) and services. This essay will review a number of consumer-related policies that the Brezhnev regime has adopted and implemented since the mid-1960s and examine its available policy options for the near term.

In reviewing the available data, it seems clear that the political leadership has had little choice but to begin attending systematically to the consumer goods sector. Wage increases coupled with deliberately restrained retail prices on basic goods have resulted in popular pressures which can be neither casually disregarded nor successfully stifled. Elite groups have become conscious of and knowledgeable about Western living standards, and increasingly they are insistent that more goods and services be made available to them, if not to the population at large;[1] the political leadership, with close ties to these

Opinions expressed or implied are solely those of the author and do not necessarily represent the views of the National Defense University, the Department of Defense, or any other government agency.

elites, cannot afford to ignore or dismiss their demands. Further, in seeking to satisfy at least partially the cumulative consumer demands that have intensified in the post-Stalin decades, without having to expend far more investment in the consumer and consumer-related sectors than current plan priorities permit or to increase imports substantially, the regime has had to resort to mechanisms which a decade ago it probably would have found unacceptable. These include encouragement of private household agricultural plot production and greater tolerance of the privately operated "grey market," which provides a considerable and growing volume of wanted goods and services.

By decreeing a host of financial penalties and administrative responsibilities, which apparently have been implemented only in incomplete fashion thus far, the leadership has sought to improve the quality, assortment, and attractiveness of consumer goods. A number of consumer survey and forecasting organizations have been created or revitalized during the past dozen years, including the All-Union Scientific Research Institute of Consumer Demand and Market Conditions, the Central Scientific Research Laboratory for Demand, and the Ministry of Trade's Council for the Study of Public Demand for Consumer Goods.[2] The regime has begun to utilize these surveys in an effort to determine current and likely future buying patterns and to relate production more realistically to consumer demand, thereby seeking to provide greater satisfaction to the citizen while simultaneously reducing the production of unwanted or shoddy quality goods which remain unsold regardless of price.

Modifying production plans by taking consumer demand into account is no simple task for policymakers, for it contradicts Soviet tradition in which consumer desires have rarely been considered. But the Soviet consumer, particularly in the nonrural areas (as almost 65 percent of the population is now categorized), has become more particular in his tastes and is no longer willing to buy whatever is offered for sale. As a Moscow department store director recently noted, "A person who has two suits won't take just any suit when he decides to buy a third. But light industry forgets this fact."[3] The consumer's basic requirements for food and clothing have been met largely, although the definition of these needs has expanded as the society modernizes and urbanizes, and he has begun to be motivated by psychological and sociological factors rather than almost exclusively by the biological dictates of earlier years.[4]

Because he has more disposable income now than in earlier decades but still limited possibilities for spending it, the Soviet consumer is inclined to buy better quality goods even if they are offered for sale at substantially higher prices than he might expect. For example, consumer demand for private automobiles, despite their inflated prices, increased costs of fuel, servicing, and spare parts (thanks to a March 1978, party-government decree), has not abated; rather, it is likely to grow as passenger car production levels off. Automobiles are considered "high demand" goods, as are motorcycles, carpets, and furs, and credit is unavailable for them; the purchase price must be paid in full before delivery. This requirement serves to siphon off some excess cash. So do savings bank deposits, and the consumer is currently inclined to save more of his income than the regime appears to favor. Both urban and rural savings have almost tripled since 1970 (and have quadrupled since 1965). Savings per capita have grown far more rapidly than income; urban workers as a whole are saving almost twice the amount they did a decade ago, while collective farmers' savings have remained relatively stable over the same period.[5] What is striking is that a significantly greater proportion of the population is saving some of its earnings now, in contrast to earlier decades. The average size of a rural dweller's savings (more than 1000 rubles) is greater than his urban counterpart's, suggesting that he has fewer possibilities for spending his disposable income.[6] In addition to reducing the volume of currency in circulation, increased savings provide the consumer with ready cash to buy goods and services through the grey or even black market, over which the regime seems able to exercise very little control.

It should be noted at the outset that official attention to the sadly neglected consumer sector has been an essential element of the post-Stalin domestic program for the past quarter century. But the Brezhnev reforms are not merely a continuation (with occasional resource shifts) of Khrushchev's policies, which were primarily of the public rather than personal variety: described as social wage benefits, they seemed designed to improve the citizen's standard of living but not to encourage him to collect personal material goods in abundance. The Brezhnev policies demonstrate greater pragmatism in confronting the consumer sector, greater willingness to disregard the ideological implications of consumerism, and recognition that the availability of desired goods acts as an important incentive for increased labor productivity (rewarded by higher wages). As Brezhnev himself emphasized to the November 1978 Central Committee plenum, "The entire course of economic development confirms again and again that group B [light] industries . . . constitute an important condition in the effective functioning of the economy as a whole, *in improving material incentives.*"[7] The regime clearly seeks to avoid the kind of mass popular unrest that manifested itself in the 1970 and 1976 Polish riots. The essential lesson of those events, which brought about the abrupt changeover in political leadership in 1970 and the hasty retraction of government price decrees in both 1970 and 1976, was that mass dissatisfaction can compel a regime to reverse policies even though such actions may be economically unsound as well as politically embarrassing. Once the precedent of successful public pressure in modifying official policy has been established, the political leadership must be ever mindful of public opinion and popular will and is likely to adopt policies more cautiously than it might wish.

Reportedly, the Brezhnev-Kosygin leadership was confronted with scattered strikes and demonstrations in 1970, just after the events in Poland, when workers in a number of cities protested the unavailability of meat and dairy products (reminiscent of the demonstrations Khrushchev encountered in 1962, when butter and meat prices were raised).[8] In response, the leaders determined that consumer-related sectors needed more financial support than had been granted them during most of the Khrushchev era and in rather rapid succession promulgated a number of decrees directly related to the expansion of personal consumer goods and services. These include consumer goods production planning on the basis of retail store orders,[9] the systematic and continual raising of real wages for all categories of workers, and the real rather than merely rhetorical emphasis on quality of goods, efficiency of enterprise operations, and expansion of edibles, consumer durables, and soft goods production and distribution. To date, there has been only limited attention paid to the inadequate retail sales network and to the necessity of expanding the maintenance and service sectors. Despite press attention, these sectors do not meet planned targets fundamentally, let alone satisfactorily.

During the past dozen years, the leadership has channeled considerable investment into the light industrial and agricultural sectors of the economy and placed particular emphasis on technological innovation and labor productivity by both managers and workers alike. Indeed, the cautious economic reforms of the middle and late 1960s, particularly as they related to production quality and efficiency, were introduced in the light industrial sector first. Among the incentives offered for innovation and efficiency were higher wages and bonuses and the unavoidable necessity of making available substantially more goods and services on which that income could be spent. At the same time, however, the regime has proved reluctant to expand the volume of available consumer goods through imports, with the exception of food. Indeed, food imports have held constant over the past decade, with some fluctuation for particularly poor harvest years. Food *exports*, on the other hand, have declined substantially since 1970, suggesting that the regime has determined that more food must be made available for domestic needs.[10] The nonedible consumer goods percentage of total imports has held constant over the past decade and forms an insignificant portion of total import volume. Clothing comprises 5-6 percent of total imports and is the only consumer item of some substance to figure in import data.[11]

Western analysts of Soviet five-year plans have noted frequently that the eighth (1966-70) and ninth (1971-75) plans allotted a greater proportion of state investment to the consumer goods sector of the economy than ever before in Soviet history. Indeed, the ninth plan was the first to call for more rapid growth in the light industrial and agricultural sectors than in the heavy industrial sector, although the latter ultimately did experience greater growth.[12] Overall state investment rose substantially in the early 1970s (from 354 billion rubles for the 1966-70 plan period to 501 billion for the subsequent plan); allocations for agriculture and light industry were proportionally larger and accounted for more than one-fourth of the 1971-75 plan's investment budget. Brezhnev and a number of other speakers at the party's Twenty-Fourth Congress, at which the ninth plan was formally presented, declared that the plan's principal task was to raise the people's living standard; this slogan became a permanent feature in most writings about the plan and its achievements. The current (tenth) plan reverts to the traditionally more rapid increase in the volume of heavy industrial production,[13] which is scheduled to grow 1 percent faster than light industry during 1978, about the same as it grew during the ninth plan.

Heavy and light industrial categorizations are frequently misleading, for a large number of heavy industrial plants have been charged with the production and marketing of consumer goods: it has been calculated that approximately 20 to 30 percent of the total consumer goods manufacturing is conducted by heavy industrial enterprises.[14] And, according to a November 1977 article in *Kommercheskii Vestnik*, nearly 75 percent of "everyday household goods" are produced by heavy industrial enterprises. The press continually laments the lack of interest that enterprise managers manifest for the production of consumer goods, which they consider strictly peripheral to their main responsibilities.

These consumer-oriented policies have scarcely begun to satisfy the steadily growing demands of the Soviet citizen. Indeed, among the economic choices the regime will need to make over the next several years is the rate at which the personal consumption sector will grow and with what consequences for other claimants on the state budget. As political leaders and economic planners face growing difficulties imposed by such factors as more costly energy supplies, more limited manpower resources in those parts of the country in which labor is and will be in even shorter supply, plant modernization needs, research and development costs, foreign trade deficits, and defense budget requirements, they are also faced with rising consumer expectations which cannot be dismissed. These expectations have been based in part upon the real increase in disposable income for most of the working force as well as for those who are eligible for retirement pensions but have been induced to remain in the labor market.

WAGE REFORMS

Briefly, the wage reforms of the past decade have been a continuation and augmentation of earlier reforms instituted during the Khrushchev period. Reforms were designed to rationalize wage scales within labor categories by reducing the number of categories within each rank and the differential between the highest and lowest categories, to reorder the relationship between basic wages and above-wage bonuses in each worker's pay package, to utilize wages more clearly as incentives for enhanced labor productivity and efficiency and as incentives for work under unpleasant conditions or in remote parts of the country where labor stabilization remains a policy priority.[15] Both the minimum and average monthly wages for most industrial, white-collar, and agricultural workers were increased in 1968 and have been raised almost continuously since that time.

The tenth plan calls for additional increases, particularly for workers in low-paying fields; collective farmers, whose (official) average monthly wage of 107 rubles (excluding income derived from household plot production) is among the lowest of all categories of workers, are scheduled to receive a 24–27 percent wage increase during the current plan period.[16] While the average monthly wage for nonfarm workers is 159 rubles, one recent Soviet source claims that the average collective farmer's monthly wage is no more than 98.5 rubles or (maximally) 124 rubles when supplemented by household plot income.[17] The average state farmer's monthly wage is 135 rubles, or 162 rubles when supplemented by plot proceeds, more nearly equal to industrial and white-collar workers' earnings. Although collective farm wages have risen more rapidly than industrial wages during the past decade (and were increased substantially during the Khrushchev years), a gap remains, as it does between collective and state farmers' income as well: the 35–40 ruble per month differential that existed in the mid-1960s has held quite constant. Moreover, official averages conceal the fact that collective farmers' income fluctuates considerably, more than either state farmers' or industrial workers', for it is based on the farm's productivity, which is highly dependent on such factors as mechanization, labor efficiency, long-term climatic and soil conditions, as well as uncontrollable year-to-year weather conditions. More than a decade ago, Brezhnev proposed (and the Central Committee decreed) that collective farmers be guaranteed wage payments relatively equal to those of state farmers, but because of its financial implications, this measure was to be implemented "gradually."[18]

The percentage of income derived from household plots has declined over the past decade as farm wages have increased.[19] Nationally, income from household plots now comprises approximately 25 percent of total collective farmer's income, compared with 36 percent a dozen years ago, although a 1976 Belorussian survey indicates that plots produce almost 40 percent of collective farmers' income in that republic.[20] Greater disposable income, through higher monetary wages (rather than payment in agricultural produce, as was the norm during the Stalin period and was gradually phased out during the 1950s and 1960s) in addition to plot sales, has encouraged the farm population to buy more consumer goods than ever before and has obliged the regime to begin to deal with the serious problem of consumer goods' maldistribution, including the wide gap in urban-rural availability of both goods and services.

Old age and disability pensions continue to be modest at best, and most pensioners would have difficulty making ends meet without supplemental income. Faced with increasing labor shortages in the predominantly Slavic-populated areas of the country which are predicted to grow more severe in the coming years, the regime has actively encouraged the rapidly growing number of pensioners to continue working beyond their legal retirement age. It is calculated that 70 percent of those eligible for retirement are physically able to continue working effectively.[21] As a practical incentive for older workers to remain in the labor force (although primarily due to budgetary limitations), pensions have been held to minimal levels and pensioners are entitled to receive 100 percent of their pension in addition to wages if the combination does not exceed 300 rubles per month. As an inducement to retain as many pension-aged but able-bodied, experienced workers on the payrolls, the 300-ruble limit will doubtless need to be modified upward. Official statistics indicate that more than 30 million people are old age pensioners, compared with 16 million just a dozen years ago; Western analysts believe that there are a considerable number of people eligible for pensions who do not collect them and thus are not included in these statistics. These people prefer to continue working if it can be arranged because the wages they receive at retirement age are higher than the pension-wage maximum.[22] Collective farmers became eligible for pensions only in 1965, and their current minimum monthly pension of 25 rubles remains almost half that of state and nonfarm pensioners. These data suggest that most pensioners are unlikely to have much impact on total consumer purchasing power, although the less dependent they are upon their families for financial support, the more likely younger family members are to spend more on goods and services for themselves.

ATTENDING TO DEMAND IN THE FOOD SECTOR

The regime's continuous efforts to expand agricultural production and heighten productivity through state investment and financial incentives to farmers are designed to satisfy both domestic consumption and foreign sales' requirements within the confines of the state and collective farm system. Included in a long series of Central Committee decrees, initiated with the one of March 1965 "On Urgent Measures for Further Development of the USSR's Agriculture," are higher state procurement and contract prices for planned and above-plan purchase of goods, respectively (the latest price increase was scheduled to go into effect on January 1, 1979);[23] greater availability of less expensive farm machinery, chemical fertilizers, and insecticides; greater investment in rural construction, including farm buildings and roads; a continued emphasis on farm personnel's acquisition and utilization agricultural technology; and substantial land amelioration projects. According to the U.S. Department of Agriculture, 1.7 million hectares of newly reclaimed (through drainage or irrigation) land went into production in 1977; Soviet data indicate that since 1970, 11 million additional hectares have been brought under cultivation.[24] Further, the regime has incrementally stressed the importance of household plot yields to overall agricultural output, despite their ideological disadvantages.

Toward this end, the Brezhnev leadership quickly moved to reverse Khrushchev's efforts to reduce and perhaps eventually eliminate the plots by stipulating some flexibility in the size of both plots and private livestock holdings. According to Soviet statistics, household plots account for approximately one-third of the milk, eggs, and vegetables, and more than half the potatoes marketed.[25] Despite these figures, private livestock holdings declined substantially during the 1970s. In 1977, farmers held 3.2 million *fewer* cows than they had in 1970, 6.4 million fewer pigs, and 3.1 million fewer sheep, although total livestock inventories (particularly cattle) increased substantially.[26] In view of its particular concern for increasing meat and poultry production and availability, the regime has been prompted to encourage expanded private livestock production for market sales. The 1977 constitution not only provides for the continued existence of household plots but holds both state and collective farms responsible for assisting citizens through the supply of fertilizers, farm implements, and livestock fodder as well as encouraging them to utilize their plots more efficiently. A press campaign during 1977 emphasized the need for each rural inhabitant to use part of his plot for fodder raising so that greater quantities would be available to him personally.[27] More recently, the Ministry of Agriculture suggested that additional fodder be made available for private livestock raising *if* the livestock were subsequently sold to the state.[28] Credit has been extended to encourage more farm families to purchase livestock (within permissible official limits) for later marketing. Collective farmers may utilize the collective's grazing lands and veterinarian services for their privately held livestock needs. As Georgian Communist Party leader Shevardnadze declared recently, "We must work out an efficient system of material and moral incentives that will give collective and state farmers a stake in enhanced output of household plot production." Indeed, he added, each farm's management must encourage maximum efficiency of household plot usage.[29]

Increased domestic agricultural production should result in less dependence on imports that soak up scarce hard currency reserves. It should also provide a more varied and qualitatively better diet than the Soviet population has enjoyed (or endured) for decades. It is in the food sector that the regime has sought most assiduously to satisfy popular demand,[30] although it has not been willing to invest or import extensively enough to begin to satisfy the demand for meat or, in lesser proportions, fresh vegetables and fruits. It has, however, been willing to import grain, including feed grains, soybeans, and potatoes, on a large scale when domestic harvests prove disastrous. In an effort to regularize annual grain sales to the Soviet Union, the U.S. government persuaded the Soviets in late 1975 to agree to buy a minimum of 6 million metric tons of grain (wheat and corn) each year. Recent Soviet purchases of feed corn have far exceeded the minimum.[31] The agreement remains in effect even during good Soviet harvest years, such as 1978, when the 235 million ton harvest exceeded both plans and predictions, particularly after the below plan 195.5 million tons of the previous autumn's harvest. Grain distribution costs have become an important item and, with the construction of major industrial projects in eastern Siberia, the regime has found it cheaper to import grain from the United States across the Pacific than to transport their own grain eastward from the Ukraine.[32] Meat remains in scarce supply, a consequence of decades of state inattention and lack of modern livestock-raising technology. More recently, the 1975 distress slaughtering (due to feed grain shortages), continuing restrictions on private holdings, and ever-scarce supply (despite foreign purchases) of feed grains and fodder have frustrated official claims that livestock production will be increased substantially each year. Meat production has been expanded since the Khrushchev years, but its growth during the 1970s has been slow and sporadic at least partially because of annual weather and harvest conditions.

Consumer demand for meat as well as other edibles has, if anything, been encouraged by the Academy of Medical Sciences' Institute of Nutrition publications, which have declared that "rational norms of consumption" in an industrialized socialist society include substantially more meat, fresh vegetables, and fruits, and considerably less starches and carbohydrates than Soviet citizens are able to buy, particularly through the retail trade and cooperative network (see Table 5.1). Even if we include collective market sales volume, which has declined in recent years but official policy seeks to stimulate, consumer demand remains far greater than supply.

The costs of efforts to satisfy consumer demand in the food sector are magnified when we consider the regime's determination to maintain stable retail prices on basic staples, apparently for political and ideological reasons. During the past decade, the regime has held prices constant on such items as bread, tea, milk, fish, meat, and margarine, while agricultural production costs have risen substantially, according to a prominent Soviet economist. One ton of grain costs 38 percent more in 1975 than it did in 1970, potatoes 25 percent more, and milk 23 percent more.[33] Not only has the state raised its procurement and contract prices for goods purchased from collective farms while holding retail prices constant, it also has increased its volume of purchases significantly in recent years. In 1977, for example, it purchased 6 million tons of potatoes more than in 1970, about 3 million additional tons (live weight) of livestock and poultry, almost 6 million additional tons of fresh vegetables and 3 million tons of fresh fruits, and 18 billion more eggs.[34] Despite

TABLE 5.1

Planned "Rational Consumption Norms" and Actual Consumption
(kilograms/person/year)

| | Plan | Actual | | |
	1980 (revised 1970)	1970	1975	1977
Meat	81.8	48.0	57.0	57.0
Milk, milk products	433.6	307.0	316.0	322.0
Bread, flour	120.4	149.0	141.0	140.0
Potatoes	96.7	130.0	120.0	122.0
Vegetables, melons	146.0	82.0	89.0	89.0
Fruits, berries	90.6	35.0	39.0	41.0
Fish	18.2	15.4	16.8	17.7

Sources: Philip Weitzman, "Soviet Long-Term Consumption Planning: Distribution According to Rational Need," Soviet Studies 26, no. 3 (July 1974); 305, 308; Tsentral'noe statisticheskoe upravlenie, SSSR v tsifrakh v 1977g. (Moscow: Statistika, 1978), p. 202. See also V. F. Mayer, Uroven' zhizni naseleniya SSSR (Moscow: Mysl, 1977), pp. 33, 102; and V. I. Raitser, Planning the Standard of Living According to Consumption Norms (White Plains, N.Y.: International Arts and Sciences Press, 1969), especially pp. 6–22.

increased state purchases, farms and farmers still retain some produce to be sold on the collective farm market at higher prices than those established by the state and cooperative network. Although additional state purchases could be interpreted as an attempt to limit collective farm market sales, it seems more likely an effort to render larger quantities of food available to the nonfarm population.

Each year the state absorbs a considerable financial burden by raising purchase prices but retaining fixed retail prices over long periods of time. One Western economist estimates that agricultural subsidies rose from 3 percent in 1965 to more than 16 percent by the mid-1970s. In addition to increasing procurement prices and the volume of purchases, the state has exempted state and collective farms from the 1967 price increases, which ranged from 5 to 20 percent, on agricultural machinery, fertilizer, processed feeds, and electric power. By the early 1970s, these subsidies may have amounted to 1.3 billion rubles annually.[35] Nikolai Glushkov, chairman of the USSR State Prices Committee, reported in February 1977, that agricultural subsidies for meat and dairy products (which account for more than 80 percent of staple subsidies) totaled almost 19 billion rubles in 1975. In the central region of the RSFSR, he revealed, one kilogram of beef sells for 2 rubles and costs the state 3.5 rubles, while one kilogram of butter is sold for 3.6 rubles and costs the state more than 5 rubles.[36] The regime has regularly avoided price increases by limiting the quantities available at the low fixed price and permitting only higher priced items to be offered for sale, usually in speciality shops where prices are routinely higher.[37] Shops regularly resort to intentionally miscategorizing items and charging customers for lower quality goods at prices established for those of higher quality.

In addition to these schemes, some items remain absent from shop shelves for months or even years. Scarce or nonexistent meat supplies in major urban centers as well as in many smaller towns are the norm, and there have been recent reports of meat rationing in some parts of the RSFSR. An American scholar who visited Moscow in early January 1979, reported a scarcity of milk and tea in retail food shops, in addition to meat.[38] Meat and poultry production have increased by almost 3 million tons since 1970, but the 16.5 million tons produced in 1977 is far below consumer demand. The leadership apparently refuses to recognize adequately that artificially low prices serve to stimulate additional demand and lengthen waiting lists and lines for wanted goods. The demand might not be as great (and remain as dissatisfied) if prices were higher and more accurately reflected production and marketing costs.

REGIME RESPONSE TO DEMAND FOR
DURABLES AND SOFT GOODS

If recent policy has failed to meet demand in the edibles sector, it has done even less well in the household appliance and clothing sectors. The early and mid-1970s saw a series of Central Committee decrees centering on consumer goods production, primarily emphasizing the need to improve quality and assortment as well as attend to the repair and servicing of household appliances. Goods are being produced in larger quantities (see Table 5.2) but are not necessarily the models that consumers are eager or even willing to buy. The problem of poor quality continues to plague production and sales, and state efforts to improve quality through financial incentives and penalties has had only limited success to date.

Since 1971, goods meeting established high standards are granted the State Seal of Quality. These goods are more costly for

TABLE 5.2

Selected Consumer Goods Guaranteed to the Population
(at year's end, per 1000 population)

Item	1965	1970	1975	1977
Watches, clocks	885	1193	1319	1408
TV sets	68	143	215	229
Refrigerators	29	89	178	210
Washing machines	59	141	189	200
Vacuum cleaners	18	31	52	64
Sewing machines	144	161	178	184

Source: Tsentralnoe Statisticheskoe Upravlenie, *Narodnoe khozyaistvo SSSR v 1975g.* (Moscow, Statistika, 1976), p. 595; Tsentralnoe Statisticheskoe Upravlenie, *SSSR v tsifrakh v 1977g.* (Moscow: Statistika, 1978), p. 204.

enterprises to produce because they are manufactured from more expensive materials, usually require more modern production equipment, have higher labor input, and the officially determined prices at which they are sold to retail trade outlets do not offset costs sufficiently. Only a small fraction of all goods produced meet the seal's standards. In 1976, for example, 4 percent of all fabrics, knitwear, footwear, and furniture merited the Seal of Quality designation.[39] Despite the higher prices at which better quality goods are offered for sale to the public, they reportedly do not gather dust on store shelves. There is virtually no incentive for enterprises to produce standard consumer goods with enhanced attention to quality and style because the prices at which they are sold to retail trade outlets remain fixed over long periods of time.[40] The traditional and oft-cited pitfalls of Soviet goods production continue. Regulations still measure plan fulfillment in terms of weight or volume and do not specify a mix of goods in size, color, or attractiveness that seeks to respond to known or presumed consumer demand.

The enterprise that produces consumer goods, rather than the retail stores to which these goods are supplied, must bear the costs of unsold goods. Discounting in order to move merchandise that does not appeal to the customer has been adopted only reluctantly and unsystematically. Selling goods at discounted prices frequently results in a loss of profits for the enterprise, although probably not as great a loss as would occur if the goods remained unsold altogether. Some particularly unwanted goods remain unsold anyway, regardless of price reductions. Soviet consumers are not accustomed to discounts and routinely assume that only defective, damaged, or unusually shoddy goods are marked down. Thus, they are reluctant to buy such goods, despite their attractive prices. Although official statistics claim that, for the country as a whole, 92 percent of reduced price goods are sold ultimately, this figure is probably inflated. According to one report, despite substantial (50–60 percent) price reductions, 94 million rubles worth of clothing and footwear remained unsold in 1974.[41] An illegal but frequently utilized scheme is the "combined offer." Consumers are told they must buy an unwanted or difficult to sell item in order to buy the item they covet.[42]

Enterprises are also liable for financial penalties if they fail to produce or deliver the goods retail stores order, based on known or anticipated consumer preferences. Fines are levied as a percentage of the ruble cost of goods, a disincentive for enterprises to produce more costly, better quality goods (in case they fail to meet delivery schedules). Considerable press discussion suggests, however, that these fines are rarely imposed and even more infrequently paid.

While consumers seek to augment their wardrobes beyond the established "rational norms," they have not yet formed the habit of replacing household appliances, especially if current models offered for sale do not differ favorably from the ones they already own. Despite the poor quality and frequent need for repair and maintenance, the typical replacement cycle for television sets is 10 years, washing machines, 15, and refrigerators, 20. Unless current models are substantially more appealing (such as color television sets rather than black and white or refrigerators with large-capacity rather than tiny freezers), the consumer has proven reluctant to buy. Indeed, the most readily available models of many household appliances have not changed for almost a decade. Thus, despite great demand for refrigerators with some freezer capacity or semiautomatic rather than manually operated washing machines, and despite retail store orders for these specific items placed with the supplying enterprises, the latter continue to produce models for which there is little or no demand.[43] To make matters even worse for the consumer, in recent years as many as 25 to 40 percent of basic household appliances have been found to be defective before they are offered for sale, according to the State Quality Inspectorate, which apparently spot checks these goods.

SALES AND SERVICE SECTORS

In addition to offering very limited supplies of high demand items, the retail trade sector suffers from the consistently lackluster quality of its sales personnel. Because it has traditionally been one of the lowest paying occupations among white-collar workers, the sector does not attract capable, energetic people who have an incentive to work either hard or efficiently. As one Soviet writer noted, the retail trade worker's wage unfortunately is not linked to quality of work.[44] In fact, there appears to be limited quality control. Sales personnel receive very little or no relevant advance training and are not paid on the basis of volume of goods sold, although there have been suggestions that piece rate wages should be adopted "to enhance the initiative of sales personnel and improve customer service."[45] Their main incentive for staying on the job may well be the bribes they receive for saving wanted goods for preferred customers or outright theft of merchandise which they subsequently sell privately.[46] Yet, if these bribes were sufficiently frequent and substantial, the sales sector might be considered more attractive than it is. There are chronic shortages of sales personnel, turnover is high, and the salesperson's lack of familiarity with the merchandise and indifference to the customer are notorious. The July 1977 Central Committee/Council of Ministers Resolution on the improvement of retail trade outlined many of the current difficulties and stressed these very points.[47]

Customers cannot avoid wasting inordinate amounts of time on each shopping expedition. Most consumer goods continue to be sold in specialty shops rather than general department stores; the latter typically carry goods of lesser quality (the internationally known GUM on Red Square is an exception), so that customers prefer the specialty stores despite accompanying inefficiencies. Specialty stores are usually better stocked because they are more easily supplied from the enterprise or the wholesale distribution point. Frequency and reliability of deliveries to retail stores remain a major problem, as does the delivery in bulk and lack of packaging facilities. Studies of time spent in shopping indicate that the average citizen is compelled to waste a great deal of time in traveling from shop to shop, waiting on various lines, and frequently discovering that the item he sought was no longer available when he finally reached the sales counter.[48] Despite press coverage, relevant data indicate that little progress has been made during the Brezhnev years to reduce consumer dissatisfaction with the sales sector; consumers now expend more time in shopping than they did a decade ago, frequently during working hours because everyone knows that popular goods available in the morning, if they are worth buying, will surely be sold out before late afternoon. Many stores close in the early evening; so customers do not have time to shop if they wait until the official close of their working day.

TABLE 5.3

Average Money Wage of Workers in Various Branches of the Economy (rubles)

Sector	1965	1970	1976
Overall	96.5	122.0	151.4
Industrial workers	101.7	130.6	168.2
Engineering, technicians	148.4	178.0	205.8
White-collar	85.8	111.6	139.2
Water transportation	135.1	169.5	220.0
Construction	119.9	149.9	181.0
Retail trade	75.2	95.1	112.3
Services	72.0	94.5	112.7
Health, social security	79.0	92.0	104.0
Culture	67.3	84.8	93.2
Science	120.6	139.5	161.6
Credit, insurance	86.3	114.4	134.2
State, economic administration	105.9	122.2	132.4

Source: Vestnik Statistiki 11 (1977): 90. (Emphasis added.)

Very similar difficulties abound in the service and maintenance of consumer durables, and demand remains largely unsatisfied, particularly for housing and household appliance repairs. The volume of services available through legally established and licensed shops is remarkably small, considering the increase in volume of goods sold, their generally poor quality, and consequent need for frequent repair. Workers are not attracted to the service sector either, where wages have remained consistently low (see Table 5.3), far below the national average, and quality work is not rewarded. Difficulties of servicing and repair result from a variety of causes apart from those associated with poor quality merchandise, including inadequate production and distribution of spare parts, lack of part standardization and interchangeability, too few trained repair personnel, and overburdened repair shops charged with handling a far greater volume of services than a decade ago. Moreover, many service establishments handle institutional rather than private orders. According to one Soviet report, only 25 percent of the work performed by laundries, dry cleaners, and furniture repair shops is based on private orders. Shops have no financial incentive to handle small private orders currently, but a policy permitting them to charge higher rates for individual orders might alleviate the situation. Official data indicate that while the number of service and repair facilities has increased modestly, the volume of services has frequently increased by seven to ten times that of a decade ago.[49]

Due to the difficulties encountered in securing service or repair of clothing, furniture, appliances, and housing (as well as automobiles, to which we shall turn presently), a private entrepreneurial sector has flourished in recent years. Always a feature of rural life (where Soviet economists now estimate that private services almost equal those provided by the state), it has spread rapidly in urban areas and has been granted a measure of legality through Article 17 of the 1977 Constitution, which provides that "individual labor activity in the sphere of handicrafts, agriculture *and consumer services* ... is permitted," although the state maintains the right to ensure that such activity "is used in the interests of society" (emphasis added). Some years ago, Brezhnev suggested that persons not regularly employed should be encouraged to work "cooperatively" in the service sector. He did not elaborate on the means by which these cooperatives would be supplied with needed materials or regulated by the state.[50]

The means by which individual consumer services currently are performed necessarily include theft or black market purchase of spare parts and materials unavailable on the retail market, private work done during regularly scheduled working hours, and acceptance of bribes to perform work quickly. These activities are illegal but largely tolerated (though subjected to sporadic abuse or harassment). According to Western estimates, such services have assumed some measure of importance in the consumer sector and must be taken into account when calculating the size of personal and, therefore, disposable income.[51] This "gray market" or "second economy" is likely to expand considerably with all its nonsocialist and dishonest characteristics, unless the regime is willing to divert substantial funding to the consumer services sector, which it has not yet shown any intent to do.

Perhaps nowhere does the "second economy" flourish as successfully as in the automobile sector, where private entrepreneurs not only procure needed parts for repair and maintenance, including windshield wipers, tires, and similar items that are difficult to replace, regularly steal gasoline and motor oil for private sale, but even steal autos for profitable disposal. Indeed, the private automobile sector has proved particularly troublesome for the regime, both practically and ideologically; the unexpectedly rapid expansion of that industry during the past decade has put an official stamp of approval on private rather than public means of transportation. A recent *Voprosy Ekonomiki* article acknowledged somewhat heretically that private automobiles "meet people's transportation needs more fully" and increase their free time, which can be spent more usefully than in traveling by public transportation.[52]

THE PRIVATE AUTOMOBILE SECTOR

In 1977, the Soviet Union produced 1.28 million passenger cars, more than six times as many as a decade earlier, and almost ten times as many as in the early 1960s.[53] Production skyrocketed in the first half of the 1970s, when the Togliatti plant, financed by Western credits, began to mass produce the Fiat-designed Zhiguli models. Concurrently, the older automobile plants at Moscow and Izhevsk were modernized, and production of the Moskvich and the more expensive Volga have been expanded.[54] In the past several years, however, automobile production has begun to level off. In 1976, only 38,000 more passenger autos were produced than during the previous year; in 1977, only 41,000 more than in 1976, and total annual production of 2.3 million for 1980 is planned. This contrasts rather sharply with a 201,000 increase between 1971 and 1972, and a 203,000 increase between 1973 and 1974.[55] Moreover, the Soviets are increasing their efforts to market more automobiles abroad, especially the Zhiguli, with its Fiat-interchangeable parts. Indeed, they recently concluded a $100-million agreement with Canada and will sell the Zhiguli (renamed Lada) for one-third its domestic price tag, at a price substantially lower than almost all similarly sized automobiles currently available in Canada.[56] The Soviets have promoted sales of the Zhiguli in Western Europe for several years, with only limited success. They also market autos to eastern Europe and have concluded agreements with several eastern European states to manufacture parts for Soviet production lines.

Reportedly, 60 percent of passenger car production is earmarked for private domestic sale, which scarcely begins to approach the ever-growing consumer demand. During the Khrushchev era, autos were to be used communally rather than privately, and most of the limited number produced were consigned for official use or taxi service. Khrushchev eschewed auto ownership as bourgeois and unsocialist, and there is no evidence that his policies were likely to change. His position was warmly supported by ideologists, who have publicly and repeatedly expressed concern about the bourgeois nature of a consumer-dominated society and the increasingly materialistic desires and attitudes of young people. As one ideologist declared, "Consumption needs must be taught, they don't simply appear spontaneously . . . if we are talking about socially valuable needs.[57] The acquisition of material possessions beyond one's "rational needs" should find no place in a socialist society, and a person's merit cannot be measured by the goods he owns. Private auto ownership, they warn, can lead to antisocialist tendencies, which must not be fostered.

In spite of the ideological difficulties, which have not been satisfactorily resolved, there is no simple explanation for the Brezhnev regime's decision to divert substantial budgetary support to auto production as well as some (but far too little) funding for the necessary accompanying infrastructure, including expansion of paved or graded highways, construction of fuel stations, service, and maintenance shops, and the training of personnel to operate them. Soviet analysts estimate that owners lose at least one full week's use of their autos due to unavoidable servicing and repair. Among the primary factors prompting expanded production appears to be the strong belief that the automobile is the sine qua non of a modern industrialized society; a country that does not mass produce autos for domestic consumption cannot properly consider itself modernized. Opinion poll data demonstrate that the Soviet citizen, particularly the urban dweller, shares this perception and wants to become an auto owner, even if it takes him years to accumulate the capital to do so. Private auto ownership may be of dubious ideological acceptability, but it is undoubtedly popular.

If we consider the obvious beneficiaries of expanded production and domestic marketing, it is obvious that autos currently and for the foreseeable future are beyond the financial reach or expectations of the average wage earner. At an initial cost of 7,000 rubles for the least expensive Zhigulis offered for sale (5,500-ruble models are theoretically available but seem to exist only on price lists) and considerably more for the more expensive Togliatti plant models as well as the Volga (disregarding the mandatory bribe for delivery, gasoline, servicing, and other necessary costs), the most likely purchasers are members of the more affluent sectors of society, including the ruling elite themselves. The decline in growth of auto production, if current trends continue, will serve as another source of dissatisfaction for large numbers of the population, and the regime will need to manage consumer expectations in this sector perhaps more carefully than in others, because production policy of the early 1970s generated an unusually large demand which might have been curtailed with more careful planning.

CONSUMER POLICY: LIKELY TRENDS

The thrust of this chapter suggests that the Brezhnev leadership has not only continued a number of consumer-oriented policies initiated during the Khrushchev years but has promulgated a number of innovative policies as well, of which mass production of passenger cars is among the most visible. The Brezhnev regime apparently found that attention to personal consumer needs was virtually unavoidable for a number of reasons. First, the basic satisfaction of shared social needs, such as health care, education, child care facilities, public transportation, recreational and cultural facilities, had been achieved for most urban areas by the mid-1960s. To be sure, housing remains seriously inadequate for most parts of the country, particularly in the urban areas, and housing utilities (central heating and indoor plumbing) remain unavailable for most of the rural population.[58] Second, industrial and agricultural productivity and efficiency had to be improved substantially, given limited resources and declining manpower. The belief persisted that higher wages would serve as a basic incentive for enhanced labor productivity. Third, necessarily following from this last was the need to provide consumer goods and services so that the incentive element of greater spending power could be realized. Fourth, citizens' awareness of their relative deprivation in the consumer sector had been exacerbated by their more frequent contact with foreigners in the Soviet Union as well as abroad. Finally, the refusal of a growing number of consumers, especially in urban areas where goods are more available, to purchase any item of clothing, furniture, or household appliance regardless of its poor quality, improper size, or color, meant that economic planners had to devise means to respond effectively to consumer demand.[59]

Two and a half decades after the close of the Stalin era, the standard of living in most sections of the country has reached a level where the average citizen is now able to insist upon both greater variety and better quality of goods. Further, the political leadership has been motivated by factors relevant to its international reputation: as a socialist developmental model and alternative to Western-style capitalism, it must in some measure substantiate its oft-stated deep concern for every citizen's well-being. Currently the Soviet Union maintains a reputation as a country which has rapidly modernized and expanded its military sector but largely ignored that portion of its domestic sector most directly related to the standard of living of its people. Consumer expectations are rising, and the political leadership increasingly will need to take them into account in order to avoid or have to quell demonstrations of mass dissatisfaction.

Indeed, faced with popular expectations rising more rapidly than the regime is willing to respond to them, the Brezhnev leadership and its successors have limited policy options. A leveling off in the consumer sector, let alone a per capita reduction in the availability of goods and services, is scarcely viable. Rather, the leadership will need to turn its attention to enhanced quality, assortment, distribution, storage, and packaging of consumer goods. If it intends to limit grey market operations, it will need to direct substantial financial resources to the service and maintenance sectors and devise more adequate methods for ensuring the production of higher quality merchandise requiring ease of maintenance and few repairs. Despite ideological difficulties, the leadership may find it economically most rational to permit or even stimulate a private repair and maintenance sector which could be regularized through expanded production of needed items (tools, spare parts) as well as personnel training and encouragement to work full-time in this occupation rather than moonlight primarily on time taken from a public sector job. By failing to deal harshly and systematically with the grey market, the political leadership has tacitly acknowledged the necessity of harnessing individual private activity; what it has not done (but could do at minimal cost) is reduce or largely eliminate the criminal aspects of that market. In an analogous development, recent official policies regarding privately cultivated household plots seem designed to regularize those efforts with the expectation of additional marketing of meat, fresh vegetables, and fruits, goods which state and collective farms are unable to supply to the population adequately.

Another closely related sector on which the leadership will need to focus considerable attention is that of retail sales. Upgrading of sales positions is urgently needed. More stringent training requirements for prospective personnel, higher wages coupled with a system of direct financial rewards, and incentives (including upward mobility) for well-performed services will render this occupation more attractive and grant it a measure of prestige. Sales positions with attractive salaries are likely to retain workers for a longer period than is currently typical. Labor conditions for sales personnel are in need of substantial improvement, which the regime has recognized, including safer and more hygienic surroundings in the work place, as well as provisions for pleasant housing with convenient transportation and shopping facilities.[60]

As the Soviet Union enters the 1980s, there is little doubt that it will continue to experience a decline in its rate of economic growth at the same time that economic planners perceive the necessity of modernizing large portions of its industrial plant as well as attend to technological advances in the agricultural sector. The Soviet leadership may be tempted to lapse into the traditional pattern of cutting back in the consumer sector, assuming (or hoping) that the Soviet citizen will be willing to tighten his belt as he has done in the past and that disguised inflation, through higher prices of those goods available for purchase, will serve to sop up excess disposable income. It is less likely now than at almost any time in Soviet history that the population will comply without mass public dissatisfaction. Although Soviet leaders are unlikely to adopt the prevalent Eastern European pattern of implementing policies that provide for greater quantities of consumer goods and services in an effort to acquire and retain a measure of popular support, they will need to attend more adequately to consumer demand in a more coherent and less piecemeal fashion than they have thus far. Rising popular expectations provide them with no viable alternative.

NOTES

1. Mervyn Matthews has described Soviet elites, their influence and expectations, in a number of writings, most recently and thoroughly in his *Privilege in the Soviet Union* (London: Allen & Unwin, 1978), especially chs. 1, 2, 4. He corrently stresses elites' *access* to goods and services, rather than merely their ability to afford them, as a crucial element of privilege.

2. See the discussion of consumer forecasting in *Pravda*, January 10, 1977; and A. Khodzhaev, "Problemy udovletvoreniya potrebitelskogo sprosa," Voprosy ekonomiki, no. 12 (December 1977).

3. *Literaturnaya gazeta*, August 23, 1978.

4. For a general discussion of consumer conduct, see, for example, James U. McNeal, *An Introduction to Consumer Behavior* (New York: Wiley, 1973), especially chs. 2, 3, 15.

5. Tsentralnoe Statisticheskoe Upravlenie, *Narodnoe khozyaistvo SSSR v 1977g.* (Moscow: Statistika, 1978), pp. 409-10. Hereafter referred to as *Nar. khoz. 1977.*

6. Tsentralnoe Statisticheskoe Upravlenie, *SSSR v tsifrakh v 1977g.* (Moscow: Statistika, 1978), p. 205. Hereafter, *SSSR v tsifrakh 1977.* See the commentary in *Literaturnaya gazeta*, December 14, 1977, on just this issue.

7. *Pravda*, November 28, 1978. Added emphasis.

8. According to Roy A. Medvedev, *On Socialist Democracy* (New York: Knopf, 1975), p. 404, there were "various spontaneous demonstrations . . . [in Ivanovo, Sverdlovsk, Gorky, and several other cities]." For a discussion of the 1962 Novocherkassk events, see Alexander I. Solzhenitsyn, *The Gulag Archipelago*, vols. 5-7 (New York: Harper & Row, 1978), pp. 507-14. The regime managed to placate the demonstrators by ensuring that local shops were supplied with butter, sausages, and a number of other items that had been missing from the shelves for a long period. It also reversed the earlier unpopular decision to reduce piece rate wages at the city's Electric Locomotive Works.

9. See the discussion in Abraham Katz, *The Politics of Economic Reform in the Soviet Union* (New York: Praeger, 1973), especially pp. 160-72.

10. *Nar. khoz. 1977*, p. 576.

11. Annual foreign trade statistics are found in Ministerstvo Vneshnei Torgovli SSSR, *Vneshniyaya torgovlya Soyuza SSR* (Moscow: Statistika, annually).

12. Gregory Grossman, "An Economy at Middle Age," *Problems of Communism*, 25, no. 2 (March–April 1976); 23.

13. See Kosygin's report to the Twenty-Fifth CPSU Congress, *Pravda*, March 1, 1976; and Baibakov's annual report to the Supreme Soviet, *Pravda*, December 15, 1977. See also Gregory Grossman, "The Soviet Economy Before and After the Twenty-Fifth Congress," in *The Twenty-Fifth Congress of the CPSU*, ed. Alexander Dallin, (Stanford: Hoover Institution Press, 1977), especially pp. 70–74.

14. See the relevant discussion in R.S. Mathieson, *The Soviet Union: An Economic Geography* (New York: Barnes and Noble, 1975), p. 167.

15. A general discussion of wage policies is found in Leonard Joel Kirsch, *Soviet Wages: Changes in Structure and Administration since 1956* (Cambridge, Mass.: M.I.T. Press, 1972). For a critique of the success in compensatory wages in less pleasant parts of the country, see Gertrude E. Schroeder, "Soviet Wage and Income Policies in Regional Perspective," *The Association for Comparative Economic Studies Bulletin*, 26, no. 2 (Fall 1974). Another useful source is V.F. Mayer, *Uroven zhizni naseleniya SSSR* (Moscow: Mysl, 1977), who notes that while industrial workers' productivity has increased more rapidly than wages, the reverse is true for collective farmers.

16. *Pravda*, December 15, 1977.

17. R. Tonkonog, "Sotsialnye aspekty industrializatsii selskogo khozyaistva," *Ekonomika selskogo khozyaistva*, no. 2 (February 1978), pp. 45ff. The author does not detail calculations of household plot income. It is unclear whether this figure represents the value of goods if sold on the collective farm market or because such goods typically are home-consumed, the figure represents a portion of income that might otherwise be spent for food.

18. Karl-Eugen Wädekin, "Income Distribution in Soviet Agriculture," *Soviet Studies*, 27, no. 1 (January 1975); 8; Mayer, *Urover zhizni*, p. 213; Bundesinstitut fur ostwissenschaftliche und internationale Studien, Köln, ed. *The Soviet Union 1975-76* (New York: Holmes and Meier, 1977), p. 31. A good review of rural earnings' growth is found in David W. Bronson and Constance B. Krueger, "The Revolution in Soviet Farm Household Income, 1953-1967," in *The Soviet Rural Community*, ed. James R. Millar, (Urbana; University of Illinois Press, 1971).

19. *Nar. khoz. 1977*, pp. 409–10.

20. V. Tarasevich and V. Leshkevich, "Znachenie lichnogo podsobnogo khozyaistva," *Ekonomika selskogo khozyaistva*, no. 2 (February 1978).

21. Bernice Madison, *Soviet Income Maintenance Programs in the Struggle against Poverty*, Kennan Institute Occasional Paper, no. 31 (Washington, D.C.: Wilson Center, 1978), especially pp. 30–37.

22. Ibid., p. 32. See also her "Soviet Income Maintenance Policy for the 1970's," *Journal of Social Policy* 2, no. 2 (April 1973); Robert J. Osborn, *Soviet Social Policies* (Homewood, Ill.: Dorsey Press, 1970), pp. 76–77; Keith Bush, "Soviet Living Standards: Some Salient Data," and M. E. Reban, "The Soviet Pensioner: An Element of the Labour Supply," both in NATO, Directorate of Economic Affairs, *Economic Aspects of Life in the USSR. Coloquium* (Brussels; NATO, 1975).

23. *Pravda*, July 4, 1978.

24. SSSR v tsifrakh 1977, p. 120. For a broad review of agricultural policies adopted during the 1960s and early 1970s, see Stephen Osofsky, *Soviet Agricultural Policy: Toward the Abolition of Collective Farms* (New York: Praeger, 1974); Werner G. Hahn, *The Politics of Soviet Agriculture 1960-1970* (Baltimore: Johns Hopkins University Press, 1972); and *Selskaya zhizn*, May 25, 1975.

25. Unsigned, "Uluchshenie torgovli—neotemlemoe uslovie podema blagosotoia-niya naroda," *Planovoe khozyaistvo*, no. 7 (July 1978).

26. Tsentralnoe Statisticheskoe Upravlenie, *Narodnoe khozyaistvo SSSR za 60 Let* (Moscow: Statistika, 1977), pp. 332-33. According to *Pravda*, January 28, 1978, 1977 registered an increase in private holdings for cattle and hogs (particularly the latter), although 1970 levels have not as yet been achieved.

27. *Pravda*, February 16, 1977.

28. A. Denisov, "Lichnoe podsobnoe khozyaistvo," *Ekonomika selskogo khozyaistva*, no. 4 (1978).

29. *Zarya vostoka*, February 4, 1977.

30. *Nar. khoz. 1977*, p. 191.

31. New York *Times*, May 22, 1978. See also D. Gale Johnson, "Soviet Agriculture and U.S.-Soviet Relations," *Current History*, 73, no. 430 (October 1977); and the weekly journal, *Foreign Agriculture*, published by the U.S. Department of Agriculture.

32. *Literaturnaya gazeta*, February 23, 1977.

33. Mayer, *Urover zhizni*, p. 214. See also Constance B. Krueger, "A Note on the Size of Subsidies on Soviet Government Purchases of Agricultural Products," *The Association for Comparative Economic Studies Bulletin*, 26, no. 2 (Fall 1974); 64.

34. *SSSR v tsifrakh 1977*, pp. 128-29.

35. U.S., Department of Commerce, Bureau of the Census, *Agricultural Subsidies in the Soviet Union*, Foreign Economic Report no. 15 (December 1978), pp. 10-11.

36. *Pravda*, February 9, 1977.

37. Hedrick Smith, *The Russians* (New York: Ballantine, 1976), pp. 92-93. See also Strobe Talbott, trans. and ed., *Khrushchev Remembers: The Last Testament* (New York: Bantam, 1976), pp. 162-64.

38. Interview with Professor Thomas W. Robinson, January 23, 1979. It is possible that the unusually cold weather (-40° F.) had an effect on goods' distribution at that particular time.

39. N. Velikova and G. Gorina, "Tsena i kachestvo tovarov narodnogo potrebleniya," *Planovoe khozyaistvo*, no. 10 (October 1977): 129-32.

40. V. V. Zotov, "Tsena v stimulirovanii proizvodstva tovarov narodnogo potrebleniya," *Finansy SSSR*, no. 6 (June 1974).

41. Ye. N. Fonarev, "O sovershenstvovanii poryadka formirovaniya i raskhodovaniya finansovykh resursov na otsenku tovarov," *Finansy SSSR*, no. 7 (July 1976): 42.

42. *Literaturnaya gazeta* 24 (June 14, 1978).

43. Ya. Orlov, "Osnovnye napravleniya vozdeistviya torgovli na promyshlennost," *Voprosy ekonomiki*, no. 7 (1978).

44. M. Makarova, "*R.A. Lokshin, spros, proizvodstvo, torgovlya,*" (book review), *Voprosy ekonomiki*, no. 10 (October 1976): 148.

45. *Pravda*, September 26, 1977.

46. Smith, *Russians*, chapter 3.

47. *Pravda*, July 19, 1977.

48. See, for example, the discussion in *Trud*, May 15, 1975; and the frequent articles in *Literaturnaya gazeta*. An authoritative, painstaking, although dated, Western source is Gur Ofer, *The Service Sector in Soviet Economic Growth: A Comparative Study* (Cambridge: Harvard University Press, 1973).

49. *Nar. khoz. 1977*, p. 482; V.M. Rutgaizer, *Resursy razvitiya neproizvodstvennoi sfery* (Moscow: Mysl, 1975), p. 202; and *Pravda*, November 15, 1977.

50. *Pravda*, June 12, 1971. See the discussion in Medvedev, *On Socialist Democracy*, pp. 270-73.

51. See, among others, Smith, *Russians*, ch. 3; Dimitri K. Simes, "The Soviet Parallel Market," NATO, *Economic Aspects*; Gregory Grossman, "The 'Second Economy'

of the USSR," *Problems of Communism*, 26, no. 5 (September–October 1977); Valery Chalidze, *Criminal Russia: Crime in the Soviet Union* (New York: Random House, 1977), especially pp. 156–201; A. Katsenelinboigen, "Coloured Markets in the Soviet Union," *Soviet Studies*, 29, no. 1 (January 1977).

52. A. Arrak, "Ispolzovanie avtomobilei lichnogo polzovaniya," *Voprosy ekonomiki*, no. 7 (July 1978): 135.

53. *Nar. khoz. 1977*, p. 167.

54. Western analysts have found Soviet automobile production of particular interest and have written extensively about it. See, for instance, Imogene U. Edwards, "Automotive Trends in the USSR," in U.S., Congress, Joint Economic Committee, *Soviet Economic Prospects for the Seventies* (Washington, D.C.: Government Printing Office, June 1973); William R. Baxter, "The Soviet Passenger Car Industry," *Survey* 19, no. 3 (Summer 1973); John M. Kramer, "Soviet Policy towards the Automobile," *Survey* 22, no. 2 (Spring 1976):

55. *Nar. khoz. 1974*, p. 249; *Nar. khoz. 1977*, p. 167.

56. New York *Times*, November 13, 1978.

57. V. Zeyle, "Razvitie potrebleniya i formirovanie vsestoronne razvitoi lichnosti," *Kommunist Sovetskoi Latvii* 11 (November 1974): 21.

58. Useful Western studies on the achievements of these sectors include Alfred J. DiMaio, Jr., *Soviet Urban Housing: Problems and Policies* (New York: Praeger, 1974); Everett M. Jacobs, "Urban Housing in the Soviet Union, in NATO, *Economic Aspects*; Willard S. Smith, "Housing the Soviet Union—Big Plans, Little Action," in Joint Economic Committee, *Soviet Economic Prospects*; William Taubman, *Governing Soviet Cities* (New York: Praeger, 1973); Osborn, *Soviet Social Policies*; J. Patrick Lewis, "Communications Output in the USSR," *Soviet Studies* 18, no. 3 (July 1976); and Susan Jacoby, *Inside Soviet Schools* (New York: Hill and Wang, 1974). A number of essays in Henry W. Morton and Rudolf L. Tokes, eds., *Soviet Politics and Society in the 1970's* (New York: Free Press, 1974), are also relevant.

59. For a more detailed discussion of these factors, see my "The Soviet Consumer in the Brezhnev Era," *Current History* 75, no. 440 (October 1978).

60. *Pravda*, February 3, 1977.

6

ENVIRONMENTAL POLICY UNDER BREZHNEV: DO THE SOVIETS REALLY MEAN BUSINESS?

Thane Gustafson

Can the Soviet state, heretofore adapted almost exclusively to heavy industrialization, protect public health, natural resources, and the environment from the effects of the industry it has created? A hammer and sickle flying on a field of ecology green is not the Soviet flag that comes most readily to mind. Until quite recently, the Soviet Union had no environmental program worthy of the name (at any rate outside Moscow and a handful of preserves), and those who wished to raise environmental issues had no regular access to the official agenda.

But now things have changed rather suddenly. In the last six years, the Soviet Union has launched a heavily funded environmental program aimed chiefly at preserving clean water. In 1973, annual investment for water quality abruptly jumped fivefold, from 300 to 1,500 million rubles.[1] In the spring of 1976, General Secretary Brezhnev announced a five-year, 11-billion-ruble program of capital expenditure for environmental protection, most of it devoted to water.[2] For the next five-year plan (1981–85), a further increase of more than 50 percent is being discussed.[3] It may be too soon to speak of the "ecology gap," but the Soviet Union may soon exceed, in money terms at least, the level of effort of the United States.

However, funding is by no means the whole story. In 1970 a national water code came into effect, followed over the next three years by detailed water legislation for each of the 15 union republics.[4] Special decrees single out high-priority areas: the Volga-Ural, the Severskii Donets, and the Caspian, Azov, and Baltic seas.[5] In 1972, enforcement responsibility for water quality was assigned to the USSR Ministry of Reclamation and Water Management (*Ministerstvo melioratsii i vodnogo khozyaistva*—often known as Minvodhkoz), one of the fastest growing agencies in the country.[6] This gave the water quality program a strong institutional defender. In 1974, environmental protection was incorporated into the national economic plan, and the State Planning Committee (Gosplan) now has a special division for the environment, with subdivisions for air and water quality.[7] Finally, at the beginning of 1978, the State Hydrometeorological Service was upgraded to the rank of a state committee, with the new name of State Committee for Hydrometeorology and Oversight of the Environment. (*Gosudarstvennyi Komitet po Gidrometeorologii i Kontrolyu Prirodnoi Sredy*). Its chairman, Yu. A. Izrael' is a member of the USSR Council of Ministers. In short, the environment, which 15 years ago had practically no standing at all, has been incorporated into every part of the government structure.[8]

But how much meaningful reform can there be—and how much do the leaders intend—when the bulk of the economy and the political system remains as pitched as ever toward rapid expansion? If the leaders really do mean business, can they implement a successful environmental program using existing institutions and mechanisms? The plan of this chapter is to try to infer what the leaders intend by observing how the new program is being designed and implemented and thus to gauge whether the new environmental policies are a Potemkin program or a genuine attempt at reform with a real chance for success.

OVERVIEW OF THE PROGRAM

The immediate cause of the new program was an impending crisis in public health. Catches of freshwater fish plummeted in southern basins, including those of important earners of foreign exchange, such as sturgeon. Massive kills occurred regularly in the spring months. Cholera, caused by untreated sewage, broke out in southern basins. These events coincided with rapidly rising demand for clean water in the southern Soviet Union caused by the spread of irrigated agriculture under Brezhnev. But until the early 1970s few countermeasures had been taken.

In 1972-73, on the eve of the present expansion of the water-quality program, only one-quarter of the industrial wastes and process water discharged into the Volga were given even the most cursory treatment, and the volume of effluent was increasing by 4 percent a year.[9] Elsewhere the picture was no better: throughout the country only 16 percent of all municipal wastes were being treated in

1970,[10] and the volume of effluent increased by 19 percent from 1970 to 1974.[11] Unless the leaders did something quickly about the humble problem of dirty water, it was clear that they would soon face major threats to the health and future development of the entire southern half of the country.

The design of the program shows clearly what the leaders are most concerned about. Moscow receives the greatest attention.[12] Outside the capital, most of the pollution control effort is directed at the 11 river basins of the country's southern zone, where over 80 percent of the country's agricultural and industrial production is concentrated.[13] In this group, top priority goes to the Volga and Ural basins. The Volga basin alone, which supports 25 percent of the country's population, industry, and agriculture, accounts for about one-third of the waste treatment capacity added during the ninth five-year plan.[14] Other areas and republics get less attention: Kazakhstan received only 56 million rubles for water quality construction in 1974;[15] Georgia was allocated 29 million for 1976;[16] Tadzhikistan got an average of just over 5 million per year from 1971 to 1975.[17]

In other words, this is not a program designed primarily to preserve wilderness or protect natural beauty, but to protect public health and facilitate further economic growth (particularly of irrigated agriculture) in the most highly developed regions of the country.[18]

How well is the program working? According to Soviet sources, water quality has already improved slightly in the areas of highest priority. The deterioration of the Volga has been halted.[19] In Moscow water quality has improved "somewhat" in the last ten years.[20] Some sources claim that waste treatment capacity is already catching up with the growing volume of industrial wastes nationwide.[21] It is hard to tell, however, which claims are real and which are inflated or overly optimistic;[22] so how can we judge the real priority and prospects of the water quality program? Fortunately, we can get a better answer by looking at the system of planning, implementation, and enforcement. Under Soviet conditions, unless human and material resources are allocated in the plan, funds for environmental protection will be returned to the state unspent, as happened routinely in the 1960s and still occurs occasionally. There must exist a specialized network for waste treatment research, design, and construction. In a system notorious for subverting plan targets from below by surreptitious "reprogramming" of personnel and resources, it is necessary to have an effective monitoring and enforcement system at the local level. Therefore, to determine the real priority and likely future of the water quality program, we must find out just how strong these new mechanisms are.

THE ENFORCEMENT SYSTEM

The center of the enforcement system is the network of basin inspectorates subordinated to Minvodkhoz.[23] They are growing rapidly; since 1972 their staff has doubled and now includes over 5,000 engineers, inspectors, and scientists. Yet, as fast as the basin inspectorates have grown, their work load has grown even faster. They are responsible in principle for every factory, farm, and municipality using more than 100 cubic meters a day of water.[24] At each location they must execute a bewildering array of tasks.[25]

But the enforcement powers of the inspectorates, at least on paper, are as formidable as their responsibilities. They are of two principal types: sanctions and power to withhold approval. I shall first discuss these powers as they exist on paper and then examine how effective they are in practice.

Sanctions Available in Theory

The basin inspectorates have an arsenal of graduated punishments at their disposal. Executives of polluting enterprises[26] can be fined up to 50 rubles on the recommendation of·the basin inspector, and the fine can be repeated at intervals of three months. Harsher penalties apply in the case of offenses considered to be criminal, such as a deliberate discharge resulting in a major fish kill. The basin inspectorates also can deprive individuals of their bonuses.[27] This is a sizable threat to an enterprise manager, whose bonuses may amount to half his total income. Such cancellation, according to the inspectors, requires no more than a letter from the basin inspectorate to the state bank. Finally, as a last resort, an enterprise, or part of it, can be shut down, or the enterprise's access to the sewage system can be closed down or its water supply shut off.

In addition to sanctions, the basin inspectorates have a potentially important weapon in the fact that their "agreement" (soglasevanie) is required at several key points in the planning, design, and construction of new enterprises and new waste treatment facilities, their level of water use and consumption, and their final commissioning on completion. In principle, this means that the basin inspectorates can prevent an enterprise from being located in an unsuitable place or from starting production if its waste treatment facilities are inadequate. Thus, on paper at least, the basin inspectorates have veto power at each of the key stages of water consumption and treatment.

Of this imposing array of formal responsibilities and powers, how many are real? To get a realistic picture, we should first inquire what resources and political support the basin inspectorates actually have.

Resources of the Basin Inspectorates: Two Examples:

The Moscow and Oka Basin Inspectorate is probably the best in the country. It is responsible for the city of Moscow and the six provinces surrounding it. But to cover a jurisdiction which includes 6,500 water-using entities and 21 million people, it has a staff of only 360 people and an annual budget of 1 million rubles, which pays mainly for salaries, operations, and upkeep of facilities.[28]

To this writer, during a visit in 1976, the Moscow-Oka Inspectorate looked somewhat like a semiamateur organization. Most of the inspectors were retired military officers, as were both the chief inspector and his chief engineer. Most of the scientists and technicians employed in the inspectorate's laboratories were women (unfortunately, in Soviet science this is a sign of low status). Inspectors earned 130 rubles a month, barely average for the Soviet Union.[29] In the inspectorate's central laboratory in Moscow, salaries were equally modest: a biological engineer earned 135 rubles per month, and the director of the laboratory earned only 170 rubles.[30] In an interview, the chief inspector acknowledged that with such salaries it was difficult to attract qualified personnel. Indeed, many of the everyday functions of the basin inspectorates were carried out by volunteers.

The basin inspectorates of the Ukraine looked much the same. About 1,000 people worked in the 11 basin inspectorates of this republic, serving a region of 55 million people.[31] Their annual budget was 3 million rubles, and their transportation, equipment, and laboratories were similar to those of the Moscow-Oka Inspectorate. They, too, had some difficulty in attracting qualified personnel. According to Ukranian inspectorate officials, only in the western Ukraine, where job opportunities are fewer and people want to stay in their home region, would young people work for the basin inspectorate. Elsewhere, in places like Moscow and the Don basin, competing job opportunities made it more difficult to attract qualified young professionals, and volunteers or retired military personnel were employed instead. The basin inspectorates, in other words, did not seem very attractive employers, and this fact suggests low status.

Compared to the Moscow-Oka and the Upper Dnieper organizations, inspectorates in lower priority regions like Kazakhstan are less

well staffed and equipped; in 1975 only 59 people were employed in
the basin inspectorates there, with responsibility for over 200,000
kilometers of streams.[32]

In sum, unless there have been major changes in the last three
years, the personnel and the resources of the basin inspectorates
seem barely adequate to cover the vast array of responsibilities they
have. If their duties were limited to water-quality monitoring alone, a
task they share with the Hydrometeorological Service, they might
perform adequately, at least in the high priority areas.[33] But when one
adds their enforcement and reporting tasks, one wonders how effective they can be in covering them all, or whether they are even
expected to. To this observer, the personnel of the inspectorates
seemed relaxed and unhurried; the central laboratory in Moscow
could actually be described as sleepy. The inspectors and their
superiors definitely did not give the impression of a harried crew
struggling desperately to cope with impossible demands.

Thus, the overall impression one gains of the basin inspectorates
is that, though they may be evolving toward real influence and real
professionalism, they are still low priority organizations. This impression is strengthened when one considers their record.

Enforcement in Practice

Enforcement is undoubtedly growing tougher. Whereas fines
were a relative rarity in the 1960s,[34] in 1973 about 5,000 enterprise
officials were either fined or deprived of their bonuses in the Volga
and Ural basins alone.[35] More than 6,000 enterprise officials were
fined in the RSFSR in 1974, and parts of 349 enterprises were shut
down.[36] In Moscow, 32 enterprises were fully or partially shut down
for brief periods in 1975, by order of the basin inspectorate.[37] In the
Ukraine, basin inspectors claim they cancelled bonuses for more than
9,000 management personnel during the ninth five-year plan
(1971–75).[38] The basin inspectorates withheld approval on more
than half of the 4,361 waste treatment facilities completed and
presented for certification in 1971.[39]

Through the figures on enforcement one can discern the same
priorities among regions already noted. Enforcement in Kazakhstan,
for example, seems much less vigorous than in the Ukraine and the
RSFSR; in 1975 only about 200 fines were levied there.[40] In Armenia
only 17 managers were fined in 1974, and there were no closings.[41]
The Ukraine ranks lower than Moscow: in contrast to the 32 closings
in Moscow, in 1975, the deputy minister in charge of water resources

in the Ukraine reported only two or three closings per year in the entire republic.[42] One can also discern enforcement priorities in the relative attention given to different industries. In enforcing the Volga-Ural decree the basin inspectorates have focused especially on the chemical industry.[43] The petroleum-refining and petrochemical industries are also prominently mentioned, both as the main causes of problems and the sources of some of the greatest strides.[44]

Shutting down a plant requires approval from higher authority. When plants are closed, it is usually for only two or three days and rarely more than a week. Most are older enterprises with obsolete technology, and the specific examples mentioned in interviews all concerned light industry, such as leather tanning, wool washing, and sugar refining. Minvodkhoz officials insist that the purpose of closing an enterprise is to give a healthy shock to its parent *glavk* (main administration). In most cases the enterprise is allowed to reopen after the *glavk* has given suitable promises that action will be taken to remedy the problem. *Pravda* reported recently the case of the Kirovakan chemical plant in Armenia, an antiquated facility and serious health hazard. Trying to shut down the worst of the plant's shops, the republic Ministry of Public Health passed a special resolution. But in vain: the USSR Ministry of the Chemical Industry had only to give assurances that something would be done, and the shop remained open. A year later, there had been no improvement, and the Armenian sanitary inspectorate took the last step remaining to it: it brought criminal charges against the enterprise director, a move everyone recognized was aimed at the wrong target.[45]

Shutting down an enterprise is clearly a measure of last resort, undertaken with great reluctance. Many cases are mentioned in which enterprise directors are fined repeatedly for the same violation, yet the enterprise continues to operate. The enormity of closure can be judged from the language of a recent article about the Tagil River in the Urals:

> If you had told Doctor Samogoltsev, fifteen years ago, that he would be putting a padlock on the gates and stopping a working plant, he would have thought you were a madman. That's right! The Plan, after all, is untouchable. And for him, as a native of the Urals, a factory is something sacred. . . . Yet, today he put lead seals on a factory shop and halted production.

The account goes on to describe a shouting match with the enterprise director. The following morning, all the parties concerned were summoned from Nizhnii Tagil to Sverdlovsk, a distance of over 75 miles, where the decision of the inspector was upheld. Clearly, water-quality inspectorates pick their targets carefully. In this case the inspector took the precaution of coming equipped with a document signed by a deputy minister.[46]

Enforcement of pollution control is not allowed to interfere with the fulfillment of high priority output targets or with local employment. Minvodkhoz will not support its basin inspectors if they try to close a high priority operation. In Moscow, for example, the inspectorate has had repeated difficulty with two copper-refining and electrolysis enterprises.[47] The Moscow-Oka chief inspector has tried on five different occasions to have them shut down temporarily but has been overruled each time by the office of the minister of reclamation himself.[48]

All in all, the basin inspectorates and other enforcement agencies do not appear very powerful. Soviet newspapers often report cases in which the protests of the basin inspectors are overridden or in which they are actually denied admittance to the plant's premises. As the chief of the Moscow-Oka inspectorate emphasized in an interview, the job of the inspectors is "difficult, conflict-ridden, and filled with tension."[49]

Part of the explanation for this weakness is that the basin inspectorates lack sufficient power, and part is that the power they have is aimed at the wrong place. Their sanctions apply mainly to the local enterprise directors, such as the hapless chief of the Kirovakan plant, who lack the means to comply. The inspectors cannot reach the real sources of the problem: the construction contractor, the research and design institutes, the supply organizations, and the higher levels of the ministries. This is not to say that enforcement has no potential role to play; we shall come back to it later on. But in the Soviet system enforcement simply is not the key to implementation. It cannot even begin to work until it is supported by materials, expertise, and incentives, and these must come from higher up, beginning with the planning process itself.

PLANNING AND IMPLEMENTATION

Prior to 1974, environmental programs had no formal place in the national plan, and consequently they received no central allocations of funds or supplies. But in the last three years the situation has changed dramatically. In 1974 a Division for the Protection of Nature was created in the State Planning Committee (Gosplan). Annual and five-year economic plans now include a section on environmental quality,[50] which assigns waste treatment and water-recycling targets to ministries and municipalities, along with the necessary material resources.[51]

The immediate consequence of these changes is that, in principle, responsibility for waste treatment construction no longer falls on the local enterprise directors but on their ministries, which are now officially accountable for the fulfillment of water quality plans. Second, the supply of equipment and materials for waste treatment becomes the responsibility of central supply organizations. Finally, there is now a recognized place in which the environmental program can be negotiated as part of the official agenda. But how do things work out in practice?

The negotiating process, as described in interviews with Soviet water-quality officials, works as follows: draft proposals for water-quality projects originate at the local level and reach Gosplan via two competing channels. The first starts from the basin inspectorates and rises through the hierarchy of the Ministry of Reclamation and Water Management (Minvodkhoz). Minvodkhoz amalgamates the local proposals into a draft water-quality plan which it sends to Gosplan's environmental division. The second channel of proposals runs up the hierarchy of the industrial ministries, or "branches," and leads to the Gosplan departments corresponding to each major type of industry.

Thus, at the draft stage of both five-year and annual plans, Gosplan must reconcile two sets of competing proposals. According to water-quality officials, Minvodkhoz's version calls for considerably more investment than do the industries' proposals—25 to 30 percent more in the case of five-year plans, 10 to 15 percent more in the case of draft annual plans.

How are these competing versions hammered together? The Division of Environmental Protection does not have actual authority to allocate resources, as the branch divisions do. The latter are given an overall "mark" by the General Division (svodnyi otdel) of Gosplan and must adjust the draft plans submitted by the ministries to fit the assigned mark. They have the power to decide for themselves what part of their investment resources to assign to environmental protection. The Division of Environmental Protection, in other words, is confined to the role of lobbyist for the environment in Gosplan, with a much weaker position in the planning process than the industrial divisions have.[52]

The same conclusion is suggested by the role that Minvodkhoz plays in this bargaining. Minvodkhoz is the main agency responsible for water use and quality, but it is not yet very effective as an institutional defender of clean water. First, Minvodkhoz, despite its budget of 7 billion rubles a year, is still nowhere near so large or so powerful as the giants it must contend with—especially the Ministries of the Chemical Industry, Oil Refining Industry, and Ferrous Metallurgy.

Second, Minvodkhoz cannot commit its full attention and political resources to water quality. Its main job is reclamation, and the reclamation wing of the ministry dwarfs the water-quality-and-use wing, in both personnel and resources.[53] By several measures, such as the relative space devoted to the two programs in the ministry's journal and in the minister's speeches or the relative number of R & D institutes working in the two fields, reclamation clearly looms far larger in Minvodkhoz's concerns than does water quality. Minvodkhoz is not likely to fight hard for its draft water-quality plans when they are whittled down by the industrial branch divisions in Gosplan.

A further reason for the weak position of water quality forces in the planning process is that their recommendations are still largely ad hoc. There is no nationwide plan for water use and quality, despite a great deal of talk about a "general scheme" being developed by hydropower planners, and regional or basin plans are still in the development stage. Quality standards are permissive: they must be reached eventually, but the exact timetable is negotiable, and the final standards themselves are still being developed.[54]

What happens next is a familiar chain of events. The subordinate position of the environmental program in the planning system signals to officials at all levels that they may safely divert resources, in case of need, to programs with higher priority. So the program's initial weakness at the top of the system is magnified in the field. Action falls then short in every department: specialists are not trained, research is not done, construction firms are not reorganized, technology is not developed, and facilities are built slowly and inadequately maintained. The final result is that the program does not move. In 1975, for example, only 23 out of 38 ministries and agencies fulfilled the plan for "physical and chemical treatment of wastewater," even in the most formal terms.[55] In 1978, a decree of the Central Committee and the USSR Council of Ministers blasted ministries and party organs alike, not even bothering with the usual ritual praise for good performers that such decrees usually begin with.[56] Obviously, from the Kremlin the situation looks grim.

As an illustration, consider the problems of constructing waste treatment facilities. The first obstacle is the structure of the industry: there are still no construction organizations specializing in pollution control, aside from one or two in Moscow. Instead, waste treatment assignments are handled by general purpose construction firms (*tresty*), operating on contract.[57]

Second, the system of incentives discourages work on pollution control. Waste treatment assignments are generally only a very small part of the total work load of construction firms and therefore a small part also of their target and bonuses. They consider waste treatment complicated, labor intensive, and exacting, and they often turn down contracts for waste treatment or put them in last place on their work schedules.[58]

The construction firms moreover, are just one link in a chain of designers, suppliers, and so on; none of these, according to the press, works particularly well. Everyone blames everyone else. The construction trusts claim that they are fulfilling their plans but are given few assignments by their ministries and inadequate supplies by supply organizations and ministries of machine building.[59] Supply offices complain that they cannot provide sets of equipment to construction firms before the systems have been designed, which the design institutes are slow to do. The USSR Ministries of Chemical and Petroleum Machine Building get the blame for not starting series production of key equipment.[60]

Clearly part of the problem is the suddenness with which the water-quality program was accelerated in 1973. Construction firms were caught unprepared. One of the firms named in the Volga-Ural decree, a petrochemical construction firm in the Ural basin town of Gurev, saw its waste treatment plan jump suddenly from 25 million rubles in 1974 to 55 million in 1975.[61] A Soviet reporter describes the firm's plight:

> To use this money is beyond the firm's capability, of course. It lacks the workers, the equipment, and the construction base. The province has only a very small casting yard for reinforced concrete items, and not a single quarry; gravel is hauled in from Aktyubinsk, hundreds of kilometers away. Bricks are shipped in from almost as far as Karaganda. Gurev urgently needs help.

The situation was much the same throughout the Ural basin. In Magnitogorsk, investment ran at only one-fourth the rate called for in the party-state decree.[62] The basin's problems have eased somewhat in the last three years, but a recent article remains highly critical and calls the quality of the water there unsatisfactory.[63]

Political priority, of course, influences the rate at which such lags are overcome. In the last five years there has been progress in the most important regions and industries, and much less in the others.

For example, one may read of a biological treatment facility for a copper-chemical combine in eastern Kazakhstan that has been under construction for ten years,[64] but such stories are now rare in the Volga basin or in Moscow. In Moscow a two-year project may take eight, but in Tadzhikistan the same project may take forever.[65] Similarly, different priorities among ministries show up in differences in construction performance. Light industry and the food industry, having little clout generally, contract with local construction firms instead of national ones.[66] This fact helps to explain the particularly poor record of these two industries.

The basin inspectorates and the other enforcement agencies can do little about these problems. They have no power to fine the construction firms or give them orders, nor do they have any leverage over the ministries' R & D and design institutes. Minvodkhoz's power of intervention is limited because it does not contribute funds, supplies, or expertise of its own.

If a new enterprise is completed but the waste treatment facilities for it are not, the inspectors have, in principle, the power to prevent the enterprise from being commissioned; that is, they can prevent it from being turned over by the construction ministry to the industrial ministry that will operate it. In practice, according to Minvodkhoz officials, the basin inspectors will not resort to such a drastic measure but will insist instead on a strict interim schedule for the operation of the enterprise, specifying a firm completion date for the waste treatment facility and permissible interim levels of discharge of untreated effluent. A reading of the Soviet press, however, suggests that such temporary variances are widespread and tend to become permanent. The participation of basin inspectorate officials on the commissioning committees and their theoretical veto power apparently are not enough to withstand the pressure of enterprise directors, who are anxious to get their facilities commissioned and operating, and of local party officials, who have every incentive to support them.

CONCLUSION

Is the new environmental program a meaningful reform? This depends on what it is intended to achieve. The program appears, in fact, to have two distinct aims. Each entails a different mix and type of costs and benefits. Each requires a different technology, administrative machinery, and level of commitment. Consequently, they differ also in their significance as departures from the traditional Soviet approach to development and in their chances for success.

The first is aimed at dealing with immediate threats: communicable water-borne diseases (such as the cholera outbreak of the early 1970s), kills of commercially valuable fish, and the like. These can be dealt with relatively quickly and simply through primary and secondary waste treatment at specific point sources, using standard techniques. This first level of aims is the easiest to implement because it relies on well-established, uniform technologies, does not affect industrial production, and demands little from the polluters themselves. Much of the current Soviet effort is of this kind. The press is filled with reports of rapidly growing waste treatment capacity, especially municipal systems.[67] This side of the program, then, is essentially a long overdue public health measure, and there is no reason to believe that it will not succeed.

The second aim is to protect resources for future economic uses, what Americans in the first half of the century called "conservation."[68] Conservation is more difficult to achieve than sanitation, because at the level of development the Soviets have now reached conservation definitely requires jostling industry. Heavy metals, chemicals, and petroleum wastes must be taken out of water or prevented from entering it. Where water is scarce (as it is in the southern half of the Soviet Union), it cannot be used as process water or as coolant with the traditional Soviet liberality. Therefore some industries must make process changes; others must be relocated or prevented from moving in. No new hydropower plants can be allowed to flood now-scarce agricultural land, and previously flooded land must be partially recovered. Conservation, in sum, means no longer giving industrial enterprises (provided they meet the plan) their accustomed complete latitude in using natural resources.

There is no reason in principle why the traditional political machinery cannot achieve such changes. Conservation involves a redirection of effort, but no fundamental change of objectives, since its aim, after all, is to facilitate further economic expansion. Making industrial process changes can be considered a type of technological innovation requiring research and development, and this in itself is no radical idea for Soviet industry. To strengthen the claims of new users of scarce water and land, the central leadership simply can strengthen the agencies concerned while whittling down those of the previously mighty. The new agencies—reclamation, for example— resemble the old; therefore they require no great adjustments of mind or procedure. In dealing with them, the party apparatus continues to play its accustomed roles of broker, troubleshooter and expediter, and therefore its power is not threatened. Conservation, then, though it stretches the traditional political system, does not require changing it.

The difficulty is that implementing conservation requires a capacity for subtlety and dosage on a massive scale which the established system of planning and administration heretofore has not shown. No two industrial plants have quite the same processes or the same wastes. Each solution must be tailor-made to local conditions. Justifying it requires a broader frame of reference and a more subtle balancing of objectives than the planning mechanism typically allows, a larger conceptual arsenal (in a system of prices for water) than Soviet economists yet use, and better measuring instruments than conservation officials yet have. Industrial executives and party officials alike concentrate on the near term and the narrow target because it has so far proved impossible to devise effective signals and levers that will cause them to behave differently. But conservation, on the contrary, requires a delicate balancing act among competing objectives at an infinity of local points.

In this respect, the requirements of the conservation program are no different from those of a multitude of other reforms the Soviet government is experimenting with, as it begins to wrestle with the problems of managing a mature industrial economy: technological innovation, computerized management, labor and demographic policies, new methods of planning, and so forth. The crucial question in all these reforms is whether the traditional political and administrative machinery, the system of "strong thumbs and weak fingers" (to borrow Charles Lindblom's phrase), can implement such reforms effectively.

When looked at in this light, the problem of enforcement stands out as crucial. Only enforcement at the local level by local bodies can guarantee the attention to detail, the case-by-case balancing, that each individual solution requires. One need not look far for reforms that would make the enforcement system more effective. Increased powers over research, design, and construction organizations would give the enforcers leverage over the entire sequence of steps leading to new processes at the plant level. Higher salaries would make it possible to attract better-qualified personnel into enforcement, especially technical specialists acquainted with the industries each inspectorate must deal with. The practice of according variances and "interim schedules" for compliance with environmental targets should be strictly limited. Enforcement would then have real teeth.

But to name these steps is to name the problem. Such powers would enable local inspectorates to coerce officials at higher levels and across organizational boundaries. Even if those powers were exercised strictly in accordance with the plan (as they would have to be), they would reverse the usual direction of authority and threaten the prerogatives of the local party apparatus, limiting its freedom of action. Such moves would represent more than a refocusing of priorities and resources; they would affect the very structure of the political system. Nothing in the fifteen-year record of the Brezhnev administration suggests the slightest willingness to try anything so bold.

In conclusion, the new environmental program is an example of the mixed record of the regime's attempts to deal with what one might call "third generation" problems, that is, the subtle tasks of managing balanced growth after two generations of nearly exclusive focus on heavy industry. Where the problem has been to ward off an immediate danger, the system has responded well. The elite has shown considerable capacity for new thinking at the top, as the very existence of the environmental program attests. But where the problem is to implement an infinity of intersectoral, hard-to-measure, partial shifts at the local level, performance has been poor, and the leadership has been unwilling so far to give environmental planners and enforcers the clout they need. Ultimately, the most important question raised by the environmental program is this: can the political system that grew up during the first two generations of Soviet rule not only devise reforms to meet the problems of the third generation but also find acceptable and effective means of carrying them out without endangering the basis of its own power?

NOTES

1. Interview with USSR Minister of Reclamation E. E. Alekseevskii, "Vodu nado berech," *Trud*, January 24, 1976.

2. L. I. Brezhnev, "Report of the Central Committee of the CPSU," *XXV s ezd Kommunisticheskoi Partii Sovetskogo Soyuza (stenograficheskii otchet)*, vol. 1 (Moscow: Politizdat, 1976), p. 67.

3. Statement by K. A. Efimov, chief of Gosplan's Department of Planning of Scientific Research and Development, at a meeting of the US-Soviet Working Group on Management of Technological Innovation, State Committee on Science and Technology, Moscow, February 1979.

4. A translation of the USSR Principles of Water Legislation can be found in Irving K. Fox, ed., *Water Resources Law and Policy in the Soviet Union* (Madison: University of Wisconsin Press, 1971), pp. 221–39.

5. On the Volga-Ural: Decree of the CPSU Central Committee and the USSR Council of Ministers, "O merakh po predotvrascheniyu zagryazneniya basseinov rek Volgi i Urala neochishchennymi stochnymi vodami," *Pravda*, March 17, 1972. On the Baltic Sea: USSR Council of Ministers decree, "O merakh po usileniyu okhrany ot zagryazneniya basseina Baltiiskogo morya," *Izvestiya*, August 20, 1976. On the Black and Azov seas: Decree of the CPSU Central Committee and USSR Council of Ministers, "O merakh po predotvrashcheniyu zagryazneniya basseinov Chernogo i Azovskogo morei," February 1976, described in I. Gasiev, "Voda i zhizn'," *Zarya vostoka*, May 21, 1976.

6. Decree of the USSR Council of Ministers and the Central Committee of the Communist Party of the Soviet Union, "Ob usilenii okhrany prirody i uluchshennii ispolzovaniya prirodnykh resursov," Decree no. 898, December 29, 1972. For background information on the reclamation program, see Thane Gustafson, "Transforming Soviet Agriculture: Brezhnev's Gamble on Land Improvement," *Public Policy* (Summer 1977).

7. P. Poletaev, "Plan i okhrana prirody," *Planovoe khozyaistvo*, no. 4 (1976).

8. For Western discussions on the beginnings of the Soviet water-quality program, see Marshall Goldman, *The Spoils of Progress: Environmental Pollution in the Soviet Union* (Cambridge, Mass.: MIT Press, 1972). See also Donald R. Kelley, "Environmental Policy-Making in the USSR: The Role of Industrial and Environmental Interest Groups," *Soviet Studies* 27 (October 1976): 4, 570–89, and Kelley, "Environmental Problems as a New Policy Issue," in *Soviet Society and the Communist Party*, ed. Karl Ryavec (Amherst: University of Massachusetts Press, 1978), pp. 88–107; *Environmental Misuse in the Soviet Union*, ed. Fred Singleton (New York: Praeger, 1976); David E. Powell, "The Social Costs of Modernization: Ecological Problems in the USSR," *World Politics* 23, no. 4 (July 1971); and John W. Kramer, "The Politics of Conservation and Pollution in the USSR" (Ph.D. diss., University of Virginia, 1973).

9. B. N. Laskorin et al., "Kachestvo i okhrana vody v basseine reki Volgi," *Vodnye resursy*, no. 4 (1975): 23–25.

10. O. M. Voronova, "Uvelichenie stoimosti ochistki stochnykh vod i tekhniko-ekonomicheskie aspekty etoi problemy," *Vodnye resursy*, no. 1 (1976): 141.

11. I. I. Borodavchenko, "Problemy ispolzovaniya i okhrany vodnykh resursov SSSR," *Gidrotekhinika i melioratsiya*, no. 4 (1976): 9

12. Secondary treatment is already the general rule there, and Moscow sanitary engineers are now moving on to tertiary treatment by means of filtration through sand and gravel. Moscow is also the first city in the country to have begun to build treatment facilities for polluted runoff from city streets.

Moscow clearly represents a special case: although it appears that more pollution control is being done there than elsewhere in the country, more also needs to be done because of the very great concentration of industry and population there and the limited natural streamflow from outside the area. To give some idea, the flow of the Moscow River inside the city limits is composed of the following sources: treated sewage water, 47 m^3/sec; industrial effluent, 8 m^3/sec; surface runoff, 10 m^3/sec; as well as the augmented inflow of the river itself, which is 40 m^3/sec. Such a large proportion of the city's streamflow consists of treated sewage water that even secondary biological treatment is not enough; much of the city's sewage is industrial in origin and contains toxic and poorly degradable substances; consequently, the efficiency of biological waste treatment is considerably lowered.

In view of these special circumstances, it is not surprising to read that, even though 400 million rubles was spent on waste treatment in Moscow from 1965 to 1975 and nearly 1,000 enterprises were equipped with waste treatment facilities, the same complaints can be heard as in the rest of the country about poor design, delays in construction, and negligent operation. A recent article concludes that the quality of the Moscow River has increased only "somewhat" in the last ten years. See A. N. Lavrenov, S. V. Ilinskii, and E. E. Scherbakov, "Vodoemam byt' chistymi," *Gorodskoe khozyaistvo Moskvy*, no. 4 (1976): 31–32.

For a background description of environmental policy in Moscow, see David E. Powell, "Politics and the Urban Environment: The City of Moscow," *Journal of Comparative Political Studies* (October 1977). See also M. G. Ryabyshev, "Okhrana vodnykh resursov Moskvy," *Vodnye resursy*, no. 5 (1975): 15–32. Finally, an account of the early history of sanitation engineering in Moscow can be found in A. Rubinov, "Saving the River," *Literaturnaya gazeta*, October 4, 1978, translated in *Current Digest of the Soviet Press* 30, no. 46 (December 13, 1978); p. 5.

13. Poletaev, "Plan i okhrana prirody." *Planovoe khozyaistvo*, no. 4 (1976).

14. This figure is derived from a comparison of nationwide net addition to capacity for the period 1971–73, with the corresponding figure for the Volga River alone during the period 1972–74. The former figure comes from Iu. P. Belichenko and Iu. G. Egorov, "Ob opyte raboty organov vodnogo nadzora," *Problemy okhrany vod*, no. 5 (1974): 13. The latter figure comes from K. I. Akulov, "Public Health Aspects of the Protection of Water Resources in the Light of the Decree of the CC CPSU and the USSR Council of Ministers, 'Regarding Measures to Prevent the Pollution of the Volga and Ural Rivers by Untreated Wastewater,'" *Gigiena i sanitariya*, no. 2 (1976): 1–7.

15. V. Golovin, "Khraniteli chistoi vody," *Kazakhstanskaya pravda*, January 21, 1975.

16. I. Gasiev, "Voda i zhizn'," *Zarya vostoka*, May 21, 1976.

17. T. Mukhamedov, "Khranite vodu v chistote," *Kommunist Tadzhikistana*, May 12, 1976.

18. The effort to protect Lake Baikal is an exception, but that is a very special case. See accounts in Goldman, *Spoils of Progress*; Kelley, "Environmental Problems"; and in my own forthcoming book, *Brezhnev's Reform: the Political Significance of the New Agricultural Policy*.

19. Laskorin et al., "Kachestvo i okhrara," p. 27. A samizdat account of environmental problems in the Soviet Union, otherwise very critical of Soviet environmental policy, agrees that the condition of the Volga has been stabilized, after an investment of "tens of millions" (Boris Komarov, *Unichtozhenie prirody* (Frankfurt: Possev, 1978), p. 53).

20. Lavrenov, Ilinskii, and Shcherbakov, "Vodoemam." At the main laboratory facility of the Moscow-Oka Inspectorate, the author had the opportunity to study data on changes in biological oxygen demand (BOD_5) for various points in the city in 1966, 1970, 1973, and 1975. These indicated a steady improvement for the Moscow River below Voskresensk. (The data, unfortunately, do not correct for variations in streamflow by indicating concentration per unit of flow.) The figures do indicate some trouble spots: for example, above Gzhelka there is a steady worsening of the BOD_5 values, owing to the presence of the Zhukovskii industrial complex and heavy agricultural runoff. Throughout the river, BOD_5 levels run between 4 and 8 ppm. Despite the general improvement, there has been little progress in dealing with synthetic detergents, which Moscow water quality officials declare to be their most worrisome problem, for the relevant ministries have done little as yet to develop biodegradable products. See also V. Varavka, "Vniz po Volge," *Ekonomicheskaya gazeta*, no. 31 (July 1975): 22.

21. During the period 1970 to 1974, says a deputy minister of Minvodkhoz,

industrial wastes increased by 19 percent, but treatment capacity grew by 37 percent (Borodavchenko, "Problemy ispolzovariya").

22. We can perform a crude calculation of our own: the same deputy minister cites the total volume of waste water produced in 1965 as 150 million m^3/day (I. I. Borodavchenko and V. R. Lozanskii, "Aktual'nye voprosy okhrany vodnykh resursov strany," *Problemy okhrany vod*, no. 1 (1972): 8. The estimate they adopt is that of Professor A. I. Zhukov, reported in "Problemy vodnykh resursov," *Trud*, September 13, 1968. This figure is higher than any of the estimates cited in Goldman, *Spoils of Progress*, which range from 50 to 100 million m^3/day (p. 83). (Undoubtedly the main reason for the wide range of estimates is that most industries have no precise idea how much water they discharge.) Assuming that this volume of waste has been growing at 4 percent annually since then, we arrive at a rough annual increase in effluent in the mid-1970s of 8 million m^3/day. This is nearly equal to the planned addition to waste treatment capacity for 1976, 8.5 million m^3/day (Poletaev, "Plan i okhrara").

In other words, 1976 was the first year in which planned incremental waste treatment capacity overtook the annual increase in effluent, at least for the nation as a whole. This assumes, however, that planned construction schedules are actually met; as we shall see, there have been problems on this score. It is probably a safe bet that the construction rate has not yet caught up with the annual growth of waste.

23. The basin inspectorates were created in 1960 (Decree of the USSR Council of Ministers, no. 425, April 22, 1960, "O merakh po uporyadocheniyu ispol'zovaniya i usileniyu okhrany vodnykh resursov SSSR"). Which major agency they should be subordinated to was a controversial issue for a long time. The question was finally settled in 1972, when they were attached to the republic-level Ministries of Reclamation. There are now 105 basin and zone inspectorates, whose activity is "coordinated and directed" by the Chief Inspectorate for the Protection of Water Sources of USSR Minvodkhoz, in Moscow (I. M. Kutyrin and Y. P. Belichenko, *Okhrana vodnykh resursov—problema sovremennosti*, 2nd ed. (Leningrad: Gidrometeoizdat, 1974), p. 49. Needless to say, several years went by before the full network was in place. It was 1967, for example, before a branch office of the Urals basin inspectorate opened in Magnitogorsk (M. Podgorodnikov and V. Travinskii, "Conflict on the Riverbank," *Literaturnaya gazeta*, no. 4 January 23, 1974, translated in *Current Digest of the Soviet Press* vol. 26, no. 4, (1974) p. 12. In addition to the basin inspectorates, there is also a network of public health inspectors with responsibility for water quality.

24. The inspectorates must check each industrial enterprise twice a year, taking samples of effluent for analysis. In 1974, according to official figures, 34,000 enterprises were inspected, and 209,000 water samples were analyzed (Alekseevskii interview in *Trud*; Belichenko and Egorov, "Ob opyte rabety," p. 12; see also Kutyrin and Belichenko, *Okhrara vodrykh resursov*, p. 48.

25. Inspectorates must verify that industrial and municipal waste treatment plants are operating properly, that industrial wastes entering municipal systems do not contain illegal levels of metals and organic compounds, and that industrial and municipalities are submitting accurate water-quality analyses, as current regulations require them to do. The inspectorates are supposed to participate in developing proposals for new waste treatment facilities and to monitor the progress of construction. They must approve plans for siting of new enterprises and must certify that new factories have adequate waste treatment capacity before the plants can be officially "commissioned" and turned over to the relevant ministry of operation. Once new plants are operating, the inspectorates are charged with monitoring their consumption of water, to induce them to economize (Y. P. Belichenko, "Vode byt. chistoi," *Izvestiya*, October 9, 1974). The general responsibilities of the basin inspectorates were estab-

lished in the December 1972 joint decree and are described in detail in the article by Belichenko and Egorov, "Ob opyte raboty," pp. 12ff. It is not clear whether the recent creation of a State Committee for Hydrometeorology and Oversight of the Environment changes this allocation of duties. A decree of the CPSU Central Committee and the USSR Council of Ministers in December 1978 (the first to describe publicly the functions of the new committee) appears to give it the lead role in dealing with air, while having relatively little to say about water. See Tsentral'nyi Komitet KPSS i Sovet Ministrov SSSR, "O dopolnitel'nykh merakh po usileniyu okhrany prirody i uluchsheniyu ispolzovaniya prirodnykh resursov," *Pravda*, January 6, 1979.

26. Such positions would include the director of an enterprise or the general director of an "association" (*ob'edinenie*) and any management positions below them, but not higher.

27. The basin inspectorates have had this authority since 1966. (USSR State Committee on Labor and Wages and All-Union Central Council of Trade Unions, special decree, "O poryadke lishenii premii pri nevypolnenii v ustanovlennye sroki meropriyatii po predotvrashcheniyu zagryazneniya rybokhozyaistvennykh vodoemov").

28. Interview with I. P. Yakovlev, head of the Moscow-Oka Inspectorate, October 1976.

29. Increases to 160 to 180 rubles a month were due in 1977, but I have not seen confirmation of this. The staff of the basin inspectorates was the last in the Minvodkhoz system to get raises, which may be an indication of their status in the ministry.

30. For purposes of comparison, a monthly salary of 170 rubles is what would be earned by a junior researcher, with a *kandidat* degree, in a research institute of the "first category," such as an Academy institute.

31. Interviews at the Ukranian Republic Minvodkhoz, Kiev, October 1976.

32. Golovin, "Khrariteli."

33. Global figures give a rough idea: if we assume that there are roughly 200 inspectors in the Moscow-Oka Inspectorate and that they inspect 6,500 water-using entities twice a year, each inspector must visit 65 per year, not an inordinate number. On the other hand, the laboratories receive effluent analysis reports from enterprises every ten days, which means a total of some 650 reports a day. This is too much for more than a perfunctory check, to which must be added the 40-odd samples contributed daily by the inspectors, assuming each inspection produces a sample for analysis.

34. Since 1961 it has been forbidden to impose fines by administrative procedure alone. Fines requested by water-quality inspectorates must be approved by the courts. In the past this step slowed down the whole procedure. T. S. Sushkov, "Pravovaya okhrana prirody," *Sovetskoe gosudarstvo i pravo*, no. 5 (1969): 3-10; and O. S. Kolbasov, "Conservation Law in the USSR," *Sovetskoe gosudarstvo i pravo*, no. 9 (1967), translated in *The Soviet Review* 9, no. 4 (1968): pp. 17-25. Only five fines were approved by the RSFSR courts in 1963, five again in 1965, 10 in 1966, and 12 in 1967.

35. Belichenko, "Vode byt' chistoi."

36. K. Kornev, "Berech' vodnye bogatstva," *Trud*, October 8, 1975.

37. Yakovlev interview.

38. Interview with V. N. Cherenichenko, chief of the Main Inspectorate for Water Quality of the Ukrainian Ministry of Reclamation, October 1976.

39. Kutyrin and Belichenko, *Okhrara vodrykh resursov*.

40. B. Ospanov, "Chistotu—vodoemam," *Kazakhstanskaya pravda*, May 7, 1976. This figure may represent a sizable increase since 1974, because another source reports that in 1974 only 117 fines were requested by the basin inspectorates, out of which 100 were approved and levied (see E. Matskevich, "Slovo o chistoi vode,"

Izvestiya, February 9, 1975). The latter figure, however, refers only to the basin inspectorates, whereas the former may include other agencies with the authority to levy fines, such as the sanitary-epidemiological stations of the Ministry of Health. Therefore, one cannot be sure that there has been any increase at all in the enforcement level.

41. Yu. Belichenko, "Za chistotu vodoemov," *Kommunist,* no. 27 (September 1975): 2.

42. Interview with K. S. Khilobochenko, deputy minister of the Ukrainian Minvodkhoz, October 1976.

43. I. I. Borodavchenko, "Problemy ispol'zovaniya i okhrany vodnykh resursov v SSSR," *Gidrotekhnika i melioratsiya,* no. 4 (1976): 9.

44. See, for example, Varavka, "Vniz po Volge."

45. Yu. Arakelyan, "Prikaz podpisan, no. . . ." *Pravda,* November 29, 1978. Earlier articles in *Pravda* on the same plant appeared in August 1977, and February 1978.

46. Boris Ryabinin, "Spasennaya reka," *Literaturnaya gazeta,* February 9, 1977.

47. Alekseevskii interview in *Trud.*

48. Yakovlev interview.

49. Ibid.

50. See V. R. Lozanskii and I. D. Pichakhchi, "Sotsialnaya znachimost vodookhrannoi deyatelnosti," *Problemy okhrany vod,* no. 6 (1975): 7.

51. According to A. K. Kuzin, a VNIIVO economist, water protection measures accounted for 10 of the 790 pages of the tenth five-year plan.

52. The *Samizdat* author of *Unichtozhenie prirody* agrees: "The Interagency Council and the Division of Conservation *(prirodopolzovaniya)* of the State Committee on Science and Technologs and the Division of Environmental Protection in Gosplan have practically no power. They are obliged to reckon with the main objectives of the agencies in which they are located, and those objectives are not directed at all toward the preservation of nature." (Komarov, *Unichtozheric prirody,* pp. 104–05.)

53. The two wings are not exactly comparable, since one builds while the other regulates. Minvodkhoz officials, in response to persistent questions, could give no precise answer about the relative size of the two wings. My own estimate is that the reclamation wing is on the order of 100 times larger, perhaps more.

54. V. Zavarzin and S. Kozhanov, "Ecology and Standards," *Ekonomicheskaya gazeta,* no. 36 (September 1978); 13, translated in *Current Digest of the Soviet Press* 30, no. 37 (1978): 12.

55. V. Shkatov and Z. Zateeva, "Ratsionalno ispolzovat bogatstva priorody," *Ekonomicheskaya gazeta,* no. 27 (July 1976); 13. The worst performance in 1975 came from the Ministries of Light Industry and Food Industry, which met their construction plan by only 80 and 70 percent, respectively, and their plan for putting waste treatment facilities into operation by 59 and 78 percent ("Berech vody" (editorial), *Izvestiya,* March 5, 1977).

56. "O dopolnitelnykh merakh po usileniyu. . . ."

57. There is a bewildering variety of such organizations, often specializing in very different fields from those of their water quality customers. For example, one of the several hundred assignments contained in the 1972 Volga-Ural decree calls for the Ministry of Agricultural Construction to build a waste treatment plant for the Aleksandrovskii radio factory in Vladimir Province (Yakovlev interview). Also see "Berech vody."

58. "Berech vodu." See also K. Solovev, "Vsem mirom," *Izvestiya,* August 19, 1975.

59. Podgorodnikov and Travinskii, "Conflict on the Riverbank."

60. K. Sharonov, "In Complete Sets and on Time: On Accelerating the Construction of Municipal Sewage-Treatment Installations and Deliveries of Equipment to

Them," *Ekonomicheskaya gazeta*, no. 49, (December 1976): 17, translated in *Current Digest of the Soviet Press*, 28, no. 49 (1976): 15. Sharonov repeats much the same criticism in a more recent article in *Ekonomicheskaya gazeta*, no. 39 (1978); 17.

61. Podgorodnikov and Travinskii, "Conflict on the Riverbank."

62. "Promyshlennost i priroda" (editorial), *Pravda*, April 3, 1975.

63. B. Suleimenov, "Vody Urala," *Kazakhstanskaya pravda*, June 25, 1976.

64. "Vazhnoe zveno okhrany prirody" (editorial), *Pravda*, January 28, 1977.

65. For an example described as "characteristic," see Mukhamedov, "Khranite vodu."

66. *Ibid.* In Gorky Province, for example, two waste treatment facilities for the Ministry of Light Industry are being contracted out to the province's agricultural trust.

67. Waste treatment capacity is scheduled to rise at a rate of 12 percent annually during the present five-year plan. During the period 1972-75, over 9,000 large new facilities began operation. "Berech vody", Poletaev, "Plan i okhrara." In addition, the level of treatment is being raised: more and more facilities are based on biological and chemical methods (secondary treatment) rather than mechanical methods (primary treatment). Of the planned capacity scheduled for the current five-year plan, 60 percent will be secondary rather than primary treatment (Poletaev, "Plan i okhrara"). Primary treatment is still the dominant method, but other methods are gaining quickly, with a corresponding increase in the unit costs of waste treatment. (The share of primary treatment dropped from 65 percent in 1970 to 52.4 percent in 1975.) The upgrading of treatment levels has been particularly striking in the chemical industry, where the share of primary treatment has dropped from 88 to 54 percent from 1970 to 1975. Chemical and biological methods rose from 12 to 43 percent during the same period (Voronova, "Uvelicherie stoimosti").

68. On the distinction between conservation and environmentalism, see Arthur Maass, "Conservation," in *International Encyclopedia of the Social Sciences*, ed. David Sills, vol. 3., (New York: MacMillan, 1968), pp. 271-79.

7

TRENDS IN THE HUMAN RIGHTS MOVEMENT

David Kowalewski

Future historians of Soviet politics during the Brezhnev era may well discover a prominent paradox. Whereas the Soviet polity under Leonid Brezhnev has displayed a relatively high level of stability, continuity, and order at the top, simultaneously there has arisen a substantial amount of instability, rapid change, and disorder from below. The disenfranchised groups comprising what has become known as the human rights movement have demonstrated their dissatisfaction with Soviet regime policies through numerous forms of verbal and physical protest.

THE HUMAN RIGHTS MOVEMENT

A protest movement can best be conceived as a relatively long-term series of collective actions by disenfranchised groups dissatisfied with regime policies and loosely united by a set of shared values in order to change those policies.[1] In the Soviet Union the set of shared values, or "basic common denominator,"[2] of the human rights movement is found in the United Nations Universal Declaration of Human Rights.[3] This document has become a staple in the underground literature archives of virtually all the groups who have displayed their dissatisfaction with Soviet regime policies. It provides not only the unifying "set of constitutive ideas"[4] for these groups but also an internationally recognized justification for their demands.

The beginning of the human rights movement can be traced to Nikita Khrushchev's secret speech to the Twentieth Party Congress in 1956. By condemning many of Stalin's practices, the Soviet premier provided a powerful stimulus to the reevaluation of the Soviet system by many groups dissatisfied with regime policies. Khrushchev's attack not only de-legitimized a good deal of past oppression but tended to legitimize dissent against these policies in the minds of members of several dissatisfied groups. Further, by suggesting a change in the rules of the political game, the secret speech made more likely both the possibility of winning the game and, thus, the mobilization of collective action in pursuit of group interests. The shift in the cost-benefit calculus of political protest is suggested by dissident Igor Golomshtok: "After Stalin's death, as soon as the threat of immediate transfer from studio to prison cell for disagreement with . . . directives was lessened, artists began intensely to create . . . that which is now called Soviet unofficial art."[5] The expectation of lower costs and higher benefits was further enhanced by Khrushchev's relaxation of political controls. Curbs were placed on the secret police, "socialist legality" was strengthened, political prisoners were rehabilitated, and other reforms were undertaken.

However, the rise to political protest certainly was not immediate. At their inception, protest movements are usually naive, diffuse, formless, and vague in purpose.[6] During this period of political maturation, individuals experiment with various forms of political activity, particularly by forming loosely knit circles and study groups in their search for new ideals.

Protest movements often undergo the transition from ferment to protest by means of a catalytic event, often in the form of a severe repressive act by regime officials. At that moment the movement's consciousness and a certain realization of its identity crystallize.[7] In the Soviet Union, the regime provided this catalyst in 1965–66 by its arrest and trial of two writers, Andrei Sinyavskii and Yuri Daniel. For the first time not only were writers tried for their literary works, but the writers steadfastly refused to plead guilty. In addition, the trial clashed markedly with the recent reforms in the rule of law which, as dissident Lidiya Chukovskaya remarked, had been the "most precious achievements" of the regime since 1956.[8]

The trial soon stimulated many groups to express their dissatis-factions with regime policies more openly and uncompromisingly in unconventional or protest behavior. Although a complete description of all the groups cannot be provided here, a thumbnail sketch of the social structure of the human rights movement can be drawn.[9]

The groups or submovements can be divided conveniently by the scope of their demands as universalist or particularist collectivities. Universalist groups advocate fundamental change for the entire polity whereas particularist groups advocate change for their special interests. Universalist collectivities in the human rights movement can best be described as civil rights groups. The Initiative Group for the Defense of Human Rights in the USSR, the Moscow chapter of Amnesty International, the Human Rights Committee, and other small groups and parties press for the defense of the rights embodied in the Universal Declaration as well as for greater democracy in the media, economy, elections, party structure, and foreign policymaking. Although most of these dissidents are Russian intellectuals, similar groups are active in Georgia, Latvia, Belorussia, and elsewhere. In the spirit of the Universal Declaration, these groups generally display a high level of political tolerance, frequently expressing the belief that freedom is indivisible, that the rights of one are inextricably bound up with the rights of all.[10]

Dissident particularist collectivities can be categorized as national, religious, labor, and professional groups. Foreign observers and Soviet protesters alike have noted a dramatic increase in national dissent.[11] According to dissident Leonid Plyushch, the nationalities problem grows in intensity from year to year.[12]

National protest groups are either repatriatory or indigenous in character. Repatriatory dissent, or "homeless nationalism"[13] has arisen among a number of groups. The Soviet Jewish movement began to gain momentum particularly after the Middle East Six-Day War in 1967. Since then numerous protest demonstrations for the right to emigrate to Israel have occurred across the Soviet Union.[14] Crimean Tatars also have managed to construct a mass movement to return from Uzbekistan and other areas to the Crimean peninsula from which they were deported during World War II.[15] Soviet Germans, another deported nationality, have also protested the regime's refusal to permit their return to their Volga homeland. One segment of the German movement, despairing of any possibility for repatriation, has demanded—and some have received—emigration visas to West Germany. Also deported from their homeland were the Meskhetians, a small national minority from the Georgian Republic. Like the Germans, some have consistently protested for return to Georgia whereas others have sought emigration to Turkey. Another deported nationality, the Soviet Koreans, has also begun agitation for its right to repatriation. Deported Greeks have been relatively successful in their repatriation movement.[16] News also has reached foreign audiences concerning the Yagnobtsi, a Tajik minority forcibly expelled from their native area in the 1960s for the purpose of supplementing the labor force for picking cotton. During this operation many perished, and presently the nation urgently desires repatriation.[17]

Indigenous protest has been expressed by many nationalities. Russian nationalists have protested the loss of Russian roots caused by the regime's intensive and frequently careless industrialization, persecution of Russian Orthodoxy, socialist realism, excessive internationalism, and distortion of Russian history.[18] A second branch of Russian nationalists has arisen which cannot be considered part of the human rights movement but should be mentioned here. An embryonic countermovement, primarily fascist in character and opposed to the human rights movement in general and the Jewish submovement in particular, has grown and apparently receives support from some members of the Soviet elite. Indeed the KGB (Committee for State Security) has attempted to turn Russian nationalist groups in a fascist direction to serve as a popular countervailing power to the human rights movement.[19]

Indigenous protests by non-Russian nations, increasingly in the form of separatist demands, have become prominent. The Baltic nationalities have demonstrated a good deal of dissatisfaction with the regime's russification policies. A number of trials in Latvia and Estonia have taken place against groups formed to combat assimilation or advocate secession from the Soviet Union. The greatest volume of political protest in the Baltic area has come from Lituanians, who have published a wide variety of dissident journals and engaged in several bloody confrontations with police and military troops.

Soviet Belorussians have been relatively quiescent, but a dissident journal (*Listok*) has found its way abroad.[20] Dissent from the Ukrainian nation, particularly in the western area of the republic, has been frequent and has taken a wide variety of organizational forms. Soviet Moldavians have also expressed their opposition to russification and their desire to be attached to Romania.[21]

A number of dissident groups have formed in the Caucasus. Whereas a small number of Armenians have sought emigration, most dissident members of this nation prefer an end to assimilation and some sort of referendum on the future status of their republic within the Soviet Union.[22] Also, Soviet Georgians have protested persecution of the Georgian Orthodox church and corruption of high officials. Of some surprise to foreign observers and Soviet regime alike was a series of bombings and attacks on army depots in 1976 in protest against russification.[23]

Some dissent has also occurred among nationalities in Central Asia. Ethnic disturbances have been reported in Uzbekistan among the Tajik minority whose internal passports had been changed to read

"Uzbek."[24] Poet Annasaltan Kelikova was placed in a psychiatric hospital for her protest against regime policies in Turkmenistan.[25] Finally, Bashkirs and Tatars have advocated a pan-Turkish movement to end discrimination by Russians in the economy, religion, education, and the media.[26]

A major role in national dissent has been played by official regime "ethnographic societies." Russian, Lithuanian, Ukrainian, and other national dissidents have proven themselves quite adept at utilizing these official organs as fronts to preserve and raise popular consciousness about their ethnic heritage. Lithuanian ethnographers, for example, were threatened with arrest by local authorities for attempts to "spread nationalistic views."[27]

Irredentist demands by national dissidents have also increased in recent years. Lithuanian nationalists have protested the lack of religious and cultural facilities for their compatriots in Latvia and Belorussia.[28] Armenian dissidents have opposed official discrimination against fellow nationals in Georgia and Azerbaijan and have demanded the return of areas now part of Turkey.[29]

Increasingly environmental issues have concerned national protesters. Estonian, Lithuanian, and other dissidents have openly criticized the regime's destruction of forests, pollution of the air, and similar side effects of breakneck industrialization and disregard for the nation's natural resources.[30]

National dissidents in the human rights movement have displayed a high level of cultural pluralism. Contrary to some popular notions of nationalism, the dissident groups display little ethnocentrism, exclusionism, chauvinism, racial hatred, or imperialism. This tolerant spirit is exemplified in the editorial policy of a recent underground Lithuanian national journal: "*Aušra* will not provoke nationalist intolerance. It regards as its friends the people of peace and goodwill of all nations who have good intentions toward Lithuanians and wish to share cultural values with her."[31] Likewise the Helsinki Watch groups, established in Lithuania, the Ukraine, Armenia, and Georgia to gather and disseminate information concerning violations of the Helsinki accords, have defended the rights of other nationalities in their republics.

Religious dissent by Orthodox, Catholic, Protestant, and other faiths also has manifested itself.[32] An increased interest in religion, particularly among young people, is evident.[33] Russian Orthodox believers have protested the lack of separation of church and state as seen in the many closures of churches and monasteries, arrests of believers, and the like.[34] Members of the Old Believer sect of the Russian Orthodox church have sent letters of dissent against police infiltration of their congregations and discrimination in housing, taxation, and education.[35] Georgian and Armenian Orthodox believers have opposed corruption within their churches and restrictions on expressions of religious belief.

Catholics in Latvia, Lithuania, Moldavia, and the Ukraine increasingly have made their dissatisfactions known. In 1975, some 5,000 Catholics in Daugavpils, Latvia, sent a letter to the West protesting the threatened closure of their church by the regime.[36] Most active have been Catholics in Lithuania, who have sent protest letters with thousands of signatures and regularly published a number of underground periodicals. Moldavian Catholics have dissented against the almost total lack of churches in their republic. A widespread and vibrant underground church life is also maintained by Uniate Catholics in the Ukraine.

Unofficial dissident Baptists or "Initsiativniki" have managed to protest persistently the severe persecution of their congregation, particularly the frequent arrests of presbyters and the faithful as well as the forced separation of children from parents.[37] Recently, however, members of officially recognized Baptist congregations have protested the close collaboration between their leaders and the regime.[38] Adventists have maintained a widespread publication network, while Pentecostals have established special councils for the purpose of emigration from the Soviet Union. Finally, a number of Buddhists were arrested in Ulan-Ude in Buratya for establishing study circles which attracted many pilgrims.[39]

The religious believers display little dogmatism in their dissent. Rather, a genuine ecumenical spirit appears to pervade the religious submovements, in spite of past antagonisms between some of the faiths.[40] Typical of this spirit was the protest of Russian Orthodox dissident Mikhail Vorozhbit against "persecution of every existing faith in the country."[41]

Strikes by Soviet workers seemingly are "no longer rare."[42] Most of these work actions, as is common in times of economic contraction, have been defensive in character.[43] However, more aggressive action has been taken by the nationwide Association of Free Trade Union Workers in the Soviet Union formed in 1975. The 200 members and 100 candidate members have protested against the "wasters of socialist property, poor work conditions, low pay, high rates of work injuries, rising work output obligations and norms leading to breakage and low-quality output, the increasing rise in prices of basic necessities and products."[44] In the spirit of the Universal Declaration, the union appears to have followed the principle of inclusive recruitment and thus is open to members of many occupations and nationalities. Indeed, the Universal Declaration document seems to have reached the hands of at least a small segment of the Soviet labor force. For instance, a blue-collar worker, Mikhail Kukobaka, was placed in a psychiatric hospital for distributing the Universal Declaration among Mogilev plant workers.[45]

Finally, a number of professional groups have dissented against regime interference with their freedom of creative inquiry. Scientists and writers have protested on behalf of greater autonomy in their work and particularly against heavy regime censorship.[46] Especially militant are dissident artists, who have formed a number of groups for the defense of artistic creativity and held several unofficial public art exhibits.[47] In general, all of these groups press for greater freedom in the search for truth in behalf of all Soviet professions.

FORMS OF PROTEST

This necessarily brief delineation of the structure of the human rights movement reveals the extensiveness of protest in the Soviet Union. No longer can the protesters be described as "a small and dwindling band of Moscow-based dissidents." Reflective of this increased dissent has been the proliferation of protest poems, short stories, novels, letters, essays, journals, and other documents in recent years. The network of underground literature (*samizdat*, or self-publication) has spread widely.[48] Indeed, some *samizdatchiki* have transcended individual publication and advocated greater cooperation among dissidents and the more extensive use of photography (*kolizdat*, or collective publication) as a more efficient means of publishing, reproducing, disseminating, and storing underground material.[49] Other manifestations include *tamizdat* (works published abroad and presently circulating in the underground), *magnitizdat* (underground tapes), *radizdat* (transcriptions of foreign radio broadcasts), *samefir* (illegal radio stations), and *kinizdat* (underground films).

Protesters have become increasingly proficient at using state-owned typographical equipment.[50] However, the actual assemblage of printing presses by dissidents is no longer uncommon. During their search of dissident Vladimir Borisov's apartment, Soviet police found "equipment for a simple, cheap printing process which can easily be set up in domestic conditions."[51] Police also found near the town of Tsesis in Latvia the Baptist "Christian Publishing House," which had 16 tons of paper.[52] The "True and Free Adventists" printing press has also become known.[53] Other modes of information-dissemination include independent press agencies [54] and the "Information Service of the Pentecostal Movement."[55] Of particular interest is the "Free Library," which began circulation in Moscow around 1976: "In spite of heavy expenditures, the Free Library charges nothing for the books it offers—they circulate freely from hand to hand. You, the reader, can pay for them by helping the family of a political prisoner, an innocent labor camp inmate, or anyone who is unjustly persecuted."[56]

As a result of this increased sophistication, the production of underground literature has reached flood proportions. Before discovery by police, the "Christian" publishing house had put out 200,000 Bibles in several Soviet languages. The National Unity Party in Armenia managed to distribute over 10,000 leaflets; even political prisoners have joined in by publishing a journal, the *Chronicle of the Gulag Archipelago*.[57] One might also mention the dissident actors, musicians, and singers, poets, and artists who present unofficial plays, concerts, readings, and exhibits in private apartments.

Of perhaps greater political importance than merely verbal dissent have been several protest demonstrations against Soviet regime policies by the groups mentioned above. For the purpose of analyzing trends in the human rights movement, I have gathered information on a sample of 497 protest demonstrations by these groups in 1965–78, from a wide variety of specialized sources.[58]

The following inclusion criteria were utilized: All events were open and public, unconventional or noninstitutionalized expressions of dissatisfactions against regime policies. All were physical rather than merely verbal expressions of dissatisfaction, such as letters of opposition, declarations, petitions, and the like. All were group protests. Expressions of dissatisfaction by lone individuals or private families, unless specifically delegated by a wider group, were omitted. The demonstrations were public; protests conducted in private dwellings or in prisons, labor camps, or psychiatric hospitals were excluded. All the events were made openly by group members making their identities known; anonymous protests, such as the secret or clandestine hangings of flags or banners, distribution of propaganda leaflets, and the like, were not included. Also omitted were protests by non-Soviet citizens. All the protests were targeted directly and primarily at regime officials or public opinion. Thus, border-escape attempts, demonstrations in front of embassies, public press conferences with foreign correspondents, and so forth were excluded. Finally, cases with insufficient data were eliminated.

At least two caveats are in order. First, since complete data are not available for 1977–78, figures for this period should be interpreted with caution. Statistics for these years will be placed in parentheses to serve as a warning to the reader. Second, since the time series is relatively short, statements concerning "trends" and the like are meant to be suggestive rather than definitive in nature.

On the other hand, since a great deal of disagreement exists regarding the rise or demise of the human rights movement, it is hoped that the quantitative data provided here will serve as a more solid basis from which to draw conclusions. The statistics also may function as a means of making tentative—very tentative—predictions about the human rights movement. In physics and politics, moving entities are much more susceptible to redirection from outside forces than are stable entities. Thus, political movements, in contrast to political structures, are highly sensitive to shocks from their environment, making their development very erratic. Instead of obeying inevitable natural historical laws of development, protest movements are best described as "sporadic rather than sustained,"[59] "markedly unstable,"[60] "mercurial,"[61] displaying "spasms and spurts,"[62] "wild oscillation,"[63] and "no characteristic life cycle"[64] but rather "considerable year-to-year variation."[65] Thus, not only should we expect a great deal of change in statistics across time, but predictions made on the basis of these statistics are likely to be very hazardous.

The following data on protest demonstrations enable us to examine the extensity and intensity of the human rights movement as well as the Soviet regime's response to protester initiatives. Protest extensity can be measured by the frequency of events and the movement's geographical and social dispersion.

Table 7.1 provides figures for the frequency of protest demonstrations. From 1965 to 1970, the number of demonstrations shows minor fluctuations until 1971, when a sharp rise occurred. Thereafter a steady decline took place until 1976, when the frequency of protest events again rose. It is interesting that, although the invasion of Czechoslovakia in 1968 "was a turning point where everyone lost faith,"[66] the protesters did not allow this defeat to discourage future activity.

Two factors—emigration and repression—can account for at least some of the decline of demonstration frequency after 1971. Whereas some 12,877 Jews received emigration visas in 1971, this figure almost tripled to 31,903 in 1972, and 34,933 in 1973. A number of non-Jewish leaders also emigrated or were expelled in this period. Worthy of note, however, is the fact that by 1976 the number of Jewish emigration visas had dropped to 14,213,[67] at which point the number of demonstrations again began to rise. A strong inverse relationship appears to hold between the regime's emigration liberality and protest demonstration frequency.

TABLE 7.1

Frequency of Demonstrations

Year	Number of Demonstrations
1965	18
1966	38
1967	18
1968	33
1969	39
1970	29
1971	77
1972	51
1973	40
1974	36
1975	34
1976	51
1977	(27)
1978	(6)
Total	497

Note: Figure for 1978 is as of May. Parentheses indicate figure based on incomplete data.
Source: Compiled by the author.

In addition, a massive regime offensive against the human rights movement began in 1972, a phenomenon noted by several observers. An increase in dissent is generally followed by an upgrading and strengthening of a regime's coercive organs.[68] Indeed, political protest sparks a tendency in "the police to see themselves as an independent . . . minority asserting itself in the political arena."[69] The growth in dissent in the Soviet Union has led to a strengthening of the KGB particularly.[70] Since Khrushchev's ouster, the KGB has increased the scope of its functions, including greater surveillance over the party, whereas the party has lost some of its administrative control over "ideological diversion."[71]

Whereas the struggle between regime and dissidents prior to 1972 could perhaps be described as a *"Katz-und-Maus Spiel,"*[72] thereafter, in response to the sharp rise in protest frequency in 1971, the regime dramatically increased its administrative repression. KGB chief Yuri Andropov was elevated to full membership in the Politburo. (Another member of the coercive organs, Minister of Defense Marshal Grechko, also rose to full Politburo membership.) In 1972-73 in the Ukraine the KGB staff increased to numbers equivalent to those in

Stalinist times, acquired more modern technology for electronic and visual surveillance, and received salary increases.[73] The KGB continues to grow to such an extent that two dissidents have claimed it to be "a power of an even greater magnitude than the armed forces of the country."[74] Furthermore, the *druzhiny* (volunteer militia) have also increased their antidissident efforts.[75]

More specifically, in December of 1971 the Central Committee initiated a wave of antidissent activity by issuing a decree ordering government organs to suppress the major journal of the human rights movement, the *Chronicle of Current Events*.[76] This general policy was supplemented by later instructions designed to cut communications among the dissidents as well as between dissidents and their supporters both in the Soviet Union and abroad. Prohibitions were placed on the use of telephones contrary to state interests; instructions were given to discourage contacts with foreigners, particularly foreign correspondents; Soviet jamming of the Voice of Israel was initiated; and censorship of foreign media was intensified.[77]

The regime's offensive was felt immediately by virtually all dissident groups. In late 1972, the *Chronicle of Current Events* failed to appear. Civil rights groups experienced heavy repression. A massive propaganda campaign was initiated against dissidents Andrei Sakharov and Alexander Solzhenitsyn. Soviet Jewry reported a secret regime instruction to police officials giving them more latitude in dealing with protesters.[78] A crackdown was ordered on Lithuanian ethnographic clubs harboring national dissidents.[79] Repression in the Ukraine, according to dissident Vyacheslav Chornovil, "was particularly massive and brutal."[80] Eight hundred cases of repression, including 100 arrests, took place in 1972.[81] Major party leaders in the republic were purged for "national deviations."[82] By the end of 1972, Ukrainian *samvydav (samizdat)* had apparently been quashed.[83] Crimean Tatars also reported that in 1972 repression "took on a sharp character."[84] Dissidents in Armenia and Georgia also experienced heavier sanctions.[85] Repression against Lithuanian Catholics increased in 1972, and on November 14, 1973, the secret police decided to liquidate the *Chronicle of the Catholic Church in Lithuania*, a decision which resulted in several trials of dissidents.[86] In places of incarceration, dissidents also were increasingly suppressed. In 1972 a previous decision to release several dissidents confined to mental hospitals was reversed.[87] Also, attempts were made to destroy contacts among political prisoners in labor camps.[88] Yet the revival of protest demonstrations in 1976 tends to support the observation that "repressive policies defeat their purposes, in the long run if not necessarily in the short run."[89]

A second measure of protest extensity is geographical dispersion.[90] Table 7.2 shows the number of republics and localities which
experienced protest demonstrations in 1965–78. The frequencies
range from a low in 1965, to highs in 1970–71 and 1976. Although
the total *volume* of protest demonstrations tended to decline in
1972–75 (see Table 7.1), geographical *dispersion* remained relatively constant in this period. Table 7.2 also reveals a slight tendency
for protest to disperse across the Soviet Union over the entire time
period.

A third measure of protest extensity is provincialization. Whereas
large cities are known for their protest frequency, an extensive
movement also reaches into the provinces. The demonstrations were
coded on a six-point urbanization scale based on the population of
the locality. Table 7.3 gives the mean of the scale for each year.
Although a slight trend toward ruralization after 1971 is visible,
generally protest demonstrations have remained a highly urban
phenomenon. Thus, whereas protest has dispersed geographically
across the Soviet Union, this movement has been more toward other
relatively large cities than toward the countryside.

TABLE 7.2

Frequency of Republics and Localities Experiencing Protest Demonstrations
(N = 497)

Year	Republics	Localities
1965	3	6
1966	6	17
1967	4	8
1968	5	11
1969	6	16
1970	7	21
1971	9	19
1972	7	19
1973	6	19
1974	7	18
1975	6	15
1976	8	24
1977	(7)	(12)
1978	(3)	(3)

Note: Figures for 1978 are as of May. Parentheses indicate figure based on
incomplete data.
Source: Compiled by the author.

TABLE 7.3

Urbanism of Protest Demonstration Locality
(N = 497)

Year	Urbanism Scale Mean
1965	5.2
1966	5.0
1967	5.4
1968	4.8
1969	4.9
1970	4.5
1971	5.2
1972	4.8
1973	5.0
1974	4.7
1975	4.3
1976	4.4
1977	(4.7)
1978	(5.7)

Note: Urbanism scale: (1) village or collective farm; (2) small town; (3) 40,000-99,999; (4) 100,000-499,999; (5) 500,000-999,999; and (6) one million and over. Figures for 1978 are as of May. Parentheses indicate figure based on incomplete data.

Source: Data on population are derived from the 1970 Soviet census as found in *Webster's New Geographical Dictionary* (Springfield, Mass.: Merriam, 1972).

A fourth measure of protest extensity is social dispersion. Long-lived protest movements usually expand their social base.[91] Table 7.4 shows the number of groups involved in protest activities. A rather strong tendency for more social groups to engage in protest demonstrations is evident. Whereas only six groups were reported to have demonstrated in 1965, by 1976 the number had risen to 13. Noteworthy as well is the slight but observable drop in group number in 1972, the period of especially heavy repression. However, the effect of this repression was only short-lived.

Yet this greater diversity in the social base of the human rights movement has not meant a significant increase in lower-class or younger participants. As Table 7.5 shows, the trend, in fact, is toward a slightly increasing *intellectualization* of the movement.[92] (Low mean scores indicate lower-class composition of the demonstrators and vice-versa.) Thus, although an increasing number of groups have made their dissatisfaction with regime policies known, they differ little in social class from previous groups. The difference in mean scores between lowest and highest years is only 1.7. Likewise Table 7.6, in which the events were coded as *one* if the majority of the demonstrators were over 30 and *two* if under 30, shows virtually no change over time.

In sum, the extensity of the human rights movement is a mixed picture. As in other long-lived protest movements, demonstrations in the Soviet Union have tended to increase in frequency, geographical dispersion, and to some extent, the social diversity of participants. On the other hand, there is little evidence of the movement extending into the provinces or to lower-class or younger populations. The human rights movement—at least as regards protest demonstrations—remains a highly urban, middle-class, and adult phenomenon.

Trends in the intensity of the human rights movement can be assessed in part by examining the size and militancy of the protest groups. The means of these scales are presented in Tables 7.7 and 7.8. The size of demonstrating protest groups has remained relatively

TABLE 7.4

Number of Groups Demonstrating
(N = 497)

Year	Number of Groups
1965	6
1966	7
1967	8
1968	9
1969	11
1970	10
1971	9
1972	8
1973	10
1974	13
1975	11
1976	13
1977	(10)
1978	(4)

Note: Includes civil rights intellectuals, civil rights students, Jews, Germans, Crimean Tatars, Meskhetians, Russians, Estonians, Latvians, Lithuanians, Ukrainians, Georgians, Armenians, Uzbeks, Lithuanian Catholics, Uniate Catholics, Russian Orthodox, Georgian Orthodox, unofficial Baptists, official Baptists, Pentecostals, workers, peasants, artists, and singers. Figures for 1978 are as of May. Parentheses indicate figure based on incomplete data.

Source: Compiled by the author.

TABLE 7.5

Social Class of Demonstrating Groups
(N = 497)

Year	Class Scale Mean
1965	3.8
1966	4.2
1967	4.8
1968	3.9
1969	4.5
1970	4.7
1971	5.5
1972	5.1
1973	5.5
1974	5.0
1975	5.0
1976	4.7
1977	(5.1)
1978	(6.0)

Note: Class scale: (1) peasants; (2) peasants and workers; (3) workers; (4) peasants, workers, and intellectuals; (5) workers and intellectuals; (6) students; (7) intellectuals. Reliability = .89. Figure for 1978 is as of May. Parentheses indicate figure based on incomplete data.
Source: Compiled by the author.

constant over time. This phenomenon is particularly remarkable in view of the widespread arrests and emigration of dissidents. Apparently new recruits to the human rights movement have more than replenished gaps in the ranks. Likewise the demonstrators have remained relatively peaceful throughout the course of the movement. Interestingly, although the regime's offensive in 1972 reduced the frequency of protest demonstrations, it had little appreciable effect on their size or militancy. Indeed, in 1971 demonstrators' militancy was higher than at any time previously and remained at approximately that level until 1974. Soviet regime repression apparently reduces dissidents' physical activity but not their psychic anger. Indeed, a number of studies have shown that regime repression of dissidents leads to their tactical radicalization.[93] However, the general distaste for disorder and violence by the anti-Stalinist dissidents, as well as the recruitment of new members to the movement who are generally found to be less militant,[94] have tended to keep the use of militant tactics to a minimum.

REGIME REACTION

We have seen that the regime reacted to increased protest frequency with enhanced administrative repressions. However, individual protest demonstrations may be subject to several ad hoc factors making regime reaction highly arbitrary.[95]

The events were divided into instrumental and expressive demonstrations. Instrumental demonstrations are those at which protesters directly confronted decision-making officials at regime structures with their demands. Expressive demonstrations are those which took place in public parks, streets, squares, and the like, during which protesters merely expressed their dissatisfaction with regime policies to public opinion in hopes of indirectly persuading the regime to make concessions at a later time. Regime concessions at instrumental demonstrations were scored on a scale ranging from total nonresponse to total response to protester demands. Concessions at expressive demonstrations were gauged by a scale ranging from immediate dispersal to complete noninterference.

Tables 7.9 and 7.10 show that the granting of concessions by the

TABLE 7.6

Age of Demonstrating Groups
(N = 497)

Year	Age Scale Mean
1965	1.83
1966	1.95
1967	1.78
1968	1.94
1969	1.90
1970	1.93
1971	1.96
1972	1.78
1973	1.88
1974	1.97
1975	1.88
1976	1.86
1977	(1.93)
1978	(2.00)

Note: Age scale: (1) majority of group under 30 years of age; (2) majority over 30. Reliability = .86. Figure for 1978 as of May. Parentheses indicate figure based on incomplete data.

Source: Compiled by the author.

TABLE 7.7

Size of Demonstrating Groups
(N = 497)

Year	Size Scale Mean
1965	4.0
1966	4.3
1967	4.7
1968	3.5
1969	4.4
1970	3.4
1971	3.0
1972	3.4
1973	3.0
1974	2.7
1975	4.0
1976	3.5
1977	(3.6)
1978	(3.3)

Note: Based on highest estimate. Size scale: (1) 1–19 demonstrators; (2) 20–49; (3) 50–99; (4) 100–149; (5) 150–499; (6) 500–999; (7) 1,000–4,999; (8) 5,000 and over. Reliability = .92. Figure for 1978 is as of May. Parentheses indicate figure based on incomplete data.

Source: Compiled by the author.

regime, as Soviet dissidents continually point out, is highly arbitrary, following little consistent pattern over time. Regime responsiveness to protest group demands at instrumental demonstrations and permissiveness at expressive demonstrations generally fluctuate widely from year to year. Concessions at individual demonstrations apparently follow no consistent general policies across time but rather result from a number of situational variables.

The repressions meted out to Soviet demonstrators by the regime can be seen in Tables 7.11–13. The mean percent of the protest group detained shows an erratic pattern until 1972, when a relatively sharp rise occurred. This level remained constant until 1975. Apparently, detentions of dissident demonstrators followed a random course reflecting regime indecision until 1972 when, as we have seen, a more deliberate antidissent policy emerged. However, injuries to protesters display a quite different pattern. The yearly results of the injury scale mean can be seen in Table 7.11. Two plateaus, 1965–68, when injuries were more common, and 1969–76, when they declined, can be discerned. The light judicial sentences against demonstrators (at least one demonstrator sentenced to 15 days for hooliganism) meted out by the regime show a decline from 1966 to 1972, when they again rose rather sharply. However, heavy judicial sentences (at least one demonstrator sentenced to over 15 days) have remained at a relatively low level.

In sum, the regime's reaction to protest demonstrations, except for detentions and light judicial sentences, which were increased in 1972, follows a relatively erratic course. If the regime has made any consistent behavioral (as opposed to administrative) response to physical protest demonstrations, one finds only partial evidence from the data presented here. One might speculate that the general moderate line of the Brezhnev leadership, which tries to maintain a balance between hard and soft wings of the political elite, has resulted in a vacillating reaction. Also, the data reveal that to some extent the 1972 offensive was relatively short-lived. Whether this rather weak staying power of repression reflects an unwillingness or

TABLE 7.8

Militancy of Demonstrating Groups
(N = 497)

Year	Militancy Scale Mean
1965	1.94
1966	1.92
1967	1.72
1968	2.03
1969	2.13
1970	1.97
1971	2.14
1972	2.00
1973	2.18
1974	1.61
1975	2.44
1976	2.22
1977	(2.26)
1978	(1.83)

Note: Militancy scale: (1) quiet negotiation and nonexhibitive demonstration; (2) exhibitive demonstration; (3) march or motorcade; (4) obstruction; (5) strike or boycott; (6) direct action; (7) attack on regime persons or property. Reliability = .87. Figure for 1978 is as of May. Parentheses indicate figure based on incomplete data.

Source: Compiled by the author.

TABLE 7.9

Concessions at Instrumental Demonstrations
(N = 303)

Year	Concession Scale Mean	N
1965	1.65	13
1966	1.00	22
1967	1.91	11
1968	1.92	25
1969	1.28	18
1970	1.36	22
1971	1.74	58
1972	1.36	29
1973	1.96	23
1974	1.36	22
1975	2.00	19
1976	1.29	24
1977	(1.17)	12
1978	(3.00)	5

Note: Concession scale: (1) demands unmet; (2) unsatisfactory offer made; (3) promises made but unfulfilled; (4) compromise; (5) near total responsiveness; (6) total responsiveness. Reliability = .94. Figures for 1978 are as of May. Parentheses indicate figure based on incomplete data.

Source: Compiled by the author.

an inability of the Brezhnev leadership to maintain a consistently high level of repression is difficult to ascertain at present.

A GROWING COALESCENCE

The growth of "propaganda of the word," by means of *samizdat,* and of "propaganda of the deed," by means of protest demonstrations, has made dissident groups increasingly aware of each other— perhaps to a degree unprecedented since the early Soviet period. This increased awareness has led to a remarkable coalescence of Soviet dissent during the Brezhnev era as seen in numerous instances of verbal support, cooperation at protest demonstrations, mutual financial assistance, and joint membership in various groups.

Verbal support by particular dissident groups for other groups is widespread both within and across general categories. Within the national dissent category, Jews have been supported by Lithuanians and Ukrainians;[96] Belorussians by Lithuanians;[97] Meskhetians by

Georgians and vice-versa;[98] and Germans by Lithuanians.[99] Indeed, Russian dissidents in Vladimir prison in 1976 called for free referenda by non-Russian nationalities concerning their future political status in the Soviet Union.[100] Within the religious dissent category, Russian Orthodox and Uniate Catholics have been supported by Lithuanian Catholics,[101] and Baptists have been backed by Russian Orthodox.[102] Across general categories, Seventh Day Adventists have protested the repression of civil rights dissidents,[103] while the latter have demanded the protection of the workers' right to form free labor unions.[104] Likewise Russian Orthodox have been supported by Jews and vice-versa;[105] Armenians and Germans by civil rights dissidents;[106] and Georgian nationalists by the ecumenical Committee for the Defense of Believers' Rights in the USSR.[107] Here one might also note the increasing support for dissidents from human rights organizations abroad, which have now reached the proportion of a large-scale international movement.[108]

In spite of the high costs and low benefits expected to result from supporting another dissident group at a protest demonstration, a

TABLE 7.10

Concessions at Expressive Demonstrations
(N = 194)

Year	Concession Scale Mean	N
1965	2.41	5
1966	2.01	16
1967	2.15	7
1968	2.76	8
1969	2.49	21
1970	2.30	7
1971	2.12	19
1972	2.18	22
1973	2.06	17
1974	1.92	14
1975	2.46	15
1976	3.41	27
1977	(2.97)	15
1978	(1.00)	1

Note: Concession scale: (1) demonstration dispersed immediately; (2) held for short while but later dispersed; (3) held for duration but harassed; and (4) held for duration without harassment. Reliability = .96. Figures for 1978 are as of May. Parentheses indicate figure based on incomplete data.

Source: Compiled by the author.

TABLE 7.11

Detention of and Injuries to Demonstrators
(N = 497)

Year	Mean Percent Detained	Injury Scale Mean
1965	3.6	1.32
1966	22.4	1.33
1967	2.4	1.43
1968	24.6	1.46
1969	12.0	1.12
1970	5.4	1.13
1971	12.6	1.07
1972	25.1	1.13
1973	27.6	1.19
1974	24.9	1.11
1975	5.3	1.08
1976	12.0	1.13
1977	(19.0)	(1.11)
1978	(7.3)	(1.31)

Note: Reliability of for mean percent detained = .95. Injury scale: (1) none; (2) 1–3; (3) over 3 or entire group if composed of 3 or fewer protesters. Reliability = .88. Figures for 1978 are as of May. Parentheses indicate figure based on incomplete data.
Source: Compiled by the author.

number of such incidents have occurred. Table 7.14 lists both supported and supporting groups for the demonstrations described above. (Since the size of the sample is small, the table should be read with caution.) Groups which protested most frequently (Jews, who account for 35.0 percent of the sample, and Crimean Tatars for 14.5 percent) also received the greatest support. The most supportive are civil rights groups and—perhaps surprisingly—unidentified onlookers. Noteworthy as well is the fact that civil rights groups, composed mainly of intellectuals of the dominant Russian nationality, often support the claims of minority nationalities. Here one should mention also the joint hunger and labor strikes by diverse dissident groups in the camps and other places of incarceration which are far too numerous to detail here.

A further indicator of coalescence is mutual financial assistance. Although dissidents have often rendered aid to families of repressed dissidents in the past, recently such help has taken organized form.[109] Typical is the Social Fund to Help Those Who Are Persecuted and Their Families established by Alexander Solzhenitsyn out of profits from his *Gulag Archipelago*.

The fund has helped hundreds of families of prisoners regardless of nationality, political views, or religious beliefs. Among those who received our assistance have been Russians, Ukrainians, Lithuanians, Jews, Germans, Armenians, Georgians, Estonians, Tatars; Orthodox, Moslems, Judaists, Baptists. The only criterion for distribution of money from the Fund is the level of need of a given family.[110]

In February 1978 it was reported that voluntary contributions to the fund from Soviet citizens had risen sharply.[111]

Finally, joint membership in dissident groups deserves mention. The son of Baptist leader Grigory Vins was named a member of the Ukrainian Helsinki Group; the Initiative Group for the Defense of Human Rights in the USSR accepts members from many nationalities. The Free Trade Union noted above describes itself as "Soviet people from different strata of society . . . of various nationalities and from different localities."[112] In a few cases the coalitions themselves have coalesced. In September 1977, the Committee for the Defense of Believers' Rights in the USSR, the Social Fund to Help Those Who Are Persecuted and Their Families, and the Initiative Group for the De-

TABLE 7.12

Light Judicial Sentences of Demonstrators
(N = 497)

Year	Light Sentence Scale Mean
1965	1.17
1966	1.24
1967	1.22
1968	1.09
1969	1.05
1970	1.04
1971	1.10
1972	1.24
1973	1.10
1974	1.08
1975	1.09
1976	1.04
1977	(1.00)
1978	(1.00)

Note: Light sentence scale: (1) none; (2) at least one demonstrator sentenced to fifteen days incarceration. Reliability = .94. Figure for 1978 is as of May. Parentheses indicate figure based on incomplete data.

Source: Compiled by the author.

TABLE 7.13

Heavy Judicial Sentences of Demonstrators
(N = 497)

Year	Heavy Sentence Scale Mean
1965	1.06
1966	1.13
1967	1.28
1968	1.09
1969	1.00
1970	1.07
1971	1.05
1972	1.10
1973	1.00
1974	1.03
1975	1.03
1976	1.04
1977	(1.04)
1978	(1.00)

Note: Heavy sentence scale: (1) none; (2) at least one demonstrator sentenced to over 15 days incarceration. Reliability = .89. Figure for 1978 is as of May. Parentheses indicate figure based on incomplete data.

Source: Compiled by the author.

fense of Human Rights in the USSR issued a joint appeal for the right of Pentecostals to emigrate.[113]

At least three factors can explain this growing coalescence. First, the emphasis on basic human rights regardless of religion, nationality, or other distinctions as reflected in the Universal Declaration has pervaded dissident circles. Thus we see the political tolerance of civil rights groups, the cultural pluralism of national dissidents, the ecumenism of religious groups, the open recruitment of labor protestors, and the demand for universal intellectual freedom by professional groups. As a result, mutual cooperation is not only possible but also welcomed. In short, the Universal Declaration comprises the "core beliefs" of the human rights movement which "make possible the system of intercell leadership exchange, temporary coalition on specific actions, a flow of financial and other material resources through nonbureaucratic channels, and an often surprising preservation of a united front in the face of external opposition."[114]

Second, the fact that all protest groups are treated by the regime with roughly similar levels of concessions and repressions has tended to create a common enemy. "If several parties face a common opponent, a unifying bond is created between them."[115] Moreover, the severity of repression has increased cohesion and thus the willingness to engage in cooperative activity.[116]

Third, in places of dissident incarceration a remarkably tolerant subculture has developed. Whereas in the past a good deal of conflict arose among political prisoners, particularly among different nationalities,[117] at present much more unity is evident. From Vladimir prison dissident Kronid Lyubarsky described this new cooperative tendency:

> We are all very different . . . Ukrainian patriots . . . Zionists . . . Lithuanians, Latvians, Estonians, Romanians . . . Armenians . . . But in spite of this diversity, we are united. We are all political prisoners in the USSR. . . . This difficult fate that we all share binds us. . . . Even with all of the . . . contrast of our aspirations, we can already now formulate a common platform with which everyone can identify.[118]

TABLE 7.14

Support Structure at Protest Demonstrations
(N = 21)

Supported Group	Supportive Group(s)
Crimean Tatars	Minority nationalities
Crimean Tatars	Civil rights
Crimean Tatars	Civil rights
Crimean Tatars	Unidentified onlookers
Crimean Tatars	Civil rights
Crimean Tatars	Unidentified onlookers
Crimean Tatars	Unidentified onlookers
Jews	Civil rights and Ukrainians
Jews	Civil rights and Ukrainians
Jews	Civil rights
Jews	Civil rights
Civil rights	Lithuanians
Civil rights	Germans
Civil rights	Baptists and unidentified onlookers
Lithuanians	Latvians and Estonians
Lithuanians	Latvians
Baptists	Unidentified onlookers
Baptists	Unidentified onlookers
Uniate Catholics	Ukrainians
Artists	Unidentified onlookers
Ukrainians	Civil rights

Note: Reliability = .88.
Source: Compiled by the author.

Thus the spirit of the Universal Declaration combined with the forced physical proximity of several dissident groups has created some semblance of a united front in places of confinement. Evidence suggests that these cooperative contacts continue after prisoners are released.[119]

Yet dissident unity certainly does not imply uniformity. Growing ideological diversity is characteristic of protest movements. Whereas at early stages dissidents can agree generally on many negative manifestations of the political system, agreement is much more difficult at later stages when positive programs are proposed.[120] Dissident Roy Medvedev makes this point succinctly;

> In 1966–68 . . . we were all united by the demands to stop political repressions . . . and discrimination . . . by protest against . . . the invasion . . . of Czechoslovakia . . . and remnants of Stalinism. . . . But no opposition movement can long act on the basis of *criticism*. . . . The necessity of *positive* programs led to the differences of opinions and to polemics among the dissidents.[121]

Although the protesters can agree generally on the need for the rights embodied in the Universal Declaration but violated by the regime, little agreement exists as to the exact political and social structures necessary to implement and preserve them. However, most dissidents appear to view ideological diversity as necessary and even functional for the movement. According to dissident Andrei Amalrik,

> The fact that Sakharov, Solzhenitsyn, Grigorenko, Maksimov, Plyushch, Orlov, Medvedev, Amalrik and others criticize each other means that after several years of forced uniformity of views we understand the importance of a diversity of views and mutual criticism, if we want to develop the best strategy for the transition of our country to democracy.[122]

So although divisions exist, they have remained primarily at the verbal level. Mutual tolerance and cooperation is by far the dominant strain in the movement.

CONCLUSION

This broad aerial view of the human rights movement has shown that Khrushchev's secret speech had deep repercussions not only throughout the Communist world but at home as well. Dissatisfied groups increasingly questioned their conditions and began to manifest their dissent in numerous forms of verbal protest. The basis of new demands was no particular ideology but rather the principles of the Universal Declaration of Human Rights. With the Sinyavskii-Daniel trial, the creed increasingly became the deed as these groups came out of their private lives and into the streets. Protest demonstrations increased in frequency, to some extent in diversity of social base, and in geographical dispersion. Widespread emigration and arrests had little effect on their size and militancy. Concomitantly, dissidents became increasingly aware of other dissatisfied groups, and the extent of mutual cooperation rose dramatically.

In response, the Soviet regime acted with a high level of vacillation until 1972, when a wide-ranging and intensive attack on the human rights movement was launched. Dissidents rightly labeled this period a "crisis" in the movement.[123] However, the depressant effect of intensified repression on the movement was short-lived. After a few years the frequency of protest demonstrations returned to high levels. The movement showed little sign of permanent damage. As dissident Valentin Moroz told his Ukrainian prosecutors, "You hurled a stone at every spark of life on the Ukrainian horizon, and every stone became a bomerang."[124]

Neither system nor movement shows any clear sign of giving in. Although the movement has won some concessions, these have been ad hoc responses to a series of particular protests rather than any change in principle. Indeed, the dissidents frequently report a widespread nostalgia for "the good old Stalinist days" on the part of many Soviet officials. A Crimean party bureaucrat was quoted as telling Jews wishing to emigrate, "It is too bad that times have passed when we could deal properly with people like you."[125] By the same token, an increasingly militant stance by the human rights movement is not improbable. In protest movements repression is often followed by greater dissident activity as well as ideological and tactical radicalization.

Although the future trajectory of the human rights movement and regime reaction is extremely difficult to predict, the possibility that the stand-off will develop into an escalating dialectic of conflict cannot be ruled out. Whatever the remote future, the dissidents have dug deeply into Soviet political ground and are not likely to be uprooted for some time to come.

NOTES

1. Charles Tilly, *From Mobilization to Revolution* (Menlo Park; Calif.: Addison-Wesley, 1978), p. 9; William Cameron, *Modern Social Movements: A Sociological Outline* (New York: Random House, 1966), pp. 7-25; Norman Fainstein and Susan

Fainstein, *Urban Political Movements: The Search for Power by Minority Groups in American Cities* (Englewood Cliffs, N.J.: Prentice-Hall, 1974), pp. xi-xvi, 237-60; and Paul Wilkinson, *Social Movement* (London: Pall Mall, 1971), p. 46.

2. Michael Lewis, "The Negro Protest in Urban America," in *Protest, Reform, and Revolt: A Reader in Social Movements*, ed. Joseph Gusfield (New York: John Wiley, 1970), pp. 151-53.

3. United Nations, *The Universal Declaration of Human Rights: A Standard of Achievement* (New York: United Nations Office of Public Information, 1963).

4. See Rudolf Heberle, "Observations on the Sociology of Social Movements," *American Sociological Review* 14, no. 2 (June 1949); 346-57.

5. "Paradoksy Grenoblskoi vystavki," *Kontinent* 1 (1974); 203.

6. Mark Hagopian, *The Phenomenon of Revolution* (New York: Dodd-Mead, 1975), p. 155; Peter Lupsha and Catherine MacKinnon, "Domestic Political Violence, 1965-1971," in *Violence as Politics: A Series of Original Essays*, ed. Herbert Hirsch and David Perry (New York: Harper & Row, 1973), p. 13; Clarence King, *Social Movements in the United States* (New York: Random House, 1956), p. 41; and Herbert Blumer, "Social Movements," in *Studies in Social Movements: A Social Psychological Perspective*, ed. Barry McLaughlin (New York: Free Press, 1969), pp. 8-10.

7. Fainstein and Fainstein, *Urban Political Movements*, pp. 93-98, 182.

8. Robert Allen and Sergius Yakobson, *Aspects of Intellectual Ferment and Dissent in the Soviet Union* (Washington, D.C.: Subcommittee to Investigate the Administration of the Internal Security Act and Other Internal Security Laws of the Committee on the Judiciary, United States Senate, 1968), p. 31.

9. An excellent comprehensive treatment can be found in Edward Corcoran, "Dissension in the Soviet Union: The Group Basis and Dynamics of Internal Opposition" (Ph.D. diss., Columbia University, 1977). See also Borys Lewytzskyj, *Politische Opposition in der Sowjetunion, 1960-1972: Analyse und Dokumentation* (Munich: Deutscher Taschenbuch Verlag, 1972); Valery Chalidze, *Prava cheloveka i Sovetskii Soyuz* (New York: Khronika Press, 1974); and Peter Smirnov, ed., *Za pyat let . . . dokumenty i pokazaniya* (Paris: La Presse Libre, 1972).

10. See Ya. Trushnovich, ed., *A. Sakharov v borbe za mir* (Frankfurt: Posev, 1973); *Politicheskii dnevnik* (for 1964-70 and 1965-70) (Amsterdam: Herzen Foundation, 1972); Roy Medvedev and Raisa Lert, eds., *Dvadtsatyi vek: Obshchestvenno-politicheskii i literaturnyi almanakh* (London: TCD, 1976); Pavel Litvinov et al., *Samosoznanie: sbornik statei* (New York: Khronika Press, 1976); Yury Glazov, *Tesnye vrate: Vozrozhdenie Russkoi intelligentsii* (London: Overseas Publications Interchange, 1973); *Dokumenty komiteta prav cheloveka* (New York: International League for the Rights of Man, 1972); Democrats of Russia, Ukraine, and the Baltics, *Programma demokraticheskogo dvizheniya Sovetskogo Soyuza* (Amsterdam: Herzen Foundation, 1970); Democratic Movement of the Soviet Union, *Memorandum demokratov verkhovnomu Sovetu SSSR* (Frankfurt: Posev, 1972); Vadim Belotserkovskii, ed., *Demokraticheskie alternativy: sbornik statei i dokumentov* (Achberg: Achberger Verlagsanstalt, 1976); Andrei Amalrik, *Prosushchestvuet li Sovetskii Soyuz do 1984 goda?* (Herzen Foundation, 1969); and N. Alekseev and S. Zorin, *Vremya ne zhdet: Nasha strana naknoditsya na povorotnom punkte istorii* (Frankfurt: Posev, 1970).

11. Walter Connor, "Differentiation, Integration, and Political Dissent in the USSR," in *Dissent in the USSR: Politics, Ideology, and People*, ed. Rudolf Tökes (Baltimore: Johns Hopkins University Press, 1975), p. 153; Teresa Rakowska-Harmstone, *Russia and Nationalism in Central Asia: The Case of Tadzhikistan* (Baltimore: Johns Hopkins University Press, 1970), p. 5; Bohdan Bociurkiw, "Soviet Nationalities Policy and Dissent in the Ukraine," *World Today* 30, no. 5 (May 1974); 214-26; Abraham Brumberg, "Dissent in Russia," *Foreign Affairs* 52, no. 4 (July 1974); 798.

12. *Le Monde*, February 4, 1976.

13. K.R. Minogue, *Nationalism* (Baltimore: Penguin, 1967), p. 15. On the Soviet nationalities problem, see Roman Kupchinsky, ed., *Natsionalnyi vopros v SSSR: Sbornik dokumentov* (Munich: Suchastnist, 1975).

14. See Avram Shifrin, *Chetvertoe izmerenie* (Frankfurt: Posev, 1973); Alexander Galich, *Generalnaya repetitsiya* (Frankfurt: Posev, 1974); and Ilya Zilberberg. *Neobkhodimyi razgovor s Solzhenitsynym* (Sussex: Ilya Zilberberg, 1976).

15. Edige Kirimal, *Der Nationale Kampf der Krimtürken* (Emsdetten: Lechte, 1952); *Tashkentskii protsess: Sud nad desyatyu predstavitelyami krymskotatarskogo naroda (1 Iyulya-5 Avgusta 1969 g.)* (Amsterdam: Herzen Foundation, 1976).

16. Jeremy Azrael, *Emergent Nationality Problems in the USSR* (Santa Monica: Rand, 1977), p. 23.

17. *Arkhiv samizdata* (Munich: Radio Liberty Research), 3199 (hereafter AS); *Khronika zashchity prav v SSSR* 29 (January-March 1978).

18. *Dve press-konferentsii (K sborniku "Iz-pod glyb")* (Paris: YMCA Press, 1975); see also John Dunlop, ed., *Vserossiiskii Sotsial-Khristianskii Soyuz Osvobozhdeniya Naroda: Programma, sud, v tyurmakh i lageryakh* (Paris: YMCA Press, 1975).

19. *Politicheskii dnevnik*, for 1964-70, p. 667, and for 1965-70, p. 153; Roy Medvedev, *Kniga o sotsialisticheskoi demokratii*, pp. 26, 101-10; Alexander Yanov, "Na polputi k Leontievu," in Belotserkovskii, ed., *Demokraticheskie alternativy*, p. 193.

20. Stephan Horak, "Belorussia: Modernization, Human Rights, Nationalism," in *Nationalism and Human Rights: Processes of Modernization in the USSR*, ed. Ihor Kamenetskii (Littleton) Colo.: Libraries Unlimited, 1977), p. 139.

21. Lewytzkyj, *Politische Opposition*, p. 38.

22. *Delo Airikyana* (New York: Khronika Press, 1977).

23. See AS 2869, 3114; *Samizdat Bulletin* 62 (June 1978).

24. *Khronika tekushchikh sobytii* 8 (June 1969) (hereafter *Khronika*).

25. *Samizdat Bulletin* 22 (February 1975).

26. AS 3085-87.

27. *Chronicle of the Catholic Church in Lithuania* 23. (June 1976).

28. *Elta Information Service* 225 (January 1978); *Chronicle of the Catholic Church in Lithuania* 24. (October 1976).

29. *Khronika zashchity prav* 28 (October-December 1977); Mikhail Agursky, "Natsionalyi vopros v SSSR," *Kontinent* 10 (1976); 157; Andrei Sakharov, *My Country and the World* (New York: Random House, 1975), p. 28; Edward Oganessyan, "On the Oppression of the Armenian People," in *The International Sakharov Hearing*, ed. Marta Harasowska and Orest Okhovych (Baltimore: Smoloskyp, 1977), pp. 227-29.

30. *Latvian Information Bulletin* 2, no. 78 (April 1970); "Protest against Soviet Industrialization Ills in Lithuania," *Baltic Review* 33 (January 1967); 22-31; *Chronicle of the Catholic Church in Lithuania* 20 (December 1975).

31. *Chronicle of the Catholic Church in Lithuania*, 20 (December 1975).

32. See D. Konstantinov, *Religioznoe dvizhenie soprotivleniya v SSSR* (London: SBONR, 1967).

33. "Iz press-konferentsii A.I. Solzhenitsyna korrespondentam Madridskikh gazet," *Kontinent* 11 (1977); 19-28; *Right to Believe* 3 (1977); Michael Bourdeaux et al., *Religious Liberty in the Soviet Union: WCC and USSR—A Post-Nairobi Documentation* (Keston: Centre for the Study of Religion and Communism, 1976), p. 5.

34. A. Levitin, *Zashchita very v SSSR* (Paris: Ikhthus, 1966); Dimitry Konstantinov, *Gonimaya tserkov: Russkaya pravoslavnaya tserkov v SSSR* (New York: All-Slavic, 1967); A. Krasnov, *Stromaty* (Frankfurt: Posev, 1972); Dimitry Dudko, *O nashem upovanii: besedy—Moskva, 1974* (Paris: YMCA Press, 1976).

35. Bourdeaux et al., *Religious Liberty*, p. 67.

36. Radio Liberty, *Roman Catholics in Latvia Petition USSR Government* (Munich: Radio Liberty Research, 1976).

37. See *Odessa-Prozess: Gerichsverhandlung gegen Gläubige der Evangeliumschristen-Baptisten in der Stadt Odessa, 2-7 Februar 1967* (Stuttgart: Missionsbund Licht im Osten, 1969).

38. Michael Bourdeaux, ed., *Religious Minorities in the Soviet Union* (London: Minority Rights Group, 1977), p. 16.

39. A. Pyatigorskii, "Ukhod Dandarona," *Kontinent* 3 (1975): 151-60.

40. Bourdeaux et al., *Religious Liberty*, p. 41.

41. *Samizdat Bulletin* 61 (May 1978).

42. Dimitry Panin, "Illegality and Arbitrary Rule in the USSR," in Harasowska and Olhovych, eds., *Sakharov*, p. 107. See also Valery Chalidze, *Lektsii o pravovom polozhenii rabochikh v SSSR* (New York: Khronika Press, 1976).

43. Edward Shorter and Charles Tilly, *Strikes in France: 1830-1968* (London: Cambridge University Press, 1974), p. 90; Jon Amsden and Stephen Brier, "Coal Miners on Strike: The Transformation of Strike Demands and the Formation of a National Union," *Journal of Interdisciplinary History* 7, no. 4 (Spring 1977): 605-06.

44. *Newsletter in the Defense of Human Rights* 1, no. 6 (April 1978).

45. *Samizdat Bulletin* 60 (April 1978).

46. Zhores Medvedev, *Mezhdunarodnoe sotrudnichestvo uchenykh i natsionalnye granitsy i taina perepiski okhranyaetsya zakonom* (London: Macmillan, 1972).

47. See Galerie Altmann Carpentier, *Mihail Chemiakin: St. Petersbourg 1976* (Paris: Galerie Altmann Carpentier, 1976); Alexander Glezer, "Dvadtsat let spustya," *Kontinent* 6 (1976): 389-410, and *Iskusstvo pod buldozerom: sinyaya kniga* (London: Overseas Publications Interchange, 1976); Alexander Glezer and Mikhail Shemyakin, eds., *La Peinture Russe Contemporaine* (Paris: Palais des Congres, 1976); and Mikhail Shemyakin, ed., *Apollon-77* (Paris: Graphic Arts of Paris, 1977).

48. For an excellent survey, see Yuri Maltsev, *Volnaya russkaya literatura: 1955-1975* (Frankfurt: Posev, 1976).

49. S. Topolev, "From *Samizdat* to *Kolizdat*," in *The Political, Social and Religious Thought of Russian Samizdat: An Anthology*, ed. Michael Meerson-Aksenov and Boris Shragin (Belmont, Mass.: Nordland, 1977), pp. 489-501; *Samizdat Bulletin* 51 (July 1977).

50. Maltsev, *Volnaya russkaya literatura*, p. 11.

51. *Samizdat Bulletin* 51 (July 1977).

52. *Samizdat Bulletin* 35 (March 1976).

53. Bourdeaux et al., *Religious Liberty*, p. 92.

54. *Khronika zashchity prav v SSSR* 28 (October-December 1977); and *Khronika* 46 (August 1977).

55. AS 1942.

56. *Samizdat Bulletin* 52 (August 1977).

57. Vyacheslav Chronovil and Boris Penson, "Dialog za kolyuchei provolokoi," *Kontinent* 6 (1976): 201; *Arkhiv Khroniki: Prilozhenie k "Khronike tekushchikh sobytii,"* no. 2 (New York: Khronika Press, 1977), pp. 5-88.

58. The events were selected on the basis of reportage in at least one source and thus cannot be considered a random sample. On the authenticity, accuracy, objectivity, and completeness of the sources and the representativeness of the sample, see the author's "Protest Uses of Symbolic Politics" (Ph.D. diss., University of Kansas, 1978).

59. Clifford Anderson and Betty Nesvold, "A Skinnerian Analysis of Conflict Behavior: Walden II Goes Cross-National," *American Behavioral Scientist* 15, no. 6 (July-August 1972): 907.

60. Seymour Lipset, *Student Politics* (New York: Basic Books, 1967), p. viii.

61. Richard Peterson and John Bilorusky, *May 1970: The Campus Aftermath of Cambodia and Kent State* (Berkeley: Carnegie Commission on Higher Education, 1971), pp. 80–81.

62. Herbert Aptheker, *American Negro Slave Revolts* (New York: Columbia University Press, 1943), p. 196.

63. Ted Robert Gurr, *Rogues, Rebels, and Reformers: A Political History of Urban Crime and Conflict* (Beverly Hills, Calif.: Sage, 1976), p. 35.

64. Cameron, *Modern Social Movements*, pp. 27–28.

65. Shorter and Tilly, *Strikes in France*, p. 48.

66. Irina Kirk, *Profiles in Russian Resistance* (New York: Quadrangle, 1975), p. 221.

67. Soviet Jewry Research Bureau, *Emigration Statistics: Soviet Jews* (New York: National Conference on Soviet Jewry, 1977).

68. Joe Feagin and Harlan Hahn, *Ghetto Revolts: The Politics of Violence in American Cities* (New York: Macmillan, 1973), pp. 227–33, 238; George O'Connor, *Civil Disorders: After-Action Reports* (Washington, D.C.: International Association of Chiefs of Police, 1968).

69. Jerome Skolnick, *The Politics of Protest: A Report to the Task Force on Violent Aspects of Protest and Confrontation of the National Commission on the Causes and Prevention of Violence* (New York: Simon and Schuster, 1969), p. 278.

70. See Jerry Hough, "The Soviet System: Petrification or Pluralism," *Problems of Communism* 2 (March–April 1972); 30; Roy Medvedev, *Kniga o sotsialisticheskoi demokratii*, pp. 194–97; Alekseev and Zorin, *Vremya ne zhdet*, p. 41; Kenneth Farmer, "Ukrainian Nationalism and Soviet Nationalities Policy: 1957–1972" (Ph.D. diss., University of Wisconsin, 1977); *Documents of the Ukrainian Public Group to Promote the Implementation of the Helsinki Accords* (Washington, D.C.: Helsinki Guarantees for Ukraine Committee, 1978).

71. Zhores Medvedev, "Since Khrushchev," *Soviet Studies* 28, no. 3 (July 1976); 432.

72. Lewytzkyj, *Politische Opposition*, p. 47.

73. *The Ukrainian Herald Issue 7–8; Ethnocide of Ukrainians in the USSR* (Spring 1974) (Baltimore: Smoloskyp, 1976), pp. 26–27, 125–27, 131.

74. T. Khodorovich and Viktor Nekipelov, in *Samizdat Bulletin* 54 (October 1977).

75. Panin, "Illegality and Arbitrary Rule," p. 107. See also William Jones, "Maintaining Public Order in the Soviet Union: The Militia and the MVD in the Post-Khrushchev Era" (Ph.D. diss., Duke University, 1976).

76. Radio Free Europe, *Civil Rights Journal Frightens the Central Committee into Action* (Munich: Radio Free Europe Research, 1972).

77. *Sbornik dokumentov obshchestvennoi gruppy sodeistviya vypolneniyu khelsinkskikh soglashenii* no. 1 (New York: Khronika Press, 1977), p. 11; Radio Liberty, *New Telephone Restrictions in the USSR* (Munich: Radio Liberty Research, 1972); Leonard Schroeter, *The Last Exodus* (New York: Universe Books, 1974), p. 33.

78. *News Bulletin on Soviet Jewry* 58 (April 18, 1975).

79. *Violations of Human Rights in Soviet-Occupied Lithuania*, vol. 3 (Glenside Pann: Lithuanian American Community, 1973), p. 23.

80. "Letter to President Ford," August 1, 1975, in *Psychiatric Abuse of Political Prisoners in the Soviet Union: Testimony by Leonid Plyushch* (Washington, D.C.: Subcommittee on International Organizations of the Committee on International Relations, House of Representatives, Ninety-Fourth Congress, Second Session, March 30, 1976), p. 80.

81. *Samizdat Bulletin* 34 (February 1976); *Trials in Ukraine 1972* (Baltimore: Smoloskyp, 1973).

82. *Ukrainian Herald*.

83. Farmer, "Ukrainian Nationalism," p. 279.

84. AS 1189.

85. Hedrick Smith, "Soviet Jewry: Carter and Human Rights," in *National Conference on Soviet Jewry Leadership Assembly: Selected Speeches*, ed. Jonathan Schenker (Washington, D.C.: National Conference on Soviet Jewry, 1977), p. 29; *Ukrainian Herald*, p. 138; Stephen Chorney, "From the Ems Ukase to the Twenty-Fifth Congress of the CPSU," *Ukrainian Quarterly* 32, no. 4 (Winter 1976); 359.

86. *Violations*, p. 53; *Chronicle of the Catholic Church in Lithuania* 8 (December 1973); *Elta* 182 (May–June 1974).

87. Sidney Bloch and Peter Reddaway, *Psychiatric Terror: How Soviet Psychiatry Is Used to Suppress Dissent* (New York: Basic Books, 1977), pp. 287–88.

88. *Samizdat Bulletin* 12 (April 1974).

89. Ted Robert Gurr, *Why Men Rebel* (Princeton: Princeton University Press, 1970), p. x.

90. Feagin and Hahn, *Ghetto Revolts*, p. 118; Alexander Astin and Alan Bayer, "Campus Unrest, 1970–71: Was It Really All That Quiet?" *Educational Record* 52, no. 4 (Fall 1971); 301–13; and John Horn and Paul Knott, "Activist Youth of the 1960s: Summary and Prognosis," *Science* 171, no. 3975 (March 12, 1971); 977–85.

91. Tse-tsung Chow, *The May Fourth Movement: Intellectual Revolution in Modern China* (Stanford: Stanford University Press, 1960); Armaud Mauss, "The Lost Promise of Reconciliation: New Left vs. Old Left," *Journal of Social Issues* 27, no. 1 (January 1971); 1–20; Skolnick, *Politics of Protest*, p. 22.

92. A random sample of 20 percent of the events was coded by an independent observer trained in Soviet politics and social science techniques but unaware of the purposes of the study. The reliability coefficients (Pearson's r's) are given under the appropriate tables.

93. James Short and Marvin Wolfgang, *Collective Violence* (Chicago: Aldine, 1972), pp. 20–21; Harold Jacobs, *Weatherman* (San Francisco: Ramparts, 1970), p. 173.

94. William Morgan, "Campus Conflict as Formative Influence," in Short and Wolfgang, *Collective Violence*, p. 291.

95. Julian Foster and Durward Long, "The Dynanics of Institutional Response," in *Protest: Student Activism in America*, ed. Foster and Long (New York: William Morrow, 1970), p. 420).

96. Algirdas Landsbergis, "Orvell i Kafka vse eshche zhivy v Litve," *Kontinent* 5 (1975); 209; *Elta* 227 (March 1978); *Documents*, p. 18.

97. *Elta* 225 (January 1978).

98. *Khronika* 45 (May 1977).

99. *Bridges* 1, no. 9 (December 1977).

100. Vladimir Bukovskii, "Russkie politzaklyuchennye Vladimirskoi tyurmy o provedenii natsionalnykh referendumov," *Kontinent* 11 (1977); 3–8.

101. *Chronicle of the Catholic Church in Lithuania* 23 (June 1976) and 28. (June 1977).

102. Bourdeaux et al., *Religious Liberty*, p. 44.

103. *Khronika* 45 (May 1977).

104. Vladimir Bukovskii et al., "Po povodu sozdannogo v SSSR svobodnogo profsoyuza v zashchitu rabochikh," *Kontinent* 15 (1978); 256.

105. Dudko, *O nashem upovarii*, p. 260; AS 3142.

106. Andrei Sakharov, *O pisme Aleksandra Solzhenitsyna "Vozhdyam Sovetskogo Soyuza"* (New York: Khronika Press, 1974), p. 12; *Delo Airikyana*, pp. 36–41.

107. *Khronika* 45 (May 1977).

108. Arthur Blaser and Stephen Saunders, "Human Rights Non-Governmental Organizations: A Study of a Social Movement," (Paper prepared for the annual meeting of the Midwest Political Science Association, Chicago, April 20–22, 1978).

109. See AS 3136 on the Fund of Donations for Assistance to Armenian Political Prisoners and Their Families.

110. Natalya Solzhenitsyna, "Pismo," *Kontinent* 15 (1978); p. 12.

111. *Samizdat Bulletin* 62 (June 1978).

112. *Newsletter in the Defense of Human Rights* 1, no. 6 (April 1978).

113. AS 3146.

114. Luther Gerlach, "Movements of Revolutionary Change: Some Structural Characteristics," *American Behavioral Scientist* 14, no. 6 (July-August 1971); 824.

115. Lewis Coser, *The Functions of Social Conflict* (New York: Free Press, 1956), p. 140.

116. Raymond Mack and Richard Snyder, "The Analysis of Social Conflict: Towards an Overview and Synthesis," *Journal of Conflict Resolution* 1, no. 2 (June 1957); 215; William Gamson, *The Strategy of Social Protest* (Homewood, Ill.: Dorsey, 1975), p. 103.

117. Alexander Dolgun, *An American in the Gulag* (New York: Ballantine, 1975), p. 147; Harasowska and Olhovych, *Sakharov*, pp. 54–56.

118. *Samizdat Bulletin* 58 (Feburary 1978).

119. Morris Brafman and Rebecca Rass, *From Moscow to Jerusalem: The Dramatic Story of the Jewish Liberation Movement and Its Impact on Israel* (New York: Shengold, 1976), pp. 117–18.

120. Clarence King, *Social Movements in the United States* (New York: Random House, 1956), p. 43; Elena Poniatowska, *Massacre in Mexico* (New York: Viking, 1971), p. 122.

121. Medvedev and Lert, *Dvadtsatyi vek*, p. 7.

122. "Pismo," *Kontinent* 10 (1976); 15.

123. Natalya Gorbanevskaya, "Neskolko Slov v 'Posleslovie,'" *Kontinent* 12 (1977); 224.

124. *Boomerang: The Works of Valentyn Moroz* (Baltimore: Smoloskyp, 1974), p. 2.

125. *News Bulletin on Soviet Jewry*, September 25, 1971.

8

DEVELOPMENTS IN IDEOLOGY

Donald R. Kelley

In its early years, the Brezhnev regime eschewed any sweeping ideological statement reminiscent of the former first secretary's penchant for devising schemata and timetables allegedly charting the future evolution of Soviet society. While the overly optimistic party program set forward at the Twenty-Second Party Congress in 1961— a program which promised the first visible stages of the transition to full communism by the 1980s—was never officially abrogated, virtually all reference to its pronouncements and promises disappeared from official writings, save only the obvious paean that communism would eventually emerge first in the Soviet Union. The program's more specific statements dealing with the emergence of the so-called all-people's state, the increasing role of public and mass organizations, and the implicit changes taking place within the Communist Party of The Soviet Union (CPSU) itself became equally invisible, in part because they, like the program itself, served as a pointed reminder of Khrushchev's once dominant presence, and also because their practical significance in terms of the continued tenure of the state as a functioning political machine and the role of the party quickly acquired disquieting implications.

Much of the new regime's reticence on ideological matters—and its conveniently faulty memory concerning the innovations of the Khrushchev era—can easily be explained by the political situation after the coup. Faced with the need to restore a degree of harmony within the party itself, and especially among the middle to higher level echelons who had felt imperiled by Khrushchev's efforts to transform the party along managerial lines, the Brezhnev regime responded with a cautious policy of stressing both the themes of stability—in other words, the "respect of cadres" approach discussed earlier—and of a return to more traditional definitions of the party's ideologically justified role in society. While the CPSU was never urged to forgo its important role as the "guiding force" in the society and economy, it was reminded, at least until the late 1960s, that its traditionally defined ideological preeminence—that is, the pre-Khrushchev notions of the party's role and the style of party leadership—had continuing relevance. It is in this realm that the regime came closest to the conservative restoration envisioned by many Western commentators. The return to ideological orthodoxy and especially the renewed emphasis placed on ideologically justified exhortations for economic performance and discipline in the place of the sorts of material incentives stressed during the Khrushchev era did seem to turn the clock backwards, at least in terms of the former first secretary's efforts to alter the party's role in society and to rationalize the levers and incentives for economic performance. Clearly the tone, as well as the mechanisms, of party rule had changed under the new regime, and in the mid and late 1960s, both Soviet and Western commentators undoubtedly were wondering where the trend toward orthodoxy would end.

It ended when the new leadership discovered that it too faced many of the problems of its predecessor and rediscovered the convenient malleability of its Marxist-Leninist heritage both to define a new sense of legitimacy and to provide the necessary fertile ground for the introduction of new notions of the CPSU's role and relationship with the society. Like several generations of Soviet leaders before it, the Brezhnev regime quickly came to recognize that while ideology per se provides only the most general prescriptions in terms of concrete guidance for public and party policy, it nonetheless can be used to legitimate and provide a receptive intellectual milieu for changes desired by top leadership. While the specifics of this reactivization of a transformationist ideology will be discussed at length below—they amount to no less than the development of a new dialectical stage of "developed socialism" to characterize the Soviet Union of the 1970s and 1980s and to chart the course of future development—one must now consider the more general place of ideology per se within the Brezhnev era.

As with so many other areas, a continuing paradox marks the regime's attempt to define the notion of developed socialism as the major theoretical centerpiece of contemporary Soviet life. On the one hand, top leadership remains committed to a fundamental political conservatism in terms of its "respect for cadres" and its unwillingness to undertake extensive personnel changes for either political or programmatic reasons. Hence developed socialism is, of political necessity, an evolutionary stage marked most significantly by its own inherent stability (one of the natural consequences of the new, higher level of maturity, Soviet theorists would argue) and by the slow-paced and untraumatic nature of its evolution toward even higher socioeconomic forms, which are set off inestimably into the future. Simply put, it is in political terms the epitome of a slowly evolving, mature system whose own inherent laws of development are at once sufficiently predictable to reassure party cadres that the capricious, "harebrained" pace of change characteristic of the Khrushchev era is a thing of the past and sufficiently flexible and forward-looking to hold forth the future of an even more mature socialist system gradually transforming itself into full communism.

But, on the other hand, developed socialism, both as a mature form of industrial society and as an embodiment of a continuing scientific and technological revolution of profound implications for all aspects of national life, itself contains its own imperatives in terms of the inexorable advance of science and industry and the commensurate changes that must occur in terms of the party's role in society and the mechanisms and style of governance. It is, in fact, a reformist imperative, containing the rationalizations and justifications needed to legitimate the regime's new-found interest in modernizing the economy and fine tuning the mechanisms of party and state rule to suit the needs of a mature industrial society tentatively on the eve of even more significant transformations as it advances through the second industrial revolution.

If, on the one hand, the doctrine is intended to reassure conservative forces within the party and state that the rationalization and modernization of political and economic life will be accomplished only with a careful regard for their views and prerogatives, then, on the other, it is intended to state in unequivocal terms the nature of the current tasks confronting the regime if it is to perform its proper progressive role and capitalize on the potential of the scientific and technological revolution to advance the society toward communism. While the notion of developed socialism carries with it no specific timetable for future transformations, as did Khrushchev's overly optimistic projections of the Twenty-Second Party Congress, it nonetheless clearly sets forth the current tasks confronting the leadership. It is not accidental, as the saying goes, that those tasks are indeed the substance of the regime's attempts to modernize the economy and state administration through the application of both Western technology and managerial methods. As a whole, the scientific and technological revolution means no less than the rationalization of the "scientific" processes of social and economic planning and a subtle alteration of the role of the party itself, which, through its mastery of the new techniques of scientific management and its acceptance of the modernization imperatives of developed socialism, is once again to assume an activist and transformationist role in social development. Unlike the frenetic and occasionally populist tone such activism attained in the Khrushchev era, the new-found role for the party is more cautious, better planned, and more "scientific" in terms of its ability to rationalize and fine tune the mechanisms of party and state. But the imperative is nonetheless clear: the party must act *now* if it is to lead in the transformation of the society and economy to higher socioeconomic forms, and it must accept *now* the need for its own internal modernization and an alteration of its style of leadership.

There is another political dimension to the concept of "developed socialism" in addition to its emergence as a theoretical justification for the modernizing and reformist bent of the Brezhnev regime from the late 1960s onward. No less than earlier Soviet leaders, Brezhnev has sought to place his stamp not only the style of regime politics during his tenure as general secretary—an impact discussed at length in previous chapters—but also upon the characterization of the epoch itself. Seen in this light, developed socialism must be read, at least in part, as an important aspect of that effort; as a distinctive and presumably forward-looking stage in the dialectical evolution of Soviet society, it embodies the sense of cautious albeit purposive reformism that has characterized virtually all other facets of Brezhnev's rule. Like the new "Brezhnev" constitution, it is meant to summarize the attainments of the regime and suggest the "business-like" tone of its further development.

THE EVOLUTION OF DEVELOPED SOCIALISM
AS DOCTRINE AND STRATEGY

The passage of the concept of developed socialism from an obscure term once used by Lenin to the centerpiece of current Soviet theory is itself an instructive study in the political usage of ideology.[1] Beginning in 1967, Brezhnev began to refer occasionally to "a developed socialist society" or to the notion of "mature communism," but there was little in his early comments to indicate the future significance of the concept. The description appeared with greater force in his opening comments to the Twenty-Fourth Party Congress in 1971, a time when the modest reform efforts of the mid-1960s had obviously failed, in part for their own conceptual shortcomings but more importantly because of the opposition of conservative elements.[2] In the period between the Twenty-Fourth and Twenty-Fifth Congresses, the concept received extensive development not only on the pages of theoretical journals such as *Voprosy filosofii (Problems of Philosophy), Kommunist (Communist*, the party's in-house theoretical journal*), and *Partiinaya zhizn (Party Life)* but in the mass media as well, which took joy in touting the emergence of developed socialism as but one further confirmation that the Soviet Union had "made it" as a major industrial power. Moreover, East European theorists were quick to take up the notion to characterize developments within their nations.[3]

While there is no disagreement that the Soviet Union presently constitutes a developed socialist society and will continue to develop within this frame of reference for the next several decades, there are considerable differences among Soviet scholars concerning the precise features of such a system and the stages of its development.[4] Some see it as a "developing concept" whose exact meaning and historical parameters are affected by the peculiarities of the specific national milieu, while others argue about the periodization and the nature of the transition process. Among Soviet commentators there are, however, three areas of consensus signifying that developed socialism entails, first, qualitative and quantitative changes in material production, including the material and technical base of industry and the transformation of "production relationships," second, advances in the "political organization and spiritual life of society," among which are the transformation of the CPSU into a "party of all the people," the creation of the all-people's state, and the improvement of party leadership over the processes of social development, and third, substantive alterations in the international situation, including the peaceful competition of the capitalist and socialist systems and the growing power and influence of the socialist bloc.[5]

Whatever their differences concerning definition and emphasis, all commentators agree on the basic proposition that as a separate historical phase, developed socialism is to be a long period marked by the gradual transformation of social, economic, and political relationships. Reporting to the Supreme Soviet on the new constitution, Brezhnev struck a tone of deliberate caution concerning both the nature of the present stage and the pace of further growth:

> The stage of the perfection of socialism *on its own basis*, the stage of mature, developed socialist society, is a necessary element of the social transformation and *constitutes a relatively long period of*

development on the path from capitalism to communism. Moreover, knowledge and utilization of all the possibilities of developed socialism *is at the same time a transition to the construction of communism.* The future does not lie beyond the limits of the present. The future is rooted in the present, and, by accomplishing the tasks of today—of the socialist present—*we are gradually entering tomorrow*—the communist future.[6]

This cautious tone is also reflected in the writings of Soviet theorists who concern themselves with the gradual evolution of developed socialism. While the specific characteristics of a developed socialist society and the changes envisioned over the next several decades will be discussed at length below, it is necessary to take note of the emphasis placed on the slow-paced nature of the transition process and the limited, embryonic emergence of future social and political forms at the present time. Three arguments are repeatedly stressed in the literature. First, it is possible to enter into the beginning stages of developed socialism without any appreciable alteration of the institutional structure. While the technical and economic forces that animate the process of further change undergo continuing evolution during this period, the institutional structure— and this clearly means both the party and the state—change only gradually, acquiring added significance and increased functions as the transformation moves inevitably forward.[7] Second, developed socialism is envisioned as a completely separate stage of development which follows its own inherent laws of growth and change; as socialism "developing on its own basis," it is neither the primitive socialism that characterized the early years of economic and social development nor the beginning stage of full communism, although it bears the marks of both either in the continued presence of social and economic survivals from the past which must be overcome during the period of developed socialism or in the nascent beginnings of the institutional and social forms which will come to maturity in a future communist society. But what is stressed is that, in theoretical terms, developed socialism has its own inherent laws of development and its own implicitly legitimate economic, social, and political configurations. It is an economic, social, and political entity in its own right, conveying legitimacy to the political and social structures developing within it by virtue of its existence as a mature industrial system.[8]

The nascent development of future social and political forms characteristic of full communism is the third feature commonly stressed.[9] Two purposes seem evident in this thinking: to articulate a "safe" and gradual process of growth toward higher socialist and eventually communist forms; and to provide a rationale for an enhanced role for party and state mechanisms, as redefined within the framework of developed socialism. Much of the practical emphasis in the literature falls on the questions of the increasingly important role of the party and state both as objects undergoing transformation during the evolution of developed socialism and as subjects whose enhanced goal-directed public role becomes the critical factor in consciously and "scientifically" directing the further transformation of society.

As a theoretical doctrine, developed socialism is at once both a statement of the current stage of development of Soviet society—and hence a descriptive account of their own view of contemporary reality—and a delineation of the social, economic, and political trends that are viewed as inexorably shaping the next several decades as developed socialism gradually enters into the beginning stages of communism. Any discussion of Soviet writings must therefore deal simultaneously with the definition of the current reality and the forces seen as shaping the future. The two are closely wedded in these writings, a conjunction which once again points to the strategic political significance of the doctrine as a statement of the party's programmatic and reformist concerns.

TECHNOLOGY AND THE ECONOMY

In general terms, the technological and economic characteristics of a developed socialist society may be grouped under the general categories of a shift from extensive to intensive development, the increasing role of the scientific and technological revolution, and the gradual construction of the material base of a future communist society.

The shift from extensive to intensive forms of economic development signifies both an alteration of the mix of capital, labor, and technological imputs required for further economic development and a reduction of the overall growth rate. Viewing a sagging growth rate over the last decade, Soviet leaders have turned to new developmental strategies emphasizing increased labor productivity and technological modernization as the key elements in further growth. No longer responsive to earlier growth strategies, which stressed massive capital and labor inputs and disproportional development of leading sectors, the economy must in the future depend on an increasingly well-orchestrated application of scientific and technological modernization, increased labor productivity, improved management, and a more balanced "proportional" development of all sectors of the economy. The process of intensification is viewed as a long-term feature whose impact will be felt throughout the entire period of developed socialism and continue well into the communist phase.[10]

Closely linked to the question of the intensification of the economy are Soviet views of the role of the scientific and technological revolution both in creating the preconditions for developed socialism and in accelerating its further transition to communism. Some of the most striking transformations are envisioned in terms of structural changes in the economy predicted over the next several decades, the most important of which is the emergence of high-technology industries as the key growth sectors. The highest industrial growth rates will be seen in the fields of electronics, instrument making, chemicals, power engineering, and other high-technology branches. These sectors will emerge as the technological vanguard for the rest of the economy, generating considerable spin-off for less rapidly modernizing branches. While little public mention is made of the defense and space industries, it is likely that they will also continue as major sources of spin-off for civilian industries.[11]

The second major structural transformation that occurs during the developed socialist phase is the growing importance of the "nonproductive" sphere. Loosely defined as including scientific research, the service industries, certain utilities, education, culture, the arts, and all other activities not directly involved in the production of material wealth, it is slated to grow even more rapidly than the high-technology sectors of industry. The highest growth levels are predicted for the areas of scientific research, which is increasingly being regarded as a "productive" enterprise. The growth of the service sector also will account for much of the increased economic weight of this sector, although Soviet planners have been understandably careful to note the distinction between the service industries and consumer goods industries as such. The latter are also slated to grow in relative proportion to heavy industry, with increasing importance attached to the consumer goods sector as the transformation of developed socialism moves forward. Particular importance is also attached to the growth of higher and other forms of post-secondary education and to other activities contributing to continuing adult education.[12]

Closely associated with the increasing importance of science and education is the third structural transformation—the growth of a "knowledge industry" or an "information industry" as one of the key characteristics of the epoch. Included are both the increasing significance of science as a direct productive force and the growing importance of information storage, processing, and retrieval capabilities. It is in this area that the impact of the scientific and technological revolution is most strongly realized, and it is upon this sector's increasing maturity and ability to translate scientific and technological achievements into production line advances and information flows into timely and informed administrative decisions that the intensification of the economy will ultimately depend. Soviet commentators leave little doubt that the creation of the "science-technology-production" link is one of the highest priorities animating current attempts to create viable research and production associations as well as one of the most serious problems facing economic planners. The further development of automated production systems, computer data gathering and control networks, and improved management systems are also seen as dependent on rapid advances in this sector, particularly in cybernetics and computer technology. In short, while among the "productive" industries the lead is to be taken by those high-technology industries discussed above, it is clear that the real leading force is now recognized as lying within·what has heretofore been labeled the "nonproductive" sphere.[13]

The scientific and technological revolution is also seen as having an extensive impact on the rationalization of management. Soviet authorities have attached great importance to the improvement of management practices at all levels, in part simply out of concern for enhanced efficiency within a bureaucracy where such behavior has been notably absent and in part to overcome time-honored "departmental barriers" to make the system more amenable to centralized direction. This new emphasis on management corresponds in theoretical terms to the increasing importance of what is termed the "subjective factor" in continued development; as distinguished from the immutable, "objective" laws of historical development, the subjective factor refers to those areas of human endeavor subject to knowledgeable manipulation by man. In simple terms, the growing importance of the subjective realm entails an enhanced role for the conscious and sophisticated planning of further economic and social development.[14] As with the impact of new and more sophisticated technology in the economy, the advent of new tools in management and in the social sciences is seen as increasing the reach of social and economic planners far beyond that of their predecessors.

Over the next several decades, as developed socialism further matures, Soviet commentators foresee definite changes in the nature of management and planning. Arguing that managerial organizations of the future will look and behave much like present-day research and development centers, they note the growing importance of common managerial skills which transcend particular sectors of the economy. Future emphasis in managerial work will fall upon the organization and control of enterprise and sectoral information networks and data banks, the selection and deployment of personnel, and the integration of complex and multisectoral activities. Particular attention is given to the latter, since the most difficult problems facing a developed socialist economy are increasingly seen in terms of relating and coordinating activities in different sectors and/or regions.[15]

It is the third important economic feature of developed socialism—the creation of the material base for a future communist society—that Soviet theorists approach with the greatest caution. In legal terms, the property relationships of a full communist society will be built gradually during this period as collective property is converted to state or all-people's property. Of far greater importance are the projected changes that are to occur in consumption levels and patterns of distribution. Despite the growing emphasis placed on the consumer and service sectors as the transformation of developed socialism goes forward, the proper formula for the distribution remains essentially "to each according to his work" throughout the developed socialist phase. However, income differentials based on skill or function will continue to narrow, and a further leveling impact will be felt from the expanded role of the social consumption fund. But it is not until the attainment of full communism that distribution according to need may be implemented, and then with the share to each individual dictated by "scientifically determined consumption levels."[16]

SOCIAL STRUCTURE

In terms of social structure, the period of developed socialism is characterized by the gradual transformation of social and class relationships formed during the period of socialist construction into the foundations of a communist society. While Soviet theorists emphasize the theme of the social unity of the "Soviet people" as an important component of developed socialism, they are quick to admit that significant distinctions remain throughout this period. At present Soviet society contains the two "fraternal classes" of workers and collective farmers and the separate stratum of the intelligentsia. Relations between these elements are held to be "nonantagonistic" because of the absence of any politically significant property interests. Rather the existing divisions are described in terms of the diminishing class differences between those whose labor is associated either with state or all-people's property (the workers and the intelligentsia) or with cooperative or collective property (collective farmers and other cooperative enterprises) or in terms of continuing social distinctions based on functional professional role, urban or rural residence, and mental or physical labor. It must be remembered that Soviet theorists speak of changes both in the *class structure* and in the *social structure* of a developed socialist society; the former are interpreted narrowly within traditional theory and are expected to disappear gradually as the transformation of developed socialism goes forward, while the latter are more broadly interpreted to include other distinctions, such as functional or professional role, type of residence, and level of consumption, and are expected to grow more complex during the developed socialist period, simplifying into a more homogeneous social structure only after the attainment of full communism.[17]

During the developed socialist period, four important distinctions continue to exist, although their intensity will diminish as developed socialism evolves, albeit at highly differential rates.

First are distinctions based upon the use of collective property or of all-people's and state property. These are the only true class divisions remaining, and these will fade from existence as collective and cooperative property are gradually converted to higher forms.

Second are distinctions between urban and rural residents. Historically this division has been closely associated with the distinction between collective farmers and industrial workers. However, as agricultural labor is gradually transformed into a form of work virtually indistinguishable from industrial labor, the significance then shifts to the impact of urban and rural life styles. Even though agricultural work will then resemble factory labor, farm laborers still will live within a rural environment and presumably possess fewer of the amenities of life or opportunities for cultural enrichment than their urbanized counterparts in industry. A second process of change is also under way in the continuing growth of existing urban areas and the creation of new population centers in rural regions reflecting the changing nature of the countryside. Some Soviet theorists envision the creation of large-scale integrated urban complexes combining several existing population centers—although current policy now obviously militates against this—while others foresee the rapid growth of towns and small cities in the countryside.

Third are distinctions between mental and physical labor. Two contradictory transformations are envisioned during the period of developed socialism. First, physical labor will itself gradually become more intellectualized as the impact of the scientific and technological revolution is felt in industry and agriculture, although Soviet theorists are careful not to absolutize this transformation to suggest the complete abolition of physical tasks. Rather they offer a distinction between "physical labor," which entails arduous exertion with minimal intellectual involvement, and "manual labor," which suggests a combination of high intellectual content and skilled craftsmanship. Second, intellectual labor will become increasingly specialized during the developed socialist period, initially growing away from any convergence downward with the gradual upgrading of manual labor. However, with the transition to the beginning phase of full communism, the level of specialization among intellectual workers will gradually fade, while the upward growth of manual labor toward higher forms will continue. Soviet theorists make it clear that the remaining distinctions between mental and manual labor will be the last to disappear and will persist long beyond the period of developed socialism.

Fourth are distinctions among nationalities. While Soviet theorists foresee the gradual erosion of the importance of nationalities in economic, social, and political terms during the period of developed socialism, they will survive in the form of secondary cultural differences long into the period of full communism. Even their importance as cultural forms is expected to diminish during the period of full communism; the tone of most writing on the topic suggests somewhat vaguely that such differences eventually will be reduced to a sense of distant cultural heritage rather far removed from the day-to-day realities of Soviet life in the twenty-first century.[18]

Soviet theorists repeatedly point out that, during the period of developed socialism, the social structure of society will grow increasingly more complex in the short run, especially to the degree to which the intellectual and occupational differentiation of society caused by the impact of the scientific and technological revolution races ahead of the emergence of highly skilled generalists within both the intelligentsia and the working class. During this period, the most significant social distinctions are those associated with the nature of work, professions, occupational identification, type of community, and comparative standard of living. While these differences are held to be devoid of any political significance—they are not, after all, classes in the traditional sense—they do give rise, especially in the transition period, to differing social interests and "contradictions." They are especially important within the intelligentsia and the professional strata of society, where the process of differentiation occurs most rapidly.[19]

Soviet theorists devote special attention to social changes within

the intelligentsia during the evolution of developed socialism. Defined as a stratum rather than a class, it nonetheless can possess a
"class character" within the nonantagonistic framework articulated
by Soviet scholars. While the intelligentsia as a separate stratum will
merge with other elements long in the distant future, during the
developed socialist period its numbers and distinctive economic and
social roles are slated to grow rapidly for a number of reasons. First,
the increasing importance of science and technology simply places a
higher premium on the role of the intelligentsia in further economic
and social development. Soviet projections hold that the scientific
intelligentsia will be the most rapidly growing stratum for the next
several decades. The increasing importance of the subjective factor in
further development is another reason for an enhanced role for the
intelligentsia; greater attention to the tasks of comprehensive and
integrated planning necessarily implies added importance for research, planning, and managerial tasks falling, at least in the transition period, into the hands of the intelligentsia. Third, the intellectualization of labor itself contributes to the growing weight of the
intelligentsia, especially as the numbers of engineers and highly
trained technicians working directly in production increases. Finally,
structural shifts within the economy lend further impetus to the
growing importance of this stratum. The expansion of high-
technology industries and of those sectors which provide highly
skilled services, such as medicine or education, inevitably demands
ever growing numbers of highly trained personnel.[20]

THE PARTY

During the period of developed socialism, the party's role and
internal composition are to be marked by three gradual developments. First, its role will increase throughout the entire period in
response both to the need for comprehensive guidance of economic
and social development and the growing importance of its work with
public organizations and in public education. Second, the style and
content of party leadership will be modernized and placed on a more
rational footing in response to the needs of the scientific and technological revolution. Last, the transformation of the party into a "party of
all the people," which began concurrently with the advent of developed socialism, will intensify, setting the stage for its survival in
redefined form long after the state has withered away.

Soviet theorists are explicit in their predictions that the role of the party will increase markedly during the period of developed socialism. While the traditional rationalizations for its leading role are ritually cited high on the list of factors justifying this growing involvement, primary emphasis in recent years has shifted to its role in guiding the scientific and technological revolution and in mastering the complexities of an increasingly differentiated economy and society. Theory holds that the complexity of the tasks facing Soviet leaders increases with the further maturation of developed socialism, requiring an augmentation of party leadership in all spheres.

While ultimately the party, too, will wither away, it is expected to persist well into the period of full communism, although its "forms of work and internal structure" will undergo even further transformation. Soviet theorists are reticent about speculating on the final withering process in the far distant future, preferring instead to argue that it will eventually turn into a "universal organization coinciding with the organs of self-administration" only when the political consciousness of all members of the society is raised to that of party members.[21]

The transformation of the party into a "party of all the people" is regarded as one of the most significant internal developments during the period of developed socialism. While party theorists promise an intensification of this trend throughout the period, two reservations are usually offered limiting the meaning of this change. The first is that while the party now embodies the interests of all segments of the community, it retains its "class essence" as a party of the working class throughout the developed socialist stage. The second limitation is that the party of all the people is slated to remain a relatively small portion of the total population; in spite of the obvious growth in total membership since the Khrushchev era, the party continues to eschew mass recruitment, and, as party leaders frequently point out, admission and probationary requirements have been tightened in recent years.[22]

It is on the question of party leadership that the concept of developed socialism has had the greatest practical impact. Stressing the constantly increasing demands made on the CPSU as developed socialism evolves, Brezhnev and other party leaders have called for a thorough modernization and rationalization of the party's leadership style. Running throughout the exhortations for improved leadership are the themes of the improvement of the party's own internal operations and the growing importance of the party as the only force capable of providing the forceful leadership necessary for translating the achievements of the scientific and technological revolution into economic and social advances. Far from witnessing a conservative restoration of a self-possessed old guard content to muddle along the road to some imprecisely articulated future, internal developments and party policies from the early 1970s onward suggest a mindful, if understandably politically cautious recrudescence of an activist and reformist style of leadership.

THE STATE AND PUBLIC ORGANIZATIONS

In their approach to the issue of the current role and ultimate fate of the state, Soviet theorists place far greater emphasis on the theme of the perfection of the state mechanism during the period of developed socialism than on its eventual withering away under full communism. Having initially ignored Khrushchev's notion of the all-people's state, they have now cautiously resurrected it as an integral part of developed socialism. Predictably, emphasis has shifted from the transitional features of the all-people's state—the rapidly growing role of public organizations and the withering away of the state, which Khrushchev alleged had already begun—to the elaboration of an all-people's state whose role and significance increases throughout the developed socialist period.[23]

The growing role of the state under developed socialism is justified primarily by its increasing importance in the creation of the material and technological base of communism. Still seen as a "main element" in building communism, it is to undergo "further perfection" during the period of developed socialism in two ways. First, it is to play an increasingly active and sophisticated role in the planning and direction of economic and social development. The argument once again centers on the growing complexity of a developed socialist system. The impact of the scientific and technological revolution and related changes in the social structure are seen as placing increasing demands on state institutions, which must undertake the task of coping with the day-to-day requirements of society. Taken within this context, the call for the "perfection of the state mechanism" is linked in instrumental terms with recent attempts at managerial and planning reforms.[24]

The second development is referred to as "the strengthening of Soviet democracy," which is best interpreted as the gradual devolution of politically nonsensitive tasks to lower administrative levels, especially the local soviets and, to a lesser degree, public organizations, and the increasing involvement of citizen-activists in the affairs of these bodies. What is significantly different from the Khrushchev years is the pace of this transfer, particularly concerning the growing role of public organizations and the involvement of citizens in pseudo-administrative functions. Not surprisingly, the role of public organizations has been scaled down and the emphasis shifted to the development of the soviets. But even with these new reservations attached, this highly selective administrative deconcentration serves both practical and theoretical needs during the transition period. In the former instance, it provides the rationale for cautious experimentation in shifting the loci of some decision making to lower administrative or territorial levels, while in the latter it demonstrates in relatively safe terms that the dialectical evolution of developed socialism continues its slow progress. As transitional institutions, the soviets are seen as sharing the characteristics of state administrative organs, public organizations, and public self-administration, with the center of gravity shifting from the first gradually through the second and eventually to the third as developed socialism matures and grows over into the beginning stages of communism.[25]

Public organizations also are expected to play an increasingly important role under developed socialism. Current literature stresses both the slow pace of any further transfer of functions to these bodies and the "supplementary" role they play in relationship to the counterpart state agency. Any further development of public organizations during the developed socialist period must depend upon the further perfection of the state agencies themselves and their success in creating the material and social foundations of a higher social order and in increasing the educational level, public involvement, and moral development of the masses, tasks which are to be shared, at least in the transition period, by both party and state.[26]

NOTES

1. V. I. Kasyanenko, *KPSS: Organizator stroitelstva razvitogo sotsializma* (Moscow: Politizdat, 1974), p. 11; the evolution of the concept is also traced in Alfred B. Evans, Jr., "Developed Socialism in Soviet Ideology," *Soviet Studies* 29 (July 1977): 409-28.
2. L. I. Brezhnev, comments to the Twenty-Fourth Party Congress, *Pravda*, March 31, 1971.
3. Evans, "Developed Socialism," pp. 412-13.
4. The discussion is summarized in Kasyanenko, *KPSS*, pp. 12-13, and also in his *Razvityi sotsializm: Istoriografiya i metodologiya problemy* (Moscow: Mysl, 1976), pp. 56-60.
5. Kasyanenko, *KPSS*, p. 13.
6. *Pravda*, October 5, 1977.
7. E. M. Chekharin, *Sovetskaya politicheskaya sistema v usloviyakh razvitogo sotsializma* (Moscow: Mysl, 1977), translated as *The Soviet Political System under Developed Socialism* (Moscow: Progress, 1977), p. 219.

8. Kasyanenko, *KPSS*, pp. 14–15; and G. E. Glezerman, ed., *Razvitoe sotsialisti-cheskoe obshchestvo: Sushchnost, kriterii zrelosti, kritika revizionistskikh kontseptsii* 2nd rev. ed. (Moscow: Mysl, 1975), p. 19.

9. Chekharin, *Soviet Political System*, p. 219.

10. Kasyanenko, *Razvityi*, pp. 107–08; Glezerman, *Razvitoe*, pp. 67–68; V. Sikorskii, *KPSS na etape razvitogo sotsializma* (Minsk: Belorussian State University, 1975), p. 123; and I. I. Kuzminov et al., *Ekonomicheskie problemy razvitogo sotsializma i ego pererastaniya v kommunizm* (Moscow: Mysl, 1977), pp. 82–96.

11. L. S. Blyakhman and O. I. Shkaratan, *Chelovek v mire truda (Sovetskie rabochie i intelligentsiya v epochu nauchno-teknicheskoi revolyutsii)* (Moscow: Politizdat, 1973), translated as *Man at Work: The Scientific and Technological Revolution, the Soviet Working Class, and Intelligentsia* (Moscow: Progress, 1977), p. 35; Glezerman, *Razvitoe*, pp. 68–85; and Kasyanenko, *Razvityi* pp. 115, 170–73.

12. Blyakhman and Shkaratan, *Chelovek*; Kasyanenko, *KPSS*, p. 186; V. V. Kosolapov, *Chelovechestvo na rubezhe XXI veka* (Moscow: Molodaya gvardiya, 1973), translated as *Mankind in the Year 2000* (Moscow: Progress, 1976), p. 126; Glezerman, *Razvitoe*, pp. 23–26; Chekharin, *Soviet Political System*, p. 292; and L. M. Gatovskii et al., *Materialno-tekhnicheskaya baza kommunizma*, vol. 2 (Moscow: Mysl, 1977), pp. 287–383.

13. Blyakhman and Shkaratan, *Chelovek*, pp. 112–15; Kosolapov, *Chelovechestvo*, pp. 153–54; and E. D. Mordzhinskii and Ts. A. Stepanyan, *Budushchee chelovecheskogo obshchestva* (Moscow: Mysl, 1971), pp. 319–20, 330–31;

14. Chekharin, *Soviet Political System*, p. 227; and Kasyanenko, *KPSS*, p. 175.

15. Sikorskii, *KPSS na etape*, pp. 130–33; Kasyanenko, *KPSS*, pp. 175–77; Blyakhman and Shkaratan, *Chelovek*, pp. 261–80; and V. G. Afanasev, *The Scientific and Technological Revolution: Its Impact on Management and Education* (Moscow: Progress, 1975).

16. Kasyanenko, *KPSS*, pp. 170–73; and Blyakhman and Shkaratan, *Chelovek*, pp. 139–41.

17. Blyakhman and Shkaratan, *Chelorek*, pp. 148–49.

18. G. I. Pivtsaikin, *Obshchestvennye otnosheniya razvitogo sotsializma* (Minsk: Nauka i tekhnika, 1973); Glezerman, *Razvitoe*, pp. 132–51; Kasyanenko, *KPSS*, pp. 181–94; and Blyakhman and Shkaratan, *Chelovek*, pp. 147–236.

19. Blyakhman and Shkaratan, *Chelovek*, p. 149.

20. D. M. Gvishyani et al., *The Scientific Intelligentsia in the USSR* (Moscow: Progress, 1976); Kasyanenko, *KPSS*, p. 192; and *Partiya i intelligentsiya v usloviyakh razvitogo sotsializma* (Moscow: Mysl, 1977).

21. Sikorskii, *KPSS na etape*, pp. 39–47, 72–78, 118–19; Glezerman, *Razvitoe*, pp. 268–77; Chekharin, *Soviet Political System*, pp. 251–68; *Partiya v period razvitogo sotsialisticheskogo obshchestva* (Moscow: Politizdat, 1977), pp. 8–20; V. S. Shevtsov, *KPSS i gosudarstvo v razvitom sotsialisticheskom obshchestve* (Moscow: Politizdat, 1974), pp. 53–60; and V. I. Lesnyi and N. V. Chernogolovkin, *Politicheskaya organizatsiya razvitogo sotsialisticheskogo obshchestva: struktura i funktsii* (Moscow: Moscow State University, 1976), pp. 36–54.

22. *Partiya v period razvitogo sotsialisticheskogo obshchestva*, pp. 12–16, 32–33; Sikorskii, *KPSS na etape*, pp. 31–42; and P. E. Burak, *Partiinoe stroitelstvo v usloviyakh razvitogo sotsializma* (Lvov: Vishcha shkola, 1976).

23. The best general discussions are in Lesnyi and Chernogolovkin, *Politicheskaya*, and Chekharin, *Soviet Political System*.

24. Kasyanenko, *Razvitoe*, pp. 165–66; L. I. Zagainov, "Povyshenie ekonomiches-

koi roli gosudarstva pri razvitom sotsializme," *Sovetskoe gosudarstvo i pravo*, no. 1 (January 1976): 17-24; and Glezerman, *Razvitoe*, p. 154.

25. Sikorskii, *KPSS na etape*, pp. 132-42, 192-227; D. A. Kerimov, *Sovetskaya demokratiya v period razvitogo sotsializma* (Moscow: Mysl, 1975), pp. 9-23; and Glezerman, *Razvitoe*, pp. 160-61.

26. Lesnyi and Chernogolovkin, *Politicheskaya*, pp. 93-104; Sikorskii, *KPSS na etape*, pp. 202-07; Chekharin, *Soviet Political System*, pp. 220-29; and *Dobrovolnye obshchestva pri sotsializme* (Moscow: Nauka, 1976).

9

CONSTITUTIONAL IMPLEMENTATION AND THE JURIDICIZATION OF THE SOVIET SYSTEM

Robert Sharlet

The Brezhnev era in Soviet political history is likely to achieve special longevity, well beyond its namesake's incumbency, through the medium of the new Soviet constitution of 1977.[1] Although this is not exclusively a "Brezhnev" constitution, he has clearly left his imprint on the document, in the sense that it describes quite comprehensively the structure and functions of the contemporary Soviet system as a party-led constitutional bureaucracy. The 1977 Constitution, successor to the constitution of 1936 and the fourth in the history of Soviet constitutions, serves as a blueprint for the post-Stalin Soviet-style *Rechtsstaat*. In keeping with the construction metaphor, the thrust implicit in the document is to bring the myriad features of the Soviet system under a single roof without, at the same time, denying the Communist Party the discretionary space to act extra-constitutionally when it deems necessary. The eventual completion of the constitutional housing of the Soviet system under the direction of the party architects will have to await the full implementation of the diverse aspects of this new Soviet constitution.

The purpose of this chapter is to examine the constitutional implementation process in its initial phase. For this purpose, I will survey and analyze the scope, direction, and content of the Soviet legal profession's learned commentary on the new constitution in the period since its ratification on October 7, 1977. Predictably, the legal press has been flooded with articles on the 1977 Constitution as scholars gird themselves for the longer term production of specialized monogrpahs. The tone and substance of this vast periodical output confirm Brezhnev's earlier remark that the new constitution was not meant to be a mere "decoration." Legal scientists invoke the continuity of Soviet legal history, judicial commentators argue that all court practice now flows from the new constitution, and publishers readily affirm that all new and forthcoming juridical literature is either about the document or at least based upon it.

The editorial article in the journal *Socialist Legality*, the organ of the USSR Ministry of Justice, the Procuracy and All-Union Supreme Court, on the occasion of the first anniversary of the new constitution, gives a fair indication of the extent and specifics of its initial implementation in the year following ratification. The impact of the constitution on the further political and sociolegal development of the Soviet system is evident in this article, published in the journal's regular section "The Constitution of Developed Socialism." In accordance with the "party hegemony" clause (Art. 6), the role of the party is understandably given first priority in the editorial: "The Communist Party of the Soviet Union, operating within the framework of the Soviet Constitution, as the ruling party has determined and will determine the political line in decisions on all major questions of governmental affairs."

The article goes on to observe that since constitutional ratification, all 15 union-republics and 20 autonomous republics have adopted new constitutions as well. In response to this development, Brezhnev is paraphrased to the effect that this completes the constitutionalization of the social and governmental systems of "mature socialism through the creation of the foundation of the entire system of legislation of the all people's state." The major legislative changes flowing from the new constitution are then recited, followed by the recitation of the specific correlation between particular constitutional articles and other narrow-gauge policy statements or legislative enactments of the past year. For instance, the requirements of Articles 21 and 24 on the state's obligation to improve working conditions and the quality of life respectively, are seen to have been "translated into life" in the resolution of the July 1978 plenum of the Central Committee on improving working conditions and raising the standard of living of those citizens engaged in agricultural production. Even more specifically, the "social security" clause (Art.43) was implemented in the 1978 all-union statute on securing the pension rights of collective farmers, while the "women's rights" clause (Art.35) is seen to have been translated into the language of legal implementation in the 1978 decree on "supplementary measures for the improvement of working conditions for women employed in the national economy." Finally, in this vein, a rather specialized piece of educational legislation is recorded as a legislative response to the constitutional principle of right to education (Art.45).

The editorial article concludes that much still remains to be done in the process of implementing the new constitution, especially with regard to strengthening socialist legality to ensure that officials in particular fulfill the constitutional norms and obey the laws of the Soviet Union. Toward this end, then, "further implementation of the provisions of the constitution" requires that all legal personnel make a thorough study of the basic law of the Soviet Union as well as systematically disseminating information about its fundamental provisions among the population at large.[2]

In the article just discussed, reference is made in passing to the positive role played by comrades' courts and juvenile commissions in the struggle for socialist legality. Neither of these institutions is mentioned specifically in the new constitution, although both are subsumed within more than one clause. This raises a related point about the constitutional implementation process. In numerous articles in the legal press, many institutions either explicitly mentioned in the constitution or implicitly subsumed enjoy a type of public certification by their identification with the new constitution. The ideal situation, of course, is to be accorded formal constitutional status, although several general clauses are sufficiently broad in scope and implication that some degree of constitutional cachet can be accorded to a number of the unmentioned institutions as well. Among those institutions basking in the glow of an enhanced or newly achieved constitutional status, as reflected in the postratification literature, are the arbitrators, advocates, assessors or cojudges, and the Young Communist League. Other groups whose institutional stature has been raised by the new constitution include the trade unions, collective farmers, and women. Additional constitutional newcomers include writers, scientists, and environmentalists, while their subsumption has given such institutions as the notary publics, the comrades' courts, and the people's voluntary patrols additional visibility and a kind of indirect constitutional legitimation within the Soviet system. The spirit and importance of constitutional notice for subsequent institutional development can be heard in the words of a senior RSFSR state arbitrator who writes "with the ratification of the USSR Constitution, the state arbitration system for the first time in the history of the Soviet state has been elevated to the rank of a constitutional organ."[3] In the words of the first deputy RSFSR minister of justice, "The USSR Constitution and the RSFSR Constitution have raised the authority of the defense bar to a new height."[4] Finally, although the claim is much more tenuous, a collective farm director effectively uses the constitution to call attention to institutions merely subsumed and not formally mentioned as he writes, "The new Constitution forces us to reevaluate the role of social organizations, the comrades' court, the people's voluntary patrol, the commission for the struggle against drunkenness, and our collective farm legal adviser in moral and legal education."[5] In conclusion, the new constitution appears to have invigorated certain institutional interest group activity in the Soviet system.

Implementing the new Soviet constitution has meant first settling the theoretical question of the conception and status of a constitution in Soviet law. The traditional view of a constitution which prevailed among legal scholars for many years up to the actual publication of the new draft constitution in the spring of 1977 held that a constitution was essentially a reflective instrument, designed to consolidate changes that had occurred and schematically reflect the revised shape of the Soviet system in constitutional language. However, during the long constitutional drafting process for the current document, an alternative conception, albeit a minority position, emerged in scholarly circles which argued that a constitution should be projective as well as reflective. The new constitution of 1977 represents the triumph of the latter dualistic position.[6]

The so-called constitutional school is now ascendant over the long dominant state law school of Soviet constitutional development. Apropos of this major shift in the theory of Soviet constitutions, a scholar analyzing the programmatic content of the new constitution keynotes his article on the Leninist legacy of this emphasis and closes with Brezhnev's statement to the effect that the new constitution should reflect past accomplishments but also provide a "clear perspective for future communist construction."[7] Another especially distinguished legal scholar argues that the 1977 document effectively completes the de-Stalinization of Soviet constitutional law. He demonstrates how the Stalinist constitution of 1936, with its emphasis on the reflective orientation of Soviet state law, distorted the Leninist constitutional orientation of including both reflective and programmatic elements. He concludes that "this mistaken view has now been corrected" in the new constitution.[8]

Inevitably, the state law advocates of a primarily reflective constitution capitulated and began to bring their views into line with the party's clear preference for a dualistic conception of the constitution. While still insisting on the constitution's fundamental reflective aspect, a representative of this school of thought conceded the positive role of programmatic elements as well. Hinging her concession on the new "conditions of the construction of developed socialism," she acknowledged that the "programmatic character of the constitution has been strengthened through the growth of the number of norms defining the goals and paths of sociopolitical development."[9] Other advocates of the traditionalist position have conceded the point by moving on to the new postratification task of developing appropriate typologies of the interrelationships of the reflective and programmatic aspects of the new constitution. The fact that the dualistic character of the constitution is no longer contested and that the predominant interest appears to be in the programmatic side of the equation is even confirmed in foreign socialist commentary on the new Soviet constitution.[10]

Now that the Soviet constitution is no longer considered a static instrument of governance, a number of scholars have begun addressing another aspect of the theoretical tasks of implementation. In the spirit of the contemporary juridical interest in Western-type systems analysis, legal scientists are beginning to conceptualize the "functions" of the new constitution. Basically, they appear to be converging toward a consensus that the constitution is much more than a mere legal instrument. The emerging consensus suggests a conception of the constitution as a "metapolicy" with broad implications for the wide gamut of policies on the various aspects of the Soviet system.[11] At a lower level of abstraction, there appears to be agreement on the "regulatory" function of the new constitution.[12] Within the regulatory function, a basic distinction is made between the political function and the juridical function of the document, with at least one scholar finding the source for this distinction in Lenin's writings.[13]

Predictably, the very vocabulary of learned discourse on the constitution is changing as the new conceptions are implemented in the scholarly literature. The phrase "Soviet constitutional law" now is employed commonly, whereas prior to 1977 it was used only occasionally by the minority advocates of the constitutional school. One even finds now in the Soviet legal press such terms as "constitutionalism" and "Soviet socialist constitutionalism" as well as the phrase "constitutional legality."[14] Adumbrating the constitution's regulatory function, the chairman of the RSFSR Supreme Court has called upon the courts, in the spirit of "constitutional legality," to help educate the citizen in "the spirit of strict obedience to the constitution of the USSR" as well as the usual legal imperatives.[15]

As Soviet legal scientists come to terms with the new conceptual and theoretical implications of the 1977 Constitution, the implementation task ahead for them will be to translate the new constitutional developments into their pedagogical and research activities. Toward this end, the major law faculties began holding working conferences shortly after ratification to discuss projected curricular changes and the consequences of the new constitution for future legal scholarship on this subject. For instance, at a conference of Moscow legal faculties (heretofore a stronghold of the state law school), it was generally agreed:

> The content of the constitution requires a new approach to the question of the subject of Soviet state law, which has been substantially enlarged; ... The main tasks of the science [of state law] include research on many new problems such as the theory of the Soviet constitution, its essential nature or essence, the interrelationship [within the constitution] of political and legal principles, the dynamic character of the development of the Soviet state, Soviet socialist democracy, the classification of Soviet governmental organs, and the interaction of authority and administration.[16]

Similar conclusions were reached in a conference at the Saratov Juridical Institute in late November 1977.[17] Finally, in a recent leading article in the major journal *Jurisprudence*, a senior legal scholar has explicitly stated that the study and teaching of state law in the Soviet Union will have to undergo a profound change in scope and content as a result of the new constitution. He added that the new problems to be addressed will in turn require new methodologies including survey research techniques, statistical analysis, mathematical methods, and a "systems analysis" approach to the legal and related social sciences in the study of the new constitution and its metapolitical implications for nearly the entire Soviet system.[18]

THE CONSTITUTION, COMMUNIST PARTY, AND POLITICAL SYSTEM

The new constitution describes the Soviet Union as an "all-people's state" (Art. 1) and explicitly sets out the role of the Communist Party in its opening chapter (Art. 6). Although Article 1 formulates in constitutional terms a new conception of the Soviet state, it is a familiar conception in recent Soviet jurisprudence and in fact has its origin in the 1961 Program of the CPSU, according to the authoritative journal of the influential Academy of Sciences' Institute of State and Law, *Soviet State and Law*.[19] Of much greater importance is that the new constitution fully articulates for the first time in Soviet constitutional history the intended and actual role of the Communist Party in the direction of the Soviet system. Previously, the party was treated jurisprudentially as an extra-constitutional entity, a kind of metajuridical institution, which is mentioned twice in the 1936 Constitution but only in terms of its less consequential roles in Soviet development. In the contemporary document the party, through its own legislative intent, has been included within the constitutional structure of the Soviet system.[20] This is probably the most significant manifestation of the increasing trend toward the reconceptualization and reconstruction of the post-Stalin system into a type of qualified Soviet *Rechtsstaat*. It can be argued that even the party has subjected itself, at least to a certain extent, to the trend of the increasing "juridicization" of the Soviet system.

Following the nationwide discussion of the draft constitution during the summer of 1977, one of the most significant and, simultaneously, cryptic amendments to the draft affected the party hegemony clause (Art.6), which was supplemented to read: "All party organizations operate within the framework of the USSR Constitution." Since there was relatively little reference to or discussion of the draft party clause, it can be assumed that this amendment arose from within the elite exclusively. Since ratification, the amended clause has been frequently explicated and clarified in the legal literature. Most significantly, it now appears that the apparent limitationist amendment is politically and historically rooted in Leninism as it is construed by the contemporary leadership. The amendment apparently was addressed to a persistent problem of the Soviet political system, that is, the tendency from time to time for particular local party organizations to preempt the functions of governmental agencies which they are primarily intended to direct and supervise.

The specific origin of the amendment is the party's first Program of 1919 proclaimed after the successful revolution. The relevant phrases are "the decisions of the party must be carried out through soviet organs *within the framework of the Soviet constitution*. The party should strive to direct the activity of the [local] soviets but not replace them."[21] In effect, the implementory message for party organizations in the new constitution is clear; the thrust of the amendment suggests not the idea of "limited government" but rather the traditional Soviet emphasis on maintaining the distinction between party and governmental functions. However, at the same time the potential symbolic and normative import of the amendment under discussion should not be ignored, since at least two commentators have suggested that through this now clarified phrase the party is expected to set an example of constitutional compliance for other Soviet institutions and citizens to follow.[22]

In its system-building role, the party is expected through the medium of the new constitution to carry forward in the future the integration of the Soviet political system through strengthening the linkage among its various parts.[23] This process of "tightening up" the system began with the ratification of the constitution and continues in the course of its implementation. For the first time in Soviet constitutional development, the political system's defense function has been given the status of a separate chapter (Chap. 5). Constitutionally, this chapter recognizes the centralization in fact as well as in theory of the USSR armed forces. As one commentator has pointed out, although the union republics no longer enjoy the constitutional right (as they did in the 1936 Constitution) to maintain their own military formations, contemporary all-union and union republic constitutional developments confirm their right "to participate in decisions on questions concerning the defense of the fatherland."[24]

However, the defense chapter of the new constitution does not exhaust the institutions available to the party and political system for the defense of the realm. Such institutions range from the paramilitary voluntary organization DOSAAF, which is implicitly subsumed under Article 7 of the political chapter of the constitution, to the Committee on State Security (KGB), which is part of the "system of governmental institutions [charged with] carrying out tasks pertaining to the defense of the fatherland" whose status is implied in Article 135 on the USSR Council of Ministers.[25]

The postratification integration of the political system under party auspices and on the basis of the new constitution, can be observed in what are the first of a long projected series of new legislative acts. I am referring to the three major new statutes, flowing from the constitution, on electoral law, the organization of the highest administrative body, and the negotiation and ratification of international treaties. Throughout the legislative discussion of these statutes in their draft form on the floor of the USSR Supreme Soviet and in the finally enacted statutes themselves, the new constitution is referenced frequently as the impetus and source of the legislation. For instance, a Supreme Soviet deputy, who also happens to be a CPSU Central Committee secretary, opened his speech on the draft statute on "Elections to the USSR Supreme Soviet" by stating that "the USSR constitution stipulates that the procedure for conducting elections to the USSR Supreme Soviet is determined by an all-union law."[26] The statute itself, in the spirit of the further constitutional and legislative articulation of the Soviet system, codifies systematically for the first time in a single legislative act of 63 articles the entire range of legal elements connected with electing deputies to the USSR's highest legislative body.[27] Under this new statute, the deputies to the Ninth Sitting of the USSR Supreme Soviet were elected by the voters in early 1979 and presumably during the course of their tenure will be carrying forward the legislative program called for in various clauses of the constitution toward the further juridicization of the Soviet political system.

In the same spirit, the new statute on the USSR Council of Ministers (the first recodification since 1950 in this area of state law) arises from, in the order indicated, "the constitution of the USSR, the decisions of the Twenty-third, Twenty-fourth and Twenty-fifth Party Congresses, the resolutions of the plenums of the Central Committee of the CPSU, and the statements of L.I. Brezhnev on the question of the development of the political system of Soviet society."[28] The responsiveness of the drafting process to the new constitution is evident in a report by a member of the legislative drafting committee of the all-union Supreme Soviet who pointed out that paragraph five of Article 3 of the new statute was directly inspired by Article 7 of the constitution, which provides for participation in the political system of the mass social organizations of Soviet society. In legislative language, the gist of this constitutional clause was translated as follows: "In cases stipulated by USSR legislation, the all-union agencies of public organizations, in accordance with their statutory tasks, take part in the examination of questions under consideration by the USSR Council of Ministers."[29] In recognition of the Soviet *Rechtsstaat*-building process underway, both of the above statutes have been referred to as facilitating the implementation of the new constitution and specifically contributing to "the full-scale development of the Soviet political system, the improvement of the socialist state system, the strengthening of the legal foundations of governmental and social affairs, and the further broadening of socialist democracy."[30]

In a similar way the constitutional origin of the new 1978 statute on international treaties is made explicit in its first article describing the objectives of the statute: "This law . . . is designed to promote the realization of the goals and principles of the USSR's foreign policy as proclaimed and codified by the USSR Constitution."[31]

At the opposite end of the spectrum, domestic policy at the local and regional level, the constitution itself provides the programmatic perspective for the enhanced status and enlarged powers of the local soviet. As the most authoritative commentator on Soviet construction states, "The new constitutions have reflected the process of the strengthening of the integration of the different administrative systems in Soviet society [and] the consolidation of the status of the soviets as the main link in the mechanism for administering governmental affairs."[32]

Finally, the postratification literature calls attention to the longer term tasks of implementing the "political culture" clause, the most programmatic article of chapter one on the political system (Art. 9).

This important projective clause proclaims that the increasing participation of citizens in the policy implementation process, the intensification of institutional interest group activity, and greater consideration for public opinion all fall within the overriding goal of the "further unfolding of socialist democracy" which constitutes, in the language of the constitution, the "basic direction of the development of the political system of Soviet society. . ."[33] In conclusion to this section on the political system, it should be noted that the vista of a participatory authoritarian system is projected within an essentially juridical framework. Key to this is the fact that the postratification literature frequently reiterates the party's role in the legal development of the Soviet system, including the enhanced legal status of the citizen, the emphasis on building an effective legal culture, and the trend toward the further sociolegal definition and articulation of the principal subsystems of the Soviet system writ large.[34]

THE ECONOMIC SUBSYSTEM

A significant agenda for implementation was written into Chapter 2 of the constitution on the economic system. As a senior commentator points out, the inclusion of the property of trade unions and other mass social organizations in the official typology of socialist property will have important implications for the traditional state and collective-cooperative types of property (Art.10). Through their "sociocultural activity," these social organizations (and their property) are expected to have a positive and substantial influence on future economic development in Soviet society.

In Article 12, which projects the eventual merger of collective-cooperative property with state property, the possibility of this long-term goal focusing attention on the creation of "agro-industrial associations" is suggested. The new constitution's planning clause (Art.16) suggests the need for greater emphasis in the future on socioeconomic planning in addition to the essentially pure economic planning of the past, as well as "the further development of the economic and legal mechanism" in order to implement this constitutional task.

Generally, the consensus in the legal literature is that the constitution makes it necessary to usher in a new stage in the development of legislation for administering the economy. For instance, the enhanced status of subnational administrative units in the Soviet system, especially with regard to economic affairs, makes necessary an ambitious program of "new legislative acts, amendments, and supplements" from the level of the union republic down to the village soviet.[35] An equally extensive program of implementing the new constitution through legislative codification is indicated on purely economic subjects themselves by the aforementioned commentator, who calls for "a statute on planning, a statute on the administration of the national economy, a statute on material and technical supplies, [and] a statute on the enterprise and production association."[36] It is evident that further legislative activity toward the increasing jurid-icization of the emerging Soviet *Rechtsstaat* appears to be the pro-jected answer to the question of constitutional implementation in the economic sector of the Soviet system as well.

THE SOCIAL SUBSYSTEM AND THE CITIZEN'S SOCIOECONOMIC RIGHTS

A common theme linking the economic and social subsystems of the Soviet Union is the state's assumption of a number of constitu-tional obligations in the interest of society. One such primary obliga-tion is the state's commitment to protect socialist property in its several forms (Art.10).[37] Even the natural environment, which is constitutionally designated as state property (Art.11), falls within the state's obligation to ensure the integrity of the economic system through the imperatives of the new constitutional "environmental protection" clasue (Art.18).[38] However, the state is not alone in its mission to protect socialist property wherever it may be found above or below ground and in whatever form it might take from factory to forest. The constitutionally heavily burdened Soviet citizen is also enjoined, to help protect socialist property in various ways, from assisting the authorities in ferreting out embezzlement and misman-agement (Art. 61) to performing the role of a civic guardian of nature (Art. 67).[39]

Conversely, the state is also constitutionally obliged to provide a vast array of socioeconomic services to the population, many of which have been enlarged upon in the 1977 Constitution and a number of which are being further amplified in the process of implementation. In addition, the new constitution has strengthened the social subsystem as a whole and afforded new opportunities for participation in certain aspects of the public business of some of its constituent components.

The family, as the basic unit of society, has received considerable attention in the new constitution compared to the relative constitu-tional silence of the 1936 document. Article 53 declares that "the family is under the protection of the state" in terms of both the sanctity of the institution and its material support, while a corresponding clause imposes the duty upon parents to rear their children as "worthy members of a socialist society" (Art.66). These two clauses are keynoting the postratification literature on family law.[40] Since the thrust of both clauses is in the traditional post-1936 direction of further strengthening the Soviet family, any reference to the spouses' right of divorce is understandably absent; therefore, the constitutional implications for divorce, child support, and the responsibilities of separated parents for the education of their offspring are being explored in the literature.[41]

Apropos of education, the implementation of the constitution in the daily life and political culture of the Soviet citizen is underway through an extensive and carefully orchestrated program of mass legal socialization. With 8 million copies of the constitution in print shortly after ratification in late 1977, schools, adult education courses, pamphlet series, documentary films, and the extracurricular activities of procurators, judges, other justice officials, and even factory directors have all been drawn into the massive effort to make the new constitution and its provisions thoroughly known to the public, young and old. A school teacher presents a series of lessons on the "Great Patriotic War," and in the course of doing so teaches the children the content of the foreign policy and defense chapters of the constitution.[42] The higher justice justice authorities recommend to all People's Universities of Legal Knowledge for adult education that they incorporate into their curricula a 34–hour course on "The Constitution of the USSR—The Basic Law of the Soviet State."[43] The publishing house "Knowledge" issues a series of inexpensive, popular pamphlets on the new constitution.[44] Even Goskino, the state film agency, produces a number of documentary films on the all-union, union republic, and autonomous republic constitutions, films which are shown in theaters throughout the country.[45] Finally, the procurator of the Moscow region, judges from Leningrad and Saratov, several regional justice officials, and even the director of the Moscow "50th Anniversary of the USSR" factory contribute to the legal socialization campaign through their various official offices.[46]

As the principal source of the political and legal codification of the Soviet citizen's socioeconomic rights, the new constitution consolidated and amplified the traditional right to work (Art. 40) and introduced at the constitutional level of the Soviet system for the first time the right to housing (Art.44). A great deal of implementory activity is underway on both of these clauses. The constitutional right to work has now been supplemented by a number of ancillary job rights which had heretofore only been guaranteed to the citizen in the general body of labor legislation.[47] Among the new job rights now constitutionally protected is "the right to choice of occupation, type of employment and work in accordance with one's primary vocation, capabilities, vocational training and education" (Art.40). Since the right to work is guaranteed to all "USSR citizens," it has been pointed out in the legal literature that the collective farmer is also entitled to enjoyment of the ancillary rights as well, although subject to the constitutional caveat of taking into consideration "social requirements."[48]

Although the caveat theoretically applies to all citizens equally, the qualification of the right implicit in the phrase appears to circumscribe the ancillary job rights of collective farmers more than industrial workers and white-collar employees. A learned commentary on the question, for instance, points out that the right of job choice is not intended to extend to the "leading cadres" of the collective farms, whose selection and assignment are subject to the *nomenklatura* and therefore constitutionally fall under the party hegemony clause (Art. 6). The ordinary collective farm member, in turn, does not enjoy an unrestricted freedom of job selection, even on the farm itself, since this would violate "the principle of the planned organization of work."[49] The collective farmer's job right is basically abridged by the restriction that he can only exercise his limited choice of jobs within the structure of collective farm work.[50] Finally, in recognition of the collective farmer's highly qualified right, a commentator projects that the new constitution will serve as the impetus for the further development of collective farm legislation in the direction of "rules for the transfer of collective farmers to other work."[51]

Article 40 also has stimulated postratification discussion on the need to implement another ancillary job right—the right of a worker to improve his job qualifications. Apropos, it is being suggested that the several hundred individual legislative enactments on advanced vocational training for workers and employees be codified into a single comprehensive statute on the subject. It is argued that this effectively would serve to implement the implied constitutional linkage between the right to work and the right to education (Art.45).[52] Other instances of implementation include the use of the right-to-work clause to call attention to the judicial errors and procedural irregularities which apparently occur with some frequency in the adjudication of cases of illegal dismissal, one of the "most serious violations of working rights."[53]

In a related sense, another legal commentator calls attention to the fact that systematic studies have revealed that a number of enterprises and other economic organizations have not been consistently observing the existing legislation designed to promote and encourage new inventions as a vital part of the ongoing scientific-technical revolution. He argues that the need to rectify this situation is now more compelling in view of the imperatives of implementing the new constitutional "freedom of scientific, technical and artistic creation" of Article 47.[54]

Looking beyond the citizen's working years, new attention is being focused on the legal aspects of the various forms of social security in light of the need to implement Article 43 of the new constitution which "has significantly broadened the fundamental rights of citizens, strengthening their guarantees [and] given a new impulse to the further in-depth working out of the problems of the right to social security" and the improvement of legislation in this sphere.[55] This includes new studies on the tasks of implementing the ancillary rights of disability and survivor benefits in the event of the loss of the family breadwinner.[56]

The right to housing, which the new constitution "elevated into the ranks of the basic socioeconomic rights of Soviet citizens," is also the object of considerable implementory attention (Art.44).[57] As the leading specialist on housing law observes, Article 44 is only one of several constitutional norms which bear directly on housing legislation in the Soviet Union. Others include the state property clause which encompasses the basic urban housing stock of the society (Art. 11), the personal inviolability clause which includes the inviolability of one's home (Art. 55), and the important new Article 58 which affords the citizen the constitutional right legally to protect and defend his interests, including his right to housing. In the commentator's informed opinion, these constitutional norms and the numerous other acts, decrees, and administrative instructions on housing require systematic codification into a set of all-union principles on housing legislation and individual union republic housing codes. This would bring the subject of housing within the framework of the post-Stalin legal reform program, which through 1979 had already encompassed the codification or recodification of all of the major and most of the minor branches of law. Apparently support for housing codification arose during the nationwide discussion of the draft constitution and during the special ratification session of the USSR Supreme Soviet in October 1977 as well. However, to the author's chagrin, support for the idea of housing codification "did not appear once in the party press" during the following year.[58]

Nevertheless, the constitutional protection of the citizen's housing right did spur the judiciary to upgrade its performance in the adjudication of housing cases. In one of its far-reaching "guiding decisions" during 1978, the plenum of the USSR Supreme Court called attention to the occurrence of errors in housing adjudication and provided the lower courts with a 20-point set of guidelines for the correct application of relevant legislation in the judicial resolution of disputes between citizens and housing construction cooperatives.[59] Since its publication, the Supreme Court's housing guidelines have been the subject of an extensive scholarly commentary and further elucidation in the spirit of bringing court practice into alignment with constitutional intent.[60]

Other legal commentaries are addressed to the implementation of the linkage between the housing clause and another of the Soviet citizen's major socioeconomic rights, the right of personal property (Art.13). This includes the individual's right to construct housing for his own needs within the frameworks of Article 44 and the personal property clause.[61] In fact, readers' questions to the answer column of the journal *Socialist Legality* are inquiring about the right to personal property in housing with moderate frequency, suggesting possibly a very widespread and lively preoccupation with personal ownership of one's residence.[62] The personal property clause is, in turn, related to the right of "individual labor activity" (Art.17). Possibly because of the great public interest in both of these clauses during the pre-ratification nationwide discussion, a prominent civil law specialist is calling for codification to clarify citizen-state and citizen-citizen relations and to implement the constitutional linkage between the two rights within a special legal framework. The proposed framework would include a general part enumerating and elucidating among other things what a citizen may own as personal property and in what amounts, and a special part that would provide legal guidelines for the lawful use of such property in the course of individual labor activity, subject to the new constitutional emphasis on the prohibition against acquiring unearned income through the use of one's personal property.[63]

Finally, the new constitution in its more programmatic aspect offers a vista of an increasingly more activist social subsystem, interacting in and acting upon the political process, which in the Soviet context is widely construed. The projected greater social activism is routed through the approved participatory channel of the "labor collective" (Art. 8) and through the programmatic ninth article, which calls for the future development of a political culture to nourish and cultivate the further flowering of "socialist democracy" (Art. 9).

In the draft constitution, the labor collective clause was originally included in the chapter on the economy, but in one of the more dramatic changes of the constitutional revision process in the fall of 1977, the institution of the labor collective was promoted to the chapter on the political system in the final version. The message encoded in this revision was that, constitutionally, more participatory space was being created in the local policy implementation process of the work places of Soviet society. The political importance accorded to this constitutional clause is being further underscored by the relatively greater amount of legal commentary being devoted to the various aspects of its implementation.

Article 8 on the labor collective contains both reflective and programmatic elements, and both are the subject of current discussion. Regardless of their varying orientations, nearly all writers are framing their discussion of the labor collective in either its present or its projected activities within the framework of local party control.[64] The labor collective and its role as a socioeconomic adjunct of the Soviet political system is being explicated in the legal literature in its two main aspects, both of which are being examined reflectively and programmatically. Through its more formal aspect of the trade union local, the labor collective contributes to the maintenance of state discipline through "the regulation of work, its oversight functions in connection with the actions of management, [and] through participation in the administration of production."[65] The constitutional intent is for even greater participation by the work collective via the medium of the trade union in the regulation of labor relations in Soviet society.[66]

The labor collective manifests its will through other less institutionalized, more ad hoc forms of activity as well. "Production meetings" actively promote production and planning discipline,[67] while the comrades' courts are seen as the cynosure of the labor collective and as an arena for the legal socialization of workers, farmers, and employees.[68]

In the further implementation of the labor collective clause, greater authority is proposed for the production meeting in the selection and assignment of executive personnel.[69] In contrast, the powers of the comrades' courts were enlarged through new legislation in early 1977 just prior to the publication of the draft constitution. These courts now are empowered to impose significant material deprivations in instances of serious violations of labor discipline by individual workers. Such deprivations now include the possible cancellation of a free vacation at a trade union-owned resort, or the loss of one's position on the waiting list for enterprise-controlled housing.[70]

However, despite the ambitious projections for the labor collective, the main thrust of its activities seems to be channeled toward the maintenance of labor discipline and the protection of public property. This impression is reinforced by the fact that the journal *Socialist Legality* has now included in its monthly pages a new section entitled "In the Labor Collective" for reports from the field, so to speak, the bulk of which concern the enforcement of work rules and the safeguarding of enterprise property. In the first report of its kind the labor collective of a factory in the Moscow region outlined the key to its success in dramatically reducing—by nearly 75 percent—the number of man-hours lost due to infractions of labor discipline. This achievement was largely credited to the collective's comrades' court, its commission on drunkenness and alcholism, and the affiliated people's voluntary patrol, all three of which worked closely together in dealing with particular problems and in following up on certain undisciplined workers.[71]

Other reports from the field reveal that individual labor collectives have organized such institutions as the "Council for the Prevention of Lawbreaking and the Strengthening of Labor Discipline" and the "Commission for the Protection of Socialist Property."[72] As an adjunct of the legal subsystem, the labor collective's auxiliary law enforcement activities are not confined to the work place. In fact, in implicit reference to the linkage between the labor collective clause and the section of the constitution devoted to the legal subsystem (Part 7), it is currently being suggested that the labor collectives should increase their participation in the legal process as well as in the political system writ large through the assignment of "social accusers" and "social defenders" in those cases before the people's courts involving members of the particular collectives (Art.162).[73] In effect, the new constitution has been designed to channel social activism into the legal subsystem as well as the political process.

THE LEGAL SUBSYSTEM AND LEGAL DEVELOPMENT

The legal subsystem draws heavily on the social subsystem to supplement its network of institutions and procedures through the constitutional mobilization of the activist citizen, who is called upon to support the law enforcement process in various ways. Many of the constitutional duties imposed upon the Soviet citizen cast him in the role of a conscripted law enforcement auxiliary. Through the labor collective, the citizen is expected to participate collectively in the enforcement of the constitutional duty to work clause (Art. 60) as well as in the provision calling upon citizens to protect socialist property

(Art.61).[74] The duty to work clause is also now being construed to imply the citizen's traditional Soviet obligation initially to accept a particular job assignment upon completion of his specialized higher education.[75] Article 60 has constitutionalized for the first time the spirit of the antiparasite legislation, and therefore the individual is put on constitutional notice that if he willfully evades "socially useful labor" he will be in violation of his duty to work and inevitably bring himself to the attention of the legal authorities.[76]

The citizen as social auxiliary to the legal subsystem is expressly described in Article 65, which obliges the individual "to be intolerant of antisocial acts, and to assist in every way in the safeguarding of public order." Commenting on the implementation of this constitutional duty, legal scholars are proposing such ideas as increasing civic participation in the appeal stage of the judicial process and more actively encouraging civic assistance to the procurator.[77] Even in construing the potential implementation of the political culture clause, the new constitution's most programmatic article, other commentators are suggesting that greater socialist democracy can be promoted through drawing the trade union locals and the people's control groups into the work of procuratorial supervision in the industrial enterprises (Art.9).[78] Or, as another writer puts it, the publicity generated by the Procuracy will help "implement the requirement of Article 9 of the USSR Constitution [of taking into] *constant consideration public opinion* as a path to the further unfolding of socialist democracy."[79]

Turning now to the institutional and procedural infrastructure, the process of constitutional implementation began quite soon after ratification. In its first "guiding decision" for 1978, entitled "The New Constitution of the USSR and the Tasks of the Further Improvement of Judicial Practice," the all-union Supreme Court addressed the lower courts on the question of the implementation of the various constitutional provisions bearing on the activity of the judiciary. Citing the new constitution and the constitutional addresses of Brezhnev in 1977, the full bench of the high court determined that these authorities "require the adoption of measures for the further improvement of justice [and] the enlargement of the role of the courts in the strengthening of socialist legality and the legal order."

The judicial directive instructed the courts to carry out "the strict implementation of the constitutional norms" concerned with the protection of state, social, and citizen interests. Specific points in the directive then discussed the problems of adjudicating the various types of cases in light of the new constitution, including public property cases, juvenile delinquency cases, and cases involving environmental, labor, housing, and family issues, among others. The high court judges also reminded the lower judiciary of its obligation to observe the constitutional rules of equality before the law and the courts (Arts.34 and 156), collegial decision making including the people's assessors or cojudges (Art.154), and the citizen's right to defense (Art.158). In addition, the lower court judges were cautioned to follow strictly the requirements of substantive and procedural criminal law in order to avoid "judicial errors, especially the conviction of innocent persons, the most flagrant violation of the rights and freedoms of the citizen." Finally, the judiciary was required to be responsive to the citizen's new constitutional rights of criticism (Art. 49) and complaint (Art.58), both of which under certain circumstances entail the possibility of recourse to and implementation through the courts.[80]

As a learned commentator points out, Article 58 has substantially broadened the constitutional basis for the citizen's resort to the courts in defense of his rights and interests. Hence, he underscores the importance of observance of the constitutional "judicial independence" clause (Art.155), the principle which will facilitate "the growth of the prestige of justice in society and encourage citizens to turn to the court for help in case of actual or alleged violations of their rights."[81] In a veiled reference to the problem of "trial by press" in the Soviet Union, the author points out that the consistent implementation and maintenance of judicial independence is also subject to the judges' compliance with the constitutional provision that the questions of guilt and punishment can be determined only through the verdict of a court within the framework of the law.[82]

However, the main thrust of this commentary is addressed to the recurring problem in the Soviet legal system of interference in the judiciary by influential persons or organizations external to the legal process. In this spirit, the author reviews the earlier higher party directives to lower party organizations on the need to observe and maintain the distinction between legitimate party supervision over the courts institutionally and the proscribed tendency for some lower party officials and organizations occasionally to interfere in the adjudication of a particular case before a court. Implicitly recognizing the distinction between "political" cases involving dissidents and other nonconformists, in which the party and KGB regularly preempt the formal legal authorities, and the great bulk of ordinary, nonpolitical cases, the author concludes that implementation of the constitutional provision for judicial independence requires that court personnel be effectively insulated from "illegal influences" in adjudicating the latter category of cases.[83]

The theme of institutional autonomy seems also to be a central preoccupation of the literature on the implementation of the constitutional provisions on the Procuracy, especially the procuratorial independence clause (Art.168). After acknowledging the relevance of the party hegemony clause for the political supervision of the Procuracy, one of the most authoritative writers on the subject adds

> The political direction of procuratorial activity and party control over the work of the organs of the Procuracy are guaranteed on the basis of laws and, most of all, constitutional norms. Accordingly the party does not permit interference in the day-to-day activity of the Procuracy, considering such interference a violation not only of party discipline but also of socialist legality.[84]

However, the main activity in connection with the implementation of the constitutional chapter on the Procuracy (Chap. 21) has been the drafting and discussion within the legal profession of a new statute on the Procuracy from the summer of 1978 into the spring of 1979. The new legislation is intended to supersede the initial post-Stalin statute of 1955. The drafting of a new statute was authorized by the USSR Supreme Soviet, which directed that the USSR Procuracy undertake the drafting process in conjunction with the all-union Supreme Court, Ministry of Justice, and Ministry of Internal Affairs as well as the Committee on State Security (KGB).[85] In addition, the legal profession, especially procurators and scholarly specialists, participated in the drafting process within the framework of the legal institutions involved and, publicly, through the running discussion conducted monthly in the journal *Socialist Legality.*

The public phase of the drafting process initially took the form of proposals for specific articles to be included in the draft statute. This phase was initiated in *Socialist Legality* by a set of general proposals drawn up by two of the leading scholarly specialists on the institution of the Procuracy. In sharp departure from the 1955 statute and congruent with the trend under Brezhnev to acknowledge and articulate the party's role in the Soviet *Rechtsstaat*, the authors proposed implementing the party hegemony clause through *"the formulation of the norms of the Communist Party's . . . role in the organization and functioning of procuratorial supervision in the Statute on the Procuracy on the USSR."*[86] Among these norms, the authors suggest spelling out the distinction between authorized party supervision of the Procuracy and illegal direct party interference in the substantive activity of the Procuracy.[87]

The ensuing discussion produced a number of interesting

proposals, virtually all of which were intended to perfect the existing juridicization of the Soviet system or to juridicize *de novo* intra or interrelationships of the Procuracy which heretofore had not been subjected to legal definition. These proposals included defining the legal status of the Procuracy's professional investigators as well as its laymen social assistants in the new draft statute.[88] Other proposals recommended extending the Procuracy's supervisory writ over the rule-making authority of social organizations, as well as its traditional supervision over the legislative output of state organizations, in the spirit of the full implementation of the constitutional procuratorial supervision clause (Art.164).[89] Several writers suggested that the new statute should include greater procuratorial supervisory responsibility and authority over the initial phases of the criminal justice process, especially from arrest through the local militia's (police) investigation.[90]

Perhaps the largest number of proposals dealt with the Procuracy's relations with state agencies and social organizations in the ongoing maintenance of socialist legality and the preservation of law and order in Soviet society. The general theme was to suggest that the state's constitutional obligation to protect socialist legality (Art.4) should be implemented in the new Procuracy statute. The function of this important constitutional principle is to advance the process of juridicizing the interrelationships of state and society within the Soviet system. In addition to the Procuracy exercising its supervisory authority over state agencies and social organizations to ensure the maintenance of administrative legality, it was pointed out several times that the Procuracy also coordinates the activities of these same institutions in the conduct of law and order campaigns and in the course of constantly attending to the task of safeguarding socialist legality in general throughout the society. Therefore it stood to reason, as one writer pointed out, that the new statute should *uzakonit*, or legally define, the Procuracy's relations with the labor collectives,[91] the People's Control organization,[92] the State Bank of the USSR,[93] local soviets, [94] and the state and social institutions in general with which the Procuracy collaborates and coordinates in the interest of socialist legality.[95]

Finally, the citizen's new constitutional right of complaint is expected to create additional demands on both the Procuracy and the *advokatura*, or defense bar, as citizens increasingly avail themselves of the opportunity to seek judicial review of "actions of officials, performed in violation of the law and exceeding their authority, that infringe on the rights of citizens." (Art. 58). In response to this potential development, a senior administrator of the USSR Academy of Sciences' Institute of State and Law argued that "the Statute on the USSR Procuracy must provide for the right of procurators . . . to bring an action in court in defense of citizens whose rights have been infringed."[96]

In addition, the defense bar, which now enjoys greater authority by virtue of its inclusion in the new constitution (Art.161),[97] is also expected to experience a rise in the demand for its services as citizens begin to exercise their right to file complaints against public officials in court. This is especially relevant to the defense bar since the deputy chairman of the RSFSR Supreme Court, among others, construes Article 58 as the "further development" of the citizen's basic constitutional right to defense (Art.159).[98] In the same vein, a senior official of the all-union justice ministry anticipates that the new constitution in general, with its increased emphasis on the rights of citizens, will generate greater need for the work of the professional legal defender. Therefore, given the higher status of the defense bar and the increased demands placed upon it by the constitution as a whole and Article 58 in particular, the all-union official concludes that the relatively low salary scale of the defense attorney should be raised commensurate with his increased prestige,[99] while his counterpart in the RSFSR Ministry of Justice concludes elsewhere that these factors will require the training of more lawyers as well.[100]

As part of the long-term process of *Rechtsstaat*-building and the increasing tendency to carry forward the emphasis on juridicization of the institutions, procedures, and linkages of the Soviet system epitomized by the new constitution, the defense bar, along with many other components and aspects of the system as a whole, has been scheduled for a new postratification statute on its organization and functions. This is but part of a vast and ambitious codification program planned by the USSR Supreme Soviet, at its first post-ratification session in late 1977, to extend into the early 1980s and virtually complete the post-Stalin legal reform program underway since the mid-1950s. Included in this extensive "plan for the organization of the work of putting into effect USSR legislation in accordance with the constitution of the USSR" are new statutes on elections to the USSR Supreme Soviet, the USSR Council of Ministers, the International Treaty Regime, and the projected statute on the Procuracy, all of which have been discussed above. In addition, new statutes are scheduled for the procedures of the all-union Supreme Soviet, the USSR Supreme Court, the People's Control, State Arbitration, regional soviets, citizenship, the rights of labor collectives, and, of course, the defense bar referred to above.

Other more specialized statutes are intended to define particular functions or procedures of the Soviet system, including the use and safeguarding of the housing fund, the procedure for all-union referenda, various aspects of the protection of the natural environment, the procedure for fulfilling voters' mandates, the procedure for transferring economic institutions from one administrative jurisdiction to another, the basic legislative principles on administrative legal violations, the hierarchy and the procedure for awarding medals, and a series of legislative acts scheduled to implement the citizen's right of complaint and resort to court (Art.58).

Beyond the scheduled new codification as implementation of specific constitutional clauses or general constitutional themes, the all-union Supreme Soviet has also ordered that certain existing general statutes be supplemented and that others, as well as the major post-Stalin *osnovy*, or all-union basic principles for legislation in the various branches of Soviet law, be amended and revised in order to be brought into conformity with the requirements of the new constitution.[101]

Finally, in the realm of legislative development, Brezhnev and the leadership have directed the jurists systematically to compile, classify, and publish by the year 1985 a multivolume *Svod zakonov SSSR*, or the collection of extant all-union legislation, the first chapter of the first volume of which is already designated for the new USSR Constitution of 1977.[102]

CONSTITUTIONAL IMPLEMENTATION
OF CITIZEN-STATE RELATIONS

The projected long-term process of implementing constitutional provisions relevant to the legal subsystem and, in the metapolitical sense, relevant to other major subsystems as well, has vast implications for jurisprudence and, in particular, legal scholarship and legal education in the Soviet Union. The jurists themselves are well aware of the ongoing and long-term juridicization process underway in the Soviet system, with its dominant emphasis on tightening the linkage between law and the state. For them, especially the academic and theoretical jurists, the principal significance of the new constitution is that "sociopolitical development in the context of mature socialism rests on the assumption that the Soviet state and all of its constituent parts operate on the basis of law."[103]

The conclusion drawn from recognition of this constitutional orientation is that the value of law as an instrument for social control and development has been greatly enhanced and, consequently, the

Soviet legal profession will benefit substantially in terms of its status and the stature of its members in Soviet society.[104] This, of course, will entail a series of major new practical and theoretical tasks for the juridical profession, including its active participation in the further development of "the entire socialist legal superstructure" through the 1980s to the year 2000, the reconceptualization of the place and functions of law in Soviet society to include such relatively new aspects as legal consciousness and legal culture, and the redefinition of citizen-state relations within the general theory of law and state.[105] In the spirit of the latter task, the resolutions of the major all-union conference in late 1978 on "The Tasks of the Further Development of Juridical Science in Light of the New USSR Constitution and the Constitutions of the Union and Autonomous Republics" specifically direct Soviet legal philosophers to work out "a theory of the legal position of the individual, [and] the state and legal guarantees for the development of the individual as the ultimate purpose of social- ism."[106]

The numerous constitutional provisions bearing on the relation- ship of the citizen to the state will, of course, serve as the point of departure in the planned theoretical undertaking. At the core of such a legal theory of man and society in the Soviet Union will be the conception of the new constitution as an explicit social compact between the state and the citizen under the aegis of the Communist Party, which occupies the Hobbesian role of a metajuridical entity above and outside of the Soviet system as a whole.[107] The essence of this contract theory is that the state fulfills designated functions and, in return, the citizenry perform specific social duties. This contractual principle was expressly included in the constitution's two so-called linkage clauses (Arts.39 and 59), the latter of which, in a phrase inspired by Marx, explicitly states that "the exercise of rights and liberties is inseparable from the performance by citizens of their duties."[108]

The constitutional counterbalancing of the state's obligations and civic duties can be seen clearly in the Soviet leadership's recent concern for the protection of the natural environment. In Article 18, the state is obligated to protect the environment in the interest of society while, reciprocally, in Article 67 "USSR citizens are obliged to protect nature and to safeguard its riches." In a more diffuse example, although one more central to the day-to-day life of the Soviet citizen, the new constitution requires that the state and its agencies "ensure the protection of law and order, the interests of society and the right and liberties of citizens" (Art.4). In effect, the Soviet state must obey the constitution and the laws, including the legal rules directly relevant to the individual in the criminal and civil process and in the administration of the society in general. In return for the constitutional protection of his rights, the citizen simultaneously is constitutionally obligated to behave within certain parameters and carry out a host of civic duties, including the requirement "to assist in every way in the safeguarding of public order" (Art. 65).

Apropos of the citizen's many constitutional rights, it must be remembered that the constitution is written in the general language and idiom of a metapolicy with systemic implications, and therefore is relatively inoperative on the practical plane. As a result, the letter and spirit of the constitution can be realized only through legislative implementation and actual practice. With reference to the analysis of various aspects of the constitutional implementation process in this chapter, it could be reasonably argued that streamlining the Soviet political system and rationalizing the economic subsystem are steps beneficial to the party and to the incumbent leadership. Similarly, the relative opening up of the social subsystem and the improvement and refinement of its legal counterpart result in a roughly equal cost-benefit ratio for the state and citizen respectively. However, this ratio is substantially tipped in favor of the citizen when the question of the constitutional implementation of citizen-state relations arises. Therefore, I would argue that the implementation of the constitutional provisions of the presumption of innocence (Art. 160), the right to defense (Art. 158), and the court-enforceable right of complaint (Art. 58), will be ultimate tests of the integrity of the new Soviet Constitution of 1977 and its implementation into operative legislation and practice.

All three of these rights were discussed by a small group of reform-minded legal scholars during the nationwide discussion of the draft constitution in 1977. The various proposed emendations to these rights as defined in the draft document were largely ignored in the preratification constitutional revision process.[109] Some of the same jurists and other like-minded ones are presently engaged in the discussion in the legal literature on the implementation of these rights. It remains to be seen whether the party leadership will be more responsive in this phase. For instance, a compromise position on the classic Western conception of the "presumption of innocence" was incorporated in the post-Stalin criminal law and criminal procedural reforms under Khrushchev and, subsequently, the higher courts for the most part have enforced the principle in the appellate and review process. Now with the implicit inclusion of the presumption principle in Article 160 and the subsequent official commentary on it by the plenum of the USSR Supreme Court, the concept of the presumption of innocence has been converted into, in the court's phrase, a "constitutional principle."[110] In the wake of the constitutionalization of the presumption of innocence, reform jurists are recommending that the criminal procedural legislation be revised to include a fully explicit and unqualified declaration of the defendant's right to enjoy the presumption of his innocence.[111] They are also beginning to explore the implications of the constitutional wording of this right for the preliminary investigation, as well as the judicial stage of the criminal process, the status of the individual before a comrades' court or a juvenile commission, and the new statute being drafted on the role and functions of the defense attorney.[112]

The constitutional principle of the presumption of innocence, in the authoritative interpretation of the all-union Supreme Court, is also secured implicitly in the constitutional right to defense (Art. 158).[113] In turn, the right to defense is seen to have been significantly strengthened (compared to the 1936 Constitution) by the higher law status now accorded to the presumption principle.[114] In addition, the citizen's right to defense has been enhanced in the new constitution in the recognition accorded the defense bar for the first time in a Soviet constitution (Art.161) and in the acknowledgment of the right of the labor collective to participate in court proceedings through the assignment of one of its members to a case as either a "social accuser" or "social defender" (Art.162). The latter roles are presently intended in the current legislation to be performed only in the initial trial phase of the criminal process, while the constitutional clause extends the labor collective's participatory right to the civil process as well, and a leading reform jurist has interpreted the clause to mean that authorized laymen may also participate, in addition, in the appellate process of both criminal and civil proceedings.[115]

However, an even more substantial enlargement of the right to defense has occurred through the inclusion of citizens' new constitutional right "to legal protection against attempts on their honor and dignity, their lives and health, and their personal freedom and property" (Art.57).[116] The "right to protection" clause also opens up the possibility for an individual personally to press criminal charges as a means of defense of his person and property.[117] Traditionally, the Soviet constitutional right to defense was accorded to the citizen as defendant within the criminal justice process. However, the expanded concept of defense in the new constitution now also includes, within the framework of Article 57, the right to file suit as a plaintiff in a civil proceeding for the purpose of protecting one's rights and interests.[118]

Ultimately, the greatest expansion of the citizen's right to defense within the Soviet system will come through the new court-enforceable constitutional right of complaint, if it is effectively implemented in the future (Art.58). Although the reform jurists' proposal to incorporate a special tier of courts for reviewing administrative actions in the draft constitution was rejected by the party leadership,[119] these jurists now are proposing the use of Article 58 as a surrogate for the extension of the principle of judicial review over a wide range of administrative acts heretofore not subject to formal appeal.

The USSR Supreme Court has alerted the lower courts to be prepared to implement correctly the right to complaint and the related right to criticism (Art.49) clauses.[120] Both the Procuracy and the defense bar are aware of the implications of Article 58 for their respective work loads, and a learned commentator argues that the demands anticipated via this clause make more imperative than ever the necessity of full implementation of the judicial independence clause (Art.155).[121] Finally, the interest in Article 58 among the legal profession is so great, the discussion over the implementation of the clause so lively and diversified, and the implications so significant that the major law journal *Soviet State and Law* devoted a substantial section of one issue to the subject, led off by a statement of the position of the prestigious Institute of State and Law of the USSR Academy of Sciences entitled "The USSR Constitution and the Broadening of the Judicial Defense of the Rights of Citizens."[122]

A number of major legal scholars have contributed to the growing discussion through individual articles. One writes that the constitutional right to complaint clause "will significantly enlarge the boundaries of judicial control over legality in the activities of the administrative apparatus." However, because of the courts' very slack past performance in this part of their jurisdiction, the author proposes that the courts themselves will have to be "checked" regularly through meetings of judicial personnel to ensure that they are carrying out their tasks in the spirit of Article 58.[123] Others write that while Article 58 will enhance the prestige of the judiciary, it will at the same time require more and better qualified judges to review citizens' complaints against arbitrary administrative actions.

Another direction in the ongoing discussion concerns the question of special legislative implementation of the right to complaint clause. Two approaches are being suggested—a global, open-ended approach to the types of complaints that would be judicially reviewable and, in contrast, a broad but specific set of categories within which a reviewable complaint would have to fall. The consensus seems to favor the latter approach.[124] In the legislative implementation phase, a very prominent reform jurist proposed that the right of complaint be broadened to include administrative agencies as well as individual officials,[125] a suggestion opening up vast possibilities, some of which are outlined by a leading administrative law specialist in another article in the same issue of *Soviet Justice*. The latter noted generally that virtually all of the rights and liberties included in the new constitution should fall within the purview of judicial protection. Specifically, he recommended judicial review of motor vehicle violations and considering the possibility of permitting citizens to bring government agencies into court in defense of the environment.[126]

Finally, a number of proposals are being put forward suggesting strategies by which the right to complaint clause can be used to help implement other constitutional clauses, as recommended by the administrative law specialist above, and defend citizens' rights already codified in current legislation. For instance, the citizen is urged to invoke Article 58 in defense of the constitutional "personal inviolability" clause (Art.56) against the illegal "interference of society and the state in his personal life."[127] In violation of existing labor legislation, a number of workers are transferred illegally from one job to another, and the courts have either ignored their protests or dealt with them ineffectively according to the RSFSR Supreme Court. Article 58 is suggested as a solution to the problem.[128] Another writer points out that the meaning of the right to complaint clause should be construed to include "inaction" as well as an administrative act as the basis for complaint and recourse to the courts. Within this broader construction, she observes that it would become possible for retired persons more successfully to challenge administrative inaction on their pension rights in violation of the spirit of implementing the constitutional "social security" clause (Art.43).[129]

In other instances, it is pointed out that administrative "action" is often the root of the problem, hence Article 58 can also be used to successfully defend the right to disability benefits within the social security clause.[130] Yet another major legal scholar suggests that the constitutional right to housing (Art.44) could also be successfully defended within the framework of the court-enforceable right to complaint clause.[131] Finally, in view of the great volume of petitions and complaints anticipated in the course of citizens acting upon their joint constitutional rights of criticism (Art.49) and complaint, better collection, classification, and statistical analysis of these civic documents is suggested in the interest of the enforcement of administrative legality in citizen-state relations.[132]

In conclusion, the eventual implementation of this single clause, Article 58, with its potentially profound implications for the internal dynamics of the Soviet system, may well serve as the critical test of how far the incumbent leadership, and eventually the post-Brezhnev leadership, will go in the process of juridicizing interrelationships within the system. The "bottom line" is likely to be whether this particular feature of the Soviet-style *Rechtsstaat* being constructed within the framework of the 1977 Constitution, helps or hinders the party in its governance of the vast constitutional bureaucracy of the Soviet Union.

Whatever the outcome, Soviet law has now secured a firm place in the process of constitutional implementation and Soviet development as "an extremely important regulator of socialist social relations and an effective instrument of social administration."[133]

NOTES

1. For a comprehensive analysis of the draft, discussion revision, and ratification of the new constitution, see Robert Sharlet, *The New Soviet Constitution of 1977: Analysis and Text* (Brunswick, Oh.: King's Court, 1978), pp. 1–71. For an English translation of the constitution, see ibid., pp. 73–131. See also John N. Hazard's analysis, "A Constitution for 'Developed Socialism,'" in *Soviet Law After Stalin: Part II—Social Engineering Through Law*, ed. Donald D. Barry, George Ginsburgs, and Peter B. Maggs (Alphen aan den Rijn, Holland: Sijthoff & Noordhoff, 1978), pp. 1–33.

2. "Konstitutsiya razvitogo sotsializma: Pervaya godovshchina konstitutsii obshchenarodnogo gosudarstva," *Sotsialisticheskaya zakonnost*, no. 10 (1978): 3–5. For English translations of Brezhnev's two principal speeches on the new constitution, see *Current Digest of the Soviet Press* 29 (July 6, 1977): 6–10; and ibid. 29 (October 26, 1977): 1–7, 13.

3. B. Puginskii and V. Orlov, "Arbitrazh i povyshenie effektivnosti khozyaistvovaniya," *Sovetskaya yustitsiya*, no. 1 (1979): 12.

4. I. Mishenin, "Sovershenstvovat deyatelnost advokatury po zashchite prav i interesov grazhdan," *Sovetskaya yustitsiya*, no. 2 (1979): 1.

5. A. Chikste, "Pravovoe vospitanie v kolkhoze," *Sotsialisticheskaya zakonnost*, no. 6 (1978): 42.

6. Sharlet, *New Soviet Constitution*. pp. 8–9.

7. S.L. Ronin, "Programmnye idei sovetskogo konstitutsionnogo stroitelstva," *Sovetskoe gosudarstvo i pravo*, no. 11 (1978): 22.

8. N. Farberov, "Vazhnoe sobytie v politicheskoi istorii strany," *Sovetskaya yustitsiya*, no. 5 (1978): 7. On the new constitution and de-Stalinization in general, see Robert Sharlet, "De-Stalinization and Soviet Constitutionalism," in *The Soviet Union Since Stalin*, ed. Stephen F. Cohen, Alexander Rabinowitch, and Robert Sharlet (Bloomington; Indiana University Press, 1980).

9. N.A. Mikhaileva, "Ponyatie i sistema printsipov sotsialisticheskoi konstitutsii," *Pravovedenie*, no. 6 (1977): 33.

10. E.A. Kiseleva, book review of K. Svoboda and S. Svobodova, *Novaya konstitutsiya SSSR* (Prague: Narodnoe izdatelstvo, 1978), in *Sovetskoe gosudarstvo i pravo*, no. 3 (1979): 169–70.

11. On metapolicy, see Robert Sharlet, "Soviet Legal Policy Making: A Preliminary Classification," in *Social System and Legal Process* ed. Harry M. Johnson (San Francisco: Jossey-Bass, 1978), pp. 209–29; and Robert Sharlet, "Legal Policy Under

Khrushchev and Brezhnev: Continuity and Change," in Barry, Ginsburgs, and Maggs, ed., *Soviet Law After Stalin*: Part II, pp. 319-30.

12. V.A. Rzhevskii, "Osobennosti sovetskikh konstitutsionnykh norm," *Pravovedenie*, no. 6 (1977): 20-28, esp. 23.

13. Farberov, "Vazhnoe Sobytie," p. 6; and I.M. Stepanov, "Konstitutsiya razvitogo sotsializma: Sotsialnaia tsennost i osnovnye funktsii," *Sovetskoe gosudarstvo i pravo*, no. 12 (1978): 8-9.

14. Stepanov, "Konstitutsiya," p. 10.

15. A. Orlov, "Zadachi sudebnykh organov v dele borby s prestupnostyu," *Sovetskaya yustitsiya*, no. 22 (1978): 1-2.

16. L.T. Krivenko, "Konstitutsiya SSSR i zadachi sovetskogo gosudarstvovedeniya," *Sovetskoe gosudarstvo i pravo*, no. 5 (1978): 140.

17. V.I. Gavrilenko, "Voprosy teorii novoi konstitutsii SSSR," *Pravovedenie*, no. 3 (1978): 127-28.

18. V.S. Osnovin, "Konstitutsiya SSSR i nauka gosudarstvennogo prava," *Pravovedenie*, no. 4 (1978): 11. See also the section "A Soviet 'Systems' Approach," in Sharlet, *New Soviet Constitution*, pp. 10-15.

19. "Dialektika razvitiya sovetskoi gosudarstvennosti i konstitutsiya SSSR," *Sovetskoe gosudarstvo i pravo*, no. 4 (1978): 4. For the influence of the party program on other articles, see Sharlet, *New Soviet Constitution*, pp. 14-15.

20. A. Kositsyn, "KPSS—yadro sovetskoi politicheskoi sistemy," *Sotsialisticheskaya zakonnost*, no. 1 (1979): 3. Compare Arts. 126 and 141 of the 1936 Constitution, translated in *Basic Laws on the Structure of the Soviet State*, ed. Harold J. Berman and John B. Quigley, Jr. (Cambridge: Harvard University Press, 1969), pp. 3-28.

21. "Dialektika razvitiya," p. 11. Emphasis is in the original as are all other italicized quotes in this chapter.

22. Ibid., p. 10; and E. Lukasheva, "Ukreplenie pravovykh osnov gosudarstennoi i obshchestvennoi zhizni," *Sotsialisticheskaya zakonnost*, no. 8 (1978): 4.

23. See generally, R. Rudenko [USSR Procurator General], a strazhe sotsialisticheskoi zakonnosti," *Kommunist*, no. 10 (1977): 57-68; and V. Kuznetsov [Candidate Member of the CPSU Politburo], "Konstitutsiya SSSR v deistvii," *Kommunist*, no. 15 (1978): 3-18.

24. V.G. Strekozov, "Zashchita sotsialisticheskogo otechestva—Funktsiya sovetskogo obshchenarodnogo gosudarstva," *Sovetskoe gosudarstvo i pravo*, no. 3 (1979): 14.

25. Ibid., p. 15.

26. "The Supreme Soviet Session—III," *Current Digest of the Soviet Press* 30 (August 16, 1978): 14.

27. "The Law on Supreme Soviet Elections," *Current Digest of the Soviet Press* 30 (August 23, 1978): 11-17.

28. P.G. Mishunin and V.I. Nekrasov, "Zakon o Pravitelstve SSSR," *Sovetskoe gosudarstvo i pravo*, no. 2 (1979): 13.

29. "Law on the USSR Council of Ministers," *Current Digest of the Soviet Press* 30 (August 2, 1978): 20.

30. Mishunin and Nekrasov, "Zakon," p. 21; and L. Saratovskikh, "Novoe v zakonodatelstve o vyborakh v verkhovnyi sovet SSSR," *Sotsialisticheskaya zakonnost*, no. 11 (1978): 10.

31. G.I. Tunkin and R.A. Myullerson, "Zakon o mezhdunarodnykh dogovorakh SSSR," *Sovetskoe gosudarstvo i pravo*, no. 2 (1979): 23.

32. G.V. Barabashev and K.F. Sheremet, "Novaya sovetskaya konstitutsiya i nauka sovetskogo stroitelstva," *Sovetskoe gosudarstvo i pravo*, no. 2 (1979): 10.

33. Lukasheva, "Ukreplenie," p. 3; and L.A. Grigorian, "Konstitutsionnoe zakreplenie politicheskoi sistemy SSSR," *Sovetskoe gosudarstvo i pravo*, no. 12 (1978): 131.

34. Lukasheva, "Ukreplenie," p. 7; and Ts. Yampolskaya, "Konstitutsiya SSSR ob obshchestvennykh organizatsiyakh," *Sotsialisticheskaya zakonnost*, no. 11 (1978): 4.

35. R.O. Khalfina, "Konstitutsionnye printsipy rukovodstva ekonomikoi," *Sovetskoe gosudarstvo i pravo*, no. 8 (1978): 10.

36. R.O. Khalfina, "Ekonomicheskaya sistema razvitogo sotsializma," *Sotsialisticheskaya zakonnost*, no. 9 (1978): 6-7.

37. K. Khasanov, "Preduprezhdenie khishchenii v potrebitelskoi kooperatsii," *Sotsialisticheskaya zakonnost*, no. 2 (1978): 20. See also, generally, Stanislaw Pomorski, "Criminal Law Protection of Socialist Property in the USSR," in *Soviet Law After Stalin: Part I—The Citizen and the State in Contemporary Soviet Law*, ed. Donald D. Barry, George Ginsburgs, and Peter B. Maggs (Leiden: A.W. Sijthoff, 1977), pp. 223-58.

38. O.S. Kolbasov, "Problemy okhrany okruzhayushchei sredy v novoi konstitutsii SSSR," *Sovetskoe gosudarstvo i pravo*, no. 5 (1978): 23.

39. R. Valeeva and E. Magnitskaya, "Nekotorye voprosy materialnoi otvetstvennosti rabotnikov torgovli," *Sovetskaya yustitsiya*, no. 23 (1978): 12; E. Nikulin, "Isk prokurora—Effecktivnoe sredstvo borby s beskhozyaistvennost yu i rastochitelstvom," *Sotsialisticheskaya zakonnost*, no. 3 (1978): 8; and Kolbasov, "Probleny," p. 25. See also, generally, Stanislaw Pomorski, "Crimes Against the Central Planner:'Ochkovtiratel'stvo'," in Barry, Ginsburgs, and Maggs, eds., *Soviet Law After Stalin*: Part II, pp. 291-317.

40. A.M. Nechaeva, "Vospitanie chuvstva otvetstvennosti pered semei," *Sovetskoe gosudarstvo i pravo*, no. 3 (1979): 39-45. See also, generally, Peter H. Juviler, "Law and the Delinquent Family: Reproduction and Upbringing," in Barry, Ginsburgs, and Maggs, eds., *Soviet Law After Stalin*: Part II, pp. 205-40.

41. V. Zhigulenkova and I. Zablotskii, "Razbiratelstvo del o rastorzhenii braka," *Sovetskaya yustitsiya*, no. 24 (1978): 9-10; and T. Evdokimova, "Uchastie roditelya, ne prozhivayushchego vmeste s detmi, v ikh vospitanii," *Sotsialisticheskaya zakonnost*, no. 3 (1978): 42-44.

42. R. Seferovskaya, "Prepodavanie prava v shkolakh moskovskoi oblasti," *Sovetskaya yustitsiya*, no. 24 (1978): 15.

43. E. Panskaya, "Narodnye universitety pravovykh znanii v sisteme pravovogo vospitaniya," *Sotsialisticheskaya zakonnost*, no. 5 (1978): 74.

44. Yu. Korenevskii, book review of T.N. Dobrovolskaya et al., *Pravosudie, arbitrazh i prokurorskii nadzor v SSSR* (Moscow: Znanie, 1978), in *Sovetskaya yustitsiya*, no. 3 (1979): 31.

45. "Goskino SSSR: Zhdem pomoshchi yuristov," *Sotsialisticheskaya zakonnost*, no. 2 (1979): 53.

46. V. Kuznetsov, "Propaganda konstitutsii SSSR—Nash professionalnyi dolg," *Sotsialisticheskaya zakonnost*, no. 5 (1978): 8-10; and *Sovetskaya yustitsiya*, no. 5 (1978): 10-24, which is devoted to a series of articles on "legal propaganda."

47. A. Stavtseva, "Pervyi kodeks zakonov o trude," *Sotsialisticheskaya zakonnost*, no. 12 (1978): 36.

48. M. Kozyr, "Razvitie sotsialnykh prav chlenov kolkhoza i usilenie ikh yuridicheskikh garantii," *Sotsialisticheskaya zakonnost*, no. 2 (1978): 12. See also generally, Peter B. Maggs, "The Legal Status of Collective Farm Members," in Barry, Ginsburgs, and Maggs, ed., *Soviet Law After Stalin: Part I* pp. 159-78.

49. G.V. Chubykov, "Pravo chlenov kolkhozov na vybor professii, roda zanyatii i raboty," *Sovetskoe gosudarstvo i pravo*, no. 2 (1979): 43.

50. Ibid., p. 41.

51. Ibid., p. 44.

52. L. Sukhareva, "Pravovye voprosy povysheniya kvalifikatsii rabochikh i sluzhashchikh," *Sovetskaya yustitsiya*, no. 19 (1978): 8-9.

53. B. Blokhin, "Isklyuchit sluchai nezakonnogo uvolneniya rabochikh i sluzhashchikh," *Sovetskaya yustitsiya*, no. 2 (1978): 11. See also generally, Zigurds L. Zile, "Soviet Law of Job Security: Controlling the Individual Employee's Choice in a Non-Market Economy," in Barry, Ginsburgs, and Maggs, ed., *Soviet Law After Stalin: Part I* pp. 259-97.

54. V. Mannanov, "Ispolnenie zakonov ob izobreteniyakh i ratsionalizatorskikh predlozheniyakh pod deistvennyi kontrol," *Sotsialisticheskaya zakonnost*, no. 2 (1978): 24-27.

55. K.S. Batygin, "Razvitie osnovnykh form sotsialnogo obespecheniya v svete konstitutsii SSSR," *Sovetskoe gosudarstvo i pravo*, no. 3 (1979): 19.

56. V. Ivanov, "Lgotnye usloviya truda rabotnikov s ponizhennoi trudosposobnostyu," *Sotsialisticheskaya zakonnost*, no. 12 (1978): 52-53; and A. Zaikin and A. Egorov, "Pensii po sluchayu poteri kormiltsa," *Sovetskaya yustitsiya*, no. 16 (1978): 26-27.

57. V. Litovkin, "Pravo na zhilishche," *Sovetskaya yustitsiya*, no. 2 (1978): 22. See also generally, Donald D. Barry, "Soviet Housing Law: The Norms and Their Applications," in Barry, Ginsburgs, and Maggs, ed., *Soviet Law After Stalin: Part I* pp. 1-32.

58. Yu.K. Tolstoi, "Konstitutsiya SSSR i Zhilishchnoe zakonodatelstvo," *Pravovedenie*, no. 5 (1978): 36-37.

59. "Postanovlenie No. 6 Plenuma Verkhovnogo Suda SSSR," *Sovetskaya yustitsiya*, no. 15 (1978): 26-28.

60. P. Ya. Trubnikov, "Zakonodatelstvo o ZhSK i praktika primeniya ego sudami," *Sovetskoe gosudarstvo i pravo*, no. 3 (1979): 53-60.

61. B. Dukalskii, "Zashchita prava lichnoi sobstvennosti na stroenie," *Sovetskaya yustitsiya*, no. 2 (1979): 18.

62. Letter from B. Butaev, *Sotsialisticheskaya zakonnost*, no. 10 (1978): 47; and Letter from B. Belikov, *Sotsialisticheskaya zakonnost*, no. 1 (1979): 28.

63. Yu.K. T lstoi, "Konstitutsiya SSSR i pravo sobstvennosti," *Sovetskoe gosudarstvo i pravo*, no. 7 (1978): 17-19.

64. See, for example, M. Gorlachev, "Ukreplenie distsipliny i obshchestvennogo poryadka—postoyannaya zabota kollektiva," *Sotsialisticheskaya zakonnost*, no. 11 (1978): 39-40.

65. Yu.P. Orlovskii, "Mesto i rol trudovogo kollektiva v sisteme trudovykh otnoshenii," *Sovetskoe gosudarstvo i pravo*, no. 4 (1979): 70.

66. Ibid., p. 68.

67. A. Sukharev, "Usilivat pravovospitatelnuyu rol trudovogo kollektiva," *Sotsialisticheskaya zakonnost*, no. 10 (1978): 8-9.

68. Ibid., p. 9.

69. Yu.P. Orlovskii, "Mesto i rol," p. 66.

70. Ibid., pp. 71-72.

71. D. Olkhov, "Vospitatelnye vozmozhnosti kollektiva," *Sotsialisticheskaya zakonnost*, no. 9 (1978): 40-44.

72. See "V trudovom kollektive," *Sotsialisticheskaya zakonnost*, no. 12 (1978): 44, 45.

73. B. Blokhin and N. Tarnaev, "Effektivnost' obshchestvennogo obvineniya i zashchity," *Sotsialisticheskaya zakonnost*, no. 3 (1979): 28.

74. E. Golovanova, "Ukreplenie trudovoi distsipliny—zalog povysheniya effektivnosti proizvodstva," *Sovetskaya yustitsiya*, no. 3 (1979): 16-18. On the array of duties constitutionally imposed on the citizen generally, see Sharlet, *New Soviet Constitution*, pp. 54-55.

75. K. Shkurov, "Prava i obyazannosti uchashchikhsya i vypusknikov profes-sionalno-tekhnicheskikh uchebnykh zavedenii," *Sotsialisticheskaya zakonnost*, no. 10 (1978): 46.

76. G. Akhverdyan, "Sudy v borbe s litsami, vedushchimi paraziticheskii obraz zhizni," *Sotsialisticheskaya zakonnost*, no. 1 (1978): 58–59.

77. G. Anashkin, book review of V.A. Teplov, *Opredelenie suda pervoi instantsii po ugolovnomu delu* (Saratov: Izd-vo Saratovskogo universiteta, 1977), in *Sotsialisti-cheskaya zakonnost*, no. 9 (1978): 91–92; and N. Bezryadin and V. Rozenfeld, "Organi-zatsiya raboty obshchestvennykh pomoshchnikov prokurora," *Sotsialisticheskaya za-konnost*, no. 3 (1978): 20–23.

78. Kh. Sanginov, "Povyshat rezultativnost aktov prokurorskogo reagirovaniya," *Sotsialisticheskaya zakonnost*, no. 12 (1978): 28.

79. S. Berezovskaya, "Demokraticheskie nachala v deyatelnosti prokuratory," *Sotsialisticheskaya zakonnost*, no. 8 (1978): 33.

80. "Postanovlenie No. 1 Plenuma Verkhovnogo Suda SSSR," *Sovetskaya yustit-siya*, no. 6 (1978): 25–27, pts. 1, 2, 4–8, 11, 13, 17, 19.

81. N.V. Radutnaya, "Nezavisimost sudei—konstitutsionnyi printsip sotsialisti-cheskogo pravosudiya," *Sovetskoe gosudarstvo i pravo*, no. 3 (1979): 147. For a study of party-court relations, see Robert Sharlet, "The Communist Party and the Administra-tion of Justice in the USSR," in Donald D. Barry, George Ginsburgs, and Peter B. Maggs, eds. *Soviet Law After Stalin: Part III—Soviet Institutions and the Administration of Law* (Alphen aan den Rijn, Holland; Sijthoff & Noordhoff, 1979).

82. Radutnaya, "Nezavisimost sudei," p. 154.

83. Ibid., pp. 149–50. For critical analysis of the problem of Soviet "political justice," which is beyond the scope of this chapter, see Valery Chalidze, "Human Rights in the New Soviet Constitution," in Barry, Ginsburgs, and Maggs, eds., *Soviet Law After Stalin: Part II.*, pp. 67–82; Christopher Osakwe, "Due Process of Law and Civil Rights Cases in the Soviet Union," in Barry, Ginsburgs, and Maggs, eds., *Soviet Law After Stalin: Part I* pp. 179–221; and Robert Sharlet, "Dissent and Repression in the Soviet Union and Eastern Europe: Changing Patterns Since Khrushchev," *International Jour-nal* (Autumn 1978): 763–95.

84. S.G. Novikov, "Konstitutsiya SSSR i prokurorskii nadzor," *Pravovedenie*, no. 5 (1978): 31. See also generally, Gordon B. Smith, *The Soviet Procuracy and the Supervision of Administration* (Alphen aan den Rijn, Holland: Sijthoff & Noordhoff, 1978).

85. *Vedomosti Verkhovnogo Soveta SSSR*, no. 51 (December 21, 1977): item 764, pt. 10.

86. V. Zvirbul and S. Novikov, "Nauchnye osnovy zakonodatelnogo regulirovaniya deyatelnosti prokuratury," *Sotsialisticheskaya zakonnost*, no. 7 (1978): 34.

87. Ibid., pp. 34–35.

88. G. Brovin, "Preemstvennost i novye polozheniya," *Sotsialisticheskaya zakon-nost*, no. 12 (1978): 57; and N. Bezyadin's proposal, *Sotsialisticheskaya zakonnost*, no. 8 (1978): 35.

89. Bezyadin proposal, p. 34.

90. See D. Bakaev's proposal on arrest, *Sotsialisticheskaya zakonnost*, no. 1 (1979): 48. See M. Guzhavin and R. Gotliv, ibid., p. 47; and A. Balashov in *Sotsialisti-cheskaya zakonnost*, no. 11 (1978): 59, on militia investigations.

91. See Bezryadin proposal, p. 35.

92. See P. Pogrebnoi's proposal, ibid., p. 34.

93. K. Skvortsov, "Konstitutsiya SSSR i zakonodatelnoe regulirovanie organizatsii i deyatelnosti sovetskoi prokuratury," *Sotsialisticheskaya zakonnost*, no. 9 (1978): 35. The author uses the term *uzakonit* on p. 36.

94. Bezryadin proposal, p. 35.

95. See Skvortsov, "Konstitutsiya," p. 36; M. Teplitskii's proposal, *Sotsialisticheskaya zakonnost,* no. 10 (1978): 59; and I. Krasnikov's proposal, *Sotsialisticheskaya zakonnost,* no. 11 (1978): 58.

96. G. Murashin and O. Lyakhovich, "Razvitie konstitutsionnykh polozhenii v zakonodatelstve o sovetskoi prokurature," *Sotsialisticheskaya zakonnost,* no. 1 (1979): 46.

97. S. Natrushkin and I. Sukharev, "Oplata yuridicheskoi pomoshchi okazyvaemoi advokatami," *Sotsialisticheskaya zakonnost,* no. 4 (1978): 31; and I. Mishenin, "Sovershenstvovat deyatelnost advokatury po zashchite prav i interesov grazhdan," *Sovetskaya yustitsiya,* no. 2 (1979): 1.

98. N. Sergeeva, "Nekotorye voprosy uchastiya advokatov v grazhdanskom sudoproizvodstve," *Sovetskaya yustitsiya,* no. 2 (1979): 4.

99. Natrushkin and Sukharev, "Oplata," p. 33-34.

100. V. Volkova, "Zadachi kollegii advokatov RSFSR v osushchestvlenii konstitutsionnykh printsipov zashchity prav i zakonnykh interesov grazhdan," *Sovetskaya yustitsiya,* no. 1 (1978): 7-8.

101. *Vedomosti Verkhovnogo Soveta,* no. 51 (December 21, 1977): item 764.

102. "Voprosy *Svoda Zakonov*: Postanovlenie Tsentralnogo Komiteta KPSS, Prezidiuma Verkhovnogo Soveta SSSR i Soveta Ministrov SSSR ot 23 Marta 1978 no. 229," *Sotsialisticheskaya zakonnost,* no. 7 (1978): 78-80; "Zadachi sovershenstvovaniya zakonodatelstva v svete novoi Konstitutsii SSSR," ibid., pp. 3-7; and A.S. Pigolkin and G.T. Chernobel, "*Svod Zakonov SSSR*—Teoreticheskie i prakticheskie problemy," *Pravovedenie,* no. 6 (1978): 25-32. See also generally, William E. Butler, "Toward A *Svod Zakonov* for the Union of Soviet Socialist Republics," in *Codification in the Communist World,* ed. F.J.M. Feldbrugge (Leiden: A.W. Sijthoff, 1975), pp. 89-111.

103. "Zadachi dalneishego razvitiya sovetskoi yuridicheskoi nauki," *Pravovedenie,* no. 6 (1978): 7.

104. Ibid.; and V.N. Kudryavtsev, "Aktualnye problemy nauchnykh issledovanii v svete novoi konstitutsii SSSR," *Sovetskoe gosudarstvo i pravo,* no. 9 (1978): 133-34.

105. Kudryantsen, "Aktualnye problemy," pp. 134-35, 138; and "Zadachi dalneishego razvitiya," p. 10.

106. "Rekomendatsii vsesoiuznoi nauchno-korrdinatsionnoi konferentsii," *Sovetskoe gosudarstvo i pravo,* no. 3 (1979): 156-57. On legal education, see V.F. Maslov and R.S. Pavlovskii, "Konstitutsiya SSSR i uchebno-vospitatelnyi protsess v vuzakh," *Pravovedenie,* no. 6 (1978): 88-92.

107. On the contract theory of the new constitution, see Sharlet, "De-Stalinization and Soviet Constitutionalism." On the metajuridical conception of the party, see Robert Sharlet, "Stalinism and Soviet Legal Culture," in *Stalinism: Essays in Historical Interpretation,* ed. Robert C. Tucker (New York: Norton, 1977), pp. 155-79, esp. 155-56.

108. V. Maslennikov, "Vzaimosviaz konstitutsionnykh prav i obyazannostei grazhdan," *Sotsialisticheskaya zakonnost,* no. 3 (1978): 3.

109. See Sharlet, *New Soviet Constitution,* pp. 38-44, 48.

110. "Postanovlenie No. 5 Plenuma Verkhovnogo Suda SSSR," *Sovetskaya yustitsiya,* no. 15 (1978): 24, pt. 2.

111. V. Savitskii, "Novyi etap v osushchestvlenii sotsialisticheskogo pravosudiya," *Sovetskaya yustitsiya,* no. 5 (1978): 9. For Savitskii's reformist proposals during the 1977 discussion of the draft constitution, see Sharlet, *New Soviet Constitution,* pp. 41-44.

112. I.L. Petrukhin, "Prezumptsiya nevinovnosti—konstitutsionnyi printsip sovetskogo ugolovnogo protsessa," *Sovetskoe gosudarstvo i pravo,* no. 12 (1978): 22-26.

113. "Postanovlenie No. 5," p. 24, pts. 1, 2. See also generally, Yurii Luryi, "The Right to Counsel in Ordinary Criminal Cases in the USSR," in Barry, Ginsburgs, and Maggs, ed., *Soviet Law After Stalin: Part I*, pp. 105–17.

114. G. Elemisov, "Konstitutsionnyi printsip obespecheniya obvinyaemomu prava na zashchitu," *Sotsialisticheskaya zakonnost*, no. 11 (1978): 15–18.

115. Savitskii, "Novyi etap." For a summary of other jurists' statements opposing Savitskii's broad interpretation, see "Obsuzhdenie problem sotsialisticheskogo pravosudiya v svete novoi konstitutsii SSSR," *Sotsialisticheskaya zakonnost*, no. 6 (1978): 70.

116. V.K. Puchinskii, "Elementy iska v sovetskom grazhdanskom protsesse," *Sovetskoe gosudarstvo i pravo*, no. 3 (1979): 46; and Yu. Lubshev, "Pravo na zashchitu i obespechenie zakonnykh interesov podsudimogo," *Sovetskaya yustitsiya*, no. 23 (1978): 8–9.

117. Yu. Lubshev, "Ugolovnoe sudoproizvodstvo po delam chastnogo obvineniya," *Sotsialisticheskaya zakonnost*, no. 2 (1978): 50–51.

118. I. Pyatiletov, "Pravo suda vyiti za predely iskovykh trebovanii," *Sovetskaya yustitsiya*, no. 18 (1978): 5–7; and M. Treushnikov, "Dokazyvanie v grazhdanskom protsesse," *Sovetskaya yustitsiya*, no. 23 (1978): 23–24.

119. See Konstantin Simis's forthcoming note on the drafting of the 1977 Constitution in a special issue on "Soviet Legal Policymaking and Policy Implementation" of *Soviet Union* (1979).

120. "Postanovlenie No. 1 Plenuma Verkhovnogo Suda SSSR," *Sovetskaya yustitsiya*, no. 7 (1978): 27, pt. 19.

121. Radutnaia, "Nezavisimost sudei."

122. See the section "Obzhalovanie v sud deistvii dolzhnostnykh lits," *Sovetskoe gosudarstvo i pravo*, no. 11 (1978): 63–80. See also generally, Donald D. Barry, "Administrative Justice and Judicial Review in Soviet Administrative Law," in Barry, Ginsburgs, and Maggs, ed., *Soviet Law After Stalin: Part II*, pp. 241–69.

123. A. Kozlov, "Sudebnoe rassmotrenie del, voznikaiushchikh iz administrativnykh pravootnoshenii," *Sovetskaya yustitsiya*, no. 4 (1978): 5–6.

124. K. Yudelson, "Konstitutsionnye printsipy sovetskogo grazhdanskogo protsessualnogo prava," *Sovetskaya yustitsiya*, no. 16 (1978): 12; and V. Savitskii, op. cit., p. 8.

125. Savitskii, "Novyi etap."

126. A. Lunev, "Sovershenstvovanie garantii prav lichnosti v sfere gosudarstvennogo upravleniya," *Sovetskaya yustitsiya*, no. 5 (1978): 21.

127. A. Vengerov, "Konstitutsionnye printsipy okhrany lichnoi zhizni sovetskikh grazhdan," *Sovetskaya yustitsiya*, no. 1 (1979): 3.

128. "S Plenuma Verkhovnogo Suda RSFSR: O voprosakh, voznikshikh v sudebnoi praktike pri premenenii st. 215 Kodeksa zakonov o trude RSFSR," *Sovetskaya yustitsiya*, no. 11 (1978): 5–8. See also Zile, "Soviet Law of Job Security," *Soviet Law After Stalin*: Part I pp. 263–65, 275–81.

129. E.G. Azarova, "O zashchite pensionnykh prav grazhdan," *Sovetskoe gosudarstvo i pravo*, no. 2 (1979): 46–49.

130. V.P. Danukin, "Trudoustroistvo i ego formy v SSSR," *Sovetskoe gosudarstvo i pravo*, no. 4 (1979): 124.

131. M. Kazantsev and Yu. Tolstoi, "Problemy sovershenstvovaniya zhilishchogo zakonodatelstva i praktiki ego primeneniya," *Sotsialisticheskaya zakonnost*, no. 4 (1978): 52.

132. V. Remnev, "Sovershenstvovanie statistiki o zakonnosti v gosudarstvennom upravlenii," *Sotsialisticheskaya zakonnost*, no. 11 (1978): 61–62.

133. V. Chkhikvadze, "Preemstvennost i razvitie idei sotsialisticheskoi zakonnosti v Konstitutsii SSSR," *Sotsialisticheskaya zakonnost*, no. 5 (1978): 6.

10

SOVIET POLICY TOWARD
THE THIRD WORLD

Roger E. Kanet
M. Rajan Menon

During the course of the past quarter century the Soviet Union has developed from an isolated bastion of Stalinist socialism with virtually no contacts with areas outside its own sphere of domination into a major world power with interests and capabilities spanning most of the globe. A significant element of this increased Soviet role in world affairs has been the expansion of Soviet interest in and contacts with the non-Communist developing countries of Africa, Asia, and Latin America. While the foundations for Soviet involvement in the developing world were laid during the years of Khrushchev's leadership, Brezhnev and his associates have continued to pursue policies that now enable the Soviets to exert influence on developments throughout much of the Third World—as in Angola, Ethiopia, and Afghanistan in recent years. The relative position of the Soviet Union in international affairs has changed substantially in the years since Brezhnev replaced Khrushchev as first secretary of the CPSU (Communist Party of the Soviet Union) in late 1964. In part this has resulted from the continued buildup of Soviet military capabilities which includes the creation of an open-water navy and merchant fleet and the acquisition of port facilities for that fleet (and for Soviet aircraft) throughout much of the Third World. By the 1970s, the Soviets were able to employ their newly developed military power in support of far-flung political and strategic goals: in Bangladesh in 1971, the eastern Mediterranean during the Arab-Israeli war of 1973, in Angola and Ethiopia (in conjunction with their Cuban allies) in 1975 and 1977–78, respectively, and, most recently, in Cambodia, where their Vietnamese allies have overthrown the pro-Chinese Communist regime of the Khmer Rouge.[1]

Soviet policy toward the developing countries has formed an integral part of Soviet leaders' overall effort to expand positions of influence throughout the world. The focus on areas of potential strategic importance, such as the Middle East and the Horn of Africa, fits well into a policy oriented toward both undermining the influence of the capitalist West—and the potential influence of the Peoples Republic of China—and establishing the role of the Soviet Union as a global power. Since the middle 1960s Soviet behavior in the developing world has been motivated by a number of important considerations: (1) the actual or potential strategic importance of a country or region for the security interests of the Soviet Union; (2) the possibility of disrupting influence patterns of the Western states, especially the United States or China in a particular region; (3) support for the position of the Soviet Union as the major Marxist-Leninist revolutionary power; and (4) the significance of a country as potential market for Soviet manufactured goods and as a source of raw materials or of relatively inexpensive manufactured goods imports.[2]

In the present study we intend to provide, first of all, a brief discussion of Soviet policy toward the developing world prior to the rise of the Brezhnev-Kosygin leadership in 1964. We shall then focus on more recent Soviet policy toward the developing countries and the place of those countries in Soviet global interests. Finally, we shall examine in more detail Soviet policy toward three regions that have proven to be of special interest to the Soviet Union: the Middle East, South Asia, and, most recently, Africa.

SOVIET POLICY IN THE KHRUSHCHEV ERA

When Stalin died in 1953, the Soviet Union was virtually isolated from the colonial and newly independent areas of the Third World. Stalin had made no effort to develop political or economic ties with the new leaders of such countries as India or Indonesia and, in fact, had alienated a number of them by supporting revolutionary activities against their governments. This situation was dramatically reversed in the mid-1950s, when Khrushchev announced that the new states represented part of a worldwide "zone of peace" and that the Soviet Union was willing to provide support both for national liberation movements struggling to achieve independence and for the new states that had recently acquired independence from the colonial powers.[3] The Soviets embarked upon efforts to expand contacts of all sorts with the new states of Asia and Africa, although the focus of that policy was on the creation of economic links as a prelude to broader political contacts. The decade from 1955 to 1965 witnessed a five-fold expansion of Soviet trade with the non-Communist developing countries, from 304 million rubles (5.2 percent of total trade turnover) to 1,743.6 million rubles (11.9 percent). In large part Soviet policy toward the developing countries was a response to U.S. efforts to create alliance systems in Asia as part of the policy of containment. Soon after Stalin's death the Soviet leadership began pursuing a "policy of denial" aimed at ensuring the neutrality of those developing countries—especially Afghanistan, India, and Egypt—which professed a nonaligned approach to foreign policy and opposed the intrusion of military alliances into their regions. The Soviets sought to expand their ties with such countries in order to prevent the uncontested growth of Western influence, ensure that gaps would remain in the U.S. alliance network, and win the support of these nonaligned countries for issues important to the Soviet Union.[4]

Since the Soviets now desired to cultivate the developing countries' good will, it was clear that their leaders could not continue to be viewed as reactionaries who ought to be swept away by the tide of revolution. In short, there existed a contradiction between the imperatives of Soviet policy and Soviet ideological assessments of these countries. While the aid and political support given to countries like Egypt and India in the mid-1950s signalled a shift in Soviet policy, a change in doctrine at an authoritative level was made with Khrushchev's introduction of the concept of the "zone of peace" at the Twentieth Congress of the CPSU in 1956. The nonaligned states no longer were regarded as mere appendages of Western imperialism but as the independent proponents of peace and, therefore, worthy of Soviet support and assistance.[5] Similarly the doctrine of "national democracy," which was developed during the next few years, recognized that the national bourgeoisie was capable of progressive internal and external policies and called upon local Communist parties to work for a union of progressive forces to complete the transition to socialism under the aegis of the national bourgeois leadership. When the Soviets realized, by the mid-1960s, that the non-Communist leaders of these countries—especially in Africa and the Middle East—had little intention of allowing a free hand to local Communists, a further doctrinal change was made. Many of the non-Communist governments were now viewed as having chosen a noncapitalist road to development. Rather than work as independent parties in opposition the Communists were told to disband their parties and seek entry into the ruling party and state structures with the view of influencing socialist-oriented policies.[6]

The primary areas of Soviet involvement in the developing world during the decade of Khrushchev's leadership were those regions of special strategic concern to the Soviet leadership—the Middle East and South Asia. Measured in terms of political contacts, economic relations (including assistance), or military aid, Soviet involvement in the areas adjacent to the southern borders of the Soviet Union expanded rapidly.[7] In addition, however, the Soviets did attempt to take advantage of a number of situations in other areas of the developing world, such as the civil war in Zaire (then, Congo-Leopoldville) and the radicalization of the governments of Sukarno in Indonesia, Nkrumah in Ghana, and Touré in Guinea.

Although the initial Soviet push toward expanding contacts with the countries of the Third World was accompanied by optimistic statements about the prospects for the development of a revolutionary climate in these countries, the immediate Soviet goal, as we have noted, was clearly the reduction of Western influence in areas of strategic significance to the Soviet Union. In spite of rhetoric about support for the construction of "scientific socialism" in developing countries, the Soviets were willing to provide assistance to such clearly non-Socialist countries as Afghanistan and the Ethiopia of Haile Selassie in the attempt to undermine the dominant Western position. However, Khrushchev's goals far exceeded the means available to the Soviet Union. The inferior military position of the Soviet Union in relation to the West—including the virtual absence of an ocean-going navy—made it extremely difficult for the Soviets to provide effective support to their friends, such as Lumumba, Nkrumah, and Keita, in periods of crisis. In addition, Soviet hopes that most—or many— developing countries would be willing to cut their economic and political relations with the West proved inaccurate. Even though such countries as Nasser's Egypt and Nehru's India had turned to the Soviet Union for military, economic, and political support, they continued to deal with the industrial West. The Soviet Union provided them with the possibility of lessening their dependence on the former colonial powers and represented an added source of military and economic assistance. It did not, however, provide a political-social-economic model that the majority of Third World political leaders were interested in following.

At the time of Khrushchev's overthrow in late 1964, Soviet policy in the developing world was in partial disarray. The optimism of the 1950s was already being questioned and replaced by a growing realism concerning prospects for political and economic developments in most of the Third World countries. Although the Soviet Union had ended its isolation from the developing countries, it had not succeeded in establishing significant influence relationships.[8]

Where Soviet goals had been partially accomplished—for example, the reduction of the Western presence in the Middle East—success resulted far more from the initiatives of the developing countries themselves than from Soviet policy. Yet the foundations for future Soviet policy in the Third World had been laid in many areas. In South Asia, India had already begun to depend upon the Soviet Union for both the military assistance deemed necessary for security with regard to China and Pakistan and support in the development of heavy industrial projects in the state sector of the economy. In the Middle East, both Egypt and Syria were now heavily indebted to the Soviets for both military and economic assistance, while Turkey and Iran both had begun to expand ties with the Soviets as a means of lessening their dependence on the United States. Throughout Asia and Africa and Soviet Union had begun to become a force to be reckoned with by Western Europe and the United States, even though the West still commanded more influence in most areas of the developing world.

SOVIET POLICY DURING THE BREZHNEV ERA

As we have already noted, the Soviets had already begun to reassess their views and policies towards the Third World prior to Khrushchev's dismissal as CPSU leader. They recognized that the prospects for the introduction of socialism in the vast majority of the new states were bleak and that the instability of many of those societies meant that leaders favorably·disposed toward the Soviet Union might well be overthrown by "reactionary elements," witness the fate of Ben Bella, Nkrumah, and Keita. The early years of Brezhnev's leadership witnessed the continued reassessment of Soviet policy. Confidence in the development of Soviet-type Socialist systems and an emphasis on economic "show projects" were replaced by the effort to develop firmly based relations with Third World countries that would begin to provide "bases of operation" from which the Soviets could expand contacts and attempt to increase their activities and build their influence. Even more than before Soviet policy focused on countries and political groupings that had inherent importance for their own purposes. First of all, they emphasized even more those countries along the southern boundaries of the Soviet Union, from India in South Asia to the Arab countries of North Africa. The importance of this area for the strategic interests of the Soviet Union is quite clear, as Soviet commentators have repeatedly noted.[9] Support for minor revolutionary groupings and for activities in sub-

Saharan Africa was downplayed—to the point where some Western commentators argued that Soviet interest in sub-Saharan Africa had virtually disappeared.[10]

In the economic realm, emphasis was now placed on projects with more than just the potential of gaining political favor. Rather, as Premier Kosygin stated in 1971, the Soviet Union would attempt to produce an "international division of labor" with the developing countries.[11] This meant an emphasis on projects that would be of economic benefit to the Soviet Union as well as to the recipient country. Finally, by the late 1960s, the Soviets had also begun the search for access to both naval and airport facilities that would enable them to expand the reach of their military capabilities.

During the 1970s, although the Soviet leaders seem to have favored providing support for revolutionary and "progressive" regimes and movements throughout the Third World, their primary focus increasingly has followed the lines laid down in the middle and late 1960s: support for states or political groups of potential importance to the Soviet Union itself and to the furtherance of Soviet interests.

In spite of the recent upsurge of Soviet involvement in sub-Saharan Africa, the major concentration of Soviet efforts has continued to be in the arc of countries that border the Soviet Union's southern flank. Here the Soviet goal continues to be the reduction of Western influence and military capabilities and the concomitant expansion of the military and political capabilities of the Soviet state. This has meant that the Soviets have continued to provide military and political support to a number of countries in the region and, in several cases, have signed treaties of friendship and cooperation with important South Asian and Middle Eastern countries.[12] The Soviets have not concentrated exclusively on the more revolutionary or anti-Western countries in the region. In fact, during the past decade they have increased their efforts to expand relations with countries formally allied to the West, such as Iran and Turkey, by offering economic and military assistance as a means of reducing these countries' dependence on their Western allies.

Throughout the last 25 years Soviet policy toward the developing countries has relied heavily on the provision of economic and military assistance as a means of developing relations. For example, from 1954 through 1977 the Soviet Union committed almost $13 billion worth of economic assistance to countries of the Third World (see Tables 10.1 and 10.2). More than 75 percent of that assistance has gone toward the construction of an industrial base in the state sector

TABLE 10.1

Soviet Economic Assistance to Developing Countries (millions of U.S. dollars)

Year	Commitments	Deliveries
Total		
1954–77	12,932	7,150
1954–67	5,664	2,555
1968	379	310
1969	476	355
1970	200	385
1971	1,126	415
1972	654	430
1973	709	500
1974	816	700
1975	1,572	500
1976	945	460
1977	392	535

Source: Central Intelligence Agency, National Foreign Assessment Center, *Communist Aid to Less Developed Countries of the Free World, 1977: A Research Report,* ER 78-10478U (November 1978), p. 6.

TABLE 10.2

Soviet Economic Credits and Grants to Developing Countries, by Region (millions of U.S. dollars)

Region	1954–77	1976	1977
Total	12,932	945	392
Africa	1,840	369	21
North Africa	901	345	0
Sub-Saharan Africa	939	24	21
Southeast Asia	156	0	0
Latin America	938	0	30
Middle East and South Asia*	9,446	249	341
Other	552	327	0

*Includes Egypt.

Source: Central Intelligence Agency, National Foreign Assessment Center, *Communist Aid to Less Developed Countries of the Free World, 1977: A Research Report,* ER 78-10478U (November 1978), pp. 5-6.

TABLE 10.3

Soviet Trade with Developing Countries
(millions of U.S. dollars)

Year	Total	Developed Countries[a]	Developing Countries			
			Total	Africa[b]	Asia[c]	Latin America[d]
1955						
Exports	3,392	552	141	13	80	24
Imports	3,029	442	194	41	94	31
1960						
Exports	5,508	1,004	334	99	170	32
Imports	5,572	1,104	529	199	294	35
1965						
Exports	8,093	1,481	1,111	329	474	48
Imports	7,978	1,616	807	249	420	107
1970						
Exports	12,672	2,369	2,019	578	653	9
Imports	11,822	2,794	1,280	530	636	77
1975						
Exports	27,359	8,255	4,471	758	1,619	194
Imports	24,840	8,102	3,145	1,146	1,790	1,013

1976						
Exports	37,363	10,445	4,987	744	1,752	157
Imports	38,308	14,429	3,740	874	1,951	891

aExcluding Communist countries
bIncluding Egypt
cExcluding Japan and Communist countries
dExcluding Cuba

Note: Exchange rates: $1.11 per ruble, through 1970; $1.32 per ruble, 1975; $1.33 per ruble, 1976. (Note that the increase in the value of the ruble exaggerates the dollar value of the growth of Soviet trade.)

Figures listed for all developing countries (especially for exports) do not agree with sums of figures for Africa, Asia, and Latin America, since Soviet statistics do not include certain types of trade (e.g. military equipment) in the country breakdowns, although they apparently are included in the totals.

In addition, a very high percentage of Soviet trade with Africa occurs with the Arab countries of North Africa. In 1976, for example, 55 percent of Soviet exports and 51 percent of imports went to or came from Egypt, Libya, Algeria, Morocco, and Tunisia.

Sources: SSSR. Ministerstvo vneshnei torgovli, *Vneshnyaya torgovlya SSSR: Statisticheskii obzor, 1918–1966* (Moscow: Mezhdunarodnye otnosheniya, 1967), pp. 62–69; idem. *Vneshnyaya torgovlya SSSR za . . . god: Statisticheskii obzor* for the years 1970, 1975, 1976 (Moscow: Mezhdunarodnye otnosheniya, annual).

243

of the economies of the recipient countries.[13] In general, the terms of Soviet assistance are relatively favorable when compared with commercial loans available to developing countries on the international market. However, since the Soviets provide virtually no nonrepayable grants and all aid is given in the form of credits for the purchase of Soviet goods and equipment (i.e. all aid is tied to purchases from the Soviet Union), the overall pattern of Soviet assistance to the Third World countries is not necessarily more favorable to recipients than that from the West.[14]

Soviet trade with the developing countries has continued to grow rapidly during the Brezhnev period. As we have already seen, trade with the Third World rose from a mere 300 million rubles in 1955 to more than 1,700 million ten years later. By 1976 Soviet trade with the developing countries had reached 6,562 million rubles, although as a percentage of total trade turnover it fell from 11.9 to 11.5 percent during that period (see Table 10.3).[15] An important aspect of Soviet trade with Asia and Africa has been the degree to which it has been related to the provision of Soviet economic assistance. With few exceptions (e.g. the sale of military equipment to Libya and the purchase of rubber from Malaysia) trade has resulted from agreements between the Soviets and their Afro-Asian counterparts which included the commitment of Soviet economic and technical assistance. Examples of this type of agreement have been those with Egypt and India which have called for the Soviet Union to provide capital equipment on the basis of long-term credits. These loans were then to be repaid with the products of the recipient country over a period of 12 years at an interest rate of 2.5 percent. Such agreements have been especially attractive to those countries which have had problems obtaining the convertible currency necessary to purchase on the world market machinery and equipment needed for economic development programs.

Probably the most important development in Soviet policy toward the Third World during the past decade has been the shift from a primary emphasis on economic assistance to a more important role for the provision of military aid. Throughout the period 1954 to 1967, the Soviets delivered an average of about $300 million of military equipment per year to developing countries. From 1968 through 1971, the figure increased to about $700 million per year. Since 1972, however, the annual deliveries have increased substantially and by 1977 totaled more than $3,200 million (compared with about $500 million per year in economic aid since 1971) (see Table 10.4). The major recipients of the recent increase in Soviet deliveries have been Libya, which pays in hard currency, Iraq, Algeria, Ethiopia, and

Angola. Not only have Soviet sales increased about fourfold during the 1970s, but the regional distribution of deliveries has also changed. Until the early 1970s approximately 90 percent of all Soviet arms deliveries went to the countries of South Asia and the Middle East. With the recent injection of Soviet involvement in sub-Saharan Africa, however, Africa has become a major recipient of Soviet military equipment (see Table 10.5).

Arms transfers have had two major benefits for the Soviet Union. First, a number of Third World countries have become heavily dependent upon the Soviet Union for their own military security. For example, Egypt (until its break with the Soviets in the mid-1970s), Iraq, and, more recently, Angola and Ethiopia have all turned to the Soviet Union for the supply of military equipment considered essential for the achievement of national interests. In addition to Soviet arms have usually come Soviet military technicians who have played an important role in training local military personnel and, in some cases, even in assisting in military operations—as in Egypt during the 1970-71 "war of attrition."[16] The presence of Soviet military advisors and the access to local naval and military facilities throughout the

TABLE 10.4

Soviet Military Commitments and Deliveries to Developing Countries (millions of U.S. dollars)

Year	Agreements	Deliveries
Total	26,050	21,035
1954–67	5,045	4,080
1968	450	505
1969	360	450
1970	1,150	995
1971	1,590	865
1972	1,635	1,215
1973	2,810	3,130
1974	4,125	2,315
1975	2,010	1,775
1976	2,890	2,445
1977	3,990	3,265

Source: Central Intelligence Agency, National Foreign Assessment Center, Communist Aid to Less Developed Countries of the Free World, 1977: A Research Report, ER 78-10478U (November 1978), p. 1.

TABLE 10.5

Soviet Military Deliveries to the Third World, by Region
(millions of U.S. dollars)

Region	1972	1973	1974	1975	1976	1977*
Total	1,205	3,010	2,250	1,685	2,190	3,265
Africa	55	75	235	600	1,070	NA
Latin America	0	10	25	55	80	NA
Middle East	970	2,655	1,785	850	830	NA
South Asia	180	270	205	180	210	NA

*A regional breakdown for 1977 is not available. However, 70 percent of Soviet deliveries in 1977 went to five countries: Iraq, Libya, Syria, India, and Peru. Ethiopia and Algeria were also major recipients of Soviet arms in 1977.

Note: The 1977 CIA study provides somewhat higher estimates of total deliveries for the years 1972–76: 1,215 (1972). 3,130 (1973), 2,315 (1974), 1,775 (1975), and 2,445 (1976).

Sources: Central Intelligence Agency. *Communist Aid to the Less Developed Countries of the Free World, 1976,* ER 77-10296 (August 1977). p. 3. for data for 1972–76: Central Intelligence Agency. National Foreign Assessment Center. *Communist Aid to Less Developed Countries of the Free World, 1977: A Research Report,* ER 78-10478U (November 1978). pp. 1–2. for the 1977 data.

Third World—for example, in Aden, Iraq, and Mozambique—has permitted the Soviets to increase substantially their potential for projecting military power in areas far from the territory of the Soviet Union.[17]

A second and increasingly important benefit of arms deliveries has been the acquisition of hard currency from military sales to such countries as Libya. It is estimated that in 1977 arms sales generated approximately $1.5 billion for the Soviet economy. Given the large deficit in Soviet trade with the West, this income helps to reduce the convertible currency trade deficit of the Soviet Union.

Before turning to our discussion of Soviet policy in the Middle East, South Asia, and Africa, a few words should be said about Soviet policy in Latin America and Southeast Asia. On the whole, even though the Brezhnev leadership has expanded its contacts with the countries of these two regions, they continue to play a far less important role in Soviet foreign policy than the countries closer to the Soviet Union. In Latin America the Soviets did view very favorably the election of the Allende government and the turn of Chile toward socialism prior to the coup d'état in 1972. More recently they have begun to sell weapons to Peru and have expanded substantially their trade—almost exclusively imports—with Brazil and Argentina. However, Soviet relations with the countries of Latin America—with the obvious exception of Cuba—remain quite limited.[18]

Soviet relations with the non-Communist countries of Southeast Asia also continue to be restricted. Needless to say, the unification of Vietnam, the Communist victory in Laos, and, most recently, the overthrow of the pro-Chinese Communist government of Cambodia have all greatly enhanced the Soviet Union's position on the Southeast Asian mainland. All three of the Communist countries in the region are now favorably disposed toward the Soviet Union and, to a substantial degree, are dependent on the Soviets for military and economic assistance and support against a potentially hostile People's Republic of China (PRC). Elsewhere in the area Soviet efforts to expand relations generally have met with only limited positive response.[19]

THE SOVIET UNION AND THE MIDDLE EAST

In the remaining pages we shall examine in somewhat more detail the development of Soviet policy in those areas on which the Soviets have focused most during the past decade. As in the Khrushchev period, Soviet policy toward the Middle East since 1965 has sought to reduce the level of Western influence and to build the foundations of a Soviet presence and of Soviet influence. Since several of the Arab states were eager to acquire Soviet economic and technical assistance, military supplies, and Soviet military advisory personnel, Moscow has been able to increase its presence in the area. There is a danger, however, in equating presence with influence. The Soviets have had to accept the fact that the Arab governments are unwilling, despite dependence on Soviet economic and military aid, to permit the Communists in their countries to emerge as serious contenders for power or to subject their own perceptions of national interest to those of the Soviet Union.

While the Arab-Israeli wars of 1967 and 1973 have provided the Soviet Union with opportunities to expand its role in the Middle East by supplying political backing, armaments, and military advisors, this has necessitated a substantial investment of Soviet resources with no guarantee of reliable and long-term returns. For example, by replenishing Egyptian arms supplies after the Six-Day War of 1967, the Soviets gained access to several port and air base facilities in Egypt. However, when Nasser's successor, Anwar Sadat, determined that Egypt's interests were not being served by Soviet policy, he expelled Soviet military personnel and reasserted Egyptian control over the military facilities in 1972. Four years later he unilaterally denounced the Soviet-Egyptian friendship treaty of 1971. More recently, when the Soviets began supporting Ethiopia, Somalia also abrogated its treaty arrangements with the Soviet Union and expelled all Soviet military personnel from the country, even though Somali military capabilities depended almost entirely on past Soviet supplies of equipment and training. It is quite clear from these examples, and others that could be cited, that mere presence and involvement have not guaranteed the Soviets the ability to influence the policies of "client" states.

A major determinant of the success of Soviet policy in the Middle East has been the Soviet willingness to underwrite and facilitate Arab aims with regard to Israel. However, this policy has also resulted in the need for the Soviets to support the Arabs in crisis situations, such as 1973, even though they have had serious reservations about the military capabilities of the Arabs and though they recognized that their involvement risked a direct confrontation with the United States.

During the Brezhnev period the Soviets have been faced with three serious problems in their Middle Eastern policy: how to ensure that Soviet military and economic aid would guarantee a Soviet presence and influence; how to achieve political gains by supporting the Arabs against Israel without also coming into confrontation with the United States; and how to reconcile Soviet military and economic assistance to bourgeois regimes with the claim of pursuing a class-based foreign policy guided by Marxist-Leninist doctrine. The complexities of these three problem areas provide a framework within which one can examine the concrete developments in Soviet-Middle Eastern relations under Brezhnev.

The first major crisis confronting the Brezhnev-Kosygin leadership in the Middle East was the Six-Day War of June 1967. Since the mid-1950s the Soviets had worked to establish close ties with the radical Arab states, in particular Algeria, Egypt, Iraq, and Syria. In the years immediately preceding the war the Soviet Union had welcomed the leftward political swing in these countries, in particular the coup in Syria that brought the radical wing of the Ba'ath Party to power. Throughout 1966 and early 1967 Moscow had encouraged the Arabs to form a united front against imperialism. When the war actually broke out, however, the Soviets provided little more than verbal and political support. They were unwilling to risk a direct confrontation with the United States and eventually voted with the West—and against the Arabs—at the United Nations on July 21, 1967 [20]

In the period immediately following the June War, the Soviets moved to regain their position of prestige in the region. In order to achieve this goal the Soviet leaders supported most of the Arab political demands, rearmed the Egyptian and Syrian armies, and stepped up deliveries of economic assistance. They also emphasized their backing of the Arabs during the war, attempted to place most of the blame for the Israeli attack on the United States, and were quite pleased by the anti-Western feeling that gripped the radical Arab states during and after the war.

The reequipping of the Egyptian military had the immediate effect of providing the Egyptians with the possibility of initiating sporadic military actions across the Suez Canal into Israeli-occupied Sinai. By 1970 this "war of attrition" had escalated to the point that the Soviets agreed to provide substantial supplies of new weapons and a Soviet-constructed and manned air defense system was installed to provide air cover for Egypt.[21] In addition, however, the Soviets gained access to naval facilities in Egyptian ports and to air bases. Given the lack of aircraft carriers in the Soviet Navy at that time and Moscow's desire to maintain an effective and continuous naval presence in the Mediterranean, this quid pro quo proved advantageous to the Soviet Union.

After Nasser's death, President Podgorny travelled to Egypt in spring 1971 to meet with Anwar Sadat, the new Egyptian president. The result was the signing of a Soviet-Egyptian treaty which provided for cooperation in both the economic and military spheres.[22] However, Sadat viewed the treaty primarily as a means to obtain the Soviet weapons necessary to make good his promise that 1971 would be the "year of decision" in which the Arab countries would regain the territories lost in the 1967 war. The Soviet refusal to provide him with the equipment he thought necessary—along with a variety of other factors, such as opposition by the Egyptian military to the behavior of the Soviet advisors—resulted in Sadat's decision in 1972 to expel the Soviet military.

At about the same time the Soviet Union faced problems in its relations elsewhere in the Middle East. In the summer of 1971, President Nimiery of the Sudan, who had established a radical government after seizing power two years earlier, was overthrown by a group of dissident army officers. Several days later Nimiery, with the aid of President Kaddafi of Libya, returned to power. In addition to executing the officers involved in the abortive coup and a number of Sudanese Communist leaders who had reportedly supported it, Nimiery accused the Soviets of having supported his opponents and recalled his ambassador from Moscow.[23]

In response to their setbacks in Egypt and the Sudan, the Soviets sought to move closer to Iraq and Syria. They already had begun to provide assistance for the development of Iraq's oil industry in support of Iraq's nationalization of Western petroleum interests,[24] and in April 1972 they signed a treaty with Iraq along the lines of their earlier agreement with Egypt.[25] Subsequently they have been granted access to naval facilities at Iraq's Persian Gulf port of Umm Qasar.

While Syria has continued to be unwilling to sign a treaty with the Soviet Union, military aid agreements were reached in 1971 and 1972, and, following the expulsion of Soviet personnel from Egypt, a major airlift of weapons was directed to Syria.[26]

By the time of the outbreak of hostilities between Israel and the Arabs in October 1973, the Soviet position in the Middle East appeared to be significantly weaker than it had been several years earlier. The expulsion of Soviet military advisors from Egypt; the development of a sense of unity among the Arabs in their relations with the West, in particular their new-found position of influence as a result of their increased control over their oil resources; and the influence of anti-Communist Arab leaders such as Kaddafi all resulted in a diminution of the Soviet role in the area.

It appears that the Soviets became aware of the Arab plans to initiate military hostilities only a few days before the attack on October 6, 1973. Initially they did nothing to restrain the coordinated offensive launched by Egypt and Syria, and, in fact, Brezhnev called upon

Arab and African leaders to support the two countries on the same day that the Soviet Union began a massive airlift of weapons to Egypt and Syria.[27] Only after the Israelis had begun pushing the Arab armies back and tension between the Soviet Union and the United States escalated did Moscow begin calling for caution and support a cease-fire.

While the Soviets in 1967 had refused to intervene actively during the course of hostilities, in 1973 they acted almost immediately to support the Arab states. In large part this was the result of the weakened position of the Soviet Union in the region. Had they failed once again to come to the assistance of the Arabs, they would have faced the distinct probability of having to write off two decades of economic, military, and political investments in the Middle East. To maintain and strengthen their position, they even were willing to run the risk of a direct confrontation with the United States and of destroying the recently established détente in U.S.-Soviet relations.

However, in spite of Soviet support during the 1973 war, Moscow has continued to suffer serious setbacks in its Middle Eastern policy. Most important has been the continued deterioration of relations with Egypt and the virtual elimination of the Soviet role in Arab-Israeli relations. Already in 1974 the United States exerted significant influence in the negotiations which resulted in the disengagement of Israeli troops from those of both Egypt and Syria. In the past year the United States has continued to play the major role in facilitating discussions between Israel and Egypt. The Soviets have strongly criticized Sadat and have supported those elements in the Arab world that have condemned his policy of negotiating a separate agreement with Israel. In supporting Arab opponents of negotiations the Soviet leaders hope not only to maintain their presence in the Middle East, but also to win support for the Soviet Union's involvement in efforts to settle the Middle East dispute.[28] Soviet-Egyptian relations, however, have continued to deteriorate, and Egypt has become, along with other former Soviet "friends" in the Sudan and Somalia, one of the most vocal critics of Soviet behavior in the Middle East and Africa in recent years.[29]

In response to the deterioration of relations with Egypt, Moscow has sought to maintain its presence in the region by supporting the more radical forces in the Middle East. In late 1973 Brezhnev for the first time referred to the "national rights" of the Palestinians, and in August 1974 the Palestine Liberation Organization opened an office in Moscow.[30] While the Soviets have provided virtually no new arms to Egypt since 1973, they have continued to supply Iraq and Syria and have added Libya as a major market. One of the more interesting developments in Soviet-Middle Eastern policy has been the rapprochement with the Libya of the strongly nationalistic and anti-Communist Kaddafi. The leaders of the two countries have entered into an "alliance of convenience" based primarily on their mutual opposition to Sadat's policy of negotiation and to Western influence in the Middle East.[31]

Since 1973 the Soviet Union has continued to develop relations with the People's Democratic Republic of Yemen (Aden). The return for Soviet military and economic assistance has been access to the naval and air facilities that are important for the projection of Soviet military power in the Persian Gulf and Indian Ocean area and were essential for Soviet support to Ethiopia in the 1977–78 war with Somalia.

Elsewhere in the Middle East the Soviets have continued their efforts to improve relations with Iran. In 1967, for example the Soviet Union sold arms to Iran for the first time, and a substantial expansion of economic relations has evolved over the last decade. This Soviet effort to woo Iran to a more nonaligned position occurred in spite of the Shah's strong anti-Communist domestic policies. The recent upheaval in Iran has resulted in periodic U.S. and Soviet warnings against interference in the troubled country. The emergence of a pro-Soviet government clearly would benefit the Soviet position in the Middle East. However, whatever the composition of the new regime in Iran, it is likely that the U.S. position will have been significantly weakened.

Over the course of the past decade and a half the record of Soviet policy successes in the Middle East has been mixed. By means of its economic and military assistance to countries of the area the Soviet Union has been able to expand its presence; by 1971, for example, it appeared that Egypt was totally dependent upon the Soviet Union. However, the Soviets have been unable to translate this presence into lasting and effective influence. Not only has Egypt broken with the Soviet Union during the past five years or so, but other countries have carried out policies strongly critized by the Soviet leadership, for instance, Syria's intervention in the Lebanese civil war against the PLO and the Syrian leftists and Iraq's execution of 20 soldiers in May 1978, on charges of setting up pro-Soviet political cells in the country.[32] While the Arab-Israeli confrontations have provided opportunities for Soviet policy in the Middle East, Moscow has not been able to influence the course of events and, in the process of backing the Arabs, has risked a confrontation with the United States.

THE SOVIET UNION AND SOUTH ASIA

As in the Middle East, the development of Soviet policy in South Asia was also closely related to regional conflicts, that is, the disputes between India and both Pakistan and China. Despite periodic overtures to Pakistan during the Khrushchev period, the Soviets pursued an India-centered South Asian policy which also sought to establish a close relationship with Afghanistan. At the beginning of the Brezhnev era, Soviet policy toward the subcontinent underwent a significant change, and an effort was made to adopt a more balanced posture between India and Pakistan. Four factors contributed to the emergence of this change: the open split between Moscow and Peking in the early 1960s and the deterioration of Sino-Soviet relations in the years that followed; the rapport that developed between China and Pakistan following the Sino-Indian war of October 1962; Moscow's uneasiness regarding the political situation in India after the 1967 general elections in that country caused an erosion of the power of the ruling Congress Party which some Soviet analysts thought portended a political move to the right; and the strains in Pakistan's relationship with the United States, its major military ally, in the years after the Sino-Indian war.

Until the Bangladesh crisis led to open warfare between India and Pakistan in December 1971, these four developments combined to produce a reassessment of Soviet policy toward the region. The deterioration of Sino-Soviet relations coupled with the growing ties between China and Pakistan suggested the need to counter Peking by setting Soviet-Pakistani relations on a new footing. In addition, the tensions that entered Pakistan's relationship with the United States also provided the Soviets with an opportunity to loosen Pakistan's ties with the West and to encourage a more neutralist posture. Taken together the four developments provide a context for understanding the specifics of Soviet policy toward South Asia from the fall of Khrushchev until the outbreak of the December 1971 Indo-Pakistan war.

Even before Khrushchev's ouster Soviet policy began to move away from its almost exclusive focus on India, as Soviet support for India on the Kashmir question appeared to wane in 1963–64. While in previous years the Soviets had supported India's claim to Kashmir as an integral part of India, the Soviet U.N. representative now maintained that a dispute over Kashmir existed and that this dispute should be settled peacefully. In addition, the communiqué issued at the end of Indian President Radhakvishnan's visit to Moscow in September 1974 included no mention of Kashmir.[33]

Under Brezhnev the search for a more balanced policy toward India and Pakistan was continued. During Prime Minister Shastri's visit to the Soviet Union in spring 1965, Kosygin avoided discussing Kashmir and impressed upon his guest the need for a negotiated settlement of the dispute. When fighting broke out between Indian and Pakistani forces in the Rann of Kutch region in April, the Soviets took a neutral position and called for an early end to hostilities. Finally, throughout the full-scale war that began in August 1965, the Soviets assumed an impartial position, emphasized the Soviet Union's good relations with both countries, and urged the settlement of all disputed issues through negotiation. In January 1966, Kosygin mediated Indo-Pakistani differences at a peace conference held in the Soviet city of Tashkent.[34] Although the conference did not succeed in resolving the sources of friction between India and Pakistan, it signalled a diplomatic victory for Moscow. While Britain, the PRC, and the United States each alienated one of the two disputants, the Soviet Union had demonstrated its ability to earn the trust of both.

In the years following the Tashkent Conference the Soviets sought to expand their relationship with Pakistan. For example, from 1965 to 1968 Soviet-Pakistani trade quadrupled in value, while an agreement signed in February 1968 envisaged a further increase. By the end of Kosygin's visit to Pakistan in April 1968 the Soviets had agreed to finance 21 projects in Pakistan.[35]

Throughout the late 1960s political relations between Pakistan and the Soviet Union also improved, and top governmental officials of the two countries exchanged visits. In 1968 the Soviets even provided Pakistan with $25 million worth of military equipment.

Although Soviet writings on India in the latter half of the 1960s exhibited an uncertainty concerning the future political direction of the country, Moscow sought to maintain its established relationship with New Delhi. In the years after the Sino-Indian war, the Soviet Union had become India's most important external source of military supplies. In the economic sphere two agreements were signed in 1965 and 1966 which provided for more than $570 million in Soviet credits for the development of Indian industry. In this period the Soviets continued to adopt a nonpartisan position on Indo-Pakistan disputes and repeatedly urged the two countries to adhere to the "Tashkent spirit" and resolve their differences peacefully.

As part of their strategy against the PRC, the Soviets sought to form regional organizations loosely linked to the Soviet Union. Efforts were made to obtain support for a regional economic cooperation scheme involving Afghanistan, Pakistan, and India, and, after Brezhnev's elliptical reference in June 1969 to the necessity of an Asian

Collective Security System, Moscow repeatedly sought the endorsement of these countries for the proposal.[36] Although neither of these initiatives ever bore fruit, both must be understood as part of an effort to contain China by creating a loose grouping of states bound together by economic and political arrangements and sponsored by the Soviet Union.

It is clear that the Bangladesh crisis of 1971 occurred at a time when the Soviets were trying to expand their relations with Pakistan and encourage cooperation among India, Pakistan, and Afghanistan. After the West Pakistani army was sent to East Pakistan to quell what President Yahya Khan viewed as a carefully planned attempt to create an independent state, large numbers of refugees from East Pakistan poured into India. The burden posed for India by the refugees, India's increasing support for the Bengali guerrilla movement, and the failure of Yahya Khan to establish a viable political settlement in the eastern wing combined to increase the chances of an Indo-Pakistani war as the year went by.

Though the Soviet Union provided $20 million to help India maintain the refugees[37] and called for an end to the military crackdown in East Pakistan, Moscow still sought to avoid giving Pakistan the impression of supporting the dismemberment of the country. It still urged a political settlement which "would meet the interests of the entire people of Pakistan."[38] Even though the Soviets signed a general treaty with the Indians in August, they continued to espouse a negotiated settlement. Only when war broke out between India and Pakistan in December did Moscow openly support India. While India's war effort was bolstered by Soviet military supplies, the Soviet veto of cease-fire resolutions in the U.N. Security Council allowed India to force the surrender of the Pakistani forces in East Pakistan.

Soviet support for India resulted in a substantial increase in Soviet popularity. However, in spite of the goodwill earned in India by the Soviet Union, there were limits beyond which Indian leaders would not go to please the Soviets. For example, they continued to refuse to support Soviet proposals for an Asian Collective Security scheme at the time of Brezhnev's visit in late 1973.[39]

Despite Soviet support for India, Soviet-Pakistani relations soon began to improve, and the Soviets viewed favorably the efforts of the new Pakistani prime minister, Mr. Bhutto, to restore stability in South Asia through a number of agreements with India and Bangladesh signed during 1972–74.

The Soviets moved quickly to establish ties with the new state of Bangladesh. Prime Minister Mujib Rahman visited the Soviet Union in 1972 and 1974, and the Soviets extended $121 million in economic assistance by 1975, plus a limited amount of military aid.[40] The coup that overthrew Mujib in 1975 displeased the Soviets, for not only was the new government more conservative and less favorably disposed toward India, but it soon moved to improve Bangladesh's relations with the PRC.

Less than two years after the ouster of Mujib, the Soviets faced a major dilemma in its relations with India.[41] On June 26, 1975, in an effort to deal with mounting political opposition, Mrs. Gandhi proclaimed a "state of emergency," jailed a large number of political opponents, and imposed press censorship. The Soviets unequivocally supported the emergency rule, hailing what they perceived to be a new sense of discipline within India. When Mrs. Gandhi and her Congress Party were defeated in the elections of March 1977 and replaced by the Janata government headed by Prime Minister Moranji Desai, the Soviets were in an uncomfortable position. Most of the leading members of the new government had been incarcerated during the emergency and traditionally had been viewed by the Soviets as representatives of the Indian right. Desai himself had been strongly condemned in the past.

However, Soviet fears were soon allayed. At the end of April Foreign Minister Gromyko arrived in New Delhi on the invitation of the new Indian government. While stressing India's commitment to nonalignment, both Desai and Foreign Minister Vajpayee thanked the Soviets for past assistance in various fields and specifically endorsed the Indo-Soviet treaty. Prior to Gromyko's departure several agreements were signed for a Soviet loan and increased trade. One prospect, however, that worries the Soviets is the possibility of a rapprochement between India and the PRC and the impact it might have on the Soviet Union's long-standing ties with the former. Since 1976 there have been numerous indications that such an improvement in relations is probable.

Given such developments as the recent change in China's relations with the West—in particular the U.S.-Sino decision to establish formal diplomatic relations—and the signing of a Sino-Japanese treaty in August 1978, Moscow has been troubled by the possibility of an improvement in Sino-Indian relations.[42]

The April 1978 military coup in Afghanistan, which led to the ouster of Prime Minister Mohammed Daoud and the formation of a new government headed by Nur Mohammed Taraki, has proved to be quite beneficial to the Soviet position in South Asia. Although the Soviet Union had maintained close ties with Afghanistan ever since the mid-1950s—the Soviets were the major suppliers of military and economic assistance to Afghanistan—the emergence of the Taraki government appears to represent a qualitative change in the situation.[43] Despite Taraki's protestations to the contrary, it is generally felt that he is a Communist and that his People's Democratic Party is Communist-dominated. Since the coup a substantial number of Soviet advisors—many from Soviet Central Asia—have become involved in the Afghan army and bureaucracy, and in December 1978, following a visit by Taraki to Moscow, Afghanistan and the Soviet Union signed a 20-year treaty which provides for continued cooperation in the economic and military fields.[44] The Soviets have hailed the coup, and Taraki in turn has spoken warmly of the Soviet Union. When the Vietnamese-backed rebel forces ousted the Pol Pot regime in Cambodia, Afghanistan joined the Soviet Union in recognizing the new government on January 10, 1979.

Overall the development of Soviet policy in South Asia has differed somewhat from that in either the Middle East or Africa. So far the Soviet Union has not acquired the kind of military position—i.e. access to base rights—that it has been able to establish in a number of Arab and African states. Even though India has depended heavily on the Soviets for arms supplies and has become a partner in numerous economic projects, it has not been willing to support the Soviet proposal for a collective security system in Asia. On the other hand, unlike the situation elsewhere in the Third World, the Soviets have not suffered any significant defeats in their relations with the countries of South Asia. On the whole the Soviets have been quite successful in establishing their presence in the region. However, at least until the coup that brought Taraki to power in Afghanistan, they have not been able to exert substantial influence—as we have employed the term—on the policies of the countries in the region.

THE SOVIET UNION AND AFRICA

Although Khrushchev had attempted to expand the Soviet presence in Africa in the early 1960s, Soviet successes were minimal. The early years of the Brezhnev-Kosygin era witnessed a substantial downturn in overt Soviet involvement in the affairs of the continent, although clandestine support for revolutionary groups operating in the white-dominated southern portion of Africa continued. In recent years, however, the overthrow of the conservative dictatorship in Portugal and the resulting collapse of the Portuguese colonial empire, the increasing political instability of the white-ruled countries of southern Africa, and the coup that deposed Emperor Haile Selassie in Ethiopia have provided the Soviets with opportunities to expand their presence in Africa.

Although Africa is not as significant for the pursuit of Soviet global interests as are the Middle East and South Asia, it does hold out the promise of assisting the Soviets in achieving some of their major foreign policy goals. Given the strategic location of the Horn in relation to the Persian Gulf and the major sources of petroleum needed by the industrial West, northeast Africa is clearly of strategic significance. As the Soviet Union developed its naval power in the Indian Ocean area, the need for port facilities arose, and Berbera, in Somalia, as well as Aden across the Red Sea from Somalia, were developed by the Soviets as virtual naval and air bases which permitted them to expand their military activities in the Indian Ocean. Mozambique and Angola also offer the Soviets possible facilities to expand naval and surveillance operations in the Indian Ocean and the South Atlantic, which serve as the major lifeline for petroleum and other raw material imports for the West.[45]

In addition to the importance of Africa for Soviet strategic interests, it already has begun to exert a modest economic attraction for the Soviet leadership. Not only does it provide a growing market for Soviet manufactured goods—as do developing countries in other regions of the world as well—but it also offers the Soviets the possibility of obtaining needed raw materials.[46] The importance of Africa as an arena in which to compete with the United States and the PRC for influence has been demonstrated clearly by developments in recent years in Angola and Ethiopia, as well as by the continuing Soviet opposition to the U.S.-sponsored programs for majority rule in Namibia (Southwest Africa) and Zimbabwe (Rhodesia). Also, as the self-proclaimed leaders of a worldwide Marxist-Leninist revolutionary movement faced with the challenge presented by the Chinese, the Soviets have found it necessary to provide some assistance to "progressive" and revolutionary states and movements in Africa in order to support these claims of revolutionary leadership.

In the 1970s, therefore, Africa has reemerged as an area of important Soviet interests, although it still trails the Middle East and South Asia in Soviet priorities. Although political ties and economic assistance have constituted an element of Soviet policy in Africa,[47] military assistance, including both arms transfers and the provision of direct military aid through Cuban troops, has become increasingly important.

Recent Soviet policy in Angola, Ethiopia, and in Africa more broadly has represented an integral part of the Soviet effort to expand positions of influence in world affairs. In 1975 Angola offered the possibility of bringing to power a political party, the Popular Movement for the Liberation of Angola (MPLA), which would be dependent upon the Soviet Union for its very existence and would, presumably, be amenable to providing the Soviets with the facilities to form a "base of operations" in southwestern Africa.[48] The value of such "bases of operation" for the Soviets—as for the United States in the past—has been clear. During the Angolan civil war, for example, the Soviets were able to use the airport facilities of Brazzaville, Congo, (where earlier they had developed strong contacts) as a staging area for supplies flowing to the MPLA. More recently Aden (South Yemen), performed the same function for the Soviet airlift of supplies to Ethiopia in late 1977 and early 1978. Port facilities in Angola provide the Soviets with the potential of operating in the South Atlantic they have lacked in the past, just as port facilities in the eastern Mediterranean gave them an advantage during the 1973 Middle Eastern war that they did not possess only six years earlier.

Soviet intervention in Angola apparently was motivated by the desire to undercut the possibility of either the PRC or the United States gaining influence in the country. In addition, the location of Angola in relation to white-dominated southern Africa presumably was a factor in Soviet calculations, for the continuing and escalating conflicts in Zimbabwe, Namibia, and South Africa provide the Soviet Union with opportunities to gain a presence in the area should national liberation movements which they support come to power. Friendship with Angola and Mozambique and a Soviet presence in these countries facilitates Soviet support for the African liberation movements. Although southern Africa is of minimal direct strategic importance for Soviet security, the availability of bases in the region would provide the Soviets with important leverage over the West in a conflict situation.[49]

After the overthrow of Emperor Haile Selassie and the rapid radicalization of the revolutionary council which seized power, the Soviets saw the opportunity to undermine the U.S. position in the Horn of Africa and to expand their own operations in the region. However, they soon discovered that their increasing support for the new Ethiopian rulers elicited strong opposition in Somalia, despite the substantial support they had supplied to the government of President Siad Barre. After unsuccessful attempts to mediate in the territorial conflict between Somalia and Ethiopia, the Soviets opted for the friendship of the larger and potentially much more important Ethiopia. By fall 1977 massive Soviet and Cuban support was flowing into Ethiopia, and during early 1978 this support was instrumental in destroying the efforts of Somali tribesmen in the Ogaden—with the direct support of the Somali army—to break away from Ethiopian control.

Clearly the Soviets decided that a unified and pro-Soviet Ethiopia in control of most of northeastern Africa was worth the risks involved in direct intervention. In general their assumptions have proved to be correct—so far at least. Despite some critical comments by the United States, U.S.-Soviet relations did not deteriorate substantially. With the exception of some verbal opposition by Arab and African countries, the Soviets have not suffered in their relations with developing countries as a result of either the Angolan or the Ethiopian events—except for their expulsion from Somalia.

As we have already argued, Soviet policy in Africa, as Soviet policy elsewhere in the Third World, has aimed at the development of ties with countries whose geographic location has immediate or potential strategic significance for Soviet interests.[50] The expansion of Soviet state power has been of far greater importance in determining Soviet policy than the "revolutionary socialist" orientation of a movement or a government that seeks Soviet support.

It is important to repeat that in Africa, as elsewhere, the results of Soviet policy have been mixed. Successes, as in Angola and Ethiopia, have been balanced by failures elsewhere. However, recent Soviet policy in Africa has indicated that the Soviets continue to be committed to a policy of taking advantage of local situations in order to expand their network of global influence at the expense of the United States and its Western allies. To date the Soviets have not been restricted in their actions by either domestic opposition to expansionist policies or by existing ties in a region. During the Khrushchev years the Soviet leadership was still restrained by its overall strategic inferiority to the West. By the mid-1970s, however, changes in the strategic balance and in Soviet military capabilities have enabled the Soviets to act forcefully in areas like Angola and Ethiopia. These actions have not only permitted the Soviet Union to establish strong ties with revolutionary regimes in the two countries but may also lead other African revolutionaries to depend more fully for support from the Soviets who have shown that they have both the ability and the willingness to provide effective assistance.

THE POLITICS OF INFLUENCE BUILDING: AN INTERIM ASSESSMENT

Since much of the discussion in the general press concerning Soviet involvement in the developing world is couched in terms of the virtually irrepressible implementation of the "grand design" of the Soviet Union, it is imperative to voice a note of caution. Although the Soviets have indeed greatly expanded their role in world affairs and in the Third World in particular, they are by no means invincible or invariably successful. To a substantial degree their policy initiatives and their successes and failures depend on local developments over which they have little control. The death of a Nasser, the seizure of power by a Mengistu, and similar developments have been extremely important for Soviet policy. Although the Soviet Union has expanded its activities and capabilities in large areas of the Third World, it is unable to dictate developments as it can in Eastern Europe.

Soviet goals in the developing world are rather clearcut: the reduction of Western military and political influence; the containment of possible Chinese influence; the development of "bases of operation" for the projection of Soviet power; and the possible economic benefits to be gained for the Soviet economy. To a very substantial degree the Soviets have succeeded in accomplishing these goals in some regions—often because of the failures of U.S. and West European policy, often because local developments provided them with substantial opportunities.

From Moscow's point of view the opportunities for the future still look favorable. The continued festering of the Arab-Israeli conflict means not only that the Soviets will continue to play a major role in supporting such countries as Libya, Syria, and Iraq, with the concomitant benefits that such support will provide, but also that Sadat may well begin to reexamine Egyptian policy if a negotiated settlement is not reached soon. Such a reexamination might well result in Egypt's turning to the Soviet Union once again for support, support which will likely come only on Soviet terms.

The escalating unrest in southern Africa provides the Soviets with expanding opportunities for involvement, and even influence, in the area. Their presence in both Angola and Mozambique provides them with facilities for supporting the major liberation movements in southern Africa which they did not possess in the early 1970s. In South Asia the Desai government has shown that, even though its political orientation is quite different from that of Mrs. Gandhi, India is not about to shift its policy away from the Soviet Union and that the Soviets will continue to be able to count on stable relations with the most important country in that part of the world. Finally, the coup in Afghanistan, the collapse of the shah's rule in Iran and the consolidation of Vietnamese control over Indochina all work to the benefit of the Soviet Union in relation to the West and the PRC.

The growth of Soviet military capabilities throughout the Middle

East, the Indian Ocean area, and the Mediterranean means that the Soviet Union possesses the capability of employing conventional military means to support Soviet interests—for example, in a conflict with the West. The growth of the Soviet nuclear arsenal and the nuclear stalemate between the Soviet Union and the United States might well, when added to the extension of conventional Soviet military capabilities, provide them with the ability to interdict Western oil supplies.

To conclude, it must be kept in mind that the Soviets still must depend upon the good will of "client" states in order to maintain the "defense system" they have constructed. As they become more involved in local developments—as in the western Sahara and Ethiopia—they will find that they cannot support two sides to a conflict and maintain good relations with both. However, as in the past, they are likely to opt for the stronger and potentially more important of the participants to a conflict.

However, Soviet dependence on local developments and the possibility of future Soviet defeats should not make the West complacent. The Soviets have shown in the past that, in spite of setbacks, they are able to rebound. Most important, however, is the fact that they have created a set of political-military relations throughout a substantial portion of the Third World which permit them to undercut Western political and economic interests. Until recently they apparently have acted on the assumption that a post-Vietnam and post-Watergate United States was so committed to inaction—and to improved relations with the Soviet Union—that it would look the other way in such "out-of-the-way" places as Ethiopia and Angola. Until now the assumption has proven essentially correct.

NOTES

1. For an excellent analysis of Soviet efforts to construct what the author refers to as collective defense systems in areas flanking the Soviet Union, see Avigdor Haselkorn, *The Evolution of Soviet Security Stratey, 1965-1975* (New York: Crane, Russak, 1978).

2. For a more complete discussion of these points, see Roger E. Kanet, "The Soviet Union and the Developing Countries: Policy or Policies," *The World Today* 31 (1975): 338-46. For an interesting survey of Soviet policy interests in the developing countries, see William H. Luers, "The U.S.S.R. and the Third World," in *The U.S.S.R. and the Sources of Soviet Policy*, Kennan Institute for Advanced Russian Studies, The Wilson Center, Occasional Paper no. 34 (1978), pp. 11-25.

3. For a more complete discussion of Soviet policy toward the developing countries during the Khrushchev years, see Roger E. Kanet, "Soviet Attitudes Toward Developing Nations since Stalin," in *The Soviet Union and the Developing Nations*, ed. Roger E. Kanet (Baltimore: Johns Hopkins University Press, 1974), pp. 27-50.

4. See Richard Lowenthal, *Model or Ally? The Communist Powers and the Developing Countries* (New York: Oxford University Press, 1977), pp. 185–86. Chapters 3 and 4 of Lowenthal's book provide an excellent analysis of the interaction between Soviet ideology and Soviet foreign policy objectives in the developing countries.

5. For an example of the adjustment and mellowing of ideological perspectives with respect to India, I. Lemin, "Plody imperialisticheskogo khozyainichaniya v Indii i Pakistane," *Voprosy ekonomiki*, no. 1 (1952): 73–89, and Modeste Rubinstein, "A Non-Capitalist Path for Underdeveloped Countries," *New Times*, no. 28 (1956): 3–6.

6. For the Soviet argument, see R. Ulyanovskii, "Nekotorye voprosy nekapitalisticheskogo razvitiya osvobodivshikhsya stran," *Kommunist*, no. 1 (1966): 113–14. For additional references to the Soviet discussion see Kanet, "Soviet Attitudes Toward Developing Nations," pp. 35–44.

7. Indications of the degree of Soviet concentration on the countries of South Asia and the Middle East (including the Arab countries of North Africa) can be found in the following statistics.

	All Developing Countries	Countries of South Asia and Middle East	Percentage, South Asia and Middle East
Exports, 1964	$777.8 million	$602.1 million	77.4
Imports, 1964	663.0 million	422.7 million	63.8
Total credits committed, 1954–64	4,268 million	3,260 million	76.4

Sources: U.S., Department of State, Bureau of Intelligence and Research, *The Communist Economic Offensive Through 1964*, Research Memorandum, RSB-65 (August 4, 1965), p. 6; idem, *Communist Governments and Developing Nations: Aid and Trade in 1965*, Research Memorandum, RSB-50 (June 17, 1966), pp. 12–19.

8. By "influence relationship" we mean the ability of the Soviet Union to cause other countries to do something that they otherwise would not do. Soviet military, economic, and political support did, however, permit individual developing countries to pursue policies that, without Soviet assistance, they would not have been able to pursue. For a fuller discussion of influence in Soviet relations with the developing countries, see Alvin Z. Rubinstein, *Red Star on the Nile: The Soviet-Egyptian Influence Relationship Since the June War* (Princeton: Princeton University Press, 1977); and M. Rajan Menon, "India and the Soviet Union: A Case Study of Inter-Nation Influence" (Ph.D. diss., University of Illinois at Urbana-Champaign, 1978).

9. See, for example, the comments of Admiral S.G. Gorshkov, commander of the Soviet Navy, in an interview printed in *Ogonek*, no. 6 (February 3, 1968). For a more complete presentation of Gorshkov's views, see his *Morskaya moshch gosudarstva* (Moscow: Voenizdat, 1976).

10. See, for example, Kanet, "The Soviet Union and the Developing Countries," pp. 344–45; and John D. Esseks, "Soviet Economic Aid to Africa: 1959–72. An Overview," in *Chinese and Soviet Aid to Africa*, ed. Warren Weinstein (New York: Praeger, 1975), p. 114.

11. For an excellent discussion in the changes in Soviet economic policy, see Elizabeth Kridl Valkenier, "New Trends in Soviet Economic Relations with the Third World," *World Politics* 22 (1970): 415–32; and idem, "Soviet Economic Relations with the Developing Nations," in Karet, ed., *The Soviet Union and the Developing Nations*, pp. 215–36.

12. At the present time the Soviets have such agreements with India, Iraq, and

Mozambique. Both Egypt and Somalia abrogated similar treaties after disputes between themselves and the Soviets.

13. See P.I. Polshikov, *Kontinent v dvizhenii* (Moscow: Mezhdunarodnye otnoshe-niya, 1976).

14. For a collection of excellent studies of Soviet economic relations with developing countries, see *Economic Relations Between Socialist Countries and the Third World*, ed. Deepak Nayyar (London; Macmillan, 1977).

15. To a substantial degree the slight drop in trade with the developing countries as a percentage of total Soviet trade is a result of the substantial increase in trade with the industrial West. From 1970 to 1976, Soviet trade with the developed capitalist countries rose from 21 percent of total trade turnover to 33 percent (See Table 10.3).

16. As of 1977, more than 10,000 Soviet and East European military personnel were working in developing countries, supplemented by an additional 22,000 Cubans. More than 4,000 of the Soviets and East Europeans were in sub-Saharan Africa, as well as all but 500 of the Cubans. See Central Intelligence Agency, National Foreign Assessment Center, *Communist Aid to Less Developed Countries of the Free World, 1977: A Research Report*, ER 78-10478U (November 1978), p. 3.

17. See W. Scott Thompson, *Power Projection: A Net Assessment of U.S. and Soviet Capabilities*, Agenda Paper 7 (New York: National Strategy Information Center, 1978).

18. For a discussion of Soviet policy in Latin America, see Roger Hamburg, "The Soviet Union and Latin America," in Karet, ed., *The Soviet Union and the Developing Nations*, pp. 179-214.

19. See Bhabani Sen Gupta, *Soviet-Asian Relations in the 1970s and Beyond: An Interperceptional Study* (New York: Praeger, 1976).

20. President Houari Boumedienne of Algeria criticized the Soviet failure to provide direct military assistance during the hostilities. Algiers Radio, June 19, 1967. *Al Ahram*, the semi-official Egyptian newspaper, reported that Boumedienne had flown to Moscow to request military aid. Cited in Suleyman Tekiner, "Soviet Policy Toward the Arab East," *Bulletin, of the Institute for the Study of the USSR* 15, no. 3 (1968): 37.

21. See Walter Lacqueur, *Confrontation* (New York: New York Times Book, 1974), p. 5. By the end of 1970, more than 12,000 Soviet military personnel were stationed in Egypt, and 4,000 military instructors were involved in an advisory capacity that included a virtual revamping of the Egyptian military.

22. For the text of the treaty, see *New Times*, no. 23 (1971): 8-9.

23. For details on Sudanese-Soviet relations during this period, see Robert O. Freedman, *Soviet Policy Toward the Middle East Since 1970* (New York: Praeger, 1975), pp. 52-55.

24. For a discussion of Soviet assistance for Iraq's oil industry, see Arthur J. Klinghoffer, *The Soviet Union and International Oil Politics* (New York: Columbia University Press, 1977), pp. 134-39.

25. The text is published in *New Times*, no. 16 (1972): 4-5.

26. Following the Soviet exodus from Egypt, there were reports that Moscow was seeking naval facilities in the Syrian ports of Latakia and Tartus. See Roger F. Pajak, *Soviet Arms Aid in the Middle East* (Washington: Georgetown University, Center for Strategic and International Studies, 1976), pp. 21-23.

27. For detailed analyses of Soviet policy during the October 1973 war, see, among others, Galia Golan, *Yom Kippur and After: The Soviet Union and the Middle East Crisis* (London: Cambridge University Press, 1973), ch. 3; and Foy D. Kohler, Leon Goure, and Mose L. Harvey, *The Soviet Union and the October 1973 Middle East War*

(Coral Gables, Fla.: University of Miami, Center for Advanced International Studies, 1974).

28. The Soviets have argued continually that it is essential that the Soviet Union participate in a Middle East settlement at all stages. See, for example, *Pravda*, October 7, 1978.

29. In March 1976, Sadat abrogated the treaty with the Soviet Union and once again denied the Soviets use of Egyptian naval facilities—there had been a partial Soviet return to Egypt in the four years since the initial "break." For a discussion of this development, see Rubinstein, *Red Star on the Nile*, p. 326.

30. For a detailed account of Soviet-PLO relations, see Galia Golan, *The Soviet Union and the PLO* Soviet and East European Research Center, Research paper no. 9 (Jerusalem: Hebrew University of Jerusalem, 1976).

31. In May 1974, during a visit of the Libyan Prime Minister in Moscow, Prime Minister Kosygin noted that what unites the two countries "undoubtedly carries much greater weight" than what divides them. *Pravda*, May 16, 1974.

32. See the editorial note on the Iraqi episode translated in *The Current Digest of the Soviet Press* 30, no. 31 (August 30, 1978); 5.

33. The text of the communiqué appears in Bimal Prasad, *Indo-Soviet Relations, 1947-1972: A Documentary Study* (Bombay: Allied, 1973), pp. 275-80.

34. For a Soviet account of the conference, see L. Stepanov, *Konflikt v Indostane i soglashenie v Tashkente* (Moscow: Izdatelstvo Politicheskoi Literatury, 1966).

35. Details of the agreement are discussed in Zubeida Hasan, "Pakistan's Relations with the U.S.S.R. in the 1960s," *The World Today* 25 (1969): 26-35; and in Y. Blinkov, "Two Countries of South Asia," *International Affairs* (Moscow), no. 10 (1970): 102-06.

36. Brezhnev's initial comment was included in his speech to the International Meeting of Communist and Workers Parties in Moscow, June 7, 1969, which was published in *International Affairs*, no. 7 (1969): 21. For subsequent Soviet statements, see Alexander O. Gebhardt, "The Soviet System of Collective Security in Asia," *Asian Survey* 13 (1973): 1075-91.

37. See Government of India, *Bangla Desh Documents*, vol. 1 (Madras: B.N.K. Press, n.d.), pp. 82-85, for data on contributions made by foreign governments to India's refugee relief efforts.

38. *Pravda*, April 4, 1971.

39. During 1973 the Soviets had provided $350 million to India for importing wheat and had signed a number of economic agreements with India during Brezhnev's visit. See Orah Cooper, "Soviet Economic Aid to the Third World," in *Soviet Economy in a New Perspective*, U.S. Congress, Joint Economic Committee (Washington, D.C.: Government Printing Office, 1976), p. 193, and *Hindustan Times* (New Delhi), December 1, 1973.

40. See William J. Barnds, "The USSR, China, and South Asia," *Problems of Communism* 26, no. 6 (1977); 50.

41. The following discussion is based on Rajan Menon, "India and the Soviet Union: A New Stage of Relations," *Asian Survey* 18 (1978): 731-50.

42. The Soviet press has dealt with Indian-Chinese relations at some length. See, for example, *Pravda*, December 19, 1978. V. Volodin, in "Vneshne-politicheskie manevry Pekina v yuzhnoi Azii," *Mezhdunarodnaya zhizn*, no. 10 (1978); especially 87-89, sought to warn India of the PRC's role of encouraging separatist movements in the northeastern part of the country and of Peking's encouragement to the pro-Maoist Communist Party of India (Marxist-Leninist) and its use of violence.

43. An excellent account of Soviet-Afghan relations since the coup appears in Gerd Linde, *Des Kremls Weg zum Khyberpass*, Berichte des Bundesinstituts fur ostwissenschaftliche und internationale Studien, no. 23 (Cologne: Bundesinstitut fur ostwissenschaftliche und internationale Studien, 1978).

44. New York *Times*, November 18, December 6, 1978.

45. For an excellent discussion of this point, see Walter F. Hahn and Alvin J. Cottrell, *Soviet Shadow over Africa* (Washington, D.C.: Center for Advanced International Studies, University of Miami, 1977).

46. For example, the Soviets are now importing substantial amounts of bauxite from Guinea which is produced in a complex constructed with Soviet economic assistance. See V. Berezin, *Cooperation Between CMEA and Developing Countries* (Moscow: Novosti Press Agency, 1976), p. 33.

47. For a recent examination of Soviet economic policy in Africa, see Roger E. Kanet and Boris Ipatov, "Soviet Aid and Trade in Africa," in *Soviet and Chinese Aid to Africa*, ed. Warren Weinstein and Thomas H. Henriksen (New York: Praeger, forthcoming). See, also, the relevant chapters in Nayyar, ed., *Economic Relations*.

48. See the excellent treatment of Soviet policy in David E. Albright, "Soviet Policy [in Africa]," *Problems of Communism* 27, no. 1 (1978): 20–39; and in Colin Legum, "The Soviet Union, China and the West in Southern Africa," *Foreign Affairs* 54 (1976): 745–62.

49. According to a recent report, the Soviets may well have already attempted to create problems for the West through their involvement in Angola. In the weeks prior to the invasion of Zaire's Shaba Province in May 1978 by Bundu rebels based in Angola and, reportedly, trained and armed by the Angolans and Cubans, the Soviets and some of their East European allies bought up abnormally large supplies of cobalt, a byproduct of copper essential to making alloys resistant to extreme heat. Nine months after the invasion, Zaire's production of copper remains crippled, and there exists a serious scarcity of cobalt on the world market. The timing of the Soviet, East German, and Polish purchase and the fact that the Soviet Union ranks second in the world in the production of cobalt and does not depend on foreign imports seem to indicate that the Soviets knew of the planned attack and that the purchases were meant to disrupt the world market. See Richard Mowrer, "Moscow's Maneuvering in Africa Causes Cobalt Shortage in the West," *Christian Science Monitor*, January 16, 1979.

50. For a more extended development of this argument, see Roger E. Kanet and William Morris [Boris Ipatov], "Die Sowjetunion in Afrika: Eine neue Phase sowjetischer Afrikapolitik?" *Osteuropa* 28 (1978): 978–85.

INDEX

ABOUT THE EDITOR AND CONTRIBUTORS

DONALD R. KELLEY is Associate Professor of Political Science at Mississippi State University. He is author of *The Solzhenitsyn-Sakharov Dialogue: Politics, Society, and the Future* (1980), co-author of *The Economic Superpowers and the Environment: The United States, the Soviet Union, and Japan* (1976), and editor of and contributor to *The Energy Crisis and the Environment: An International Perspective* (Praeger, 1977). He has also contributed articles to anthologies and various journals, such as the *American Political Science Review, Journal of Politics, Polity, Soviet Studies,* American *Behavioral Scientist,* and *Canadian Slavonic Papers.*

Dr. Kelley received his A.B. and M.A. from the University of Pittsburgh and his Ph.D. from Indiana University.

VALERIE JANE BUNCE has been Assistant Professor of Political Science at Northwestern University since 1977. From 1976 to 1977 she was Assistant Professor at Lake Forest College. Dr. Bunce has published articles and reviews in *Comparative Political Studies, Comparative Politics, Soviet Studies, The Journal of Politics, The American Political Science Review,* and *The Russian Review. Changing Leaders and Changing Policies* are forthcoming. Dr. Bunce received her B.A., M.A. and Ph.D. from the University of Michigan.

JOHN M. ECHOLS III is Assistant Professor of Political Science at the University of Illinois at Chicago Circle. He has published several articles in the areas of Soviet and comparative politics, including pieces in the *Journal of Politics, Comparative Political Studies,* and *Public Finance.* Dr. Echols holds a B.A. from the University of Virginia and a Ph.D. from the University of Michigan.

GEORGE R. FEIWEL is Professor of Economics at the University of Tennessee, Knoxville. He is author of *The Economics of a Socialist Enterprise: A Case Study of the Polish Firm* (1965), *The Soviet Quest for Economic Efficiency: Issues, Controversies, and Reforms* (1972), *New Economic Patterns in Czechoslovakia* (1968), *Industrialization and Planning under Polish Socialism* (1971), *Essays on Planning in Eastern Europe* (1973), *The Intellectual Capital of Michal Kalecki: A Study in Economic Theory and Policy* (1975), *Growth in a Supply Constrained Economy* (1975), and *Growth and Reforms in Centrally Planned Economies: Lessons from the Bulgarian Experience* (1977). Dr. Feiwel received his Ph.D. in economics from McGill University.

THANE GUSTAFSON is Associate Professor of Government at Harvard University and Research Associate at the Rand Corporation,

Santa Monica, California. His writings on U.S. and Soviet politics have appeared in *Science, Survey, Problems of Communism,* and *Public Policy,* as well as several joint collections. He is currently completing a book on the Brezhnev programs in agriculture and environment. Dr. Gustafson received a B.A. from the University of Illinois and a Ph.D. from Harvard University.

ROGER E. KANET is Professor of Political Science and a member of the Russian and East European Center of the University of Illinois at Urbana-Champaign. Until 1974 he was on the faculty of the University of Kansas. Professor Kanet has published widely on various aspects of Soviet and East European foreign policy. His publications include edited books on *The Soviet Union and the Developing Nations* (1974), *Soviet Economic and Political Relations with the Developing World* (Praeger, 1975, with Donna Bahry), and *Policy and Politics in Gierek's Poland* (forthcoming, with Maurice D. Simon). Dr. Kanet holds a Ph.B. from Berchmanskolleg (Pullach-bei-Munchen, FRG), an A.B. from Xavier University (Cincinnati), an M.A. from Lehigh University, and an M.A. and Ph.D. from Princeton University.

DAVID A. KOWALEWSKI is Assistant Professor of Political Science at Benedictine College, Atchison, Kansas. He has contributed articles on Soviet affairs to *Armenian Review, Lituanus,* and *Nationalities Papers.* Dr. Kowalewski received his Ph.D. from the University of Kansas.

ROY D. LAIRD, Professor of Political Science and Soviet and East European Area Studies at the University of Kansas, founded the ongoing (informal) Conference on Soviet and East European Agricultural and Peasant Affairs and authored *The Future of Agriculture in the Soviet Union and Eastern Europe* (1977 with Joseph Hajda and Betty A. Laird), *To Live Long Enough: The Memoirs of Naum Jasny, Scientific Analyst* (1976 with Betty Laird), and *The Soviet Paradigm: An Experiment in Creating a Monohierarchical Polity* (1970). Dr. Laird received his Ph.D. from the University of Washington.

M. RAJAN MENON is Assistant Professor of Political Science at Vanderbilt University, Nashville, Tennessee. Dr. Menon has contributed articles and reviews to *Asian Survey, Current History, Osteuropa,* and other journals. Dr. Menon holds a B.A. from Delhi University, an M.A. from Lehigh University, and a Ph.D. from the University of Illinois at Urbana-Champaign.

JANE P. SHAPIRO is Professor of Foreign Affairs at the National War College, Washington, D.C. She is on leave from Manhattanville College (Purchase, N.Y.), where she is Professor of Political Science. Dr. Shapiro has coedited several volumes on communist affairs, including *Change and Adaptation in Soviet and East European Poli-*

tics and *From the Cold War to Detente* (both Praeger, 1976), and *Communist Systems in Comparative Perspective* (1974). She has published articles and reviews in *Problems of Communism, Soviet Studies, Pacific Affairs, Studies in Comparative Communism,* and *The Russian Review.*

Dr. Shapiro holds a B.A. from Cornell University, and an M.A. Certificate of the Russian Institute, and Ph.D. from Columbia University.

ROBERT SHARLET is Professor of Political Science at Union College, Schenectady, New York. He is author of *The New Soviet Constitution of 1977* (1978); co-author (with Zigurds L. Zile and Jean C. Love) of *The Soviet Legal System and Arms Inspection* (Praeger, 1972); coeditor (with Stephen F. Cohen and Alexander Rabinowitch) and contributor to *The Soviet System Since Stalin* (1980); coeditor and coauthor of the introduction (with Piers Beirns) to *E.B. Pashukanis: Selected Writings on Marxism and Soviet Jurisprudence* (1980); and has contributed numerous articles and essays on Soviet law and politics to scholarly journals and book-length symposia. Dr. Sharlet received his Ph.D. from Indiana University.